Physics for O.N.C. Engineers

Consulting Editor

D. R. Browning

Principal Lecturer, Department of Science,
The Bristol Polytechnic

Other titles in the Technical Education Series

Hancox: Basic Mathematics for Engineers
Bezzant: Basic Organic Chemistry
Bennett: Introduction to Modern Biology
Brown: Comparative Inorganic Chemistry
Titherington and Rimmer: Applied Mechanics
Titherington and Rimmer: Mechanical Engineering Science
Lunt: Basic Mathematics for Technical College Students
Ward: Electrical Engineering Science

PHYSICS
for O.N.C. Engineers

Walter Schofield
Head of Science Department, East Hertfordshire College of Further Education.

McGRAW-HILL · LONDON

New York · St. Louis · San Francisco · Toronto · Sydney · Mexico
Johannesburg · Panama · Düsseldorf · Kuala Lumpur · Montreal
New Delhi · Rio de Janeiro · Singapore.

Published by

McGRAW-HILL Book Company (UK) Limited
McGraw-Hill House · Maidenhead · Berkshire · England

07 094267 6

Revised first edition.

PRINTED AND BOUND IN GREAT BRITAIN

Preface

This book provides a background of up-to-date physics to meet the needs of students of the Ordinary National Certificates and Diplomas in Engineering. It caters for the Heat, Light, and Sound requirements of Part I of the Engineering Institutions Examination, and also contains an account of the structure of matter and related topics which are commonly included in College syllabuses. Throughout the book SI units (Système International d'Unités) and conventions are used. Certain non-coherent metric units whose use may continue have been included, e.g., the torr (mm Hg) and the litre. British units are mentioned only in the appendix, where a table of conversion factors is given.

A student's first thought is to prepare for an examination and, to help him in this, there are many worked examples in the text and, at the end of each chapter, a large number of questions and problems of the type set by Colleges and Engineering Institutions. Many errors in problems arise from uncertainty about units and so a review of basic SI units is given in the first chapter. Quick location of material is essential during revision and a full index is provided for easy reference.

The approach used in the book is direct rather than historical, and I have concentrated more on the explanation of basic concepts than on mathematical derivations. A knowledge of calculus, though sometimes useful, is not needed to understand the subject matter.

Students find difficulty at the same points in physics and, therefore, to some extent these points can be anticipated. As a check, however, a draft of the book has been read by Ordinary National Certificate students at East Ham Technical College. In the light of their detailed observations, I have varied the pace of the final version, explaining the difficult points at length and describing easier topics more concisely. It appears that students usually ignore cross references in the text and so these have been kept to a minimum. Instead, I have repeated material in the various places where it is needed.

In the past, there has been a tendency for subjects to be studied in isolated compartments, which makes students reluctant to apply the principles learned in one subject to the problems raised in another. Thus, engineering students often regard physics as quaint and even irrelevant to their other subjects. Sometimes, this is because the relevance of science to the work which the engineer knows to be valuable is not given sufficient emphasis. At other times, the examples selected to illustrate fundamental principles appear rather too artificial or contrived. In the text I have taken every opportunity to integrate theory with practice, and I have selected problems which either involve real applications or illuminate the theory particularly well.

Physics has its own part to play in the education of any specialist engineer who wishes to understand more fully his own field and to contribute to its development. However, I feel that the presentation of physics should not contrast too much with the more empirical approach adopted in engineering subjects. My aim in writing this book is not only to show that physics is useful to the engineer, but also to show that it has a vital interest of its own.

ACKNOWLEDGEMENTS

Ron Hale	drew the illustrations
Roland Rosser	helped and advised at every stage
Robert Bell	improved the clarity of the text and read the proofs
Mildred Schofield	produced the typescript

My thanks are also due to my colleagues and students at East Ham Technical College for their help and encouragement.

Finally, I should like to thank the Institution of Electronic and Radio Engineers for permission to reproduce questions from their examinations.

Walter Schofield

Contents

1 Fundamentals

Physics and Engineering

Physics is the study of matter and energy, and of the relation between them. In view of this very broad definition of physics, it can claim, more than any other science, to be the basis of both science and engineering. Like all scientists, the physicist is concerned with investigating natural phenomena and with understanding the laws underlying them. At one time, in fact, physics was known as natural philosophy. Engineering, on the other hand, like all the applied sciences, is more directly concerned with the practical application of natural laws, that is, with developing and putting to use the discoveries which have been made. Physicists and engineers do not work entirely independently of each other, of course. A constant interchange of ideas and discoveries stimulates both in their continual search for a clearer understanding and more complete mastery of the forces of nature. We in society need the scientist and the engineer to reveal the secrets of nature and to improve the comfort, variety, and security of our lives.

Once the inventor has made use of a discovery, it often happens that the new application leads to yet other discoveries. When the applied science of the optical instrument maker, Lippershay, produced the first refracting telescope in 1608, it became possible for Galileo in the following year to direct his improved version of it towards the sky and to see for the first time the moons of Jupiter. This discovery led naturally to new ideas in astronomy, and to a demand for more powerful and more efficient telescopes, which in their turn probed deeper and deeper into the universe. Again, although it was known since the days of ancient Greece that the world was round, not until the fifteenth century had marine engineering developed sufficiently to enable explorers to embark with confidence across the unknown thousands of miles of ocean and circumnavigate the earth.

The reverse of this process is also true; the physicist working alone, can make discoveries which pose an entirely new set of problems for the engineer. In modern times, radio engineers developed the manufacture of radio valves to a very high degree of precision, but independent research by physicists into the nature of semi-conductors led to the invention of the transistor. (Fig. 1.1.) It was clear at once that a discovery

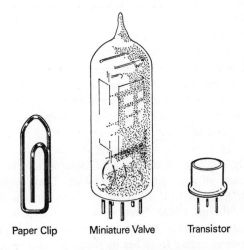

Paper Clip   Miniature Valve   Transistor

Fig. 1.1. Valve and Transistor.

of major importance had been made, transistors being small, compact, light, and very robust, yet at first it was difficult to mass-produce identical transistors in large quantities. This was the problem

1

that engineers had to take up and work at, until they finally found ways of producing transistors accurately, cheaply, and in large quantities.

Thus science and engineering are at their most productive when there is a constant interchange between the two. In the same way, physicists are more versatile when they know of the developments in engineering, and engineers are more effective when they have the background knowledge to appreciate the potentialities of new discoveries.

From the beginning of recorded history we can trace the development of man's curiosity in the face of the mysteries of nature, as he sought to lay bare the fundamental patterns of natural order, and to explain the causes of all the effects he observed. At first, all mysterious occurrences in nature were attributed to a large number of gods, a sort of divine working-party whose job it was to operate all the mechanisms of nature. The sun was the god Apollo, driving a flaming chariot across the sky, and the moon the goddess Diana, bringing illumination to hunters at night. So long as men accepted this explanation of natural events, they could not expect to find a system in the universe, for the gods, they believed, had human whims and motives, and were able to indulge these by reason of their immortality and magical powers. It took a long time for men to adopt a new approach to the problem of uncovering the basic structure of the universe.

A new approach first became evident in ancient Greece, where a race of men with inquisitive and sceptical minds began to observe nature objectively, to analyse and classify their observations, to discuss them, and to formulate theories about them. They laid the foundations of many of the subjects we study today, and made valuable contributions to the sciences of logic and mathematics. They applied their mathematical discoveries to the construction of buildings which have never been excelled in beauty. But they rarely attempted to wrest the secrets of nature from her by force of experiments; they rarely did more than think about the natural events which presented themselves during the course of normal human experience. Archimedes was an exception and he discovered the laws of levers and invented the Archimedean screw. (Fig. 1.2.)

The Romans, who took the lead after the decline of the Greek civilization, were fine engineers who put into practice, in their construction of superb

Fig. 1.2. Archimedes screw was designed to pump water for irrigation.

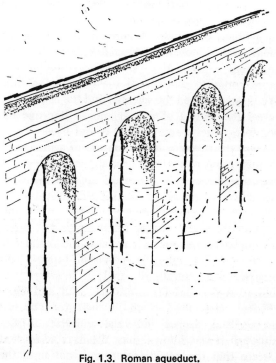

Fig. 1.3. Roman aqueduct.

2

military roads, bridges, water supplies, and systems of sanitation, the principles that the Greeks had discovered; but they made no contribution of their own to the advancement of theoretical science. (Fig. 1.3.)

Not so very far from Rome in 1500 A.D. lived a man who combined the abilities of scientist, engineer, and artist in a way never equalled before or since. His name was Leonardo da Vinci. He described a possible diving helmet, portable bridges, a flying machine, and a parachute. (Fig. 1.4.) He hated war, although he invented several

Fig. 1.4. Da Vinci's design for a helicopter.

guns and an armoured car, and he would not publish the details of his submarine for fear it might be used to sink ships. He invented roller bearings, a sprocket chain, a screw-cutting lathe, and many other things, but despite all of these he is remembered most for his artistic work, notably his painting of the Mona Lisa.

Da Vinci was hundreds of years in advance of his time, and it was not until the seventeenth century that the foundations of modern experimental science were laid, and scientists began to train themselves in those habits of mind and work which have led in modern times to the rapid expansion of human knowledge.

The progress of science has been retarded during certain periods in man's history when it was held to be wrong to challenge the authority of the government, the church, and the opinions of certain ancient scientific writers. Even worse than this have been those periods when scepticism was re garded as a sin, and publishing factual discoveries a punishable crime. We hope, now that science is quite respectable, that this stage in the development of science is over. You can find a similar situation, however, in present day social and economic science which is in its infancy. The belief that public ownership leads more efficiently to the things which man values is regarded as a crime in some Capitalist countries, just as the belief that private ownership is more efficient is a crime in some Communist countries. One day we may come to regard the question as a matter for objective experiment.

Francis Bacon, the Elizabethan courtier, scholar, and writer, was one of the first to advocate the experimental method. He himself died as the result of an experiment in refrigeration. One winter's day in 1626, as he was travelling from St. Albans to London, thinking perhaps of how organic decay is retarded in winter, he was struck by the idea that snow might preserve meat just as well as salt. He stopped his coach at a roadside cottage and bought a chicken, which he proceeded to stuff with snow. The experiment worked, but exposure to the snow and cold made Bacon ill. He contracted bronchitis, and died a few weeks later.

The Scientific Method

The work of the pioneer scientists of the seventeenth century paved the way for the development of the scientific method. This is a method which scientists follow in investigating natural phenomena, and in demonstrating to the limit of present knowledge the laws which govern the ceaseless flow of energy in the universe. The five stages of the scientific method listed below will repay careful study and constitute an approach which has proved unrivalled in scientific investigation.

1. *Observation:* Any event or experiment must be subjected to careful and systematic scrutiny, and not simply given a passing glance.

2. *Experiment:* By this means we verify phenomena under controlled conditions, and establish that we are not dealing with an illusion or an effect of coincidence.

3. *Analysis:* We search for a pattern into which all observations can be fitted.

4. *Prediction:* We examine the possible consequences of the deductions in 3, and apply them to other circumstances.

3

5. *Verification:* All predictions must be checked by further experiment.

The scientist must bear in mind that, in applying the scientific method to his investigations, he is still an animal, and, like all animals, is limited by his own fallible and unreliable senses. While his brain is the most wonderful organism in creation, it depends for information on messengers that sometimes deliver garbled and inaccurate messages. Your eyes, for example, convey one impression of the pattern in Fig. 1.5 which a few measurements

more quickly, clearly, and precisely will we arrive at the truth about what we are observing. Quite small differences in measurement can point to errors in scientific theories that have been accepted up to now, so that it becomes a duty of every scientist and engineer to take meticulous care over his measurements. This is a fundamental principle of science which William Thomson summarized about 100 years ago: 'When you can measure what you are speaking about and express it in numbers you know something about it; but when you cannot measure it, and when you cannot express it in

Fig. 1.5. Optical illusion associated with the sharp contrast of light and shade.

made with a ruler will correct. This is an example of an optical illusion, but it is not only the eyes that make mistakes. If you put your right hand in hot water at the same time as you put your left hand in cold, and then plunge both hands simultaneously into a bowl of luke-warm water, your right hand will tell you the water is cold, and your left hand that the water is hot.

Some method must obviously be found of accurately informing the brain of the actual measurements of length, mass, temperature, and time which relate to any particular investigation. Scientists are consequently very much concerned with instruments of measurement, and are constantly striving to find new methods for measuring the effects of physical phenomena, and to make the instruments which are already available even more accurate. Today, in response to these modern requirements, measuring instruments are manufactured with a very high degree of skill and precision.

Measurement

Obviously, the more accurately we can measure the effects we are studying in any experiment, the

numbers, your knowledge is of a meagre and unsatisfactory kind.'

The degree of accuracy we aim at, however, depends on the purpose of the measurement. It will sometimes be costly for an industry to work to very close tolerances, and may also lead to an unnecessary waste of valuable time. The need for exactness of fit can often be reduced by careful design, for instance, a three-legged stool will never wobble, but there are cases in which precise measurement is essential. Parts mass-produced in one factory must correspond closely with parts manufactured in another. The complete interchangeability of spare parts is only possible when all the parts are exactly alike, and this naturally means that all instruments of measurement must be made to conform as accurately as possible with a universally acceptable standard.

A final point is made here about the expression of measured values. The accuracy of a measurement can be indicated, when we express it, if we adopt the following convention. The error must be less than half a unit of the last significant figure quoted, i.e., more accurate measurement would never produce a revision of the last figure.

For example,

15 m   means   14·5 m to 15·5 m

                    (i.e., $\pm 0\cdot5$)

15·0 m   means   14·95 m to 15·05 m

                    (i.e., $\pm 0\cdot05$)

15·00 m   means   14·995 m to 15·005 m

                    (i.e., $\pm 0\cdot005$)

A result of say 524,000 accurate to ± 500, is better expressed as $5\cdot24 \times 10^5$ so that we can employ the above convention.

Basic Units

The basic units which we adopt are really a matter of choice, and different branches of science and engineering in different countries have chosen various systems. Scientists have previously based their system on the basic units of the centimetre, the gramme, and the second (cgs). Mechanical and civil engineers and the general public in English speaking countries have used the foot, pound, second (fps) system of units.

In May 1965, the British Government decided to give the signal to industry in the United Kingdom to go metric! The movement, which started after the French Revolution and which has spread to every corner of the Earth, will at last cross the Channel. The change will be received with mixed feelings, but although the cost will be great, the benefits will be even greater. We can easily abandon the bushel or the peck, and the rod, pole or perch will soon be forgotten, but the miles, the pints, and the tons will die hard.

The greatest confusion arises during the change-over when both systems are in use together. The simplicity of the new system will only become obvious when the conversion is complete. Hence the quicker we grasp the nettle the sooner we will gain the benefits.

We are fortunate that the United Kingdom is changing to the metric system at a time when a newly rationalized set of metric units is coming into use internationally. (See the British Standards Institution publication BS 3763: 1964.) This system is called the International System (SI) of units, and it closely follows the MKSA system which has been used for some time by electrical engineers.

All measurements are simply comparisons with some convenient standard or unit. The International System of units, is based on the kilogramme, the metre, and the second, and also on three other units: the ampere, the kelvin, and the candela (see Table 1.1). These last three units will not be defined at this stage. All six units are referred to as arbitrary units because their values were given to them by a decision and not as a result of a deduction. Once these six basic units have been defined, all other units can be defined in terms of them without making any further arbitrary decisions.

When an instrument is checked against any of these standards, the degree of standardization must be more accurate than any measurement the instrument may be called upon to make. The standardization, therefore, sets a limit on the accuracy of any instrument. For example, it would be nonsense to quote a measurement accurate to 1/100,000,000th part of a metre if the standardization of the gauge were only possible to 1/10,000,000th part. Any engineer involved in accurate measurement must be aware of this, and this is why we attach great importance to the processes of standardization.

Measurement of Mass

The standard unit of mass is the *kilogramme*. The kilogramme was first defined as the amount of matter

Table 1.1. Basic SI Units

Quantity	Name of unit	Unit symbol	Dimensions
Length	Metre	m	L
Mass	Kilogramme	kg	M
Time	Second	s	T
Electric current	Ampere	A	A
Thermodynamic temperature	Kelvin	K	θ
Luminous intensity	Candela	cd	I

contained in one thousand cubic centimetres of pure water at 0°C. Today, the standard kilogramme is the mass of a particular lump of platinum, which is kept in the International Bureau of Weights and Measures in Paris. Other countries keep replicas of this standard kilogramme, using them to standardize their weighing instruments.

We must be very careful to distinguish between *mass*, which is a measure of the inertia of a body, and *weight*, which is the force exerted by a body when it is supported at the Earth's surface. The mass of a body determines its reluctance to accelerate when a force is applied to it. Thus a body, which accelerates to the same extent as the platinum standard when the same force is applied to it, has the same mass.

The major contribution to the weight of a body is the force of gravity which is strictly dependent on the environment. The force exerted by the Earth's gravity varies from one place to another on its surface. For example, it is slightly greater at the poles than at the equator because of the Earth's departure from a spherical shape. Similarly, it is greater in areas where the surface rock is very dense than in areas where the surface rock is lighter. A further minute variation is introduced by the differing effect of the Earth's rotation at the equator and at the poles. These variations cannot be measured using a beam balance, no matter how accurate it is, but they register on a spring 'balance'. (Fig. 1.6.) Weight is a relative term; the standard kilogram would weigh far less supported on the Moon than it does here on Earth (about $\frac{1}{6}$). A man in an orbiting space craft appears to have no weight at all because both he and the craft are unsupported and subject to the same body forces. Remember, however, that the *mass* of the kilogramme is constant, because a certain force would give it the same acceleration in all of these places.

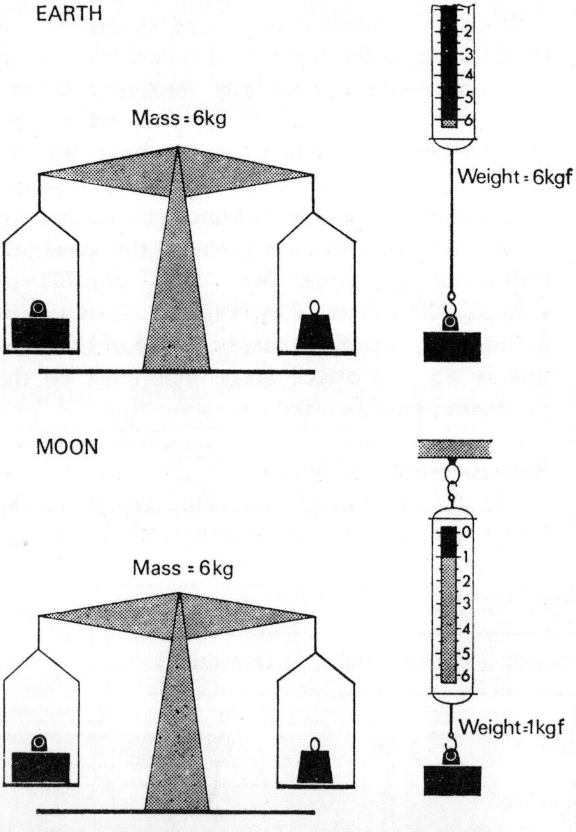

Although the kilogramme provides a convenient basis for a system of measurement, there are some branches of science which deal with such small particles of matter that a much smaller unit of mass is more convenient. Physicists express the masses of atoms in terms of the unified atomic mass unit (u). This is roughly equal to the mass of one hydrogen atom or, more precisely, to one twelfth of the mass of an atom of the main isotope of carbon. To a close approximation:

$$1 \text{ u} = 1 \cdot 66 \times 10^{-27} \text{ kg}$$

Units of Length

The basic unit of length is the metre. When French scientists first established the metric system in the late eighteenth century, they defined the metre as one ten-millionth part of the distance from the Equator to the North Pole on a line through Paris. Since then, more accurate measurement has shown that the distance is actually rather more than ten million metres, but the original metre has been the basis of measurement ever since. It was fixed as the distance between two lines engraved on a ruler of platinum–iridium kept, like the standard kilogramme, in the International Bureau of Weights and Measures, and, as with the kilogramme, other countries possess replicas of this standard.

EARTH

Mass = 6kg

Weight = 6kgf

MOON

Mass = 6kg

Weight = 1kgf

Fig. 1.6. Showing how mass and weight of an object are affected by a change in position.

No matter how carefully made, however, no ruler can be trusted to provide the perfect definition of a distance. Metal rulers expand and contract, wood and plastic warp. In 1961, therefore, an international congress redefined the metre in terms which are not subject to variation, and presented the world with a new standard of length. This is the wave-length of the orange-red light emitted by the gas krypton, there being by definition 1,650,763·73 wave-lengths in the standard metre. It is more convenient, however, to express some lengths in terms of fractions and multiples of this standard metre (Table 1.2).

Table 1.2

Name	Symbol	Definition
kilometre	km	1000 m
centimetre	cm	10^{-2} m
millimetre	mm	10^{-3} m
micron	μm	10^{-6} m
Nanometre	nm	10^{-9} m

Units of Time

To establish a standard of time, we require a process which is repeated endlessly and with absolute regularity. The most obvious recurrent phenomenon in human experience is the fact that day follows night, and the time it takes for the cycle to be completed is divided into hours and minutes, and finally seconds. One second, which is our unit of time, is approximately $1/60 \times 60 \times 24$th of a mean solar day. For the purposes of precise, scientific definition, however, this method of arriving at the length of a standard second is far too vague and inexact. The time taken for the Earth to rotate on its axis, that is, the average day as measured on a sundial, is not constant. The viscous effect of the tides slows the rotation down by about $3\frac{1}{2}$ seconds every 1000 years. Even the length of the year is not absolutely constant, and, in any case, different methods of measuring it produce slightly different values. The second therefore, was defined as a fraction of one particular year, as measured by one particular method. (1/31,556,925·9747 of the year of 1900.)

Since the discovery of the regularity of the swing of the pendulum by Galileo, this device has been the main method of controlling the movements of clocks. Like all mechanical processes, however, the swing of the pendulum is subject to factors such as variations in the temperature and the viscosity of the air, which influence slightly the length of time it takes to swing.

In recent years, clocks have been developed which are accurate to within one second in every 300 years. These are controlled by the natural vibration of atoms of caesium or of molecules of ammonia, which have, as far as we can judge, a constant frequency. The present definition of the second is the duration of 9,192,631,770 periods of the radiation from transitions between the two levels of the ground state of the caesium 133 atom.

Motion

Velocity. A body in the process of movement possesses a velocity which is defined as the distance moved per unit time in a certain direction. For a body moving with a uniform velocity v

$$v = \frac{S}{t}$$

where S is the distance moved by the body in a certain time t. Sometimes the term 'speed' is used to mean the same as velocity, but conventionally we use speed in cases when the direction of the motion is not important. A car lapping a circular track at a constant rate has a constant speed but a changing velocity, because the direction of the motion is continually changing. Velocities are expressed in metres per second or kilometres per hour.

Problem: A motorist covers the distance from London to Birmingham, a distance of 180 km, in 6 hours. Calculate his average speed in km/h and m/s.

Solution: $V = \dfrac{180}{6} = 30$ km/h

$$= \frac{30 \times 1000}{60 \times 60} = 8 \cdot 3 \text{ m/s}$$

Acceleration. Rarely do objects have a uniform velocity; they are usually changing either their speed or their direction of motion. This change in velocity is called an *acceleration* and we define it as the *change in velocity per unit time.* An object

7

moving in a straight line, which increases its velocity from u to v in a time t, has an acceleration a given by the equation

$$a = \frac{v-u}{t}$$

which can be expressed in metres per second, per second (m/s² or ms⁻²).

Problem: A grand prix racing car reaches 60 km/h from a standing start in 8 seconds and then takes a further 12 seconds to reach 140 km/h. Calculate the average acceleration in ms⁻² during these two periods.

Solution:

Now 60 km/h = 16·6 m/s
and 140 km/h = 38·9 m/s
Using $a = (v-u)/t$

In the first period $a = \dfrac{16\cdot6 - 0}{8} = 2\cdot07$ ms⁻²

In the second period $a = \dfrac{(38\cdot9 - 16\cdot6)}{12} = 1\cdot86$ ms⁻²

Momentum

Imagine that we are investigating the collision of objects, and trying to find a relation between quantities before and after collision. We might try to find a quantity which is conserved in the collision. We expect the mass to be conserved, but the sum of the velocities before and after does not remain constant. We might investigate the conservation of various quantities such as acceleration, or products such as m^2u, or mv, or mv^2, etc. Proceeding in this way, we would discover that the quantity which remains constant before and after every collision is the product mass × velocity. This quantity is called the momentum and, having magnitude and direction, it is a vector quantity. We can express our findings in the form of a law of conservation of momentum. *When objects collide, the sum of the momenta before impact is equal to the sum of the momenta after impact.*

In calculating the momentum, the velocities in one direction must be reckoned positive, and those in the other direction negative. We will illustrate this by considering how the law applies in two common cases.

Consider what happens when two trucks of masses m_1 and m_2 collide. (Fig. 1.7.)

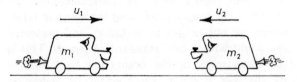

Before collision

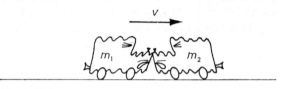

After collision

Fig. 1.7. Momentum is conserved when objects collide.

Total momentum before collision

$$= m_1 u_1 + m_2(-u_2)$$

Suppose that they do not rebound on collision but have a common final velocity v in the direction of u_1.

Total momentum after collision

$$= m_1 v + m_2 v$$

By the law of conservation of momentum

$$m_1 u_1 + m_2(-u_2) = m_1 v + m_2 v$$

The recoil of a rifle is explained by this conservation of momentum. (Fig. 1.8.) The initial momentum of the rifle and bullet is zero, so that, after firing, the nett momentum of the rifle and the bullet must also be zero.

$$m_1 v_1 + m_2(-v_2) = 0$$
$$m_1 v_1 = m_2 v_2$$

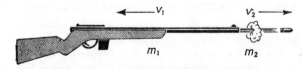

Fig. 1.8. At the instant of separation, the rifle and the bullet have equal momenta.

Problem: A rifle weighing 3 kg fires a 2 g bullet with a muzzle velocity of 500 m/s. Calculate the velocity of recoil of the rifle.

Solution: $m_1 v_1 = m_2 v_2$

$$3 \times v_2 = \frac{2}{1000} \times 500$$

$$v_2 = \frac{2}{1000} \times \frac{500}{3} = 0 \cdot 33 \text{ m/s}$$

Force

When a force is exerted on an unrestricted object, its velocity is changed. If the body is rigidly held or its motion otherwise resisted, the body changes its shape somewhat under the influence of the applied and resisting forces. Thus, when a mass is suspended from a spring balance it is the gravitational force on the mass and the opposing force on the support which stretch the spring. An unbalanced force, such as that exerted by the engine of a motor car, causes an acceleration.

Newton investigated force and expressed his findings in terms of three laws.

1st Law Every body continues in its state of rest or of uniform motion in a straight line unless acted on by a force.

2nd Law The rate of change of momentum (mv) of a body is proportional to the impressed force and takes place in the direction of the force.

3rd Law When a force acts on one body, a force equal in magnitude and opposite in direction must act on another body

The first law tells us something about the nature of a force, while the third law is based on the fact that all forces arise from the interaction of pairs of bodies.

The second law relates the magnitude of a force to the momentum.

force ∝ rate of change in momentum

Usually the mass remains constant, in which case

force ∝ mass × rate of change in velocity

i.e., force ∝ mass × acceleration

We use this relation to define the unit for force, which is called a *newton* (N).

force (newtons) = mass (kg) × acceleration (ms⁻²)

i.e.,
$$F = ma$$

Thus the newton is the force which produces an acceleration of 1 ms⁻² in a mass of 1 kg.

Problem: If the force of gravity produces an acceleration of 9·80 ms⁻² relative to the Earth's surface when applied to a mass of 1 kg, what is the magnitude of the force?

Solution: $F = ma$
$$= 1 \times 9 \cdot 8$$
Force $= 9 \cdot 8$ N

In general, at a place where the acceleration produced by gravity is g, the force exerted on a mass of m kilogrammes is given by:

$$F = mg \text{ newtons}$$

When we are dealing with forces which are a result of applying weights, such as the loading of beams, we find it convenient to express force in gravitational units. The force of gravity on 1 kg we call the kilogramme weight. However, since the force of gravity varies slightly from one place to another so does the value of the kilogramme weight. We overcome this inaccuracy by adopting a standard value for g which gives us a technical unit called the kilogramme force (kgf)

$$1 \text{ kgf} = 9 \cdot 80665 \text{ N}$$

The kgf must not be used to express the value of forces in basic formulae where the proper unit of force, the newton, should be used.

Work

The last hundred years have seen the proportion of the work of industry performed by manual labour change from over 90 per cent to under 10 per cent. In physics, work has a precise meaning, which is not related to mental or physical fatigue. Pushing an object which doesn't move or holding an object still against the pull of gravity may produce fatigue, but it does not constitute work. Work is done only when a force moves in the direction in which it is applied.

$$\text{Work} = \text{force} \times \text{distance}$$
$$W = F \times S$$

The SI unit of work, the *joule, is the work done when a force of one newton moves a distance of one metre.*

The meaning of the unit is illustrated in Fig. 1.9.

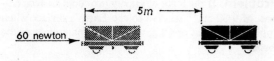

$$W = F \times s = 60 \times 5 = 300 \text{ joules}$$

Fig. 1.9. The joule as a unit of work.

When a mass of 30 kg is moved 20 m against the force of gravity as in Fig. 1.10, the work W is given by:

$$W = \text{force} \times \text{distance}$$
$$= (30 \times 9 \cdot 8) \times 20$$
$$= 5880 \text{ J}$$

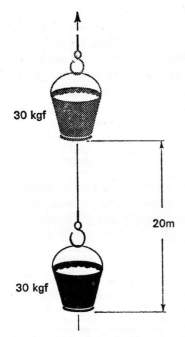

Fig. 1.10. Work done against the force of gravity.

Only movement in the direction of the force contributes to the work done. Thus, when calculating the work done, we either resolve the force in the direction of movement (Fig. 1.11a) or find the distance moved in the direction of the force (Fig. 1.11b).

10

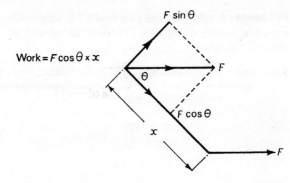

$$\text{Work} = F \cos \theta \times x$$

(a) Resolving the force

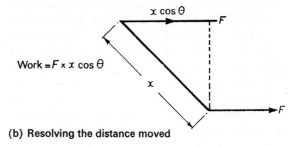

$$\text{Work} = F \times x \cos \theta$$

(b) Resolving the distance moved

Fig. 1.11. Work done in moving a force at an angle to its direction in which it is applied. *(a)* Resolving the force. *(b)* Resolving the distance moved.

Energy

A person who performs a hard day's work is said to have expended energy. This use of the word energy coincides with its meaning in physics, where energy is defined as *the capacity to do work.*

This capacity to do work may take many forms. Heat supplied to a steam engine results in the performance of work and therefore heat is a form of energy. A moving mass may do work as it is slowed down by a force and is said to have *kinetic energy*, i.e., energy due to motion. A compressed spring and an elevated mass possess energy because they could perform work in returning to their original position. Before they do this work they are said to have *potential energy*, or energy due to position. There are, of course, many more kinds of energy, such as chemical energy (fuels), electrical energy (batteries), and atomic energy (nuclear reactors). They all have the one thing in common, that is, when suitably harnessed, they can be made to do work.

Energy is generally measured in the same units as work, namely the joule. Other units of energy may be used, such as the calorie ($=4.1868$ J) which is useful when dealing with the thermal properties of water.

We can derive a simple expression for the kinetic energy of a mass m moving with a velocity v as follows: Suppose a body initially at rest is accelerated by a force F, which continues to be applied whilst the body moves a distance S. The kinetic energy acquired by the body is equal to the work done by the force ($F \times S$).

To obtain a value for S we use the equation

$$v^2 = u^2 + 2aS$$

where the initial velocity $u=0$ and v is the final velocity,

rearranging $\quad S = \dfrac{v^2}{2a}$

Also $\qquad F = ma$

thus $\quad$ K.E. $= F \times S = ma\dfrac{v^2}{2a} = \frac{1}{2}mv^2$

The energy will be expressed in joules when m is in kilogrammes and v is in m/s.

The potential energy of a mass m, relative to some level a distance h below it, is equal to the work done in raising it against the force of gravity.

Potential Energy = Work = Force × distance

To obtain the potential energy in joules we must express the distance in metres and the force of gravity in newtons, in which case:

Force $= mg$ and distance $= h$

thus

P.E. $= mgh$

Earlier science was based on two separate laws of conservation: the law of conservation of mass, and the law of conservation of energy. Nowadays, we know that neither law holds true in isolation, although both are valid if we consider a big enough system. In a nuclear explosion, a very large amount of energy is released, which is not apparently converted from any other form and, at the same time, a small amount of mass dis-

appears. Both conservation laws are contradicted unless—and this idea opens up astonishing new fields of investigation—the small amount of mass and the large amount of energy are in some way related. We now believe that they are, in the sense that mass is a property of energy. Any form of energy has mass associated with it. Thus, a given force accelerates an object less when it is hot than when it is cold. For example, a sphere of iron 2 m in diameter, which is glowing red hot, is about a tenth of a milligramme more massive than when it is at room temperature. Einstein was the first to express the relation between mass and energy in an exact way by the equation

Energy = mass × (velocity of light)^2
$$E = mc^2$$

E is given in joules when m is expressed in kilogrammes and c is in m/s. The value of c is 3×10^8 m/s, so that $c^2 = 9 \times 10^{16}$.

This large constant of proportionality accounts for the apparently large difference between the energy and the mass associated with it.

Problem: How much energy is equivalent to a mass of a millionth part of a gramme?

Solution: 10^{-6} g $= 10^{-9}$ kg.
We use $E = mc^2$
$\qquad\qquad = 10^{-9} \times (3 \times 10^8)^2$
$\qquad\qquad = 9 \times 10^7$ joules

Power

In these days when, as we say, 'time is money', we are concerned with not only doing a job, but doing it within a given budget and within a certain time. Thus, the rate at which energy can be supplied, the power, is as important to us as the total energy which is required. Power is defined as the *rate of doing work*

$$P = \frac{\text{work}}{\text{time}}$$

The SI unit of power is the *watt, a rate of working of 1 joule per second.* Where this unit is too small, the kilowatt (1000 watts) is used.

The old unit of power; the horsepower, is roughly the power that a horse can muster flat out for a short time. Of course, we don't define it in terms of the horse, but in terms of the watt:

$$1 \text{ hp} = 745 \cdot 7 \text{ W} \approx \tfrac{3}{4} \text{ kW}$$

Motor vehicle engines produce from about 30 to 300 kW (40 to 400 hp), aircraft engines several thousand kW, and some marine engines about 100,000 kW. Electric motors will develop 20,000 kW or more, but it is generally more convenient to use a number of small ones of low power than to use one large motor.

Problem: A jet plane weighing 5,000 kg can climb vertically at a rate of 200 km/h. What power is being expended? ($g = 9 \cdot 8$ m/s).

Solution: Power = work/time = $\dfrac{\text{force} \times \text{distance}}{\text{time}}$

$$= \text{force} \times \text{velocity}$$
$$F = mg = 5,000 \times 9 \cdot 8 \text{ newtons}$$
$$v = 200 \text{ km/h} = 55 \cdot 6 \text{ m/s}$$
$$\text{Power} = 5,000 \times 9 \cdot 8 \times 55 \cdot 6$$
$$= 2,724,000 \text{ W} = 2,724 \text{ kW}$$

Pressure

A force acting over a surface may be thought of as exerting a pressure on the surface. The pressure is defined as the normal force per unit area.

In many cases, the pressure is as important a quantity as total force. For example, in a cutting process the edge of the tool must be sharp in order to reduce the area of contact and thereby increase the pressure.

$$\text{Pressure} = \frac{\text{force}}{\text{area}}$$

The SI unit of pressure is the newton per square metre (N/m^2). Stresses are sometimes expressed in kgf/m^2 where

$$1 \text{ kgf/m}^2 = 9 \cdot 8 \text{ N/m}^2$$

In fluids, which means gases and liquids, the pressure is exerted equally in all directions. In liquids, which do not compress much under the influence of gravity, the pressure increases uniformly with depth. To obtain an expression for the pressure at a depth h in a liquid of density ρ we proceed as follows:

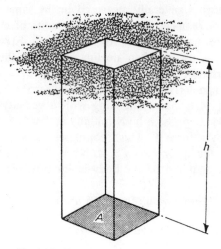

Fig. 1.12. The pressure at a depth in a liquid is due to the weight of the liquid.

Consider a column of length h and area of cross-section A (Fig. 1.12).

$$\text{Volume} = hA$$
$$\text{mass} = \text{volume} \times \text{density} = hA\rho$$
$$\text{pressure} = \frac{\text{force}}{\text{area}} = \frac{\text{mass} \times g}{\text{area}} = \frac{hA\rho g}{A}$$
$$p = h\rho g$$

This gives the pressure in N/m^2 when h is in metres ρ is in kg/m^3 and g is in m/s^2. If g is ommitted from the expression for pressure, then the units of pressure will be kfg/m^2.

Instead of expressing pressure as a force per unit area, we often express it in terms of the height of a column of a reference liquid, which would exert the same pressure. For example, the length of a column of water is commonly used to specify pressure in the gas industry, and also, since atmospheric pressure is measured with a mercury barometer, it is convenient to express this pressure directly as the height, in millimetres, of a column of mercury, of density $13 \cdot 6 \times 10^3$ kg/m^3

$$1 \text{ mm Hg} = h\rho g = \frac{1}{1000} \times 13 \cdot 6 \times 10^3 \times 9 \cdot 8 = 135 \text{ N/m}^2$$

1 mm Hg is sometimes called a torr.

1 atmosphere = 760 mm Hg = $h\rho g$

$$= \frac{760}{1000} \times 13 \cdot 6 \times 10^3 \times 9 \cdot 8$$
$$= 1 \cdot 0 \times 10^3 \text{ N/m}^2$$

Coherent Units

Difficulty arises in calculations because of our uncertainty as to which units to use when applying basic formulae. For example, do we use kilogramme-force or newtons as units of force in the equation

Force = mass × acceleration?

This difficulty is reduced if we know what is meant by a coherent system of units. A system of units is coherent if the product or quotient of any two unit quantities in the system is the unit of the resulting quantity. In the coherent SI system each unit is defined in terms of the basic units, as shown in Table 1.1, and not any multiple of them. Thus the unit of volume is the cubic metre and not the cubic centimetre, and the unit of force is the newton and not the kilogramme-force.

Often non-coherent units are more convenient for everyday use and thus the litre $\left(=\dfrac{1}{1000}\,m^3\right)$ is used for fluid measure. (Who wants to buy beer in cubic metres?) Formulae may be designed to take units which are not part of a coherent system, e.g.,

$$\text{Power (kW)} = \frac{\text{Work done (J)}}{3\cdot6\times10^6\times\text{time (h)}}$$

More general formulae are only valid when coherent units are used. Thus each time a quantity is introduced, we should be aware of the unit of the quantity which forms part of a coherent system.

Dimensions

Every quantity can be expressed in terms of its basic dimensions of mass, length, time, etc. (Table 1.3.) The procedure for doing this is first to write down the equation defining the quantity, then to express each component of the defining equation in its dimensions.

$$\text{Velocity} = \frac{\text{distance}}{\text{time}} = \left[\frac{L}{T}\right] = [LT^{-1}]$$

$$\text{Acceleration} = \frac{\text{change in velocity}}{\text{time}}$$

$$= \left[\frac{LT^{-1}}{T}\right] = [LT^{-2}]$$

The square brackets indicate that only the dimensions of the quantities are being considered.

Problem: Find the dimensions of force.

Solution: Force = mass × acceleration

$$= (M)\times\frac{\text{(change of velocity)}}{T}$$

$$= \left[\frac{ML/T}{T}\right]$$

$$= [MLT^{-2}]$$

Apart from emphasizing the dependence of all units on the basic units, this reduction of a quantity to its dimensions can be useful in checking equations involving physical quantities. Each of the

Table 1.3. Derived SI Units

Physical quantity	SI units	Unit symbol	Dimensions
Area	Square metre	m²	L^2
Volume	Cubic metre	m³	L^3
Density (mass density)	Kilogramme per cubic metre	kg/m³	ML^{-3}
Velocity	Metre per second	m/s	LT^{-1}
Acceleration	Metre per second squared	m/s²	LT^{-2}
Pressure	Newton per square metre	N/m²	$ML^{-1}T^{-2}$
Thermal conductivity	Watt per metre, kelvin	W/(m K)	$MLT^{-3}\theta^{-1}$
Force	Newton	N = kg m/s²	MLT^{-2}
Work, energy, quantity of heat	Joule	J = N m	ML^2T^{-2}
Power	Watt	W = J/s	ML^2T^{-3}
Electric charge	Coulomb	C = A s	AT
Frequency	Hertz	Hz = s⁻¹	T^{-1}
Luminous flux	Lumen	lm = cd sr	
Illumination	Lux	lx = lm/m²	

terms in such an equation must have the same dimensions if it is to be valid, e.g.,

work done on body = kinetic energy acquired

i.e., force × distance = $\frac{1}{2} mv^2$

$$[MLT^{-2}][L] = [M][L^2\,T^{-2}]$$
$$[ML^2\,T^{-2}] = [ML^2\,T^{-2}]$$

When we reach this equality, we conclude that the equations are dimensionally consistent. Some quantities have no dimensions. They are merely ratios between quantities of equal dimensions.

e.g., $Strain = \dfrac{\text{increase in length}}{\text{unit length}} = \dfrac{L}{L}$

$relative\ density = \dfrac{\text{mass of a substance}}{\text{mass of an equal volume of water}}$

Problem: Only one of the following equations gives the distance S travelled by a body with initial velocity v, and acceleration during a time t.

$$S = vt + \tfrac{1}{2}\,at^2$$
$$S = vt + \tfrac{1}{2}\,at$$

Confirm that one of them is incorrect by showing its dimensions to be dimensionally inconsistent.

Solution: For the first equation

$$[L] = [LT^{-1}][T] + [LT^{-2}][T^2]$$
$$[L] = [L] + [L]$$

∴ The terms are dimensionally constant and the first equation could be correct.

For the second equation

$$[L] = [LT^{-1}][T] + [LT^{-2}][T]$$
$$[L] = [L] + [LT^{-1}]$$

∴ The equation is incorrect.

Questions

1. What is the difference between basic units and derived units?

2. What are the advantages of the metric system?

3. What is the effect of (a) the Earth's shape, (b) surface rocks, (c) the Earth's rotation on the force on a constant mass at different places on the Earth?

4. If you were in space, drifting away from your capsule, how would you get back?

5. Explain the difference between mass and weight.

6. How could you compare the masses of two objects without weighing them?

7. Suggest how the importance of the quantities $\frac{1}{2}mv^2$ and mv could be established experimentally.

8. Can you increase your power by the use of a lever?

9. A bird is perched in a cage which is hanging on a spring balance. What happens to the balance reading when the bird leaves its perch and flies around the cage?

10. Work and torque are both defined as force × distance. What is the difference between them?

Problems

1. A spring bathroom scale reads 68 kg when a man steps on it in a lift. What does it read (a) if the lift cable snaps. (b) If the lift accelerates up at 10 m/s²? ($g = 9.81$ m/s²).
Answer: (a) 0. (b) 135 kg.

2. A man weighing 70 kg is sitting in a car which accelerates at 2 m/s². What horizontal force does his seat exert on him?
Answer: 140 N.

3. How much coal could a 1 kW motor lift up a 60 m shaft in 1 minute?
Answer: 102 kg.

4. The resistance to motion of a car travelling at 100 km/h is 400 N. What power is the engine producing?
Answer: 1·1 kW.

5. A shell of mass 0·5 kg is fired from a cannon at a muzzle velocity of 200 m/s. If the recoiling part of the gun weighs 300 kg, what is the velocity of recoil?
Answer: 3·33 m/s.

6. A pile-driver of mass 350 kg falls 6 m before striking the pile; the blow drives the pile 200 mm into the ground. What average force is exerted on the pile?
Answer: 103 N.

7. A stream of water from a hose 50 mm in diameter, hits a wall at 8 m/s. What force is exerted on the wall if we ignore splashing?
Answer: 125·6 N.
What would be the effect on the force of the splashing back of the water?

8. An electric motor develops 19 kW and consumes 20 kW. What is its efficiency?
   Answer: 95%.

9. A bathyscaphe went down 10 km into the Pacific. What was the water pressure on it at this depth? (Specific gravity of sea-water=1·03, density of water=1,000 kg/m³).
   Answer: 10·3 MN/m². (i.e., $10·3 \times 10^6$ N/m²).

10. Check the following equations for dimensional consistency
    (i) $v^2 = u^2 + 2\,aS$.
    (ii) Pressure = height $\times$ density $\times g$.

11. What air pressure, acting on a 200 mm diameter ram, is necessary to lift a car weighing 900 kg on a hoist weighing 100 kg?
    Answer: 310 N/m².

12. A mass of 5 kg is hung on one end of a string, and the other end is passed over a pulley, and a 7 kg mass is tied to it. What is the acceleration if the masses are released, and what is then the tension in the string? ($g = 9·81$ m/s²).
    Answer: 1·63 m/s², 57·2 N.

13. If a man weighing 77 kg slides down a rope with a breaking load of 45 kgf, what is his smallest possible acceleration?
    Answer: 4·07 m/s².

14. A bullet weighing 18 g strikes a 0·6 kg block of wood at 550 m/s, penetrates it, and leaves at 250 m/s. What is the velocity of the block after the bullet has passed through?
    Answer: 9 m/s.

15. The lift cage in a coal-mine has a mass of 1200 kg. What is the tension in its supporting cable if it is accelerated up the mine shaft at 0·70 m/s²?
    Answer: $1·26 \times 10^4$ N.

16. If a water pressure of 262 kN/m² is required in a main, how high up must the storage tanks be? (Density of water=1,000 kg/m³).
    Answer: 26·7 m.

17. Distinguish clearly between the terms energy, work, and power. Show that for a mass falling under gravity from rest, the sum of its potential and kinetic energies is constant throughout its fall.

    (I.E.R.E. mechanics.)

18. The results of nuclear fusion occurring in the interiors of stars is the production of energy and the conversion of hydrogen into helium. Calculate the energy release if 0·993 kg of helium result from 1·0 kg of hydrogen.
    Answer: $6·3 \times 10^{14}$ J.

2 Temperature

Everyone has an intuitive idea of the meaning of temperature, but we have difficulty when it comes to putting a concise explanation into words. One thing we do know is that temperature is the quantity which determines the direction of heat flow. Heat flows from objects at a high temperature to objects at a lower temperature, and where there is no heat transfer we know that the objects are at the same temperature. Recognizing the difference of temperature is not enough, however; we need to devise a means of defining and measuring temperature precisely. The human body is sensitive to temperature differences, but it is quite unreliable as a means of temperature measurement. The skin is sensitive not so much to temperature, as to heat flow into the skin (warm sensation) or out of the skin (cold sensation).

Certain fixed temperatures we can define, because under constant conditions a substance always changes from solid to liquid, or liquid to vapour at the same temperature. For example, we can talk about the temperature at which mercury freezes and know that we are referring to a specific temperature. This change of state can be used to classify temperatures as shown in Fig. 2.1. We could specify the temperature at which ice melts or water boils in the same way, but how do we specify temperatures in between these points?

Unmelted Cones   Melted Cones

Fig. 2.1. Clay cones having different melting points are used in ovens to indicate that the temperature lies between certain limits.

As a substance gets hotter, certain of its properties change. Most substances, when they are heated, expand in size, change their electrical resistance, and, if they are glowing hot, change colour. We can use the variation in a property of a material to bridge the gap between any fixed points. In fact, we find that, using a varying property in this way, we need only two fixed points to define any temperature. The two fixed points we choose are the melting point of ice and the boiling point of water. The property which is most commonly used to measure temperature is the expansion of mercury in a glass tube.

Mercury-in-Glass Thermometer

This thermometer consists of a sealed glass tube of narrow bore with a bulb at one end containing mercury, which fills the bulb and extends up the tube. To calibrate the thermometer, we immerse the bulb first in melting ice, and then in the steam from water boiling at standard atmospheric pressure, in each case marking the level of the mercury on the stem (Fig. 2.2). The distance between the two fixed points is called the fundamental interval of the thermometer, and it is divided up into a number of equal parts.

Celsius was a Swedish physicist and he devised the mercury thermometer 250 years ago. He divided the fundamental interval between the ice and boiling point of water into 100 parts. Perhaps because he was from Sweden, he originally took the boiling point as 0°C and the freezing point as 100°C and thus measured degrees of cold! Later these were reversed, and this method of dividing up the interval produces the *Celsius* or *centigrade* scale of temperature.

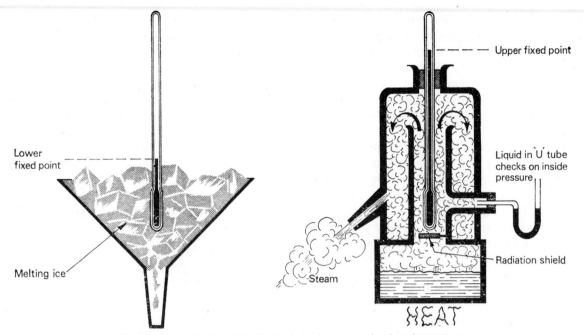

Fig. 2.2. Determination of the fixed points of a mercury-in-glass thermometer.

Marking the thermometer in degrees allows us to make direct readings of temperature between 0°C and 100°C. If we know the length of mercury thread at 0°C (L_0) and at 100°C (L_{100}), we can obtain the temperature corresponding to any other value (L_t) by using a straight line graph drawn through the fixed points (Fig. 2.3). Alternatively, we can derive an equation to do the same job.

Since $t° \propto L_t - L_0$

and $100° \propto L_{100} - L_0$

$$\frac{t}{100} = \frac{L_t - L_0}{L_{100} - L_0}$$

This equation defines temperature and gives it a value in degrees Celsius [°C], on the mercury-in-glass scale.

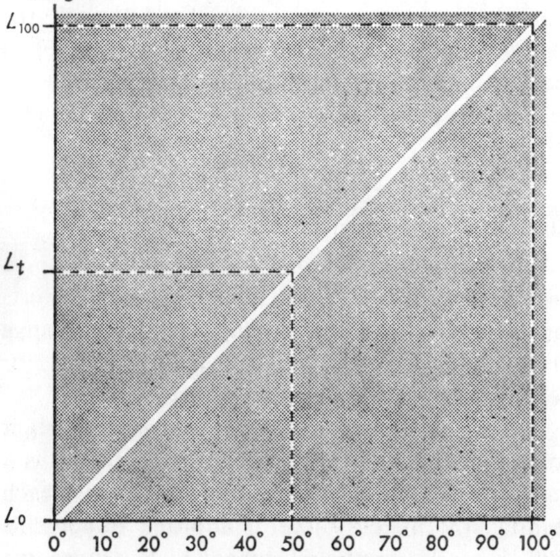

Problem: A mercury thread has lengths of 20·0 cm and 21·7 cm at the standard freezing and boiling points of water. What is the temperature when the length is 21·1 cm?

Solution: $\frac{t}{100} = \frac{L_i - L_0}{L_{100} - L_0} = \frac{21\cdot1 - 20}{21\cdot7 - 20} = \frac{1\cdot1}{1\cdot7}$

$$t = \frac{1\cdot1 \times 100}{1\cdot7} = 64\cdot7°C$$

Accuracy of Mercury Thermometer

Mercury-in-glass thermometers are subject to errors which are difficult to eliminate. For example, the glass bulb and stem, being slightly plastic, take some time to contract when cooled. The pressure of the mercury thread causes different readings in

Fig. 2.3. Calibration graph relating the lengths of the thread to the temperature for a mercury-in-glass thermometer.

17

the vertical and horizontal positions, and irregularities in the bore produce variations between thermometers in the size of degrees. Mercury thermometers are very convenient, however, and we can achieve an accuracy of 0·01°C by using a thermometer which has been calibrated against an accurate thermometer at the National Physical Laboratory.

The range of the mercury thermometer extends from the freezing to the boiling point of mercury, −39°C to 356°C. Alcohol-in-glass thermometers are used to measure atmospheric temperatures below −39°C. More accurate and more convenient thermometers than the liquid-in-glass variety exist and are preferred for many applications in science and industry.

Absolute Zero and the Kelvin Scale

The freezing point of water is quite an arbitrary point at which to fix our zero of temperature. Is there a more natural zero we could use? Yes there is. There does exist an absolute zero of temperature at which no more internal energy can be extracted from a body. This is used as the lower fixed point of the kelvin scale of temperature.

The upper fixed point on the kelvin scale is the triple point of water. The triple point is the temperature of transition of ice and water, when

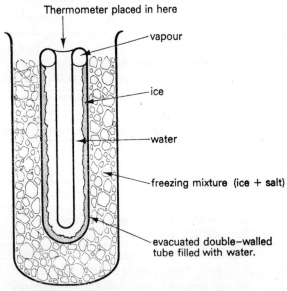

Fig. 2.4. The Fahrenheit and Celsius temperature scales compared.

they are subject only to the pressure of water vapour. This temperature is chosen because it can be accurately determined with the apparatus of Fig. 2.4.

By definition the temperature of the triple point is 273·16 kelvins. It is 1/100 of a kelvin above the melting point of ice at atmospheric pressure (273·15 K). The size of a kelvin and a degree Celsius is exactly the same, it is just that the starting points of the numbers are different as shown in Fig. 2.5.

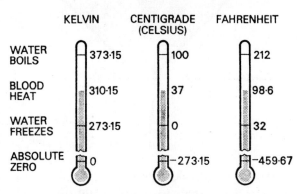

Fig. 2.5. The product *PV* for a gas is not strictly constant but changes slightly with pressure. The constants *A* and *B* vary with temperature so each line applies to one temperature.

For all purposes except the most accurate measurements we can assume that 0°C=273K and that absolute zero, 0K=−273°C. Although the centigrade scale is defined in terms of the kelvin scale we often standardize thermometers at the ice and steam points.

The Gas Thermometer

When a gas, maintained at constant volume, is heated from 0°C to 100°C the pressure it exerts increases by about 36 per cent. This large change in pressure serves as an excellent property for defining and measuring temperature.

Figure 2.6 shows a simple form of constant volume gas thermometer. A capillary tube joins a bulb to a flexible U tube of mercury. Before each reading, the mercury level is adjusted to coincide with a mark on the U tube which defines the constant volume. The gas pressure *p* is equal to atmospheric pressure *A* plus the pressure of the

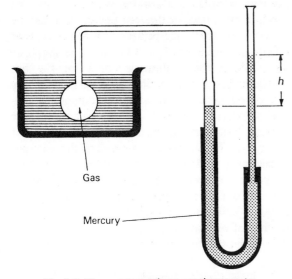

Fig. 2.6. The constant volume gas thermometer.

The Platinum Resistance Thermometer

A rise in the temperature of a metal produces an increase in its electrical resistance. Since we can measure resistance very accurately, we can use this property as an accurate measure of temperature. Pure platinum is commonly used as the resistive material, being extremely unreactive chemically. The resistance of platinum increases by about 40 per cent between 0°C and 100°C.

The platinum resistance thermometer consists essentially of a fine platinum wire coil wound on a mica former. (Fig. 2.7.) A sensitive ohmmeter serves to measure the resistance as it varies with temperature. Commercial instruments are often calibrated directly in degrees, but the change in resistance may be used to define a temperature scale quite independently of any other thermometer by using the equation

$$\frac{t}{100} = \frac{R_t - R_0}{R_{100} - R_0}$$

For more accurate work we measure the resistance on a Wheatstone bridge net. The copper leads to the platinum coil, passing near to the heat source, are heated to some extent and introduce an error into the measurement of resistance. We eliminate this by including a pair of identical leads, which experience the same temperature differences, into the opposite arm of the bridge (Fig. 2.8). Usually, the standard resistance available cannot be varied in small enough steps so a slide wire and contact are incorporated between S and R (Fig. 2.8).

The range of the platinum resistance thermometer extends from −200°C up to 1500°C (70K to 1800K) if high melting point materials are used in its construction. It is highly suitable for measuring the high temperatures of heat-treating and annealing processes in the metallurgical industry, and it adapts easily for automatic recording or

mercury column h. The defining equation may be stated in terms of P or h.

$$\frac{t}{100} = \frac{p_t - p_0}{p_{100} - p_0}$$

Expressing the pressure as a height of mercury

$$\frac{t}{100} = \frac{(h_t + A) - (h_0 + A)}{(h_{100} + A) - (h_0 + A)}$$

$$\frac{t}{100} = \frac{h_t - h_0}{h_{100} - h_0}$$

We rarely use the gas thermometer to measure temperature directly because of its awkward size and mode of operation. When pure hydrogen is the gas used, the range of the thermometer extends from −240° to 1500°C (approx. 30K to 1800K), and between the fixed points it can measure accurately to 0·005°C. Its range and accuracy make the thermometer an ideal standard with which to calibrate other more convenient types of thermometer.

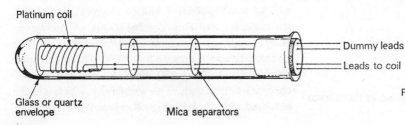

Fig. 2.7. The platinum resistance thermometer is sometimes evacuated to prevent oxidation.

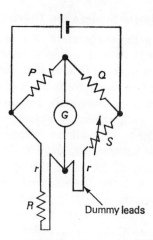

Fig. 2.8. Platinum resistance thermometer circuit. The resistance r of the leads to the platinum coil R is cancelled out by the dummy leads in the opposite arm of the Wheatstone bridge.

control systems. It has the disadvantage of responding slowly to temperature variation because of the thermal capacity and low thermal conductivity of the bulb. This is one of the reasons why it is not used so widely in industry as the thermoelectric thermometer.

Thermocouple

At the point of contact between two different metals there exists an electrical potential difference which depends on the temperature of the junction. When we complete the circuit with a second junction at a different temperature, a current flows round the circuit. (Fig. 2.9.)

This thermoelectric effect is called the *Seebeck effect* after the man who discovered it, and the

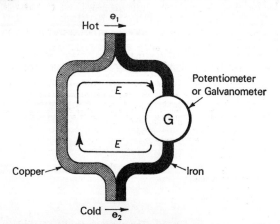

Fig. 2.9. Thermoelectric e.m.f.s are generated at the junction between different metals.

20

junction is called a *thermocouple*. Either the net e.m.f. in the circuit or the resulting current may be used to measure temperature. When the cold junction is maintained at 0°C, then the graph of Fig. 2.10 is the calibration curve for the hot junction. The cold junction may be held at any desired temperature, and the corresponding calibration curve obtained by drawing new axes through this point on the curve. The graph is not linear, so that we must standardize the thermocouple at a sufficient number of points to draw the curve. To avoid ambiguity, we usually operate only on one side of the maximum of the graph. When a measuring instrument is included in the circuit, other junctions between different metals may be introduced, but they do not influence the

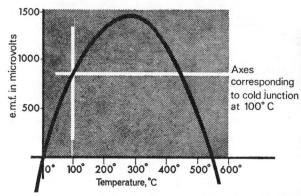

Fig. 2.10. The calibration curve for an iron–copper thermocouple with the cold junction at 0°C. The white axes show how we adjust the graph when the cold junction is at any other temperature.

readings provided they are all at the same temperature. For less accurate measurements, we can dispense with the cold junction completely, and replace it by the measuring instrument (Fig. 2.11.) The thermocouple then behaves as though its cold junction were at room temperature.

The robustness, low thermal capacity, and compact size of the thermocouple make it the most widely used thermometer in industry. It lends itself well to remote control and to automated systems. By choosing suitable combinations of metals or alloys, such as platinum–rhodium alloy, we can measure temperatures up to 1500°C. Other common combinations (thermels) are iron–constantan and chromel–constantan. The sensitivity which can be achieved by combining thermocouples into a

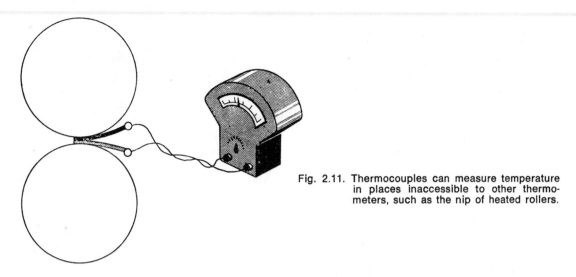

Fig. 2.11. Thermocouples can measure temperature in places inaccessible to other thermometers, such as the nip of heated rollers.

thermopile (Fig. 2.12) must be seen to be believed. Such an instrument with several hundred junctions can detect the heat of a candle flame a hundred feet away.

Pyrometers

The thermometers we have so far described have an upper limit of measurement of about 1500°C (1800K). Devices for measuring high temperatures are called pyrometers. In one form of pyrometer, the *radiation pyrometer*, heat rays from the hot object are received on one set of junctions of a thermopile. Under fixed conditions, the reading of a sensitive galvanometer connected across the thermocouple correlates with the temperature of the radiating object. A calibration graph for the pyrometer up to 1800K may be extrapolated to measure temperatures beyond this limit.

The heat radiation emitted by objects at a high temperature includes visible light, and the brightness of the light emitted increases with temperature. In the *optical pyrometer* we usually match the light from a filament of known temperature with that of the glowing object. (Fig. 2.13.) The match is made by increasing the current in a filament until it cannot be distinguished against a background of the light from the hot object. For this reason we sometimes refer to the optical pyrometer as the 'disappearing filament pyrometer'. The filament current produces a deflection on a meter marked directly in degrees, and the instrument is capable of an accuracy of about 0·4 per cent.

Pyrometers are calibrated against gas thermometers up to about 1800K. Their range can be extended up to about 3000K by the use of sectored discs which cut down the radiation in a known

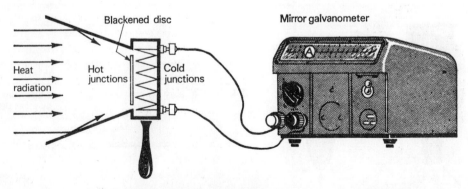

Fig. 2.12. In a radiation pyrometer, a thermopile made up of many thermocouples connected in series is used to measure the heat radiation.

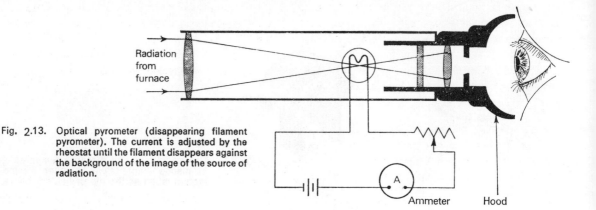

Fig. 2.13. Optical pyrometer (disappearing filament pyrometer). The current is adjusted by the rheostat until the filament disappears against the background of the image of the source of radiation.

ratio. (Fig. 2.14.) Pyrometers are very convenient for measuring the surface temperatures of molten metals and the interiors of volcanoes or furnaces, at a safe and comfortable distance.

Temperature Definitions

When we graduate the scale of a thermometer as °C or kelvins, we are merely using different methods of numbering; but every time we use a property, say X, to define temperature we are defining a unique temperature scale by the equation

$$\frac{t}{100} = \frac{X_t - X_0}{X_{100} - X_0}$$

All such scales coincide exactly at 0°C and 100°C, but away from these temperatures the different properties do not change exactly in step. For example, three thermometers, depending on different properties and standardized at 0° and 100°, could read, 49·8, 50·0, and 50·1 for the same

temperature, and all be correct according to their own definitions.

We eliminate this ambiguity either by stating the property we use, e.g., 24°C (platinum resistance scale), or by correcting all temperatures to one standard scale. But, since each scale is equally correct, which scale shall we adopt as a standard? One standard scale of reference is that obtained by using the lightest gas, hydrogen, at very low pressure in a constant volume gas thermometer. Ideally, we would prefer a scale which does not depend on any particular property and, in fact, such a scale exists in theory. It is called the thermodynamic scale because it depends only on energy considerations. On this scale, however, we cannot arrive at a temperature without a lengthy procedure.

There is a scale, the International Practical temperature scale (IPTS 1968) which approaches very near to the thermodynamic scale. Its importance lies in that it is used internationally for

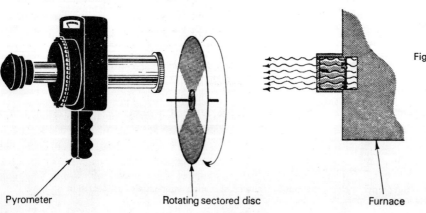

Fig. 2.14. Use of a sectored disc to extend the range of pyrometers beyond those which can be checked by a gas thermometer.

Pyrometer   Rotating sectored disc   Furnace

22

legal purposes, such as the **registering** of patents where ambiguity must be avoided at all costs. The feature of the international practical scale is that it has not two but a number of fixed points. Extrapolation between these points is made in a specified way with different thermometers (Table 2.1.)

Table 2.1. Some fixed points on the International Practical Temperature Scale 1968

Substance	Point	Temperature		Coverage
		K	°C	
Hydrogen	triple	13·81	−259·34	
Hydrogen	boiling	20·28	−252·87	platinum
Oxygen	triple	54·361	−218·789	resistance
Water	triple	273·16	0·01	thermometer
Water	boiling	373·15	100	
Zinc	freezing	692·73	419·58	
Silver	freezing	1235·08	961·93	thermo-
Gold	freezing	1337·58	1064·43	couple
	above		1064·43	radiation pyrometer

The Ideal Gas

If we had a gas which obeyed perfectly the relation $PV = A$ where A is a constant (Boyle's law), then temperatures measured with a gas thermometer using this ideal gas would coincide exactly with the thermodynamic scale. We take it that:

$$T \propto pV$$

or more strictly

$$T \propto A$$

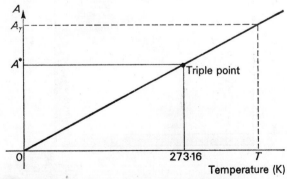

Fig. 2.15. Calibration graph for the ideal gas scale of temperature.

To obtain a calibration graph we would measure A at the triple point (273·16K) and use the fact that $A = 0$ at 0K. (Fig. 2.15.) We may measure any other temperature by determining A for that temperature and reading its value from the graph.

Unfortunately no such gas exists!

Real gases obey a relation;

$$pV = A + Bp$$

where B is a constant, and thus Bp is a correction term which increases with the pressure.

For a real gas the thermodynamic temperature T is not proportional to the product pV, but still it is true that

$$T \propto A$$

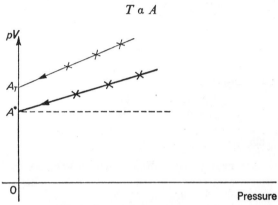

Fig. 2.16. The value of A for a particular temperature is obtained by projecting back to zero the graph of pV against p for a real gas.

If we could operate a gas thermometer at zero pressure then Bp would be zero and we could obtain A directly, but that is not possible. Instead we obtain several values of p and V at a particular temperature and plot the graph of pV against p. (Fig. 2.16.) We then project back to zero pressure to get A. Carrying this out at the triple point gives A^*, and we can draw the graph of Fig. 2.15. Repeating the procedure at a temperature T that we wish to measure, gives A_T, and with the aid of Fig. 2.15 we can find the value of T.

Perhaps after following this procedure you will see why, in practice, we prefer to standardize on the hydrogen scale or to use the International scale. The concept of an ideal gas which obeys $pV = A$ is, however, a useful one, and you may meet it again in the study of thermodynamics.

23

Temperature Coefficients

Several physical properties, such as length, pressure, and electrical resistance, vary with temperature, and we must make allowance for the variation in the design of a countless number of devices. The change in a property is not always directly proportional to the change in temperature, but we can describe all those changes which are approximately so, in a similar way. The variation in each property is described by a temperature coefficient, defined as the fractional change in the property per unit rise in temperature.

We will illustrate the method of approach for the specific case of linear expansion.

The coefficient of linear expansion α is the fractional change in length per unit rise in temperature.

$$\alpha = \frac{\text{change in length}}{\text{original length} \times \text{temperature rise}}$$

$$\alpha = \frac{l_2 - l_1}{l_1 \times \theta}$$

change in length $= l_1 \alpha \theta$

new length = original length + change in length

$$l_2 = l_1 + l_1 \alpha \theta$$
$$l_2 = l_1 (1 + \alpha \theta)$$

A change in temperature of a rigidly held body can cause a change in the constraining force. This may be either compression or tension and, in both cases, it is dependent on the expansion coefficient and the elasticity of the material.

Young's modulus $= E = \dfrac{\text{stress}}{\text{strain}}$

$$= \frac{\text{force/area}}{\text{fractional change in length}}$$

Also $\qquad \alpha = \dfrac{\text{fractional change in length}}{\text{temperature change}}$

If no movement occurs, we can equate the fractional changes in length

$$\frac{\text{Force}}{\text{Area} \times E} = \alpha \times \text{temperature change}$$

i.e.,
$$\text{Force} = EA\alpha t\theta$$

Note that the original length does not influence the force set up.

Problem: An iron girder of cross-sectional area 8,000 mm² is held rigidly in position. Calculate the change in the compressional force in the girder when the temperature changes from 0°C to 30°C.

$$\alpha = 12 \times 10^{-6}/°C, \quad E = 20 \times 10^{11} \ N/m^2$$

Solution: $F = EA\alpha\theta$

$$= 20 \times 10^{11} \frac{8,000}{10^6} \times 12 \times 10^{-6} \times 30$$

$$= 5 \cdot 76 \times 10^5 \ N$$

Area and Volume Coefficients

The change of area with temperature can be described by a coefficient of superficial (area) expansion, β. Adopting the procedure above we have:

$$\text{Change in area} = A_1 \beta \theta$$

$$\text{New area} = A_1(1 + \beta\theta)$$

For a regular shape we can calculate the new area by considering the linear expansion. (Fig. 2.17.)

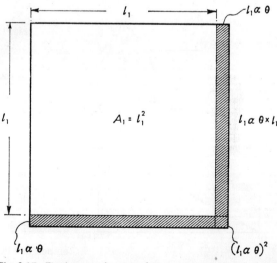

Fig. 2.17. The increase in area of a square may be calculated from the increase in length of its sides.

24

New area $= [l_1(1+\alpha\theta)]^2$

$\qquad = l_1^2(1+2\alpha\theta+\alpha^2\theta^2)$

Now $\alpha^2\theta^2$ is very small compared with $(1+2\alpha\theta)$ and $A_1 = l_1^2$.

$\qquad$ New area $\simeq A_1(1+2\alpha\theta)$

Comparing this with the expression above, involving β we see that

$$\beta \simeq 2\alpha$$

When dealing with the volume changes, we use the volume coefficient γ in our calculations.

$$\text{Change in volume} = V_1\gamma\theta$$

$$\text{New volume} = V_1(1+\gamma\theta)$$

By calculating the volume change in terms of the linear expansion of a cube of side 1, we can show that

$$\gamma \simeq 3\alpha$$

i.e.,

$$\text{New volume} \simeq V_1(1+3\alpha\theta)$$

The volume and area coefficients for solids are not quoted in reference tables since they are easily calculated from the linear coefficients. (Table 2.2.) Volume coefficients are quoted for liquids and they are generally higher than those for solids. A complicating factor in the case of liquid expansion is the expansion of the liquid container, which makes the expansion of the liquid appear to be less than it really is.

Usually, it is the apparent expansion we are interested in, and so we calculate an apparent coefficient of expansion for the liquid relative to the material of its container.

$$\gamma_{apparent} = \gamma_{absolute} - \gamma_{material\ of\ container}$$

Problem: A volume of $500\ cm^3$ of mercury is contained in a glass tube graduated in cubic centimetres. What increase in volume will be registered when the temperature is increased from $20°C$ to $200°C$, if the average coefficients of expansion over this temperature range are

$$\gamma = 0.182 \times 10^{-3}/°C \text{ for mercury}$$
$$\alpha = 8.3\ \times 10^{-6}/°C \text{ for glass}$$

Solution: $\gamma_{glass} = 3\alpha = 3 \times 8.3 \times 10^{-6}/°C$
$\qquad\qquad\qquad = 24.9 \times 10^{-6}/°C$.

Apparent coefficient $\gamma_{app} = \gamma_{mercury} - \gamma_{glass}$
$\qquad\qquad\qquad = 0.182 \times 10^{-3} - 24.9 \times 10^{-6}$
$\qquad\qquad\qquad = 0.157 \times 10^{-3}$

Apparent expansion $= V_1\ \gamma_{app}\ \theta$
$\qquad\qquad\qquad = 500 \times 0.157 \times 10^{-3} \times 180$
$\qquad\qquad\qquad = 14.1\ cm^3$

Temperature Coefficient of Resistance

The resistance of metals and alloys increases with temperature while that of insulators decreases. The temperature coefficient of resistance is defined as *the fractional increase in resistance per unit rise in temperature*, and it is therefore positive for metals and negative for insulators. (Table 2.3.)

$$\sigma = \frac{\text{increase in resistance}}{\text{initial resistance} \times \text{temperature rise}}$$

$$\text{Change in resistance} = R_1\sigma\theta$$

$$\text{New resistance} = R_1(1+\sigma\theta)$$

Table 2.2. Coefficients of expansion in range 0–100°C

Solids	α (°C^{-1})
Aluminium	23.8×10^{-6}
Brass	18.7×10^{-6}
Copper	16.8×10^{-6}
Glass (soft)	8.5×10^{-6}
Iron	$12\ \times 10^{-6}$
Plaster	$10\ \times 10^{-6}$
Platinum	$9\ \times 10^{-6}$
Wood	along grain $\simeq 8\ \times 10^{-6}$
	across grain $\simeq 40\ \times 10^{-6}$
Liquids	γ
Glycerine	$0.51\ \times 10^{-3}$
Mercury	$0.18\ \times 10^{-3}$
Petrol	$0.95\ \times 10^{-3}$
Water	0.207×10^{-3}
Gases	
Air	3.67×10^{-3}
Carbon dioxide	3.72×10^{-3}
Hydrogen	3.66×10^{-3}
Nitrogen	3.67×10^{-3}
Water vapour	4.19×10^{-3}

Table 2.3. Temperature coefficients of resistance at 20°C

Material	σ (°C^{-1})
Aluminium	$3.8\ \times 10^{-3}$
Brass	$2.0\ \times 10^{-3}$
Carbon (graphite)	$-0.5\ \times 10^{-3}$
Copper	$3.9\ \times 10^{-3}$
Eureka	0.05×10^{-3}
Nichrome	$0.4\ \times 10^{-3}$
Platinum	$0.3\ \times 10^{-3}$

Variation of Coefficients

Where the greatest accuracy is necessary, consideration must be given to the following points.

1. All the temperature coefficients vary with temperature, and the range of temperature to which they apply must be specified.

2. The way in which temperature is defined affects the temperature coefficients.

3. The property may vary regularly but not linearly with temperature and a more complex relation may apply, e.g.,

$$\text{New length} = l_1(1 + \alpha\theta + \beta\theta^2)$$

Questions

1. What are the advantages and disadvantages of a mercury-in-glass thermometer as an instrument for measuring temperature?

2. Prove that the thermal coefficient of volume expansion of a material is about three times the coefficient of linear expansion.

3. If you were inventing a temperature scale, would you use the ice point and steam point as its fixed points? Why? (or why not?).

4. Devise the equations for converting temperatures from kelvin to Celsius and Celsius to kelvin.

5. Why does there seem to be a lower limit for temperatures, but no upper limit?

6. A temperature of 50°C measured on a mercury thermometer is different from 50°C measured on a platinum resistance thermometer. Why?

7. Why is the gas thermometer not used for industrial temperature measurements?

8. How would you measure the temperature of the Moon's surface?

9. Why are dummy leads used in a platinum resistance thermometer circuit?

10. Write down the equation defining temperature in terms of a property X, which has values of X_0 and X_{100} at the ice and boiling points of water at S.T.P.

11. What happens to the volume of the space inside a steel tank when its temperature is raised?

12. Suggest five situations where the engineer must take account of the effect of thermal expansion.

Problems

1. What temperature has the same numerical value on both centigrade and kelvin scales?
Answer: approx. 136·5 k.

2. The length of the mercury thread of a thermometer is 32 mm at 0°C and 210 mm at 100°C. At what temperature is the length 86 mm?
Answer: 30°C.

3. The pressure of the gas in a constant volume gas thermometer at 0°C is 325 mm of mercury, and at 100°C it is 458 mm. What temperatures are represented by pressures of 410 mm and 543 mm?
Answer: 64°C, 164°C.

4. The resistance of a platinum coil is 13·5 ohms in melting ice and 14·7 ohms in steam at normal atmospheric pressure. What is its temperature on the platinum scale when its resistance is 13·692 ohms?
Answer: 16°C.

5. The following table gives the e.m.f.'s in a copper-iron thermocouple circuit for various temperatures of the hot junction (the cold junction is at 0°C).

temp. (°C)	0	50	100	150	200
e.m.f. (mV)	0	+0·62	+1·15	+1·60	+1·90
temp. (°C)		250	300	350	400
e.m.f. (mV)		+2·10	+2·05	+1·87	+1·60
temp. (°C)		450	500		
e.m.f. (mV)		+1·15	+0·60		

Plot a graph and deduce the two temperatures giving an e.m.f. of +1·75 mV. How would you tell which was the correct temperature in practice?
Answer: Approx. 170°C, 375°C.

6. A constant volume air thermometer gave the following results

Temp. (°C)	8	32	54	78	99
Pressure (mm Hg)	783	849	911	977	1037

By drawing a graph, find the air pressures at 0°C and 100°C and calculate the coefficient of increase of pressure of air at constant volume.
Answer: 760 mm Hg, 104 mm Hg, 0·0037 per °C.

7. A thermometer reads 1·5°C in melting ice and 99·4°C in steam at a pressure of 760 mm of mercury. If its bore is uniform, what is the correct temperature when the thermometer reads 30°C and −20°C?
Answer: 29°C and −22°C.

8. The cross-sectional area of a steel rod is 650 mm². Calculate the force required to prevent it contracting if its temperature changes from 50°C to −10°C. (Coefficient of linear expansion of steel $=12 \times 10^{-6}$/°C. Young's modulus for steel $=1·72 \times 10^{11}$ N/m².)
Answer: 80·5 kN.

9. A line 29 km long is measured at a temperature of 50°C, using an invar-steel tape 30 m long, standardized at 15°C. Calculate the error caused by the expansion of the tape. (Coefficient of expansion of invar-steel$=0·9 \times 10^{-6}$/°C.)
Answer: 0·914 m.

10. A steel wire, length 300 m is cooled to 0°C from 60°C. What is its change in length? (Coefficient of thermal expansion of steel = 0·000012/°C.)
Answer: 0·216 m.

11. A mass of gas at constant pressure has a volume of 0·4 litres at the temperature of melting ice, 0·5464 1 at the temperature of boiling water, and 1·0502 1 at the temperature of melting sulphur. At the same set of temperatures, a platinum wire has resistances of 1·000, 1·389, and 2·640 ohms. Compare the values of the melting point of sulphur given by the two sets of results.
Answer: 444°C, 422°C.

12. A centigrade thermometer is wrongly calibrated, and reads 1·30°C in melting ice and 99·2°C in boiling water. At what temperature does the thermometer give the right reading?
Answer: 61·9°C.

13. The equation connecting the resistance of platinum R with the gas scale temperature T is
$$R_T = R_0 \ (1+\alpha T - \beta T')$$
$$(\alpha = 3·8 \times 10^{-3}/°C, \ \beta = 5·6 \times 10^{-7}/°C)$$

What temperature on the platinum scale corresponds to 300°C on the gas scale?
Answer: 291°C.

14. A neutralization tank contains corrosive liquor whose temperature may be between 20°C and 90°C. Temperature is indicated locally and recorded at a remote supervisory position. In the first case the sensing element is a mercury-in-steel filled system, and in the second a resistance thermometer. The less accurate local indicator is marked with the kelvin notation whereas the recorder is marked with the Celsius notation. When the recorder shows 90°C the indicator reads 365 k. Express the error as a percentage.
Answer: 2.2 per cent.

3 Heat

A man expends about 3 million calories of energy a day, which he could produce by consuming about one kilogramme of sugar. The Electricity Authority would describe this same amount of energy as four kilowatt-hours. The Gas Board, on the other hand, might describe this energy as 0·012 therms, while fuel oil suppliers would quote it as 12,000 British thermal units. (Fig. 3.1.) 'Quite a variety of units', you might say, 'and, anyway, since heat is a form of energy, shouldn't we measure it in joules?'

These units were developed by technologists, at different times, to suit the convenience of particular industries operating in isolation from each other. The isolation of industries, like that of countries, is a thing of the past and there are overwhelming advantages in having one unit for all forms of energy in all situations. In the future different industries in different countries will all use the same unit of energy, the joule. The unit of heat flow will be the joule per second, i.e. the watt. Where the older units of heat are still used they are defined in terms of the joule. (Table 3.1.)

Wherever you can you should think and work in joules directly.

The realization that all forms of energy are interchangeable did not happen overnight. Like many revolutionary discoveries it had to be fought for with experimental evidence and argument. In the sections below we trace back the development of the theory; perhaps you will find this interesting, even amusing.

Table 3.1. Value of heat units

1 calorie	$=4{\cdot}1868J \approx 4{\cdot}2J$
1 kilocalorie or Calorie	$=4186{\cdot}8J \approx 4000J$
1 kilowatt-hour	$=1000 \times 60 \times 60 = 3,600,000J$
1 British Thermal unit	$=1,055,000J \approx 10^6J$
1 Therm	$=10^5 \text{ Btu} \approx 10^{11}J$

The Caloric Theory of Heat

Two hundred years ago the prevailing theory among scientists was that heat was an invisible fluid. They thought that this fluid, which they called

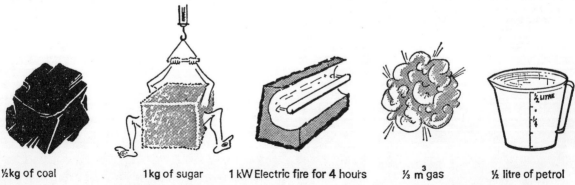

½kg of coal   1kg of sugar   1 kW Electric fire for 4 hours   ⅓ m³ gas   ½ litre of petrol

Fig. 3.1. Approximate equivalents to the energy expended by a man in one day.

caloric, filled up the spaces between the molecules of a body and flowed from hot bodies into cold bodies when they came into contact. They attributed the fact that bodies expand when heated to the increased quantity of caloric that flowed into them. The caloric theory worked reasonably well in accounting for heat flow. Early engineers visualized heat engines as operating on a flow of caloric, in the same way as a hydraulic turbine operates on a flow of water.

Count Rumford, an international adventurer and engineer, who was engaged in boring out cannon barrels for the Bavarian Army dealt the caloric theory a severe blow. He attacked the assumption that the rise in temperature produced during sawing or drilling was a result of the caloric squeezed out of the sawdust or grindings. By using a blunt drill, which removed very little metal, he showed that the heat had more to do with energy expended by the horse which turned the drill than with the drillings produced.

Molecular Vibration Theory of Heat

The modern theory of the nature of heat associates heat with mechanical energy. The internal energy of a body is the sum total of the energy of vibration of the molecules making up the body. (Fig. 3.2.) When heat is added to a body its molecules vibrate more energetically. It is this increased vibration that causes the effects, such as thermal expansion, that we associate with

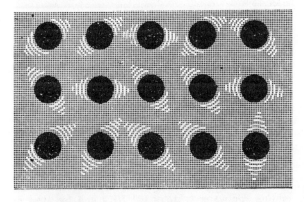

3.2. Molecules of a solid vibrating with thermal energy.

temperature rise. The vibrations can be increased by contact with a body at a higher temperature or by mechanical activity such as hammering or rubbing.

The theory was slow to gain support, but eventually it became accepted as a result of experiments made by James Prescott Joule at Peel Park, Salford. He established accurately that the amount of work done on a system is directly proportional to the heat which would produce the same temperature rise:

Quantity of heat $\propto$ work done.

Joule's Experiments

The measurement of the mechanical equivalent of heat fascinated Joule, and he improved his methods, time and time again. In his first experiments, he allowed descending weights to turn a paddle against the viscous drag of water in a container. (Fig. 3.3.) The churning of the water

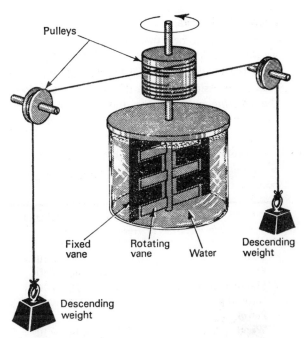

Fig. 3.3. The apparatus which Joule used to determine the mechanical equivalent of heat.

caused a rise in temperature, which Joule measured with a thermometer. Considering that he had to make his own thermometer, it is amazing that his value for the energy required to heat 1g of water

29

by 1°C differed by only $\frac{1}{4}$ per cent from the present accepted value of 4·187J.

Energy to heat
1g of water by 1°C =

$$\frac{\text{Work done}}{\text{mass of water} \times \text{temperature rise}}$$

Joule later investigated the relation of electrical energy and heat energy. His contribution to science is recognized by naming the SI unit of energy, the *joule*, after him.

Once heat became accepted as a form of energy, the principle of the conservation of energy could be formulated. It states that *energy cannot be created or destroyed but only converted from one form to another*. Thus, heat can be converted to or derived from mechanical, electrical, or kinetic energy, etc.

Calorific Values

To choose the best fuel for a particular purpose, we must consider very carefully such factors as the cost, the convenience, and the availability of the fuel. In assessing the cost, it is important to know the *calorific value* of the fuel, i.e., *the heat of*

Table 3.2. Calorific values of fuels and foods

Round figures are quoted because large variations can occur in the quality of the sample.

	Calorific value (J/kg)
Fuels	
Coal	30 $\times 10^6$
Fuel oil	46 $\times 10^6$
Manufactured gas	28 $\times 10^6$
Natural gas	55 $\times 10^6$
Petrol	46 $\times 10^6$
Wood	14 $\times 10^6$
Foods	
Bread	11 $\times 10^6$
Butter	34 $\times 10^6$
Milk	3·0 $\times 10^6$
Potatoes	40 $\times 10^6$
Sugar	16 $\times 10^6$

combustion per unit mass. These are quoted in Table 3.2 for some common fuels and foods.

We measure calorific values by burning a measured quantity of fuel in a strong steel container, called a bomb calorimeter. (Fig. 3.4.) An electrical filament ignites the fuel, and, to ensure complete combustion, the calorimeter is filled with oxygen under pressure. The heat produced increases the temperature of the bomb calorimeter and the surrounding water, all of which is in an insulated container to prevent loss of heat. Having made allowances for the heat supplied by the filament, and the heat absorbed by the calorimeter, we can calculate the calorific value of the fuel from:

$$\text{Calorific value} = \frac{\text{mass of water} \times \text{temp. rise}}{\text{mass of fuel}}$$

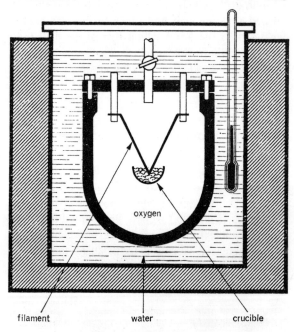

Fig. 3.4. In the bomb calorimeter fuel is burnt in oxygen under pressure and the heat produced is measured.

Problem: 5 g of coal is ignited in a bomb calorimeter by passing a 10 A current at 12 V for 10 seconds. The calorimeter is made of steel, and weighs 5 kg and is immersed in 3 kg of water. If the temperature of the water rises 10°C, what is the calorific value of the coal? (The energy required to produce a 1°C rise in temperature for water is 4·2 $\times 10^3$ J/Kg and for steel in 0·5 $\times 10^3$ J/Kg.)

Solution: Let X be the calorific value in J/kg

$$\text{Energy released} \begin{cases} \text{by fuel} = \dfrac{5}{1000} \times X \text{ J} \\ \text{by current} = 120 \times 10 = 1200 \text{ J} \end{cases}$$

$$\text{Energy absorbed} \begin{cases} \text{by water} = 3 \times 4.2 \times 10^3 \times 10 = 126 \times 10^3 \text{ J} \\ \text{by calorimeter} = 5 \times 0.5 \times 10^3 \times 10 = 25 \times 10^3 \text{ J} \end{cases}$$

Equating energy released to energy absorbed

$$\frac{5X}{1000} + 1200 = 126 \times 10^3 + 25 \times 10^3$$
$$X = (151 \times 10^3 - 1200)1000/5.$$
$$= 30 \times 10^6 \text{ J/kg}.$$

Specific Heat Capacity

When we heat equal masses of copper and aluminium in the same flame, the temperature of the copper rises about twice as fast as that of the aluminium. The aluminium accepts the same amount of heat but shows less of a change in temperature. We say that the aluminium specimen has a greater *thermal capacity* than the copper specimen. As usual, we want to express this property of a substance in a precise way and we therefore define a unit of measurement, basing it on a unit mass of the substance and unit temperature change. This property is called *specific heat capacity*, and it is defined as *the heat required to raise 1 kilogramme of a substance by 1°C* (Note that whenever we use the word 'specific' before a quantity we mean 'per unit mass', e.g., specific volume means the volume of unit mass of a substance.)

From Joule's experiment we saw that 4.2 J were required to heat one gramme of water by 1°C. Hence, the specific heat of water is 4.2×10^3 joules per kilogramme per degC ($\text{Jkg}^{-1}°\text{C}^{-1}$ or $\text{Jkg}^{-1}\text{K}^{-1}$). The symbol for specific heat is C and its value for some common materials is given in table 3.3.

From the definition of specific heat:

$$\text{Specific heat} = \frac{\text{Quantity of heat energy } (Q)}{\text{mass of substance } (m) \times \text{temperature } (\theta)}$$
$$C = Q/m\theta$$

We use this equation to calculate quantity of heat in the form

$$Q = mC\theta.$$

Q is given in joules when m is in kilogrammes, θ is in degrees C or K, and C is in $\text{Jkg}^{-1}°\text{C}^{-1}$.

Specific heats vary slightly according to the temperature at which they are measured, and for accurate work we use values which apply to the particular temperature we are dealing with. Water is no exception to this, and its specific heat varies by about 1 per cent between 0°C and 100°C. For very accurate work we take the specific heat capacity of water to be 4.1868×10^3 $\text{Jkg}^{-1}°\text{C}^{-1}$ at 15°C. However, for most purposes we can assume a value of 4.2×10^3 $\text{Jkg}^{-1}°\text{C}^{-1}$, and ignore any variation with temperature. If we express specific heats in kilojoules, the 10^3 term is not required, e.g.,

$$4.2 \times 10^3 \ \text{Jkg}^{-1}°\text{C}^{-1} = 4.2 \ \text{kJkg}^{-1}°\text{C}^{-1}$$

Table 3.3. Specific heats
$(\text{Jkg}^{-1}°\text{C}^{-1})$

Substance	Sp. ht.	Substance	Sp. ht.
Air*	7.1×10^3	Iron	0.5×10^3
Ethyl alcohol	2.5×10^3	Lead	0.13×10^3
Aluminium	0.92×10^3	Mercury	0.14×10^3
Copper	0.39×10^3	Steam*	1.4×10^3
Glass	0.13×10^3	Marble	0.88×10^3
Hydrogen*	10×10^3	Water	4.2×10^3
Ice	2.1×10^3	Wood	17×10^3

Since specific heat varies with temperature the values are approximate.
* The values quoted are for the case of constant volume.

Problem: An aluminium pan of mass $\frac{1}{2}$ kg and containing 3 kg of water is heated from 10°C to 100°C. How much heat has been received by the pan and contents?

Solution: Using equation $Q = mC\theta$, quantity of heat received by pan is:

$$Q_p = 0.5 \times 0.92 \times 10^3 \times (100 - 10) \text{ J}$$
$$= 4.1 \times 10^4 \text{ J}$$

Quantity of heat received by water:

$$Q_w = 3 \times 4.2 \times 10^3 \times (100 - 10) \text{ J}$$
$$= 113 \times 10^4 \text{ J}$$

Total heat received $= Q_p + Q_w$

$$= 117 \times 10^4 \text{ J} = 1.17 \text{ kJ}.$$

Thermal Properties of Water

The specific heat of water is very high compared with most other substances, which makes it an

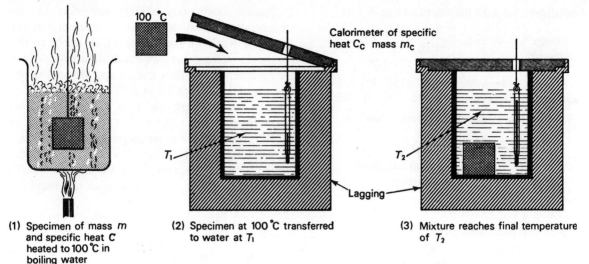

(1) Specimen of mass m and specific heat C heated to 100 °C in boiling water

(2) Specimen at 100 °C transferred to water at T_1

(3) Mixture reaches final temperature of T_2

Fig. 3.5. Measurement of specific heat by the method of mixtures.

excellent medium for storing heat. The heat absorbed by lakes and oceans in the summer is released during the winter, and this reduces the extremes of temperature in both seasons. Thus the climate of Edinburgh is very different from that of Moscow although they are situated at the same latitude.

Heat exchangers, ranging from boilers to hot water bottles, use water because of its high thermal capacity. Although it is corrosive, it is cheap, readily available, and non-inflammable, and hence it is universally used for transferring heat in industry.

Measurement of Specific Heat (C)

The simplest way of measuring the specific heat of a solid is to heat it and then immerse it in a calorimeter containing say W kg of water. Heat flows from the specimen into the water and calorimeter until they are all at the same temperature.

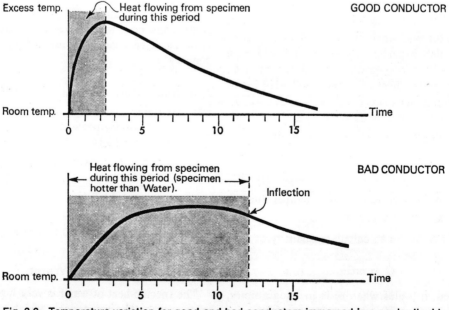

Fig. 3.6. Temperature variation for good and bad conductors immersed in a cooler liquid.

32

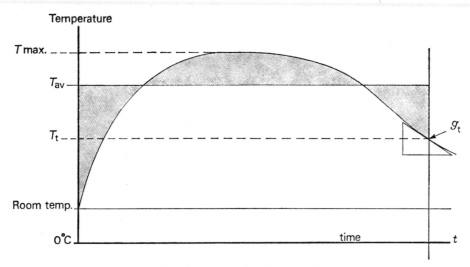

Fig. 3.7. Calculation of cooling correction.

Using the symbols of Fig. 3.5,
heat gained by
calorimeter and contents = heat lost by specimen,
i.e.,

$$m_cC_c(T_2-T_1)+WC_{water}(T_2-T_1)$$
$$=mC(100-T_2)$$

We calculate the specific heat of the specimen from this equation. When thermal capacity of the calorimeter is small compared to that of the water it contains, we neglect the term $m_cC_c(T_2-T_1)$.

A specimen which is a good conductor quickly reaches the same temperature as this water and little heat is lost to the surroundings. On the other hand, a poor conductor takes longer to reach thermal equilibrium with the water, and during this time an appreciable quantity of heat may escape from the calorimeter. (Fig. 3.6.) The first stage in correcting for this heat loss is to plot a graph of the temperature of the water over a period of time after adding the hot specimen. (Fig. 3.7.)

The graph can be used to estimate the cooling correction by proceeding as follows:

1. Draw a vertical line at any time t beyond the inflection in the curve.

2. Measure the rate of cooling g_t (slope of graph) and the temperature T_t at this time.

3. Estimate the average temperature ($T_{av.}$) during this time.

To find $T_{av.}$ draw a horizontal line in such a position that areas above and below the line between it and the cooling curve are equal.

Assuming that the rate of cooling is proportional to the excess temperature, i.e., $g \propto T$,

$$g_{av.} \propto T_{av.} \text{ and } g_t \propto T_t$$

or

$$\frac{g_{av.}}{g_t} = \frac{T_{av.}}{T_t}$$

temperature correction
= average rate of loss of temp. × time,
i.e.,

$$\text{temperature correction} = g_{av.} \times \text{time}$$

This correction is added to the average temperature to give the maximum temperature that would have occurred if there had been no heat loss.

Measuring the Specific Heat of Liquids

We can use the method of mixtures to measure the specific heats of liquids by immersing a hot solid of known specific heat in a quantity of the liquid. Equating the heat lost and the heat gained we have

$$m_cC_c(T_2-T_1)+m_{liquid}C_{liquid}(T_2-T_1)$$
$$= mC(100-T_2)$$

In a more convenient method, the liquid is heated by an electrical element. (Fig. 3.8.) The electrical

33

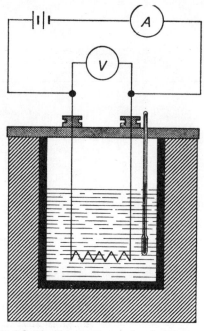

Fig. 3.8. Liquid heated by an electrical element.

energy supplied, VIt joules, is absorbed by the calorimeter and the contained liquid.

$$m_c C_c(T_2 - T_1) + m_{liquid} C_{liquid}(T_2 - T_1) = VIt$$

Alternatively, the heat can be continuously absorbed by a flow of liquid. (Fig. 3.9.) After the liquid has flowed for some time at a constant rate, the thermometers give steady readings and if a mass m flows in a time t then

$$m_{liquid} C_{liquid}(T_2 - T_1) = VIt$$

The vacuum jacket reduces heat loss to a low value and, since the temperature of the calorimeter remains constant, its heat capacity does not enter into the calculation.

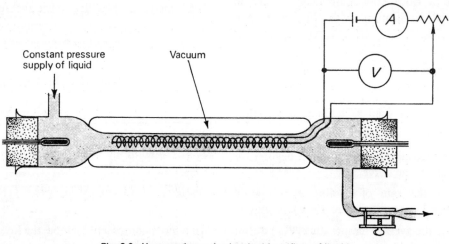

Constant pressure supply of liquid

Vacuum

Fig. 3.9. Heat continuously absorbed by a flow of liquid.

Questions

1. Does a hot-water bottle filled with water contain more internal energy than a brick of the same mass at the same temperature?

2. What errors would you have to guard against in determining the mechanical equivalent of heat?

3. Explain how the principle of conservation of energy makes it impossible to construct a perpetual motion machine.

4. What factors would you consider in choosing a heating system for a house?

5. Why is water chosen for comparison in specifying specific heats?

6. Why is it necessary, in accurate work, to define the temperature at which specific heats are measured?

7. What are the advantages of continuous flow methods of measuring specific heats over the method of mixtures?

8. Explain the difference between heat and temperature.

9. Explain why we can never extract all the internal energy contained in a body.

10. Why, on the coast, does the wind often blow towards the shore in the daytime, and towards the sea at night?

Problems

1. How many joules are produced by 2 kW heater operating for 1 hour?
   Answer: 7·2 MJ.

2. How much heat is needed to heat 4 kg of lead from 20°C to 100°C? (Specific heat of lead =126 J/kg°C.)
   Answer: 40·3 kJ.

3. What change in temperature is produced by 400 joules of heat added to 1 g of (a) mercury, (b) iron, (c) wood? (Specific heats: mercury =126 J/kg°C; iron=480 J/kg°C; wood= 1750 J/kg°C.)
   Answer: (a) 3174°C; (b) 834°C; (c) 228°C.

4. If lead shot at 100°C is poured into 1 litre of water at 25°C, how much is required to raise the temperature to 50°C? (Specific heat of lead=126 J/kg°C.)
   Answer: 16·7 kg.

5. A litre of boiling water is poured into an aluminium teapot at 20°C. If the final temperature of water and teapot is 86°C, what is the mass of the teapot? (Specific heat of aluminium=890 J/kg°C.)
   Answer: 1 kg.

6. A man weighing 90 kg slides 3 m down a rope before coming to rest. How much heat is produced? (Acceleration due to gravity=9·8 m/s².)
   Answer: 2·7 kJ.

7. By how much is the temperature of water raised in going over Niagara Falls (51 m high)? (g=9·8 m/s².)
   Answer: 0·12°C.

8. A spanner weighing 0·7 kg is dropped from an aeroplane flying at 3000 m. How much heat is produced when the spanner hits the ground Neglect forward motion. (Assume that g=9·8 m/s².)
   Answer: 21 kJ.

9. If a car weighing 1455 kg, travelling at 27·4 m/s, is brought to rest by the brakes, how much heat is generated?
   Answer: 547 kJ.

10. 2 kg of coal is consumed in a burner, which is 85 per cent efficient, during a test using a continuous flow calorimeter. 300 kg of water flows during the run, entering at 15°C and leaving at 65°C. What is the calorific value of the coal?
    Answer: 36·7 MJ/kg.

11. What is the upper limit to the power of an engine burning 18 kg of diesel oil per hour, if the calorific value of the oil is 50 MJ/kg?
    Answer: 250 kW.

12. The brick walls of a house have an area of 200 m², and are 200 mm thick. If the bricks have a density of 2000 kg/m³ and a specific heat of 837 J/,kg°C, how much heat is required to raise their temperature by 30°C?
    Answer: 2009 MJ.

13. How much does this cost, burning coal of calorific value 29·4 MJ/kg in a 30 per cent efficient furnace, if the coal costs £1 per 100 kg?
    Answer: £2·28.

14. How much coal of calorific value 29·4 MJ/kg burned in a 50 per cent efficient stove, would heat 5000 m³ of air at constant pressure from 20°C to 30°C? (Density of air=1·2 kg/m³; Specific heat of air at constant pressure=1000 J/kg°C.)
    Answer: 4·08 kg.

15. How much water at 100°C and how much at 20°C must be mixed together to give 100 kg of water at 50°C?

    Answer: 37·5 kg at 100°C, 62·5 kg at 20°C.

16. In a continuous flow calorimeter, at a flow rate of 5 g/s, a temperature rise of 3°C is produced in water by a current of $\frac{3}{4}$ A at 100 V. The same temperature rise is produced by $\frac{1}{2}$ A at 100 V at a flow of 3 g/s. What is the specific heat of water?

    Answer: 4·17 kJ/kg°C.

17. A high-energy beam of hydrogen atoms, each weighing $1·67 \times 10^{-24}$ g, is directed at a thermally insulated brass target weighing 500 g. If 2×10^{15} atoms strike the target per second, with an average velocity of 2×10^7 m/s, how long will it take to raise the temperature of the target by 200°C? (Specific heat of brass = 378 J/kg°C.).

    Answer: 57 sec.

18. Describe a continuous flow method for determining the specific heat of a liquid. Explain how errors due to heat losses are eliminated. In such a determination the temperature rise along the flow tube is found to be 2·5°C, when the rate of flow is 60 g/min and the heating power consumed is 13·5 watts. When the rate of flow of liquid is increased to 90 g/min, the power has to be increased to 18·8 watts in order to maintain the same rise in temperature. What is the specific heat of the liquid?

    (I.E.R.E.)

    Answer: 4·2 J/kg°C.

4 Heat Transfer

Everywhere in Nature heat energy is on the move. The heat moves from high to low temperature regions tending to produce a uniform temperature throughout the universe. On the scale of the universe, heat transfer occurs slowly, and temperature differences will exist for all the foreseeable future. Viewed on a smaller scale heat transfer can be violently rapid, as in a nuclear explosion.

The control of heat flow has always been of importance to man. From the most primitive times, he has needed to protect his body from the extremes of heat and cold but, although this remains his first consideration even today, he now wishes to control the transfer of heat in a far wider variety of applications, from the incubation of bacteria to atomic energy reactors. We recognize three basic processes of heat transfer; conduction, convection, and radiation, but the processes of evaporation and condensation often make an important contribution and we could well include them in the list. The human body, in particular, relies on evaporation to keep its temperature down in hot climates.

In some instances, we try to promote heat flow as in a boiler or heat exchanger while, in other cases, we try to reduce heat flow as in homes in winter. Sometimes we delicately control the heat flow both in and out as in a manned satellite. In practice, engineers solve heat transfer problems by analysing the transfer into its component processes and dealing with each one separately. We will adopt the same approach and consider each of the processes in turn.

Conduction

In conduction, heat flows down temperature gradients from places of high temperature to places of lower temperature. When heat has been passing through a conductor for some time, temperatures along the conductor may reach steady values.

In a bar which is lagged at the sides, the heat flows longitudinally in at one end and out at the other. The temperature gradient is uniform as shown in Fig. 4.1a. This distribution of temperature would also be typical of a conductor of large cross-section, such as a boiler plate.

In a conductor which is not lagged at the sides, the temperature quickly falls away from the hot end, owing to the heat escaping through the sides. (Fig. 4.1b.) Such a distribution would apply to the case of the cooling fins on an air cooled engine. The optimum length of the fins may be deduced from a knowledge of the temperature distribution along the fins.

Thermal Conductivity k

The rate of heat conduction through a material is measured in joules per second, i.e., watts, or kilowatts. The rate depends on three factors. (Fig. 4.2.)

(a) The temperature gradient $\dfrac{T_1 - T_2}{x}$.

(b) The area A.

(c) The material.

If a quantity of heat Q flows during a total time t, then:

$$\text{Rate of flow } \frac{Q}{t} \propto \frac{A(T_1 - T_2)}{x}$$

If we introduce a constant of proportionality k this will depend on the material

$$\frac{Q}{t} = kA\frac{(T_1 - T_2)}{x}$$

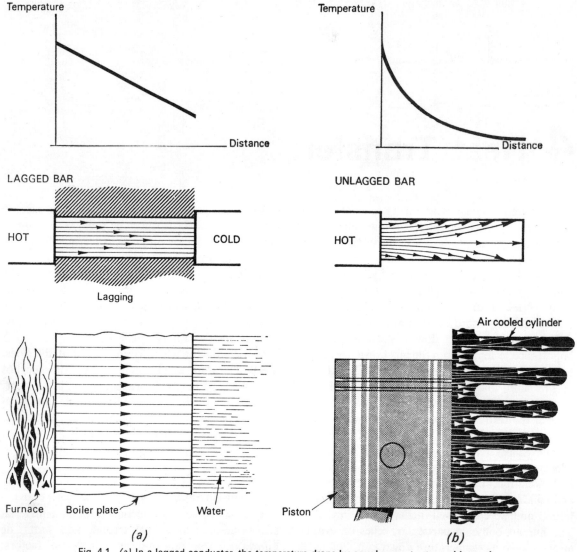

Fig. 4.1. *(a)* In a lagged conductor, the temperature drops by equal amounts at equal intervals along the conductor. *(b)* In an unlagged conductor, the heat flow is not parallel and the temperature gradient is not linear.

The constant k is called the thermal conductivity of the material and is defined quite adequately by this equation. Alternatively, it could be defined in words as '*the rate of flow of heat through the material, per unit area, per unit temperature gradient*'.

This latter equation can be more precisely written in calculus notation

$$\frac{dQ}{dt} = -kA\frac{d\theta}{dx}$$

This equation is true even when k varies with temperature, in which case the gradient would not be uniform and

$$\frac{T_1 - T_2}{x} = \frac{d\theta}{dx}$$

The particular units used to express conductivity vary according to the application. Generally, for more precise specifications we use watts per square metre per (°C/metre), sometimes written as W/m°C or $\text{Wm}^{-1}\text{°C}^{-1}$, or W/mK or $\text{Wm}^{-1}\text{K}^{-1}$.

Table 4.1. Thermal conductivities

The figures should be taken as approximate because of variations of k with temperature and with the particular state of the material.

Material	Thermal Conductivity, W/m°C
Copper	400
Aluminium	210
Iron	67
Glass	1·1
Concrete	0·92
Brick	0·63
Water	0·59
Alcohol	0·21
Wood	0·17
Hydrogen	0·17
Cork	0·046
Wool felt	0·042
Air	0·025

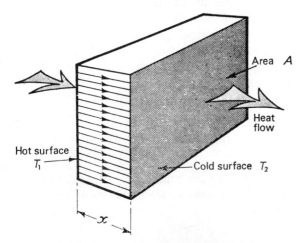

Fig. 4.2. Factors involved in the heat flow through a section of material.

Problem: An icebox has an area of 2·4 m² and its inner surface is maintained at 2°C when the outer surface is at 17°C. If the box is insulated with cork 50 mm thick, how much heat flows into the box per hour?

Solution: $Q/t = kA \times$ temperature gradient

$$= 0·046 \times 2·4 \times (17-2)/0·05 \text{ J/second}$$
$$= 60 \times 60 \times 0·046 \times 2·4 \times 15/0·05$$
$$= 10·8 \times 10^4 \text{ J/hour}$$

Problem: The plaster ceiling of a centrally heated house is 6 m × 10 m × 12 mm thick. Calculate the heat flow through the ceiling with and without a 36 mm thick layer of insulating fibre glass, if the inside and outside surfaces are at a temperature of 24°C and 4°C. (k (plaster) = 0·63 W/m°C; k (fibreglass) = 0·04 W/m°C).

Solution: In general, rate of flow = $kA \times$ temp. grad.

(a) Flow through insulated ceiling

Let the temperature of the plaster felt interface be T. The rate of flow is the same for the two media.

$$\text{Rate of flow} = \frac{0·63 \times 6 \times 10 \times (24-T)}{0·012}$$
$$= \frac{0·04 \times 6 \times 10 \times (T-4)}{0·036}$$

which gives a value of 23·6°C when we solve for T.

$$\text{Rate of flow} = \frac{0·63 \times 6 \times 10 \times (24-23·6)}{0·012}$$
$$= 1·3 \text{ kW}$$

(b) Flow through uninsulated ceiling

$$\text{Rate of flow} = \frac{0·63 \times 6 \times 10 \times (24-4)}{0·012}$$
$$= 6·3 \text{ kW.}$$

[Why is this figure so ridiculously high?]

U Values

Where we are dealing with standard structures such as a 9 in. brick wall or ¼ in. plate glass, it is simpler to give a figure for the structure as a whole rather than to quote the conductivities of its materials. (Table 4.2.) Such a figure is called a *U value* and is defined as the *rate of flow of heat per unit area, per degree of difference of temperature between its surfaces.*

Table 4.2.

Structure	U value, W/m²°C
Solid double brick wall	2·8
Solid double brick wall, plastered one side	2·5
Plate glass (6 mm)	10
Plastered ceiling	2·0

In practice, when heat is flowing through a solid surface which is in contact with a liquid or gas, a large part of the temperature change occurs in the fluid near the surface. These surface layers strongly affect the rate of conduction through a barrier such as a boiler plate or a window. (Fig. 4.3.) If the heat flow is calculated on the assumption that the temperatures of the surfaces of the barrier are the same as those in the body of the fluids, it could be hundreds of times too great. Thus, the U value of a barrier obtained by experiment is more useful than a knowledge of thermal conductivity.

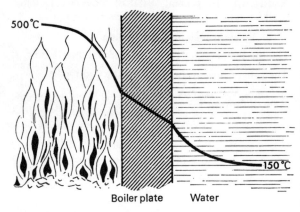

Fig. 4.3. Most of the temperature drop associated with a boiler plate is in the fluid layers near its surface.

Problem: Calculate the U value of the uninsulated ceiling in the previous example [assuming that the surface layers reduce the heat flow to $\frac{1}{10}$ of that value.]

Solution:

$$U \text{ value} = \frac{\text{rate of heat flow}}{\text{area} \times \text{temperature difference}}$$

$$= \frac{6 \cdot 3 \times 1000/100}{6 \times 10 \times 20}$$

$$= 0 \cdot 53 \text{ W/m}^2 \, ^\circ\text{C}$$

Measurement of Thermal Conductivity

To determine the thermal conductivity k of a material, we must measure the quantities in the equation:

$$k = \frac{\text{rate of heat flow}}{\text{area} \times \text{temperature gradient}}$$

Because the temperature gradients in good conductors are small, they are difficult to measure accurately. This is overcome in *Searle's apparatus*, by using a test specimen about 40 cm long which gives an appreciable change in temperature at two widely separated points. (Fig. 4.4.) A regular flow of water through a spiral coil, which is soldered on to the bar, extracts the heat from the cold end of the bar. We measure the rise in temperature of this water and its rate of flow, and calculate the rate of conduction of heat along the bar. Apart from demonstration apparatus, the measurement is made only in specialized laboratories because the apparatus must be constructed around the specimen.

$$Q/t = (\text{mass of water}/t \times C \times (T_4 - T_3)$$

and temperature gradient $= (T_1 - T_2)/L$.

$$\therefore \quad k = \frac{(\text{mass of water}/t) \times 4 \cdot 2 \times (T_4 - T_3)}{A(T_1 - T_2)/L}$$

In measuring the conductivity of insulators, the problem is to make a measurable quantity of heat flow through the specimen. The *Lee's Disc*

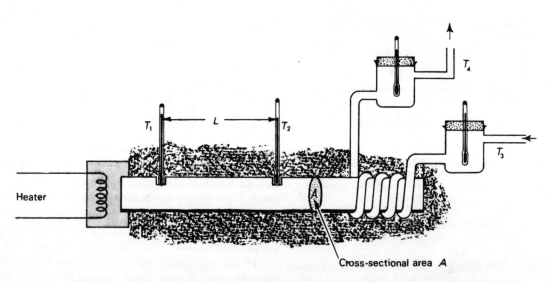

Fig. 4.4. Searle's apparatus. Heat is prevented from escaping through the sides of the bar either by evacuating the space around it or by filling the space with insulating material.

apparatus makes the flow of heat appreciable by applying heat to a specimen of large cross-section and small thickness. (Fig. 4.5a.) We supply electrical power or steam to the upper surface of the specimen and allow the apparatus to reach a steady state. The temperatures of the brass plates are effectively those of the specimen surfaces, since temperature gradients in the brass are small. In the most convenient form of the apparatus, the heat flow is measured electrically. The brass plate containing an electrical heater is bounded by the specimen on one side, and on every other side by surfaces at the same temperature as itself. (Fig. 4.5b.) Therefore, all the heat from the heater passes through the specimen.

$$Q/t = VI = k \times \frac{\text{Area of specimen } (T_1 - T_2)}{\text{thickness}}$$

$$\therefore \quad k = \frac{VI \times \text{thickness}}{\text{Area} \times (T_1 - T_2)}$$

The apparatus may be used to measure the conductivities of liquids and gases provided the heater is above the specimen. The upper layers are hotter and therefore less dense than those below, which prevents any circulation.

Using the simpler form of the apparatus (Fig. 4.5a), which is common in colleges, the rate of flow of heat through the specimen is measured in a second experiment, as follows: remove the upper brass plate, leaving the specimen in position, and by means of a gas flame gently heat the lower disc. Note the time for its temperature to drop from say 5°C above to 5°C below T_2, the previous steady state temperature. Knowing the rate of loss of temperature at T_2, we can deduce the rate of loss of heat. This is the rate at which heat passes through the specimen in the steady state.

Quantity of heat
= mass × specific heat × temperature change

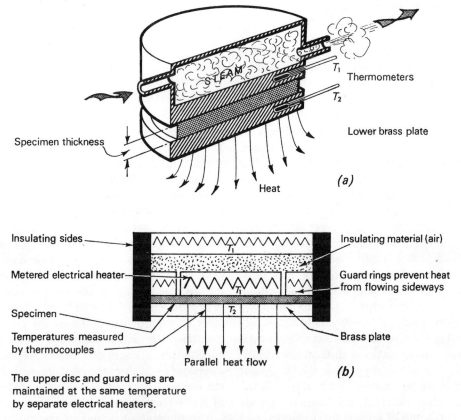

The upper disc and guard rings are maintained at the same temperature by separate electrical heaters.

Fig. 4.5. Measurement of the thermal conductivity of insulators by Lee's disc apparatus. *(a)* Simple form of apparatus. *(b)* Electrical form of apparatus.

Quantity of heat$/t$

$$= \frac{\text{mass} \times \text{specific heat} \times \text{temperature change}}{\text{time}}$$

Rate of loss of heat

$$= mC \times \text{rate of loss of temperature}$$

Again, this relation can be neatly expressed in calculus notation

$$\frac{dQ}{dt} = mC\frac{d\theta}{dt}$$

Conduction in Metals

Metals are very good thermal conductors, just as they are good electrical conductors. We can, in fact, say more than this because measurements show that the ratio of the thermal to the electrical conductivity is a constant for metals at the same temperature. The ratio itself is proportional to the absolute temperatures, so that we may express this as

$$\frac{\text{Thermal conductivity}}{\text{Electrical conductivity}} = ZT$$

The simplicity of this relation is not just a coincidence but suggests some underlying similarity between the processes. What is behind this similarity? Electrical current in metals is known to be a flow of electrons. The conductivity is high because in metals there are large numbers of electrons not rigidly bound to particular atoms. We strongly suspect that these same highly mobile electrons are responsible for passing on the heat so quickly by their rapid reaction on each other and on the lattice of metal atoms.

It appears that conduction proceeds by two mechanisms, one involving the atoms, and the other a much more rapid one involving any loosely bound electrons which may be present.

One of the best conductors is the metal sodium which is known to have electrons which are highly mobile. Unfortunately, it is also highly chemically reactive, and ignites spontaneously even at normal temperatures, which makes it difficult to handle. We use it as a conducting material in special cases where it can be enclosed, for example, in the valves of certain internal combustion engines (Fig. 4.6.) The group of metals, silver, copper, and gold combine high electrical and thermal conduc-

tivity with great resistance to corrosion, but unfortunately only copper is cheap enough to be widely used.

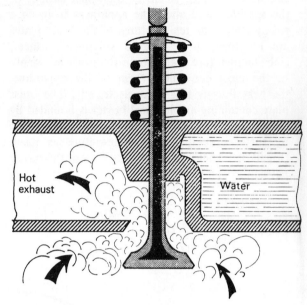

Fig. 4.6. Some high performance engines have sodium cored valves to conduct the heat away rapidly.

Conduction in Non-Metals

Insulators are generally materials which contain comparatively few free electrons, and heat flows entirely by means of the interaction of the atoms. In comparison with electrons, these atoms are massive, and the transfer of heat by this process is usually very much slower.

The atoms have a vibratory motion about an equilibrium position but each atom keeps its place in the lattice. Atoms at a higher temperature have more energetic vibrations and, by jostling their neighbours, cause them to vibrate more energetically. They, in turn, influence other atoms and so the energy is passed on through the material. When the temperatures have stabilized, the molecules at a particular point on the conductor will maintain the same degree of vibration, being simultaneously activated by molecules in the direction of higher temperature and damped to the same extent by the molecules in the direction of lower temperatures. (Fig. 4.7.)

The thermal vibrations of the molecules is not entirely irregular. In non-metals, the heat flows

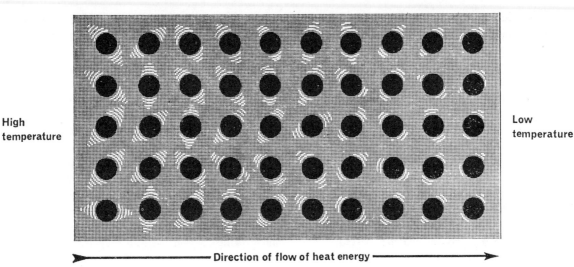

High temperature

Low temperature

Direction of flow of heat energy

Fig. 4.7. Molecules at a certain point in a material receive energy from the molecules on one side and give up energy to the molecules on the other side.

predominantly by means of very high frequency elastic waves sent out in short bursts called *phonons*. These can provide a very effective means of heat transfer, especially at low temperatures when they are scattered less by the random thermal vibration of the atoms. For example, at about $-180°C$ some materials, such as synthetic sapphire (Al_2O_3) are better thermal conductors than copper. Even at room temperature some non-metals conduct heat better than some metals. These waves are scattered strongly by free electrons and so they contribute less to the conduction of heat in metals.

Conduction in Fluids

Since in most liquids the process of heat conduction, as distinct from convection, is rather sluggish, it is thought that conduction in liquids is similar to that in solid insulators. There are some notable exceptions such as mercury and other molten metals. The Dounreay Fast Reactor for producing atomic power uses a liquid sodium–potassium alloy as its coolant.

Gases, too, are generally good insulators. Heat travels in them rather differently from the way it travels in solids and liquids. The highly mobile gas molecules convey heat by a process of diffusion which differs subtly from the process of convection, which will be explained later. In practice, we find it difficult to divorce the effect of convection from our examination of conduction in gases. At very

low pressures, the molecules of gas are so scattered that they rarely collide, and convection and conduction become indistinguishable. Many solid structures, such as cork, wool, and expanded polystyrene, act as good insulators because of the pockets of still air trapped inside them.

Convection

Convection is the transfer of heat in which the material moves taking the heat with it. Liquids and gases, which are poor conductors, can transfer heat very effectively by this means. Natural convection occurs because of the reduction in density which usually accompanies heating. By the principle of flotation, the hotter (lighter) material rises displacing or mixing with the cooler material above. (Fig. 4.8.) Household hot water systems use natural convection to circulate the water. Chimneys promote convection by insulating the hot gas from the cooler atmosphere.

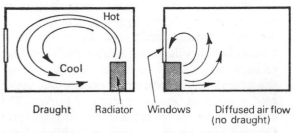

Draught   Radiator   Windows   Diffused air flow (no draught)

Fig. 4.8. Natural convection in a room may cause a draught if the 'radiators' are not well situated.

Where natural convection is too slow for a certain purpose, the fluid velocity may be increased by mechanical means such as a fan or pump. We call this *forced convection* and use it to produce a more rapid replacement of the fluid in contact with the heat source. It allows apparatus to be smaller than would be necessary using natural convection. The small bore central heating system is an example of the use of forced convection in this way, while the cooling system of a car engine uses forced convection of water and air. (Fig. 4.9.)

The effectiveness of convection depends very largely on the viscosity of the fluid concerned. Thus, thin soup can be left to simmer in the pan but porridge will surely burn if not stirred.

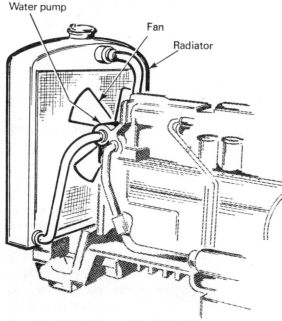

Fig. 4.9. To keep it as small as possible, the cooling system of a car engine uses forced convection of water and air.

Evaporation Transfer

A further means of heat transfer is that of evaporation and its reverse process condensation. Whenever exposed liquid surfaces are involved, evaporation may occur and extract the latent heat of vaporization from the remaining liquid. If, on the other hand, condensation occurs, this latent heat is given up at the condensing surface. The effect of evaporation is likely to be very pronounced when the liquid involved is volatile, or is near to its boiling point.

A boiling kettle is a good example of evaporation and condensation transfer. The source of heat provides the latent heat to change the water into vapour, whilst the temperature remains constant. The vapour diffuses away from the kettle until it encounters perhaps the cold surface of a wall or ceiling. Here it condenses to a liquid, at the same time giving its latent heat to the wall. The net result has been a rapid transfer of heat from the source to the wall. Unfortunately for some wall coatings, the water has also been transferred.

The excess heat from the human body is effectively dissipated by evaporation. Each gramme of water evaporated extracts about 2000 joules, and in a hot climate a man may sweat away 3 kg per day.

Radiation

Molecules in a surface vibrating with thermal energies generate electromagnetic waves. The waves travel away at the speed of light, taking energy with them and leaving the surface cooler. When the waves encounter some other material, they produce a disturbance of the surface molecules, thus raising their temperature. The radiation requires no intervening material between transmitter and receiver and, in fact, travels best in a vacuum.

Radiation is particularly important because it is the process by which heat is received by the Earth from the Sun. When the Sun is directly overhead it provides about 1 kW/m². The level of radiation is less in polar regions of the Earth because it meets the surface obliquely and traverses a longer path in the atmosphere. (Fig. 4.10.) A similar level of radiation is received by the Moon's surface but, because the Moon revolves only once in four weeks, each point on the Moon enjoys two weeks sunshine followed by two weeks of darkness. The temperature extremes produced on the Moon by this long day and night are much wider than on Earth. This provides one of the major problems for manned landings. The solution may not be in elaborate insulation but in keeping to the twilight zones where the temperature is moderate.

Nature of Heat Radiation

Heat radiation contains a large spread of wavelengths, the average value of the wave-length

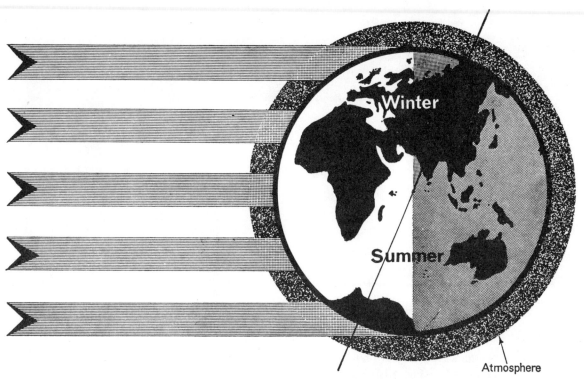

Fig. 4.10. The oblique incidence of the Sun's rays in the polar regions increases their path in the atmosphere and spreads them more thinly over the surface.

emitted depending on the temperature of the radiating surface. The larger part of the energy in heat radiation has a wave-length falling in the infra-red region of the complete electromagnetic spectrum. At higher temperatures, about 1000K, the proportion of shorter wave-length radiation increases sufficiently to be seen by the eye. (Fig. 4.11.) Because infra-red radiation and light are

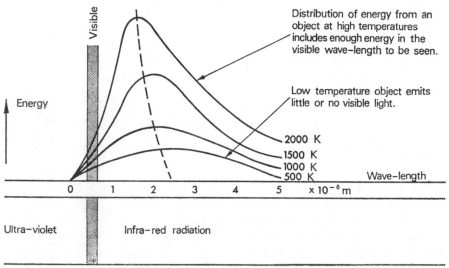

Fig. 4.11. At higher temperatures, the radiant energy includes increasing amounts of shorter wave-length radiation.

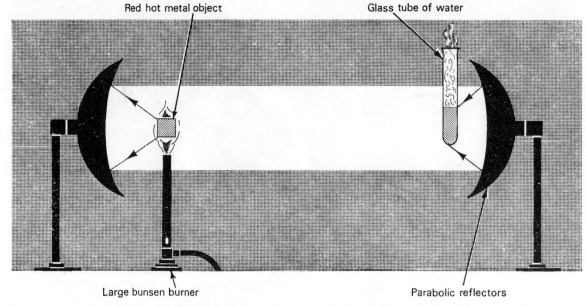

Red hot metal object   Glass tube of water

Large bunsen burner   Parabolic reflectors

Fig. 4.12. The water in the glass tube may be boiled by the reflected radiant heat.

both electromagnetic waves, they are reflected and refracted in a similar way. (Fig. 4.12 and 4.13.)

The materials of prisms and lenses used to examine heat radiation must be carefully chosen to transmit the wave-lengths required. For example, glass is transparent only to light and the shorter wave-lengths of infra-red radiation. It is opaque to the longer wave-length components. Quartz, on the other hand, is transparent to a wider range of wave-lengths extending far into the infra-red.

The cold frame or greenhouse is a clever means of trapping heat radiation. The radiation from the Sun at a temperature of 6000K contains a large proportion of short wave-length radiation which is admitted by the glass. (Fig. 4.14.) The interior of the greenhouse at a temperature of 300K radiates longer wave-length radiation, to which the glass is more opaque. Thus, the temperature of the interior rises considerably above that of the surrounding atmosphere.

Effects of Nature of Surface

The rate of radiation of heat from a body depends on the nature of its surface. A polished metal surface is a poor radiator, while a white painted surface is only slightly better. Radiation increases as the shade of the surface darkens and loses its shine, until a matt black surface is the

best radiator of all. (Fig. 4.15.) If these surfaces are exposed to radiation, it is found that the best radiating surface, the matt black one, is also the

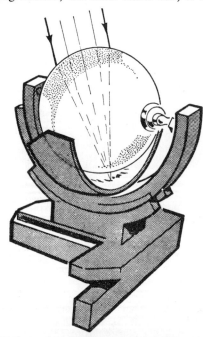

Fig. 4.13. In a sunshine recorder, a glass sphere focuses the heat radiation which scorches a line on a paper during the hours of sunshine. Glass strongly absorbs infra-red radiation, so to examine the radiation in detail, we use instruments which have quartz or rock salt components.

46

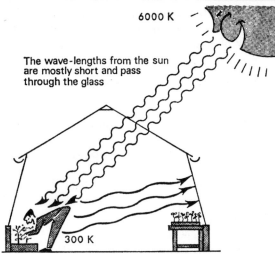

6000 K

The wave-lengths from the sun are mostly short and pass through the glass

300 K

The longer wave-length radiation from the greenhouse interior is blocked by the glass

Fig. 4.14. Glass acts as a one way trap for the Sun's radiant energy.

most effective absorber. The same order is preserved up to the polished metal surface which absorbs least. Polished metal surfaces reflect heat best and they are used on electric fires and the outside of satellites. To keep out the heat in the tropics. people wear white clothes and live in whitewashed houses. The so-called household radiators should be matt black for maximum heat transfer but people prefer to paint them to match their

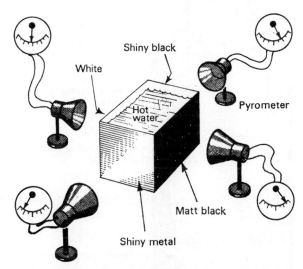

Shiny black

White

Hot water

Pyrometer

Matt black

Shiny metal

Fig. 4.15. Leslie's cube allows the comparison of the radiant energy from four different surfaces at the same temperature.

walls. This makes little difference because most of the heat from these 'radiators' is lost by convection.

Stefan's Law of Radiation

After the discovery of infra-red rays in 1800, many quantitative measurements were made on the radiation. Stefan carefully examined some of these measurements and discovered a relation between the rate of radiation of energy and the temperature. He discovered that the *rate of heat radiation from a full radiator is proportional to the fourth power of its absolute temperature*. That is, energy radiated/unit area/second = σT^4.

$$Q/t = A\sigma T^4$$

The constant of proportionality, σ in the above equation, is called Stefan's constant and it has a value of $5\cdot7 \times 10^{-8}$ Jm^{-2} s^{-1} K^{-4} (or Wm^{-2} K^{-4})

A full radiator has a standard distribution of energy among the wave-lengths that it emits (Fig. 4.11). Many surfaces have this distribution and, in a sense, the radiation is independent of their individual properties. A small hole into a cavity acts as a full radiator irrespective of the nature of the surface lining the cavity. Since a full radiator absorbs all the radiation falling on it, we sometimes refer to a full radiator as a 'black body'. Other surfaces emit radiation which differs from this standard distribution and is characteristic of the particular surface. Stefan's law of radiation holds only approximately true for surfaces which are not full radiators.

All bodies, at any temperature above absolute zero, radiate heat energy. This rate of radiation does not, as one might expect, reduce the temperature of a body to absolute zero. When a body is surrounded by surfaces at the same temperature, it absorbs and emits energy at the same rate, and there is no net change in temperature. When a body (T_1) is hotter than its surroundings (T_2), it radiates more heat than it recovers and its temperature drops.

Rate of loss of heat
$$= \sigma[T_1^4 - T_2^4]$$
$$= \sigma[T_1^2 - T_2^2][T_1^2 + T_2^2]$$
$$= \sigma[T_1 - T_2][T_1 + T_2][T_1^2 + T_2^2]$$

47

(a)

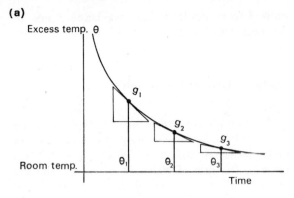

(b)

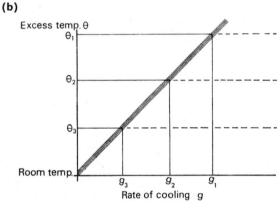

Fig. 4.16. The slope, *g*, of the cooling curve, *(a)*, at any point, is proportional to the excess temperature, θ, at that point, i.e., *g* α θ. The slope, *g*, at any point on the cooling curve *(a)* is directly proportional to the excess temperature θ. This is shown by the straight line graph *(b)* and it is a statement of Newton's law of cooling.

For small temperature differences, the net heat radiated is directly proportional to the excess temperature $(T_2 - T_1)$. Note that changes of a few degrees in T_1 make only a small proportional change in the terms $[T_1 + T_2]$ and $[T_1^2 + T_2^2]$.

At high temperature excesses, the background temperature makes very little difference to the rate of loss of heat. This can be seen from the first expression, where if $T_1 \gg T_2$, then T_2^4 is negligible compared to T_1^4. Substituting figures for excess temperatures of, say, 5K, 10K, and 1000K over an ambient temperature of 300K will show up this dependence.

At the surface of the Sun (6000K), the flow of radiation energy is colossal: $\propto (6000)^4$. In the interior of stars where the temperature is of the order of millions of degrees the radiation is so intense as to exert a substantial physical pressure.

This radiation pressure opposes the gravitational contraction and is an important factor in the stability of stars.

Problem: The filament of an evacuated light bulb requires 40 W to maintain it at 2000°C. How many watts would be needed to maintain it at 2200°C, assuming that the heat lost by conduction is negligible?

Solution: Let T_1 = filament temperature and T_0 = room temperature.

Rate of radiation $\propto (T_1^4 - T_0^4)$. That is, rate of radiation $= K(T_1^4 - T_0^4)$ where K is a constant of proportionality.

Since $T_1 > T_0$ we can neglect T_0^4.

Rate of radiation $= KT_1^4$.

At the lower temperature, $40 = K \times 2273^4$.

At the higher temperature, $X = K \times 2473^4$

Hence power required $= X$ watts $= 40 \times \dfrac{2473^4}{2273^4}$

$$= 56\text{ W}.$$

Newton's Law of Cooling

The rate at which a body loses heat is proportional to the excess temperature of the body over its surroundings.

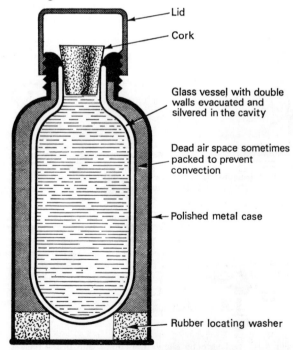

Fig. 4.17. The vacuum flask is a container which is designed to minimize heat flow either in or out.

48

The law is an approximation, which only applies when the temperature excess is small and when the body is not allowed to surround itself with a warmed layer of still air, i.e., provided there is forced draught over the object.

We use the law to predict heat losses of a body at various temperatures so that we can design suitable heating systems or make corrections for any losses which may occur during heat measurements. First, we plot a cooling curve over a convenient range of temperature. (Fig. 4.16a.) The rate of cooling at any instant is given by the corresponding slope, g, of the curve, which is proportional to the excess temperature at that instant:

$$g_1 \propto \theta_1, \quad g_2 \propto \theta_2, \text{ etc.,}$$

or, generally,

$$g = K\theta.$$

We obtain the rate of cooling at a particular excess temperature by extrapolating a graph of g against temperature. (Fig. 4.16b.) Alternatively, we find the value of the constant K in the above equation. Using either of these procedures, if the average temperature and duration of a process is known, then the heat loss may be calculated.

Total heat loss = average excess temperature × rate of cooling × specific heat × time.

Figures 4.17 and 4.18 show how a knowledge of heat transfer processes has been applied to insulation problems.

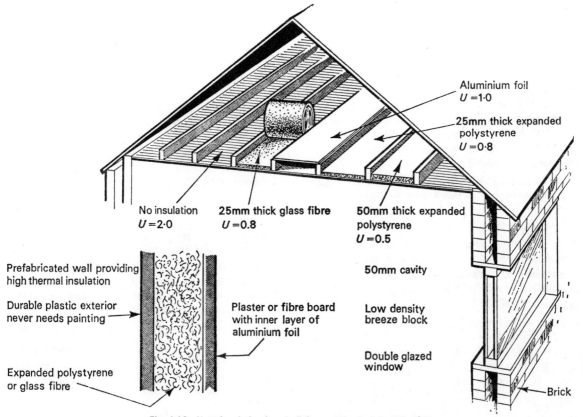

Aluminium foil
$U = 1.0$

25mm thick expanded polystyrene
$U = 0.8$

No insulation
$U = 2.0$

25mm thick glass fibre
$U = 0.8$

50mm thick expanded polystyrene
$U = 0.5$

50mm cavity

Prefabricated wall providing high thermal insulation

Durable plastic exterior never needs painting

Plaster or fibre board with inner layer of aluminium foil

Low density breeze block

Double glazed window

Expanded polystyrene or glass fibre

Brick

Fig. 4.18. Heat insulation in a building. (*U* values in W/m²°C)

Questions

1. A ladle of molten metal at 1600°C is taken from a furnace. Which process of heat transfer accounts for most of the heat loss?

2. Why does a tall chimney draw better than a short one?

3. Explain why brass conducts heat better than wood.

4. Why is steel wool a worse conductor than the steel from which it is made?

5. What are the advantages of forced convection over free convection for cooling and heating systems?

6. Why does a metal spoon at 0°C feel colder to the touch than a wooden one at the same temperature?

7. Why does damp air feel warmer than dry air at the same temperature?

8. Why does a cube cool quicker than a sphere of the same mass and material under identical conditions?

9. How is solid carbon dioxide used to keep ice-cream cool?

10. Explain why water can be boiled in a paper bag.

11. Explain how a metal spoon placed in a thick glass tumbler prevents it cracking when boiling water is poured into it.

12. Explain the significance of the term 'a black body' used in connection with heat transfer and indicate how the energy radiated from such a body is distributed over different wave-lengths.
Describe and explain the action of an instrument used for measuring high temperatures, which is based on the above concepts.

(I.E.R.E.)

13. What is meant by 'black-body radiation'? State the principal laws relating heat radiation to the temperature of the radiating surface. Discuss the relative importance of radiation, conduction, and convection in the heat transfer occurring in the following processes:

(a) the heating of a room by a conventional domestic radiator;

(b) the cooling of an engine by water circulation;

(c) the dissipation of heat from the anode of a high-power transmitting triode.

(I.E.R.E.)

Problems

1. The glass in the windows of a house has a total area of 20 m². If the glass is 4 mm thick and the temperature differences between its two surfaces is 1°C, how much heat is transmitted in 24 hours? (Thermal conductivity of glass = 105 W/m°C.)
Answer: 4.5×10^8 J.

2. If the Earth, 150,000,000 km from the Sun, receives 1400 $Jm^{-2}s^{-1}$, how much heat is radiated by the Sun per sec?
Answer: 39.5×10^{25} J.

3. A blackened spherical retort at 727°C has a diameter of 1·2 m. At what rate must heat be supplied to balance radiation losses? (Stefan's constant = 5.67×10^{-8} $Wm^{-2}K^{-4}$.)
Answer: 256 J/s.

4. Compare the rate of loss of heat between the walls and windows of a room, if the room measures 6 m × 3·5 m × 3·5 m high with two windows 2 m × 1 m (ignore doors, ceilings, and floors). How much power would be required to maintain the inside temperature at 20°C if the outside temperature is 0°C? (U values: wall, 2·8 W/m²°C; windows, 5·7 W/m²°C.)
Answer: Ratio 8·7:1; total power 4·3 kW.

5. The ceiling of a building measuring 9 m × 7·5 m is insulated with fibreglass. The temperature below the ceiling is 30°C and above it is 0°C. What is the rate of heat loss through the ceiling? (U value = 0·6 W/m²°C.)
Answer: 1·2 kW.

6. Water flows at a rate of 150 litres/min through a 20 mm thick plastic hot-water pipe of length 80 m and outer diameter 40 mm. Over this length the temperature falls from 80°C to 79°C. Calculate the thermal conductivity of the pipe if the outer surface of the pipe is at a temperature of 15°C.
Answer: 0·16 W/m°C.

7. A heating element of 2 kW is enough to maintain a closed cylinder of liquid measuring 3 m × 1 m diameter at a temperature of 60°C when the air temperature is 20°C. How many kilowatts will be needed to keep a similar vat of 6 m × 1 m diameter at a temperature of 50°C at the same air temperature? (Assume the rate of heat loss is proportional to the surface area and obeys Newton's law of cooling).
Answer: 2·8 kW.

8. A filament is supplied with 100 watts which maintains its temperature at 1200°C. To what temperature would it rise if it were supplied with 150 watts?
Answer: 1360°C.

9. A 37·5 kW steam engine which is 30 per cent efficient, is driven by a boiler in which the water temperature is 250°C. The temperature of the outside of the boiler is 400°C. What is the minimum surface of the boiler exposed to the furnace if the thickness of the wall is 4 mm? One-tenth of the total temperature drop occurs in the metal itself. (Conductivity of boiler material = 378 W/m°C.)
Answer: 0·088 m².

10. A copper hot-water cylinder having a total area of 2·5 m² contains water which is maintained at an average temperature of 75°C by an electric immersion heater. It is lagged with an insulating jacket of thickness 30 mm and when the temperature of the outer surface is 15°C it is found that the heater consumes electrical power at an average rate of 30 watts. Calculate the thermal conductivity of the material of the lagging.
Answer: 6×10^{-3} W/m°C.

11. A rectangular equipment room with four outside walls is 12 m long, 6 m high, and 5 m wide. In one of the long walls are double steel doors 2.5 m wide and 6 m high. There are no windows. Calculate the total electrical loading required to maintain an inside temperature of 15°C when the minimum outside temperature is -7°C and there are two air changes per hour.

	U value W/m²°C
Floor (concrete over air spaces on piles)	1·1
Ceilings (concrete)	2·3
Doors (steel)	8·5
Walls (brick)	2·6

(Heat capacity of air = 1000 J/m³°C.)
Answer: 22·9 kW.

12. It is required to keep the oil in an arc furnace regulating transformer, while out of service, at a temperature of 15°C. Calculate the rating of a suitable immersion heater in kilowatts. Assume a minimum outside temperature of -7°C and the heat loss through the transformer tank for a temperature difference of 21°C as 218 W/m². Dimensions of the tank are height 3·4 m, width 2 m, depth 1 m.)
Answer: 3·9 kW.

13. Plastic moulding is left to cool in a room at 17°C and cools from 60°C to 50°C in 10¼ min. What is the time taken for its temperature to fall from 50°C to 40°C under conditions of forced convection (Newton's law) and natural convection. (Langmuir's law, $\dfrac{Q}{t} = K(\theta - \theta_0)^{5/4}$ where Q/t is cooling rate,

K is a constant, θ is the temperature of the moulding, θ_0 is room temperature.)
Answer: 14 min 15 s, 15 min 21 s.

14. A brick wall 200 mm thick is plastered 20 mm thick. Calculate the number of watts flowing per square metre if the inside surface temperature is 20°C and the outside surface temperature is 0°C. (Thermal conductivity of brick = 3×10^{-2} W/m°C; of plaster = 3×10^{-1} W/m°C.)
Answer: 2·97 W/m².

15. What is the temperature difference across a window 4 mm thick if 250 J/h escape per square metre? How much would it cost per day to replace it at 1½p per kilowatt-hour? (Thermal conductivity of glass = 1·1 W/m°C.)
Answer: 0·9°C; 9p.

16. A heater at the centre of a metal sphere is supplied with 100 watts of electricity. What is the temperature gradient 10 mm from the centre, once a steady state has been reached? (Thermal conductivity of the metal = 8·42 W/m°C.)
Answer: 9·45°C/mm.

17. In a Lee's disc experiment, a circular piece of glass, 3 mm thick and 110 mm in diameter is used· Its lower surface is at 95°C and its upper surface at 100°C. If the rate of cooling of the lower disc is 0·05°C/s at 95°C, its mass is 1 kg and its specific heat is 420 J/kg, what is the thermal conductivity of the glass?
Answer: 1·34 W/m°C.

18. Describe how you would measure the thermal conductivity of a poor conductor. Calculate the percentage reduction in heat lost by conduction brought about by replacing a single glass window by a double window, consisting of two sheets of glass separated by an air layer 10 mm thick. The glass is 2 mm thick in each case. (Thermal conductivities of glass and air are 1·7 and 0·58 units respectively.)

(I.E.R.E.)

Answer: 94 per cent.

5 Vibrations and Waves

Most matter is neither held absolutely rigidly in position, nor is it completely free to move. Each particle is restrained by its environment, and force of one kind or another is capable of moving it. A force sufficiently strong will entirely overcome the restraining influences and completely tear the particle away from its environment. A weak force, on the other hand, will merely distort the surroundings until their resistance counteracts the applied force. By 'environment' here we mean the adjacent parts, either internally or on the surface, of a solid, liquid or gas.

When the applied force is removed, the environ-ment pushes the particle back towards its original position. In returning, the particle gathers speed until, when it reaches the equilibrium position, where no forces act, it overshoots it and distorts the environment on the other side. This action is repeated back and forth giving rise to a common event in nature – periodic motion. Such motion exactly repeats itself in successive equal intervals of time, that is, the time taken by the particle to cover each swing of the vibration is always the same. The greatest distance from the equilibrium position reached by the particle is called the amplitude a. (Fig. 5.1.)

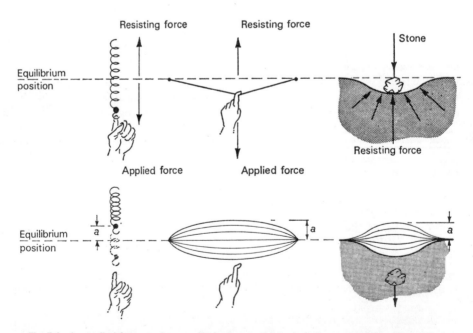

Fig. 5.1. An applied force produces a displacement which gives rise to a resisting force. When the force is removed, vibration occurs about the equilibrium position.

Simple Harmonic Motion (S.H.M.)

Frequently, the restoring force exerted on a particle is directly proportional to the displacement of the particle from its equilibrium position. We call the particularly simple kind of vibration which results in such cases *simple harmonic motion*. The vertical oscillations of a mass on a spiral spring is an example of this type of motion. (Fig. 5.2.) The acceleration of the mass is proportional to the force acting on it and is directed towards the equilibrium position.

$$\text{Force} = \text{mass} \times \text{acceleration} = ky$$

$$T = 2\pi \sqrt{\frac{m}{k}}$$

Note that the period is unaffected by the amplitude. If the amplitude of the motion is increased, the average velocity is also increased and the period remains constant. The number of vibrations per unit time, the *frequency n*, is equal to the reciprocal of the period.

$$n = \frac{1}{T}$$

The mass on the spring is an example of a

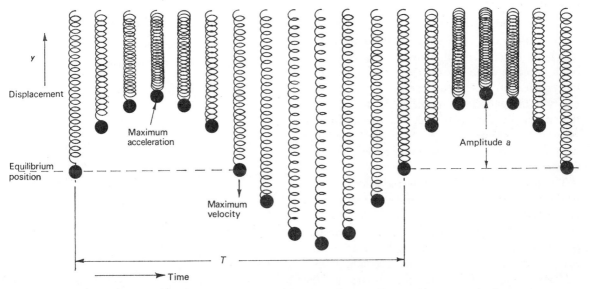

Fig. 5.2. The position of the mass on the spring is shown at different instants as it vibrates with simple harmonic motion.

where y is the displacement from the equilibrium position and k is the spring constant, i.e., the force exerted when the spring is extended by unit length.

When $y = 0$ the acceleration is zero and the velocity is greatest. When $y = a$ the acceleration is a maximum and the particle is instantaneously at rest. The time taken for the particle to perform a complete cycle, starting and ending with the same velocity and position, is the *period* of the motion, T.

The period depends on the restoring force represented by k and on the inertia of the particle represented by its mass, as follows:

linear vibration. Figure 5.3 shows examples of *angular vibrations* which may also be simple harmonic motion.

Problem: A rubber ball of mass 100 g is hanging from a rubber strip. If a force of 2 newtons will pull it down 400 mm find its period.

Solution: $T = 2\pi \sqrt{\dfrac{m}{k}}$ where $k = \dfrac{\text{force}}{\text{displacement}}$

$$= 2\pi \sqrt{\left(\frac{0 \cdot 1}{2/0 \cdot 4} \right)}$$

$$= 0 \cdot 9 \text{ s}$$

53

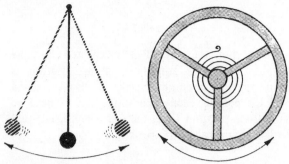

Fig. 5.3. The pendulum bob and watch balance, oscillations of which are examples of angular simple harmonic motion.

Energy Associated with S.H.M.

At the equilibrium position, the energy of a particle oscillating with simple harmonic motion is wholly kinetic. As it moves away from this point, work is done against the restoring force at the expense of the kinetic energy. In its extreme position the particle is momentarily at rest, and the energy is wholly potential. The proportions of kinetic and potential energy of the particle change with its position, but the total energy remains constant.

The work done in converting the kinetic energy of the particle into potential energy is the product of the average restoring force and the distance moved by the force. Each of these is separately proportional to the amplitude and, therefore, the energy possessed by a particle oscillating with S.H.M. is proportional to the square of the amplitude.

$$\text{Energy} \propto (\text{amplitude})^2$$

Problem: What fraction of the energy of a swinging pendulum remains when its amplitude is reduced from 10 cm to 4 cm?

Solution: Original energy $\propto 10^2$
Final energy $\propto 4^2$

Fraction remaining $= \dfrac{4^2}{10^2} = \dfrac{16}{100}$ or 16 per cent.

Equation of S.H.M.

The variation with time of the position of a particle vibrating with simple harmonic motion (Fig. 5.2) is the same shape as the graph of $\sin \theta$

against θ (Fig. 5.4). (The graph of $\cos \theta$ against θ would serve equally well.)

Starting with the equation $y = \sin \theta$ we can modify it to make it describe the motion of the particle. Now $y = \sin \theta$ has a maximum value of 1. Therefore, to give y a maximum value equal to the amplitude of the vibration, a, we write

$$y = a \sin \theta$$

If we compare Fig. 5.4 with Fig. 5.2 we see that $360°$ corresponds to T the period. Any other value of θ will correspond to a lapse of time t such that

$$\frac{t}{T} = \frac{\theta}{360°}$$

i.e.,

$$\theta = \frac{360t}{T} \text{ degrees}$$

or

$$\theta = \frac{2\pi t}{T} \text{ radians}$$

Hence the equation for y becomes

$$y = a \sin \frac{2\pi t}{T} \qquad (1)$$

We use this equation to predict the position of an object vibrating with S.H.M. at any time after it has passed through the equilibrium position.

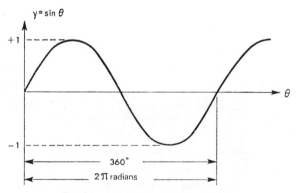

Fig. 5.4. Graph of $y = \sin \theta$ against θ.

Problem: What is the displacement of a particle vibrating with S.H.M. of period 0·5 s and of amplitude 8 cm at an instant 0·1 s after passing through the zero displacement position.

Solution: We use $y = a \sin \dfrac{360°t}{T}$

$$y = 8 \sin 360° \times \frac{0·1}{0·5}$$

$$= 7·6 \text{ cm}$$

Circular Motion and S.H.M.

The motion of a particle in a circle is related to S.H.M. in a very simple way, which gives some insight into both types of motion.

A radius OP of a circle rotating steadily about the centre O describes equal angles in equal intervals of time. (Fig. 5.5.) The number of degrees or radians described per second is the angular velocity ω

$$\omega = \frac{\text{angle described}}{\text{time taken}} = \frac{\theta}{t}$$

After a time t has elapsed, θ will have the value ωt. The projection y of OP on a vertical straight line is given by

$$y = OP \sin \theta = OP \sin \omega t$$

or

$$y = a \sin \omega t \qquad (2)$$

where $a = OP$, the radius of the circle.

frequency will be imposed on the particle. The amplitude of the particle will not be large, however, because it is not able to store much energy at frequencies other than its natural frequency. The incident energy is dissipated as random vibration, i.e., heat.

Should the forced frequency coincide with the natural frequency, the particle increases its amplitude and stores the energy. This situation is called resonance. (Fig. 5.6.) Minor resonances can occur when the forced frequency, n, is a simple fraction or multiple of the natural frequency n_0, e.g., $n = 2n_0$ or $n = \frac{1}{2}n_0$, etc.

Damping

There are two ways of driving a vehicle over an unmade or washboard road surface—either fast or very slow. At a certain intermediate speed the frequency of the road irregularities is near to the

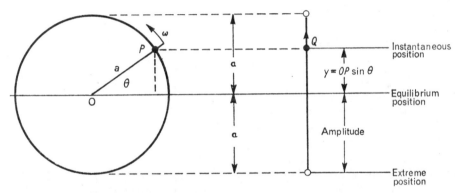

Fig. 5.5. Simple harmonic motion may be considered as a projection of uniform circular motion.

Equation (2) is the equation of motion of the point Q. By comparing it with equation (1) which represents S.H.M. we see that they are the same except that ωt replaces $2\pi t/T$. We therefore conclude that point Q performs S.H.M. of period $T = 2\pi/\omega$ and of amplitude a equal to the radius of the circular motion.

Free, Forced, and Resonant Vibrations

A particle which is free to vibrate will assume a natural frequency of vibration which will depend on the mass of the particle and the elasticity of the medium. If a force fluctuating at a frequency other than the natural frequency is applied, its

natural frequency of the springing or the steering, and the vibration builds up and makes control difficult. Even on apparently smooth roads, a recurring irregularity of the surface has been known to shatter car windscreens, a phenomenon sometimes attributed to poltergeists by people who do not realize the effects of vibration. This tendency to resonate can be reduced by providing a means of absorbing the undesirable energy of vibration. In motor vehicles, the energy is absorbed by hydraulic dampers (shock absorbers). (Fig. 5.7.) Movement in either direction is resisted by the viscous forces as the liquid passes from one side of a piston to the other through a restricted aperture, called the transfer channel.

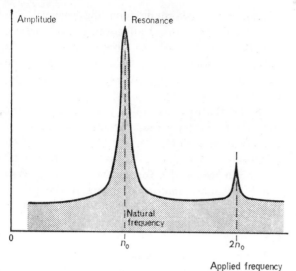

Instruments with moving pointers, such as balances and electrical meters, are damped to curtail oscillation about the final rest position. The damping may be provided by viscous, frictional, electrical, or magnetic forces.

It is important to provide just the right degree of damping. This is usually the damping which returns the system to the equilibrium position in the shortest possible time without oscillation. The condition is called *critical damping*. The graphs of Fig. 5.8 illustrate the effect of varying degrees of damping.

You can roughly check a car or motorcycle for critical damping by applying your weight to the suspension and then quickly removing it. The vehicle should return quickly to its original position without oscillating.

Energy Dissipation and Wave Motion

The energy supplied at a point of disturbance such as we have described is transmitted to adjacent particles by the forces between the particles. If there is little internal friction or damping, the energy travels away from the point in the form of a pulse. If the pulse is confined to one direction, like a ripple along a piece of rope, each particle in its path will, in turn, assume the movement of the original particle. (Fig. 5.9.) If the internal

friction is considerable, the kinetic energy of the pulse will be converted to heat in a short distance. (Fig. 5.10.)

If the energy which causes the disturbance carries on producing recurrent complete vibrations, then a continuous periodic wave is generated. We can form an accurate picture of such a wave by plotting the position, at one instant in time, of each particle in its path. (Fig. 5.11.) The distance between the wave crests or between corresponding points on the curve is the *wave-length*. As the wave profile moves, it displaces the position of each particle on its path. All the particles on the wave vibrate with S.H.M. but each one lags

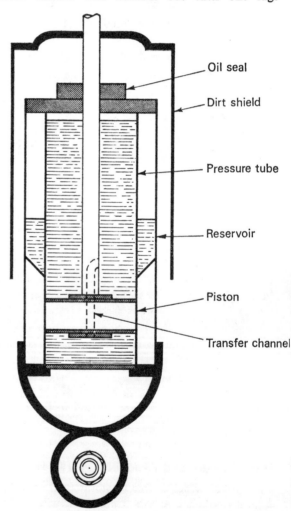

Fig. 5.7. Hydraulic dampers are used on motor vehicles to absorb the energy of the suspension. Limited resistance to vertical motion is provided as the liquid passes through the transfer channel.

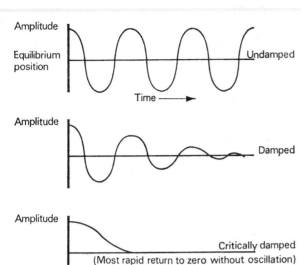

Fig. 5.8. The graphs show the behaviour of a particle which is displaced from its equilibrium position and released under varying degrees of damping.

slightly behind the one on the left because of its inertia. Figure 5.12 shows two positions of a wave separated by a short time interval. The wave profile travels from left to right, but note that each particle moves up and down about its equilibrium position.

$$\text{Velocity of wave} = \frac{\text{distance travelled by wave}}{\text{time taken}}$$

$$= \frac{\text{number of waves} \times \text{wave-length}}{\text{time}}$$

i.e.,   velocity = frequency × wave-length

$$v = n\lambda$$

Problem: One end of a rope is vibrated at 8 H_z and the waves generated measure 600 mm from crest to crest. How fast do they travel and what is the period of the vibration of any part of the rope?

Solution: $v = n\lambda$

$$v = 8 \times 0{\cdot}60$$

$$\text{velocity} = 4{\cdot}8 \text{ m/s}$$

$$\text{period} = \frac{1}{n} = \frac{1}{8} \text{ s}$$

Intensity of a Wave

The amount of energy flowing per second, per unit area normal to the direction of a wave, is called the *intensity* of the wave. The energy of a wave resides in the simple harmonic motions of the particles along its length. The energy of each of these component S.H.M.s is proportional to the square of the amplitude as explained earlier. Hence *the intensity of a wave is proportional to the square of its amplitude.*

$$I \propto a^2$$

If a wave diverges in all directions from a source, the intensity reduces with the distance from the source according to an *inverse square law.*

$$I \propto \frac{1}{d^2}$$

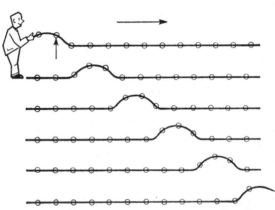

Fig. 5.9. A single pulse travels away from a source of energy. The pulse shown is only half a complete cycle and, in an elastic material, the amplitude remains constant.

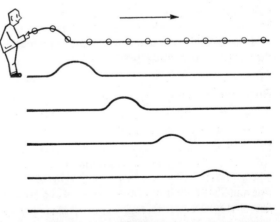

Fig. 5.10. A pulse is shown travelling in a non-elastic medium. The shape is preserved as before but the amplitude gradually reduces because of the internal friction.

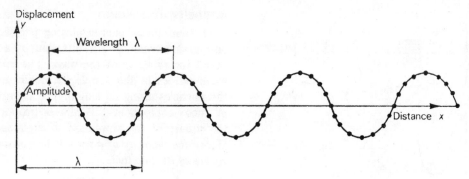

Fig. 5.11. A picture of a wave frozen at an instant in time showing the displacement of particles along its path.

where d is the distance from the source. You can deduce from these two relationships that the amplitude of a divergent wave falls off linearly with distance.

$$a \propto \frac{1}{d}$$

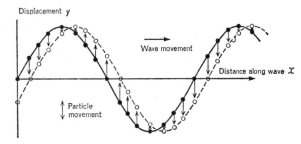

Fig. 5.12. Pictures taken of a wave at two close instants of time show that the particles do not move in the direction of the wave but at right angles to it.

Problem: The intensity of waves at a distance of 20 m from their source is 25 W/m². What is the intensity at a distance of 50 m and how do the amplitudes of the waves compare at the two places?

Solution: Intensity $\propto \dfrac{1}{d^2}$

$$\frac{I_2}{I_1} = \frac{d_1^2}{d_2^2}$$

$$I_2 = 25 \times \frac{20^2}{50^2} = 4 \text{ W/m}^2$$

The amplitudes are in the inverse ratio of the distances from the source

$$\frac{\text{amplitude at 20 cm}}{\text{amplitude at 50 cm}} = \frac{50}{20}$$

Wave Equations

If we can find an equation which describes a wave, it will help us to appreciate the relation between the wave variables and enable us to calculate the precise values of these quantities in given circumstances. The curve on Fig. 5.11 is the same shape as a sine curve, i.e., the graph of $y = \sin\theta$. How can we change this equation to make it give us the value of the displacement y of a particle distance x along the wave? We start with $y = \sin\theta$ which has a maximum value of one. To make the vertical scales match and give y a maximum value of a, we write

$$y = a \sin\theta$$

To make the horizontal scales match, 360° on the sine curve must correspond to λ the wave-length on the wave profile. Therefore x must have the same relation to λ, as θ has to 360°,

i.e.,
$$\frac{\theta}{360} = \frac{x}{\lambda}$$

or
$$\theta = \frac{360}{\lambda}x \text{ degrees}$$

$$= 2\pi\frac{x}{\lambda} \text{ radians}$$

$\therefore$
$$y = a \sin 2\pi\frac{x}{\lambda}$$

General Wave Equation

The displacement y at a distance x along the static wave profile, is given by $y = a \sin 2\pi\dfrac{x}{\lambda}$. Imagine that the profile moves from right to left with a velocity v, then after a time t it will have travelled a distance vt. The displacement of the particle at the distance x will be that at $(x+vt)$ on the static profile Fig. 5.13.

Substituting $(x+vt)$ for x in the wave profile equation, we have

$$y = a \sin \frac{2\pi}{\lambda} (x+vt)$$

This is equivalent to moving the axis a distance of vt to the left.

Phase Difference and Path Difference

The angle which is the subject of the sine in the wave equation is called the *phase* of the wave at the point. The phase determines at what stage a particle is in its S.H.M. cycle. The phase varies at different instants in time and at different positions on the wave, i.e., when x or t varies. Particles which have an integral multiple of 360° or 2π phase difference are said to be *in phase* while those which are an odd multiple of 180° or π difference of phase are *out of phase*.

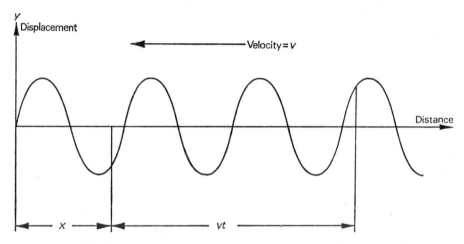

Fig. 5.13. The progressive wave moves a distance vt to the left during a time t.

This equation describes a wave progressing through a solid. Its use is in answering the question: 'What is the displacement y of a particle situated a distance x from the origin after a time t has elapsed?' For a wave travelling in the opposite direction the equation becomes:

$$y = a \sin \frac{2\pi}{\lambda} (x-vt)$$

In fact, the equation of a progressive wave can be expressed in several forms, e.g.,

substituting for v from $v = n\lambda$

$$y = a \sin \frac{2\pi}{\lambda} (x-n\lambda t)$$

$$= a \sin 2\pi \left(\frac{x}{\lambda}-nt\right)$$

substituting for n from $n = 1/T$

$$y = a \sin 2\pi \left(\frac{x}{\lambda}-\frac{t}{T}\right)$$

The distance between two points on a wave, expressed in units of λ the wave-length, is called the *path difference*. Particles which are $n\lambda$ apart are also $2\pi n$ different in phase.

phase difference $= 2\pi \times$ path difference

i.e.,

$$\varphi = \frac{2\pi(x_1 - x_2)}{\lambda}$$

Problem: Calculate (a) the path difference, (b) the phase difference at two points a distance 5 mm apart on a wave of wave-length 40 mm.

Solution: path difference $= \dfrac{\text{separation of points}}{\lambda}$

$$= \frac{5}{40}$$

$$= 0.125 \text{ wave-length}$$

phase difference $= 2\pi \times 0.125$

$$= 0.785 \text{ rad} = 45°$$

Wavefronts

If we join together the points on a wave which are in phase, we form a wavefront, and can subsequently predict its movement and direction. As a rule, the energy exerted by a wave flows at right angles to the wavefront, and it is sometimes simpler to represent the direction in which the energy is flowing by means of the straight lines bounding the wavefronts, that is, by means of a beam or, if the beam is very narrow, a single straight line, representing a ray. (Fig. 5.14.)

This simplified representation of wave motion is not valid when dealing with the minute detail of overlapping waves (interference) or with waves which are being restricted by an obstacle (diffraction). In these cases, we must consider not only the flow of energy, but also the detail of the periodicity of the waves.

In this chapter we have described the way in which vibration can generate waves and how the motion can be represented graphically and by an equation. The next chapter describes other kinds of waves and explains their general behaviour.

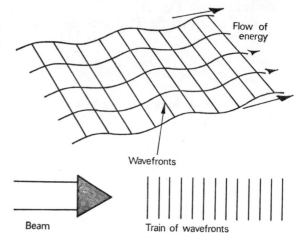

Fig. 5.14. A wavefront is a line on a wave joining points of equal phase. Waves may be represented by a train of wavefronts or more simply by a beam or ray.

Questions

1. Why do you think simple harmonic motion is so common?
2. How could you tell whether a vibration was a simple harmonic one?
3. Why is a difference in phase given as an angle?
4. How would you increase the damping exerted by a shock absorber?
5. Does a light beam obey the inverse square law?
6. When the driver gets into a car, what happens to the vibration period of the springs?
7. Given a motor, how would you use it to drive a platform up and down with simple harmonic motion?
8. Why does a car designer try to keep down the unsprung weight?
9. Explain how the general equation can describe both the instantaneous profile of the wave and the motion of one point in the wave.
10. How do resonance and damping affect loudspeaker design?

Problems

1. A man weighing 80 kg gets into a car, which sinks 4 mm on its springs. If the driver and the sprung part of the car weigh 400 kg, what is the period of vibration of the car?
   Answer: 0·28 s.

2. The period T of a pendulum is given by the formula
   $$T = 2\pi \sqrt{\frac{l}{g}}$$
   (l = length, g = acceleration due to gravity). If $T=1$ s and $l=250$ mm on the Earth, what length of pendulum would make $T=1$ s on the Moon, where the force of gravity is $\frac{1}{6}$ that on the earth?
   Answer: 42 mm.

3. A platform moves up and down with simple harmonic motion having an amplitude of 300 mm. What is the maximum frequency of the platform for which a box placed on top of the platform would maintain contact with it?
   Answer: 0·9 Hz.

4. What is the wave-length of a radio station broadcasting at 1000 kHz frequency? (Speed of radio waves $=3 \times 10^8$ m/s.)
   Answer: 300 m.

5. A weight of 45 kg vibrates with simple harmonic motion at the end of a spring. Its amplitude is

3000 mm and the period of its vibration is 0·8 s. What is its maximum kinetic energy?

Answer: 125 J.

6. What is the steady speed of a particle moving in a circle whose projection describes simple harmonic motion of period 5 s and amplitude 1 m?

Answer: 1·26 m/s.

7. A weight of 20 g vibrates with simple harmonic motion of period π seconds and amplitude 100 mm. What force is acting on it when its phase is 0° (maximum speed position), 30°, and 90°?

Answer: 0, 0·4 × 10⁻³ N, 8 × 10⁻³ N.

8. A particle vibrates with simple harmonic motion at 120 Hz and 1·0 mm amplitude. What is its speed through the equilibrium position, and 1·39 × 10⁻³ s later?

Answer: 0·76 m/s, 0·38 m/s.

9. One end of a string is vibrated at 50 Hz at an amplitude of 15 mm and a wave moves along the string at 2 m/s. What are the displacements of a particle 40 mm from the source at $t=0·040$ s, 0·045 s, 0·050 s, and 0·055 s after the vibration starts? (Assume no energy is dissipated by the string.)

Answer: 0, 15 mm; 0, −15 mm.

10. With the same wave, calculate the displacements of particles 0, 10, 20, 30, and 40 mm from the source at a time 0·02 s after the wave starts.

Answer: 0, −15 mm; 0, 15 mm; 0.

11. The period T of a pendulum is given by the formula $T = 2\pi \sqrt{\dfrac{l}{g}}$; where l is the pendulum length and g is the acceleration due to gravity. From the data given in the table, plot a graph and determine g.

Period (s)	3·96	3·66	3·34	3·16	3·00	2·80
Length (m)	3·92	3·36	2·80	2·52	2·24	1·96

12. A 0·5 kg weight is hung on a spiral spring and produces a deflection of 40 mm. A second 0·5 kg weight is suddenly added to the first. What is the maximum deflection and what is the period of the vibration of the double weight?

Answer: 120 mm, 0·88 s.

13. At high tide at 5 p.m. the water at a harbour entrance is 10 m deep, and at low tide, 6¼ hr before, it was 6·4 m deep. What is the earliest time a ship could enter if it needs 8·7 m depth? Assume the water level varies with simple harmonic motion.

Answer: 2.20 p.m.

14. Write down the equation of motion for an object moving with simple harmonic motion. Derive an expression for the velocity of the object at any instant and define the terms period and amplitude. A spring fixed at its upper end is stretched vertically downwards 10 mm when a mass is suspended from it. The mass is set in vertical oscillations of small amplitude. Determine the periodic time of oscillation.

(I.E.R.E. mechanics)

Answer: 0·2 s.

15. (i) How may a simple pendulum be used to determine the acceleration due to gravity? Discuss the limitations of the method.

(ii) A tuning-fork spring is vibrating at 500 Hz with an initial peak-to-peak amplitude of 1 mm. Calculate (a) its maximum speed and (b) the fraction of the energy lost when the amplitude has fallen to 0·5 mm.

(I.E.R.E. mechanics)

Answer: (ii) (a) 3·14 m/s; (b) ¾ (if amplitude is 1 mm).

6 Wave Behaviour

When energy of any kind involving a regularly fluctuating quantity travels along, it is called a wave. Wave motion is the most important means of energy transfer in the universe, whether it be from the Sun to the planets or from one end of a room to the other. Little wonder, then, that an understanding of wave motion is essential to both scientist and engineer.

The different kinds of wave which exist have many features in common. Thus, having considered one type of wave, we can apply the same methods to describe the behaviour of other waves, such as sound waves, light waves, or waves on liquid surfaces.

Longitudinal Waves

In the previous chapter, we described waves in which the movement of the particles is at right angles to the direction in which the waves travel. These are *transverse* waves. Equally important are *longitudinal waves*, in which the particles vibrate in the same direction as the wave travels. (Fig. 6.1.) As in the case of the transverse wave, each particle on the path of a longitudinal wave performs S.H.M. about its average position as the wave moves through it. Although both types of wave may pass through the same material, their velocities are generally different because of the different physical properties of the material which are involved in

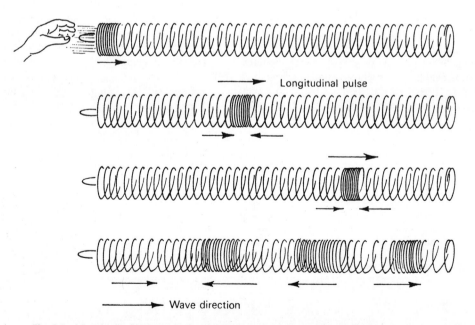

Longitudinal pulse

Wave direction

Fig. 6.1. A longitudinal pulse and a longitudinal wave are shown travelling along a spiral spring. Individual coils move back and forth about their undisturbed positions.

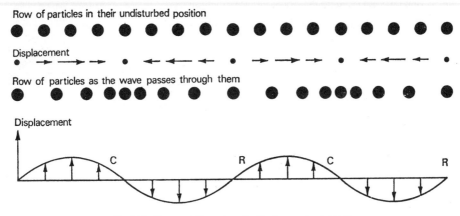

Row of particles in their undisturbed position

Displacement

Row of particles as the wave passes through them

Displacement

Fig. 6.2. Representing a longitudinal wave by a graph.

propagating them. When the appropriate constants are inserted in the wave equation which has already been given, it will describe both transverse and longitudinal waves equally well. Evenly spaced particles are displaced as the wave passes through them to the positions shown in Fig. 6.2. When we plot this displacement as ordinate against the horizontal equilibrium position of the particles, we obtain the familiar sinusoidal graph.

Note that a complete wave-length includes a compression and a rarefaction. The instantaneously undisturbed particles are at the centre of the compressions and rarefactions.

Light Waves

We are familiar with the way in which light energy travels from a source to arrive eventually at some other point which it illuminates. What is happening in the region through which the light is passing? Were it possible to stop such a light wave and take minute measurements along its path, we would detect two influences, a fluctuating electric field at right angles to the direction of the beam and a fluctuating magnetic field at right angles both to the beam and the electric field. (Fig. 6.3.)

Note that the electric and magnetic fields have

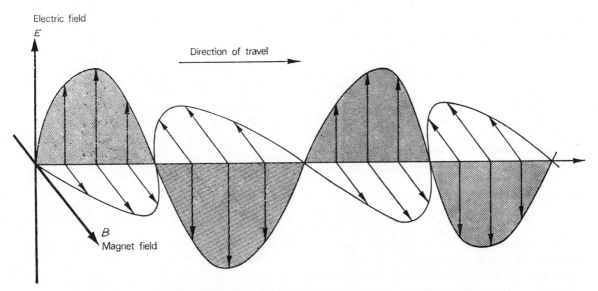

Fig. 6.3. The magnetic and electric field variations in a light wave are at right angles to the direction of the wave.

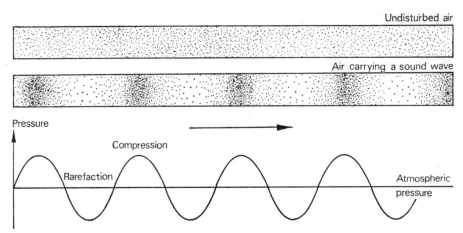

Fig. 6.4. Along the path of a sound wave in air, the longitudinal to and fro movement of the particles produces alternate compressions and rarefactions.

the same wave-length and they keep in phase. The energy of the light is stored in these two fluctuating fields, the pattern of which is preserved as it travels along. If one could read an electrometer and a magnetometer as the light passed through them, they would give readings first in one direction, reaching a maximum, and then in the other direction, reaching the same maximum in a similar way to the motion of a particle performing S.H.M. In fact, electromagnetic waves may be produced by a vibrating charged particle, such as an electron, which creates a varying electric field.

Sound Waves

Encouraged perhaps by the answer to the question 'what is light?', let us pose the question 'what is sound?' If we were to employ the same tactics and take suitable instruments between source and receiver while the wave is frozen in time, what would we find there? The instruments would show that the pressure along the wave changes regularly, alternating from a little above average to a little below average. (Fig. 6.4.)

The compressions and rarefactions move through the material with the velocity of the wave. For a sound wave in air this is about 350 m/s, i.e., 1250 km/h, depending on the temperature of the air.

The particles in the path of the wave move from their equilibrium position first in the direction of the wave and then in the reverse direction. This type of to and fro movement along the direction of travel makes sound a longitudinal wave.

Light waves are, in contrast, transverse waves because the fluctuation is across the wave perpendicular to the direction of travel.

Waves in Strings

When a stretched string is pulled to one side, the tension tends to return it to its equilibrium position. The higher the tension, the quicker the string is restored to this position when it is released and the faster the resulting wave travels along the string. The mass of the string tends to retard its return and so slows down the wave. The velocity of a transverse wave in a string is given by the equation

$$\text{Velocity} = \sqrt{\left(\frac{\text{Tension}}{\text{mass/unit length}}\right)}$$

Surface Liquid Waves

Liquid surface waves can be quite complex, like sea waves generated by a storm centre in the

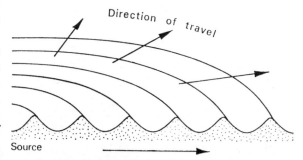

Fig. 6.5. Liquid surface waves are transverse waves not having the same shape as the simple sine curve.

great oceans, or they can be more regular like the waves on a still pond when a stone is dropped into it. (Fig. 6.5.) A wave on a liquid combines both longitudinal and transverse vibration which give each particle on its path a cyclic motion. The waves can be analysed into simple sinusoidal variations such as we have dealt with in this chapter. The principal restoring force acting on particles in a sea wave is the force of gravity, whereas for ripples the surface tension plays a greater part.

Refraction of Waves

A change in medium or a change in conditions may cause a wave to slow down as, for example, when rays of light strike the surface of a block of glass, or when sea waves meet a shelving beach. This slowing-down has the effect of shortening the wave-length, that is, the distance between the crests of the waves, although the frequency of the waves remains the same. This is shown for normal incidence in Fig. 6.6 which also shows what

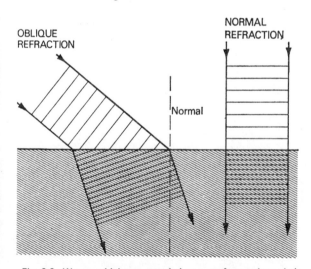

Fig. 6.6. Waves which are retarded at a surface reduce their wave-length and are refracted towards the normal.

happens when the wavefronts meet the surface obliquely. One end of each wavefront, the end which touches the obstacle first, slows up before the other, and the whole wavefront is made to swing round. The retardation of the waves causes deviation towards the normal at the surface. Conversely, if the waves travel faster in the second medium they deviate away from the normal. This phenomenon is called *refraction*. It may occur

sharply as, for example, when light waves enter a glass block, or it may occur gradually as is the case for sea waves approaching a shelving beach. The velocity of the waves reduces as the depth increases, and the waves are bent around to face the shore. (Fig. 6.7.) The shortened wave-length causes the waves to break as they become too steep-sided to support themselves.

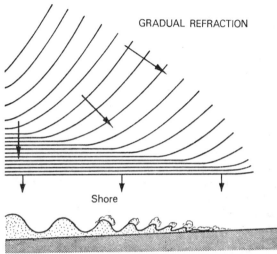

Fig. 6.7. Sea waves retarded by a shelving beach swing round and break on the shore.

Reflection of Waves

When a wave meets a surface separating two materials in which its velocity is different, some of the energy of the wave is reflected. The reflected wave has the same velocity, frequency, and wave-length as the incident wave, and the two waves are symmetrical with the surface. (Fig. 6.8.)

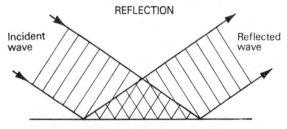

Fig. 6.8. The reflected wave and the incident wave are symmetrical with the surface.

In some cases of reflection, a change of phase occurs which is of importance when considering the detail of sound and light waves. Imagine a compression approaching a boundary at which its

65

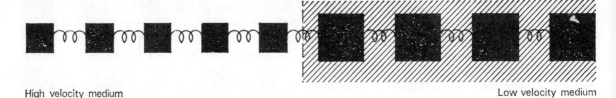

High velocity medium   Low velocity medium

Fig. 6.9. Two media represented by particles of different masses linked by equal springs.

velocity reduces. This is represented in Fig. 6.9 by a series of masses linked by identical springs. When the link connecting the two media is compressed, the more massive particle moves to the right carrying some of the energy into the second material. Being more massive, however, the particle does not move sufficiently to relieve all the compression on the spring, and the less massive particle bounces back from the boundary. The recoil produces a pulse in which the displacements

are exactly opposite in phase to those on the incident wave. Thus, at external reflection, the phase of a wave changes by 180°. (Fig. 6.10a.)

A compression approaching the boundary from the material in which it travels slower (right to left) corresponds to internal incidence. In this case, compression of the connecting link moves the lighter particle so readily that the more massive particle overshoots and stretches the link behind it. This generates a pulse of extension which

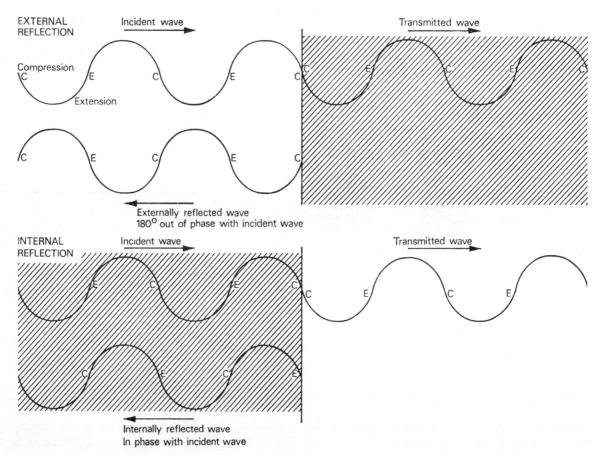

Fig. 6.10. A phase change occurs on external reflection but no phase change on internal reflection.

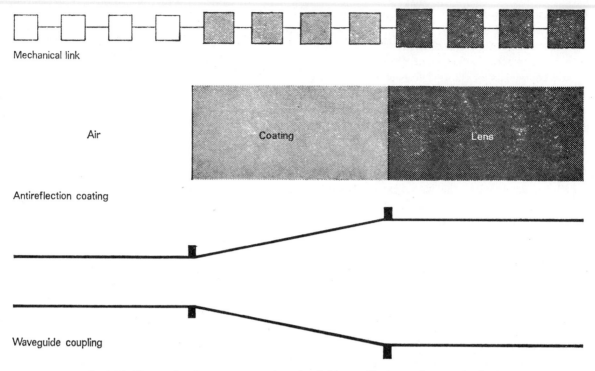

Mechanical link

Air   Coating   Lens

Antireflection coating

Waveguide coupling

Fig. 6.11. The transfer of energy across a boundary is increased by interposing a section having intermediate properties which reduces reflection.

reflects back into the more massive particles. In the case of internal reflection, therefore, the incident and reflected waves are in phase. (Fig. 6.10*b*.)

The greater the change in conditions at a surface, the greater is the fraction of incident energy reflected. Where we require a wave to cross a boundary with minimum reflection, we try to reduce the abruptness of the change. We do this in several ways depending on the kind of wave we are dealing with. (Fig. 6.11.)

Interference

Two wave trains will pass through the same region and each will emerge on the other side quite unaffected by the other. Where they actually overlap however, they do interact or interfere with each other. In practice, if we wish to detect and examine the interference, the two wave trains must be simply related and have the same frequency and amplitude, but we can appreciate the principle of interference by considering the interaction of single pulses travelling along a string of particles. Two crests travelling in opposite directions produce

a maximum amplitude where they coincide and then move on unaffected. (Fig. 6.12*a*.) The

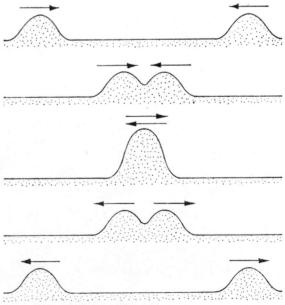

Fig. 6.12. *(a)* Two approaching crests produce a maximum where they coincide.

67

coincidence of two troughs would also produce a maximum amplitude, but, where a crest and a trough coincide, they cancel each other and result in a point of zero displacement. (Fig. 6.12*b*.)

The complexity of the interference pattern from two sources of continuous waves may be appreciated from Fig. 6.13. The coincidence of two crests or two troughs produces a maximum amplitude or *antinode*. Where crest and trough coincide, a minimum amplitude or *node* is produced. The nodes and antinodes are not points but lines which remain fixed as the waves move outwards.

The different parts of a single wave train can give rise to interference when they are restricted by some obstacle. This type of interference is given the name *diffraction* and it produces a variety of wave patterns depending on the nature of the obstacle.

Stationary Waves

Directly between the sources of Fig. 6.13 the interference produces a rather special type of wave which forms whenever two waves of equal frequency and amplitude travel in opposite directions through the same space. Figure 6.14

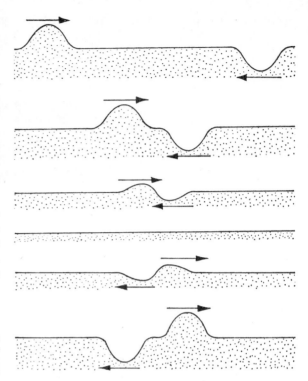

Fig. 6.12. *(b)* The coincidence of a crest and a trough produces destructive interference.

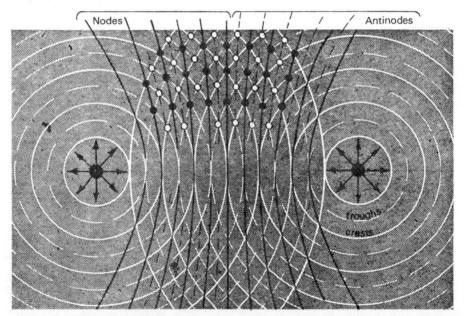

Fig. 6.13. As the waves of equal amplitude *and* frequency radiate from the sources, a pattern of lines of minimum amplitude (nodes) and lines of maximum amplitude (antinodes) is produced.

shows two such waves and their combined effect in different positions.

At every stage in their motion, the waves sum to zero at certain fixed points, the nodes, situated half a wave-length apart. Because of these fixed nodes we call the resulting wave a *standing* or *stationary wave*. The amplitude is not constant

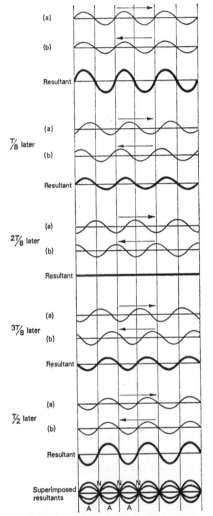

Fig. 6.14. A stationary wave is formed when two identical progressive waves travelling in opposite directions are superimposed. The waves interfere destructively at the nodes and supplement each other at the anti-nodes.

along the wave but varies from zero at the nodes to a maximum at the antinodes midway between the nodes. All the points between two successive nodes are in phase and each antinode is exactly out of phase with its neighbour.

Stationary waves are very common because they are generated whenever a progressive wave is reflected at right angles to a boundary. A transverse stationary wave is shown in Fig. 6.14. Longitudinal stationary waves are described in chapter 17.

A rather dramatic example of transverse standing waves was the destruction of the Tacoma Suspension Bridge, U.S.A., in 1940. The centre span of 850 m was slung between towers 130 m high, which were anchored by cables to blocks containing 15,000 m³ of concrete. Even during construction it was found to have a tendency to vibrate and an effort was made to reduce it. When completed it resonated to a standing wave with eight or nine nodes at a frequency of 36 or 38 vibrations/minute. When it was completed, it lasted just four months and seven days, before one mildly windy day the amplitude of the standing wave rose to several metres, exceeding the elastic limit of its construction members, and the bridge broke up.

Shock Waves

Just as an object has a natural frequency of vibration, so in each medium a wave has a natural velocity of propagation. It is in some cases possible for a body to move through the medium at a higher speed than waves. Bullets, shells, and projectiles travel much faster than sound and, now, our manned aircraft can maintain supersonic velocities. Ships often exceed the velocity of water waves but, in contrast, no object can ever travel faster than light waves in a vacuum.

When a body exceeds the speed of waves in a medium, no wave travels ahead of it to produce a mild disturbance. The air is undisturbed until the body itself arrives. The sudden disturbance which the object produces is called a *shock wave* and this travels away from the leading edge of the object at the wave velocity. The bow wave of a ship travelling faster than water waves is another example of a shock wave. We often express supersonic velocities in units of the speed of sound, called *mach numbers*.

$$\text{mach number} = \frac{\text{velocity of body}}{\text{velocity of sound}}$$

Since the speed of sound varies with atmospheric conditions, so does the speed indicated by a certain mach number. Under normal conditions, a speed of mach 1 would correspond to about 1250 km/h and speeds of about mach 5 have been achieved by prototype 'planes, such as the American X15.

The mach number of a missile can be deduced from the shape of its shock wave. (Fig. 6.15.) During the time that the body travels at a velocity v from x to y, the wave travels at c, the velocity of sound, to z.

$$\sin \theta = \frac{xz}{xy} = \frac{ct}{vt} = \frac{c}{v}$$

$$\text{mach number} = \frac{v}{c} = \frac{1}{\sin \theta}$$

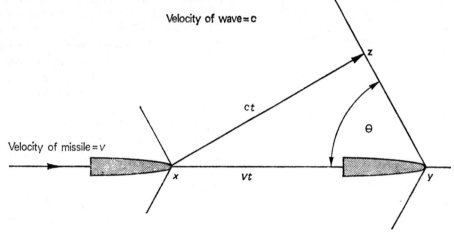

Velocity of wave = c

ct

θ

Velocity of missile = v

x

vt

y

z

Fig. 6.15. Shock wave from a supersonic missile.

Questions

1. What is the difference between progressive and standing waves?

2. What decides whether a medium will transmit longitudinal or transverse waves?

3. How can a longitudinal wave be represented on a transverse graph?

4. When a transverse wave travels along a rope, each particle moves only at right angles to the rope. What is it that moves along the rope?

5. What is the effect on the velocity of a wave along a string if the tension and density of the string are both halved?

6. Does light travel in straight lines?

7. What effect does the phase-change introduced by reflection from a denser medium have on interference effects?

8. If the wavefronts of a light beam are closer together in a block of glass than in air, why does the light not change colour?

9. Sea waves are mostly transverse—what propels a surfer?

10. In a monophonic record player, does it matter which wire goes on which terminal of the speaker? Does it matter on a stereophonic one?

Problems

1. If waves travel along a rope weighing 0·15 kg at 8 m/s and the rope is 3 m long, what is the tension in the rope?
Answer: 3·2 N.

2. A rope weighing 4·5 kg and 18·3 m long is stretched horizontally with a tension of 1360 N. How long will a transverse wave take to travel from one end to the other?
Answer: 0·246 s.

3. A bullet travels at 550 m/s in air. What is the bow-wave angle if the velocity of sound is 335 m/s.
Answer: 63°.

4. A jet aircraft is travelling at 300 m/s. What is its mach number, if the velocity of sound is 340 m/s?
Answer: 0·88.

5. A jet is flying horizontally at mach 2, 2000 m up. How far away will it be when its shock wave reaches an observer on the ground?
Answer: 4480 m.

7 The Structure of Matter

An apparently endless variety of materials exists in nature. Added to these, the materials produced by man raise the number to a staggering total. Yet, despite the diversity in the appearance of matter, men have always cherished the idea of an underlying simplicity. Long before science developed to the stage of experiment, the scientists of the ancient world speculated about the basic substances from which all matter was made, and formulated the theory that there were four elements—earth, water, fire, and air.

This theory obviously sprang from common human observation; if we interpret the four elements as solid, liquid, heat, and gas, they include the whole of man's ordinary experience, and by means of this theory men succeeded for many centuries in accounting for most natural phenomena. For example, they explained the fact that steam rises contrary to normal gravity by pointing out that steam is a mixture containing more fire than water, so that it shares with flames the property of rising. Differences in the appearance of materials, they explained, result from differences in the proportions of the four elements contained in them, and all they felt they had to do to change one material into another was to find a way of altering the proportions of the constituent elements. By adding a sufficiently large dose of the element of fire to the correct mixture of sand, alkali, and lead, they produced glass, and for several wasteful centuries alchemists tried continually to change worthless materials into gold by similar processes of mixing and heating.

To us the speculative methods of the early scientists, mixing and stirring their quaint ingredients like so many adventurous cooks, and making new discoveries only once in a long while—and then only by accident—seem naïve and amusing. Yet this was, in general, the state of science before the vigorous new approach, which we call the Scientific Revolution, began in Western Europe in the seventeenth century. Then, for the first time, scientists started using systematic experiments to seek out the underlying structure of matter, and slowly revealed the existence of, not four, but about one hundred elements, of which all other substances are composed.

The Elements

The elements which occur in nature range from hydrogen, which is the lightest, to uranium, which is the heaviest. Rarely does any one of the elements occur separately from other elements. When an

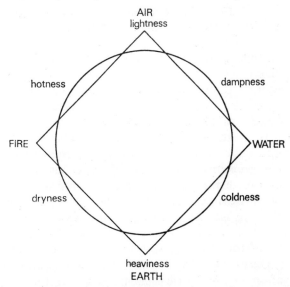

Fig. 7.1. The four element theory of the nature of matter.

element does appear in its pure form it is usually to be found mixed with other matter, as gold-dust is with river-sand, and oxygen with the other gases in the atmosphere. More often, the elements only exist in chemical combination with other elements, and their isolation requires a series of chemical reactions. All the naturally occurring elements have been isolated and identified. They have been given names and symbols, as shown in the complete list given in the appendix at the end of the book.

Mixtures and Compounds

It is important to distinguish between a physical mixture and a chemical compound. In a mixture, the components make only superficial contact, retaining their separate identity, and being capable of separation from the mixture by physical means. A mixture has something of the properties of its components and its percentage composition may vary. A mixture of peas and beans illustrates these points well.

A compound, formed of two or more elements, involves a much more fundamental change. The combination is accompanied by the absorption or emission of heat, and the properties of the compound produced may be quite different to those of either component. For example, hydrogen and oxygen are quite unlike water, which is the compound they produce when they combine chemically. The proportions of the components are constant in every part of a compound, and separation can only be achieved by chemical means.

The difference between a compound and a mixture can be illustrated very neatly with iron filings and powdered sulphur. These two components mixed in any proportion can be separated by using a magnet or by placing the mixture in a liquid in which the sulphur either floats or dissolves. If the mixture is heated, however, a compound of iron and sulphur, ferric sulphide, is formed which has properties quite unlike those either of the iron or of the sulphur. The compound has fixed proportions of iron and sulphur, any surplus of either in the mixture being left unchanged.

The Atom

Question: If it were possible to take a quantity of any one of the elements and to divide it into a large number of very small amounts, is there any

limit to the size of the parts, or could we go on dividing indefinitely? The answer is that eventually we would come to a dead stop. We would reach a stage at which we could not divide the element any further. Heating or cooling, chopping or cutting would make no permanent change in this basic particle. Each of the elements has such a basic unit called an *atom*. It is defined as *the smallest part of an element which can take part in a chemical change.*

The Molecule

When elements combine together, the atoms join to form a basic unit of the new substance. This unit is called a molecule. It is the *smallest part of a substance which can have a separate stable existence.*

Even atoms of a single element may be more stable when they are joined together into a molecule. Oxygen atoms, for example, are more stable when they join together in pairs. (Fig. 7.2.) The

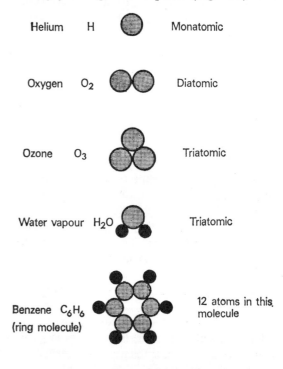

Helium	H	Monatomic
Oxygen	O_2	Diatomic
Ozone	O_3	Triatomic
Water vapour	H_2O	Triatomic
Benzene C_6H_6 (ring molecule)		12 atoms in this molecule
Polyethylene (Polymer) $n(CH_2)$		Polyatomic

Fig. 7.2. Atoms combine together to form molecules.

molecule of oxygen is then said to be diatomic. It is represented by writing a suffix after the symbol for the element, e.g., O_2 for a molecule of oxygen, and H_2 for a molecule of hydrogen, which is also diatomic.

The atoms of many elements are quite stable when they exist singly and so they are both atom and molecule at the same time. Such elements are *monatomic*.

In some circumstances, oxygen atoms combine together to form a triatomic molecule, that is, a molecule containing three atoms, which we represent by the symbol O_3. This form of oxygen is produced near electrical equipment where sparks occur. It has the special name of *ozone*, and can be distinguished from oxygen, which is odourless, by its smell. (Ozone is produced in the ionosphere of the Earth, where cosmic rays from outer space produce an electrical disturbance as they encounter the Earth's atmosphere.) Some atomic groups combine together to form chains of great length called polymers. (Fig. 7.2.) Such molecules are the basis of many plastics and synthetic textiles, and chemists can tailor molecules to give required properties.

The Weight of Atoms and Molecules

The mass of an atom expressed in kilogrammes is a very small quantity. For example, the mass of a carbon atom is 2×10^{-26} kg. A much smaller unit of mass is more convenient for expressing the masses of atoms. The hydrogen atom is the lightest, so that by taking its mass as one unit, we can express the mass of all the other atoms as numbers greater than one.

1 unified atomic mass unit (u)$=1.67 \times 10^{-27}$ kg.

On this scale the carbon atom's mass is 12 u. The mass of an atom expressed in atomic mass units is referred to as the *atomic weight* of the element.

The atomic mass unit also serves as a unit for measuring the masses of molecules and, in this case, they are referred to as *molecular weights*.

Chemical Equations

We have a shorthand method of writing down a chemical reaction which is both clear and concise. For example, an oxygen atom combines with two hydrogen atoms to give a molecule of water and this can be represented by

$$2H + O = H_2O.$$

Since oxygen and hydrogen molecules are diatomic, however, it is better to deal in molecules and write

$$2H_2 + O_2 = 2H_2O.$$

Such equations must balance, that is, they must show the same number of atoms of each substance on each side. Here are some other examples of the use of equations of this type to describe simple reactions.

$$2Na + Cl_2 = 2NaCl$$
sodium + chlorine = sodium chloride (common salt)

$$C + O_2 = CO_2$$
carbon + oxygen = carbon dioxide

$$2C + O_2 = 2CO$$
carbon + oxygen = carbon monoxide

$$Fe + S = FeS$$
iron + sulphur = ferrous sulphide

The numbers in front of the chemical symbols indicate the number of molecules, while the suffixes indicate the number of atoms in each molecule.

The Phases of Matter

Having recognized atoms and molecules as the basic building blocks from which matter is constructed, we turn our attention to the different arrangements of the molecules and the binding forces which hold them together.

An important feature of a substance is the phase in which it exists, i.e., whether it is a solid, a liquid, or a gas. The phase of a substance depends on the conditions of pressure and temperature which prevail. For example, an increase in temperature will change a solid into a liquid and ultimately into a gas or vapour. Substances tend to be classified according to their phase under normal conditions. We class water as a liquid, but an Eskimo might not agree. The molecules in each phase influence each other to different extents. We will describe the structure of solids first, and then examine the transition to other phases later.

The Solid State

In a solid the molecules and atoms hold each other into a regular three-dimensional pattern.

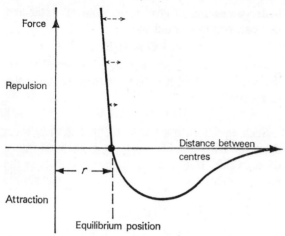

Fig. 7.3. The resultant force between atoms changes from being attractive at long range to being strongly repulsive at short range. The amplitude of vibration and the average distance between atoms increases with temperature.

The mutual attraction of molecules increases as they approach each other, but it turns to strong repulsion, if they get very near. (Fig. 7.3.) At a certain distance apart the molecules are in equilibrium. The forces holding the molecules in position form links which can be stretched or compressed rather like springs. (Fig. 7.4.)

When an overall compression or stretching is applied to a body, its elastic properties depend on its structure and on the strength of the links between molecules. The links can be very strong, as is demonstrated by a 40 mm diameter steel hawser which supports 50,000 kg (50 tons) quite safely.

Part of a solid's internal energy is due to the vibration of its molecules about their average

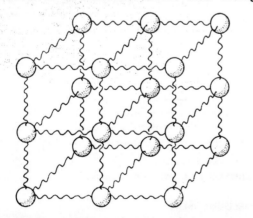

Fig. 7.4. [In a crystalline solid, the links hold the atoms into a regular pattern.

position. There is a continual exchange between the kinetic energy of vibration and the potential energy of the stretched linkages. The amplitude of the vibration increases as heat is added and usually the dimensions of the solid increase. This can be explained by referring to Fig. 7.3 which shows that the repulsive forces increase more rapidly than the attractive forces, with the displacement from the equilibrium position. Thus a temperature rise increases the amplitude of vibration more on the extension side of the equilibrium position, and the average distance of separation of the atoms increases.

Crystal Structure

For the sake of convenience, molecules and atoms are often represented by spheres. In fact,

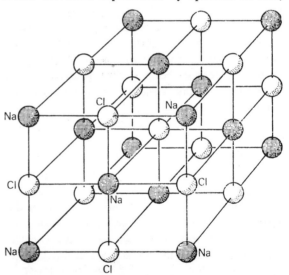

Fig. 7.5. Sodium and chlorine ions fit together forming a cubic structure.

they are not spherical but have definite and characteristic shapes, and a tendency to link together in characteristic ways. The molecules of any particular substance have a set number of links, which reach out from the nucleus of the molecule in certain directions. For these reasons most solids are crystalline, that is, they are made up of a characteristic pattern of atoms. (Fig. 7.5.)

The particular crystalline pattern is a very important factor in determining the properties of a solid. The difference between two arrangements of the same atoms can be very pronounced.

Graphite and diamond are solids having two different arrangements of the carbon atom. One is an excellent lubricant and the other a superlative abrasive. (Fig. 7.6.)

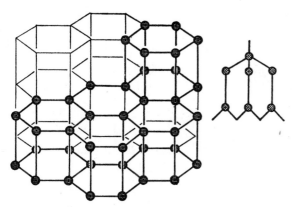

Fig. 7.6. Graphite and diamond are two crystalline forms of carbon.

The carbon atom has four links, and in graphite three of these links lie in a plane joining up with other atoms to form a sheet structure. The sheets are only loosely joined together by the fourth link of the atoms and it is very easy for the sheets to slide over each other. In diamond the four links are arranged symmetrically around each atom, forming a stable pyramid structure.

There are seven basic crystal systems in all. The crystal structure of a solid can often be deduced from the shape of its crystals (Fig. 7.7), or by a microscopic examination of a fractured surface. (Fig. 7.8.) At one time, only the more obvious and simply shaped solids were thought to be crystalline but more rigorous examination shows the majority of solids to be crystalline. It was also held that the movements and positions of the molecules of liquids and gases were completely random. Recent researches have produced statistical evidence of pattern and indicate the possibility of an underlying crystalline structure in these states of matter also.

Crystal Defects

Although many crystals appear quite symmetrical, absolutely perfect crystals are extremely rare. Most crystals possess defects which are so small that they may not be visible even with the most powerful microscopes, but which nevertheless exert a very strong influence on their properties. (Fig. 7.10.) Thermal vibration causes the defects to diffuse at random about the crystals (Fig. 7.9). When under stress the defects tend to accumulate and cause deformation of the crystal under much less force than that which would deform a perfect crystal. (Fig. 7.11.) To make a material remain elastic under greater stress, we must either reduce the number of dislocations or stop their movement.

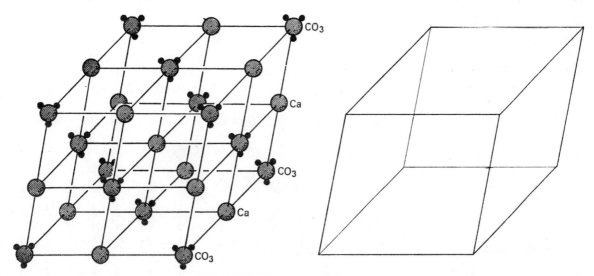

(Calcium carbonate $CaCO_3$)

Fig. 7.7. Naturally occurring calcite (calcium carbonate $CaCO_3$) compared with the crystal structure.

75

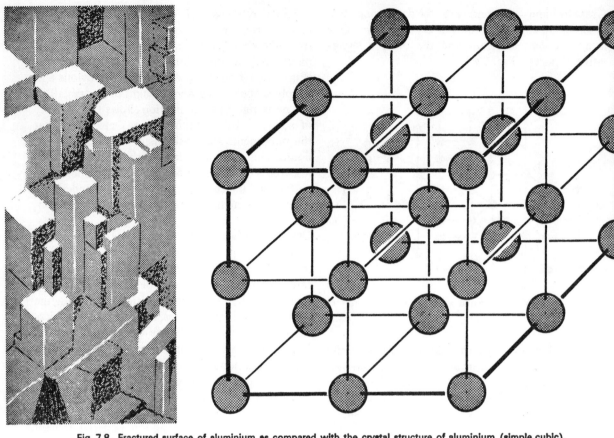

Fig. 7.8. Fractured surface of aluminium as compared with the crystal structure of aluminium (simple cubic).

Whiskers

Until *whiskers* were discovered, scientists thought it would be impossible ever to produce crystals which were free from the effects of dislocations. Whiskers are minute metal filaments, which grow on the metal coatings of electronic components, and during experiments aimed at eliminating these filaments, it was found that the whiskers on tin were about 1000 times as strong as tin wire of the same diameter. We attribute this strength to the fact that each whisker is a single dislocation-free crystal. Unfortunately, they are so minute, only about 10^{-5} mm in diameter, that we cannot as yet make use of their strength. Further development,

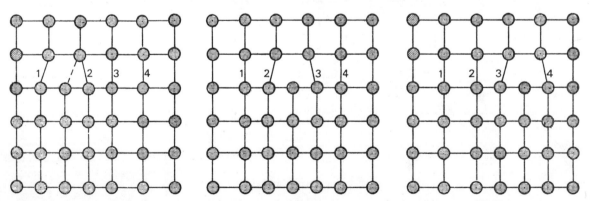

Fig. 7.9. The edge dislocation moves to the right as links 2 and 3 transfer in turn to the left.

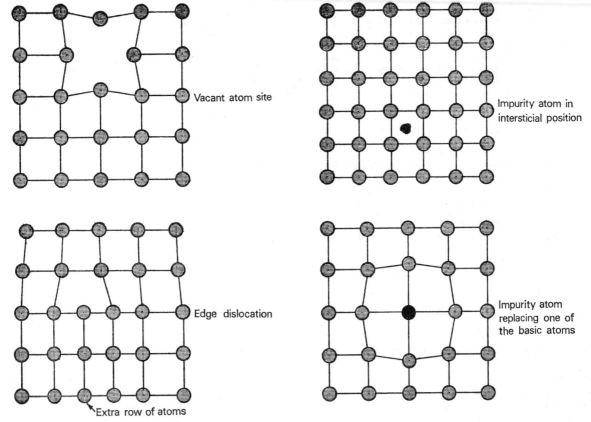

Fig. 7.10. Types of crystal defects.

Vacant atom site

Impurity atom in intersticial position

Edge dislocation

Extra row of atoms

Impurity atom replacing one of the basic atoms

however, may one day produce a material of unprecedented toughness from these whiskers.

Polycrystalline Materials

The usual methods of hardening materials aim at immobilizing the dislocations. Most materials are polycrystalline, that is, they are made up of a large number of crystals joined at the boundaries. (Fig. 7.14.) These boundaries restrict the movement of the dislocations and give strength to the material. The greater the number of boundaries the stronger the material becomes and vice versa. If we wish to harden a material, we cool it rapidly and it crystallizes in many places at once. To make it softer, we cool it slowly after heating (annealing) and larger crystals form. (Fig. 7.15.) Metals are sometimes hardened by cold working, that is, by being hammered or rolled into sheets, which increases the area of the boundaries between crystal zones and restricts the movement of dislocations. This prestressing of the material allows

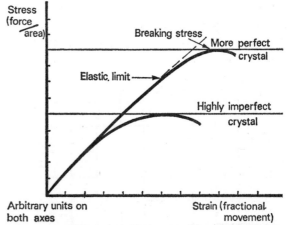

Fig. 7.11. Imperfections in a single crystal lower its elastic limit and breaking stress.

the more mobile defects to move and, perhaps, become fixed before the material is machined to shape.

The introduction of impurity into a crystalline

77

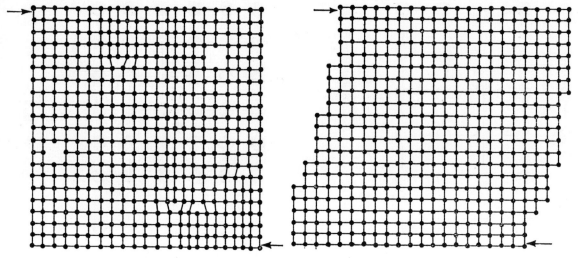

Fig. 7.12. A shear stress may cause a deformation by the movement of lattice defects. (Vertical forces have been omitted.)

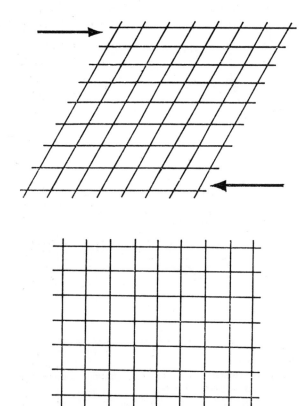

Fig. 7.13. Shear of perfect crystal.

Fig. 7.14. Most materials are polycrystalline and are made up of crystallites of different lattice orientation.

material can make it stronger. For example, brass is harder than either of its copper and zinc constituents and carbon steel is stronger than mild steel which contains less carbon. The impurity makes the lattice irregular and prevents the even movement of the dislocations. (Fig. 7.16.)

In the design of structures, such as bridges and machines, a very large margin of safety must be allowed between the maximum load to be applied in use and the breaking strength of the structure.

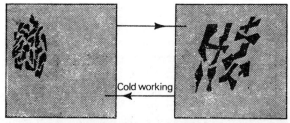

Fig. 7.15. The result of annealing a specimen of cold worked brass is an increase in the size of the crystal which makes the brass less brittle.

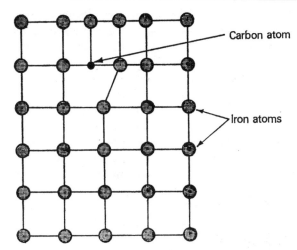

Fig. 7.16. An edge dislocation may be fixed when it encounters an impurity atom. The smaller carbon atom fits into the restricted space better than an iron atom.

The ratio of breaking strength to maximum load, called the safety factor, is usually about four for steel structures and about ten for brick structures.

Materials which are subject to repeated stresses over a period may break or become deformed under loads well below the breaking strain. This phenomenon is called *fatigue* and is caused by the accumulation in use of dislocations in one particular plane or direction. (Fig. 7.17.) This type of failure could be disastrous in an aeroplane. Thus, components subject to fatigue are replaced after a certain period of use, even though they may show no superficial signs of wear or deterioration.

Change of State

The linkages between the atoms or molecules of a solid can only restrain the atoms to a limited extent. Thus, if the thermal vibrations exceed this limit, the interatomic attractive forces are overcome and the atoms are less rigidly held in position. This is the case when a solid reaches its melting point.

For every atom of a solid which becomes liquid, energy must be provided, even if there is no increase in temperature. The energy is called the *latent heat of fusion* of the material.

The boiling or melting point can be obtained by plotting the graph of Fig. 7.18.

Crystalline substances which are pure, or which contain a uniform distribution of impurities, produce well defined horizontal sections. Non-crystalline or amorphous substances such as glass, paraffin wax, and many kinds of 'plastic' material, do not have a well-defined melting point. They become softer or more plastic as the temperature rises. Even at low temperatures they flow and they may be regarded as liquids of very high viscosity. Glass windows taken from very old

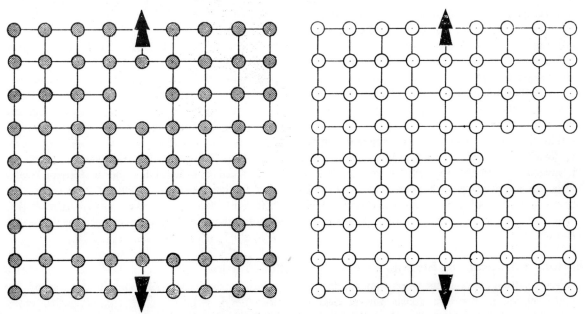

Fig. 7.17. Surface defect acts as a point at which other defects collect and develops into a crack.

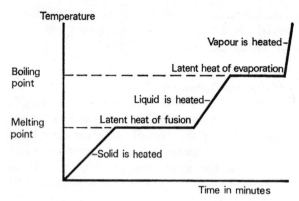

Fig. 7.18. When a substance is supplied with heat at a constant rate, the temperature rise is delayed at the melting and boiling points, due to the absorption of latent heat.

houses are sometimes misshapen because, for centuries, they have been subjected to strong pressures due to the settlement of the building.

The Liquid State

But what of the cohesive forces between the molecules in a liquid? The cohesion is different in solids and liquids as can be appreciated by comparing the cutting of a solid with the drawing of a knife through a liquid. However, cohesive and repulsive forces do exist between the molecules in liquids as we can see from the way in which liquids hold together. For example, the surface tension in a droplet is a result of such forces making the surface behave like an elastic film under constant tension.

The forces between the molecules of a liquid are comparable to those in the solid but they are continually being broken up by thermal vibrations. The obvious pattern disappears and molecules move through the extent of the liquid.

The rigidity of a solid has its counterpart in the viscosity of a liquid. A liquid flows under the influence of even the smallest external force, the viscosity affecting only the speed of flow. Thus under the force of gravity a liquid assumes the shape of its container and acquires a horizontal surface.

Effect of Pressure on Melting Points

Most substances contract when they solidify, so that increase in pressure assists the process of solidification, making it occur above the normal

melting point. A few substances, including cast iron and water, expand on freezing, and an increased pressure lowers their melting points. The depression of the melting point of water by 1°C requires a pressure of about 10^7 N/m². Pressures of this order are produced under sledge runners and ice-skate blades. The ice melts momentarily and the runner slides on a film of water.

The melting point of a substance is usually lowered by the presence of an impurity. Sea water freezes well below 0°C, and most alloys of two metals melt at a lower temperature than that of the major constituent.

When a liquid is heated, the increased amplitude of vibration of its molecules increases their average separation and the liquid expands. There are exceptions to this and water actually contracts as its temperature rises from 0°C to 4°C. The behaviour of water near its freezing point is very important for animals and plants in water. As

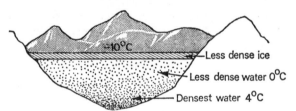

Fig. 7.19. Unless it freezes solid, the water at the bottom of a lake will be at 4°C.

the water cools at the surface, it becomes denser and falls to the bottom. This produces convection currents which continue until the water reaches a temperature of 4°C at which temperature water has a maximum density. Any further cooling below 4°C produces expansion and the cooled water remains on the surface. Eventually, ice forms and, being less dense than the water, it floats on the surface and insulates the underlying water from further heat loss. Thus, the water at the bottom of ponds and lakes may remain at 4°C all throughout a long cold winter permitting the survival of underwater life. (Fig. 7.19.)

Evaporation

During the continual random motion of the molecules in a liquid, collisions with other molecules and with the bounding surfaces are frequent.

Some of the faster molecules colliding with the exposed surface break free to become gaseous molecules. Thus, the loss of the more energetic molecules reduces the average temperature of the liquid left behind. To put this in another way, latent heat of evaporation has been extracted from the liquid to change the substance from liquid to vapour.

Evaporation can occur directly from solid to vapour, the rate of evaporation being less and the latent heat being greater than evaporation from the liquid.

In the gaseous state, the momenta of the molecules is large compared to the influence of the attractive forces between them. Thus, when gas molecules do collide, they may approach nearer to each other than the molecules in a solid or liquid. The pressure exerted by a gas on a surface is a result of a continual bombardment by the rapidly moving molecules. In colliding with each other, or with a solid surface at the same temperature, the molecules rebound without any net loss of energy. Gas molecules occupy uniformly any space into which they are introduced. At normal pressures, the volume of the molecules themselves is only a minute fraction of the space in which they move about.

Both gases and liquids are classed as fluids because they have certain features in common. The pressure exerted by a fluid increases with depth owing to the gravitational field. At any point in a fluid, the pressure is exerted equally in all directions.

Latent Heat

The *latent heat of a substance is the heat required to convert unit mass of the substance from one state to another at a constant temperature.*

Each substance has a latent heat of fusion (melting), and a latent heat of evaporation. Latent heats are quoted in joules per kilogramme at either the melting point or the normal boiling point.

The graph of Fig. 7.18 indicates the temperature of a solid which is heated by a steady source of heat. The graph shows quite clearly the pause in temperature rise as the heat is used to change the solid to liquid, and the liquid to the vapour.

The values of the latent heats of several substances are given in Table 7.1.

Table 7.1. Latent heats of fusion and evaporation (J/kg) at the standard melting and boiling points

Substance	Latent heat of fusion	Latent heat of evaporation
Alcohol, Ethyl	105×10^3	857×10^3
Alcohol, Methyl	69×10^3	1105×10^3
Carbon dioxide	190×10^3	367×10^3
Glycol	182×10^3	802×10^3
Mercury	$11 \cdot 8 \times 10^3$	286×10^3
Naphthalene	$8 \cdot 4 \times 10^3$	297×10^3
Oxygen	$13 \cdot 9 \times 10^3$	214×10^3
Water	335×10^3	2270×10^3

Questions

1. Distinguish between mixtures and compounds.

2. Give an example of molecules which are (a) monatomic, (b) diatomic, (c) triatomic, (d) polyatomic.

3. What basic unit do we use to express the mass of atoms and molecules?

4. What is the difference between an amorphous and a polycrystalline substance?

5. What property of water allows it to freeze on the surface while the body of the liquid is several degrees above freezing?

6. Is air a mixture or a chemical compound? Why?

7. Why is heat given out or absorbed in a chemical reaction?

8. What characteristics of an atom or molecule will determine the shape of a crystal of which it is a constituent?

9. Explain how dislocations reduce the strength of a crystal.

10. Why is metal heated before forging?

11. Why do engineers avoid sharp angles and small radii when designing components to resist fatigue failure?

12. How do latent heats of fusion and vaporization help in calibrating thermometers?

13. If you had a sealed cylinder, which you could not open or see through, how could you tell whether it contained a solid, a liquid, or a gas?

14. Why do crystals have 'planes of cleavage' along which they split more easily than in other planes?

15. Under what conditions would you form a crystal to keep it as free from dislocations as possible?

16. To reveal the grain structure of alloys, a metallurgist will polish a specimen and treat it with acid. The acid attacks the grain boundaries more than the crystals themselves. Why is this?

17. Balance the following equations

$$C + O \longrightarrow CO_2$$
$$U + O \longrightarrow UO_3$$
$$KM_nO_4 \longrightarrow K_2M_nO_4 + M_nO_2 + O$$

Problems

1. Freon, which is often used in refrigerators, has a latent heat of vaporization of 168 J/kg. How much freon is vaporized if 336 kJ of heat are transferred from the storage compartment of a refrigerator?
   Answer: 2 kg.

2. A boiler delivers steam at atmospheric pressure to a radiator, where it condenses and cools to 80°C before returning to the boiler. How much steam must be circulated to supply 9.4×10^6 J of heat?
   Answer: 40 kg.

3. A heater supplying 168 W is lowered into 200 g of water at 20°C and removed after 14 min. If 30 g of water have boiled away, what is the latent heat of vaporization of water?
   Answer: 2.5×10^6 J/kg.

4. What is the least amount of heat that will melt 6 kg of lead, initially at 20°C? (Latent heat of fusion of lead $= 24.7$ kJ/kg; specific heat of lead $= 1.26 \times 10^2$ J/kg°C; melting point of lead $= 327$°C.)
   Answer: 378 kJ.

5. How many Joules are needed to change 60 g of ice at -40°C into steam at 140°C at atmospheric pressure? (Latent heat of fusion of water $= 334$ kJ/kg; latent heat of vaporization of water $= 2260$ kJ/kg; specific heat of water and ice $= 2.14$ kJ/kg°C; Specific heat of steam $= 2.01$ kJ/kg.)
   Answer: 17.8 kJ.

6. What results if you remove 3000 kJ from 1 kg of saturated steam at 100°C? (Latent heat of fusion of water $= 334$ kJ/kg; latent heat of vaporization of water $= 2260$ kJ/kg.)
   Answer: 0.66 kg of ice and 0.34 kg of water at 0°C.

7. Sketch the cooling curve which would be obtained if molten soft solder is allowed to cool. Discuss the effect on the solidification process of changing the proportions of the components of the solder. A 200 watt heating element is embedded in a lump of tin weighing 0.5 kg. Calculate the minimum time required to melt all the tin, assuming the initial temperature to be 20°C. (Specific heat of tin $= 0.21$ kJ/kg°C; melting point of tin $= 232$°C; latent heat of fusion of tin $= 59$ kJ/kg.)

   (I.E.R.E.)

   Answer: 4.3 min.

82

8 The Structure of Atoms

Having established that all matter is composed of only about one hundred different sorts of atoms, one might think that man's mind would rest content. His curiosity knows no bounds, however, and there arose the inevitable question: 'what are atoms made of?' At the time when this problem was approached, the modern scientific method of enquiry was well established. Certain similarities in the chemical properties of different elements seemed to point to a similarity in structure. Step by step, by painstaking and inspired experiment, a picture of atomic structure was developed, and is still developing. The most adequate theories are highly mathematical, but a useful picture which appeals to common sense and yields a good measure of understanding of matter, is given by the orbiting electron model of the atom.

The Value of Models

You may wonder why we bother to explain at length a mental picture of the atom which is known to be ultimately inadequate. To answer this question we can look to the history of science which has developed by a series of concepts each one improving on the earlier ones. For example, the corpuscular theory of light gave way to the wave theory, and the caloric theory of heat gave way to the kinetic theory. Even today simplified theories, although they may contain half truths, are useful stepping stones to our understanding of complicated phenomena.

We often call a mental picture a 'conceptual model' or simply a 'model'. We find a model useful if it connects in a rational way experimental facts which are within our experience. A model which tells no lies but neither introduces any order into our experience will be of little use to us. An engineer might judge a model by its effectiveness in aiding his thinking but a scientist is often more interested in its deficiencies because they may lead to an entirely new theory. Thus, over-emphasis on an inadequate model could inhibit a scientist from making further progress.

In the early part of this chapter a model of the atom is developed which, though difficult in parts, can be understood using a knowledge of elementary mechanics. The model is not truly historical in approach, but it is easy to visualize and it explains some of the properties of atoms. It shares some features with the more advanced theories and it is often used alongside them because they are more difficult to imagine.

The Orbiting Electron Model of the Atom

Every atom has a massive central nucleus, which carries a positive electric charge. Around the nucleus, and at a comparatively long distance away from it, revolve the electrons. These are minute, negatively charged particles which whirl around the nucleus much as the planets orbit around the Sun. (Fig. 8.1.)

We can assume that the electrostatic attraction between the negative electrons and the positively charged nucleus provides the central force required to maintain the electrons in their orbits. In other words, the force prevents the electrons from escaping while the motion prevents it from plunging into the nucleus.

We cannot show on a diagram just how small the nucleus is compared to the electron cloud. Even a large nucleus has a volume which is less than a millionth of a millionth of the volume of the atom as a whole. The masses of nuclei commonly found in nature vary from one atomic mass unit (1.66×10^{-27} kg) in the case of hydrogen to 238 a.m.u. in the case of uranium. The mass of the electron (9.11×10^{-31} kg) is only about one two-thousandth part of the mass of the hydrogen nucleus.

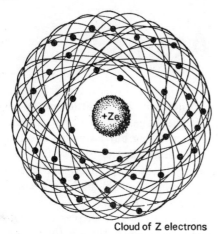

Cloud of Z electrons

Fig. 8.1. Atom of element no. Z (not to scale).

Each electron carries the same basic unit of charge (-1.6×10^{-19} C) and the positive charge on the nucleus is always an integral multiple of this unit. That is,

$$\text{nuclear charge} = +(Z \times 1.6 \times 10^{-19} \text{ C})$$

In any particular atom, Z, the actual number of charges on the nucleus, is a very important quantity and is called the *atomic number* of the element.

The number of orbiting electrons equals the number of positive charges on the nucleus, thus preserving the electrical neutrality of the atom as a whole. For example, the hydrogen nucleus carries one positive charge and therefore has only

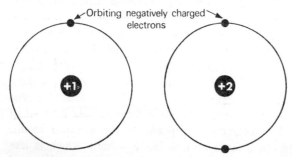

Fig. 8.2. The atoms of hydrogen and helium.

one orbiting electron. (Fig. 8.2.) The helium atom has a doubly charged nucleus and two electrons and so on, each successive element having a progressively greater number until we reach uranium, which has ninety-two positive charges on the nucleus and ninety-two orbiting electrons. A complete list of the elements is given in the appendix but the first twenty are shown in Table 8.1.

Table 8.1

At. no. (Z)	Element	Symbol
1	Hydrogen	H
2	Helium	He
3	Lithium	Li
4	Beryllium	Be
5	Boron	B
6	Carbon	C
7	Nitrogen	N
8	Oxygen	O
9	Fluorine	F
10	Neon	Ne
11	Sodium	Na
12	Magnesium	Mg
13	Aluminium	Al
14	Silicon	Si
15	Phosphorus	P
16	Sulphur	S
17	Chlorine	Cl
18	Argon	A
19	Potassium	K
20	Calcium	Ca

Quantum Theory

Both the number and the arrangement of electrons outside the nucleus play a major role in the determining of the chemical and physical properties of the atom. The orbits available to electrons in a particular atom are strictly defined and limited in number. The electrons in these orbits possess energy: potential energy due to the electrostatic attraction of the nucleus and the repulsion of other electrons, and kinetic energy due to their motion. While they are in a particular orbit, the electrons do not lose energy but they may gather or lose energy when they transfer to another orbit. A particular electron which changes its orbit must go from one of these fixed orbits to another. This is strongly supported by the fact that the light which is released or absorbed by this type of transition has a limited number of components, whose energies correspond to the differences in energy between the permitted orbits.

Table 8.2. Grouping of electron orbits according to size

Shell	1	2	3	4	5	n
Number of electrons	2	8	18	32	50	$2n^2$
Designation	K	L	M	N	O	

The orbits are sometimes referred to as *energy levels* and they are important in spectroscopy which is a study of light emitted by atoms. The restriction on the energies permitted to electrons in an atom is part of the *quantum theory* of the atom. The energy is said to be *quantized*.

The electron orbits may be divided according to their size into a number of groups of shells. Each shell has a limited number of vacancies for electrons. The first shell can accommodate two electrons, i.e., 2×1^2; the second shell can accommodate eight electrons, i.e., 2×2^2. In general, the nth shell will hold a total of $2 \times n^2$ electrons. (Table 8.2.)

The shells may be referred to by the letters K, L, M, N, etc., or else by the number n. The value of n for a shell is called its *principal quantum number*. Thus electrons in the 3rd (M) shell have a principal quantum number of 3.

The electrons required to match the nuclear charge first populate the orbits nearest the nucleus of lowest energy, leaving the upper shells vacant. Because more energy is required to detach electrons in the lower shells from the atom, they are said to be more tightly bound.

The electronic structure of some of the simpler elements is shown diagrammatically in Fig. 8.3. Hydrogen is the simplest element and contains a single electron in the first shell. Helium, of atomic number 2, has two electrons which occupy and fill the first shell. The next element lithium has three electrons, one of which begins the 2nd shell. Beryllium, boron, carbon, oxygen, and fluorine progressively have one more electron in the 2nd shell, until with neon the shell is full. The third shell begins with sodium and so on. In all there are seven major shells which normally accommodate the electrons of the 100 or so elements.

When a new shell contains a single electron, for example, lithium (Fig. 8.4*a*), this electron is screened off from the nucleus by the inner shell of electrons and its attachment to the nucleus is weak. The next element, beryllium, has an additional charge on the nucleus but only the same screening, so that there is a greater net attractive force. (Fig. 8.4*b*.) Thus the two electrons in the outer shell of beryllium are more tightly bound to the nucleus than the solitary electron in the outer shell of lithium. Each further increase

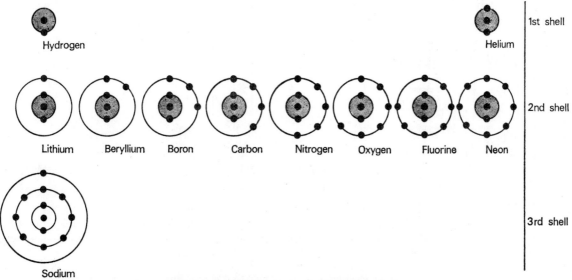

1st shell

Hydrogen   Helium

2nd shell

Lithium   Beryllium   Boron   Carbon   Nitrogen   Oxygen   Fluorine   Neon

3rd shell

Sodium

Fig. 8.3. Electronic structure of some simple atoms.

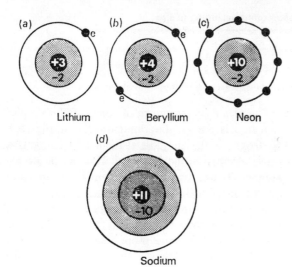

Lithium Beryllium Neon

Sodium

Fig. 8.4. The net attractive force on outer electrons increases as the shell is filled.

maximum as the inert gas neon is reached. (Fig. 8.4c.) The next element, sodium, (Fig. 8.4d) has a single electron in the third shell which again is easy to remove because of the shielding of the inner electrons.

Ionization Potential

The ionization potential of an element is the energy in electron-volts, required to remove the most loosely bound electron from the atom in its normal state. The electron-volt, the energy acquired by an electron in falling through a potential of 1 volt, is a convenient unit for expressing the energies of elementary particles.

$$1eV = 1 \cdot 6 \times 10^{-19} \text{ J}$$

The variation of ionization potential with atomic number is shown in Fig. 8.5. Notice how the ionization potential alters sharply with the atomic number.

Helium ($Z = 2$) and neon ($Z = 2+8$) have peak potentials because they have filled outer shells. They are followed by lithium and sodium, which

in atomic number produces an increase in the binding of the electrons in the outer shell. As the shell approaches completion, the binding of the electrons becomes very strong and reaches a

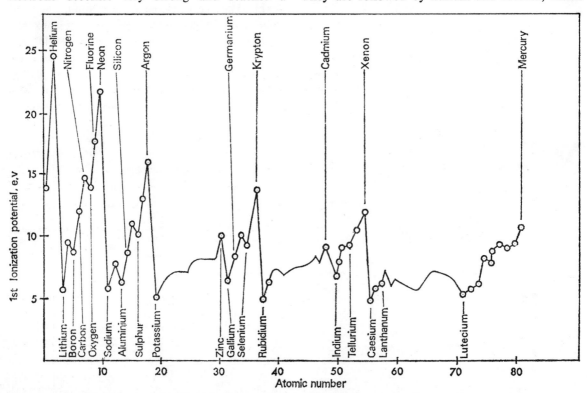

Fig. 8.5. Ionization potentials of the elements. (These potentials refer to isolated atoms and not to atoms grouped as in a molecule or a solid.)

have low ionization potentials in keeping with their having a single electron in the outermost occupied shell.

Electrical Conductivity

Electrical conductivity depends on the existence of large numbers of mobile charge carriers. Substances such as sodium and aluminium, having only one or two electrons in the new shell, are good conductors and are classed as metals. The application of even a small electric potential causes the electrons to drift freely in the direction of the field.

There is a gradual change in the electrical properties as the shell becomes filled. An almost completely filled shell structure results in a material which is an insulator. Then at an intermediate stage there are materials which can be classed as neither metals nor insulators, the so-called semi-conducting materials such as carbon, silicon, and germanium. Characteristically, the ionization potentials of semiconductors lie between 8 and 10 eV.

Chemical Properties

The extent to which the outermost occupied shell of an element is complete is very important in determining its physical and chemical properties. When a main shell (or a particularly important subshell as explained later) is completely full, the element is very stable and rarely reacts with other elements. These inert substances are all gases at normal temperatures and pressures and comprise helium, neon, argon, krypton, xenon, and radon. When atoms combine chemically they tend to do so in a way which imitates the structure of the inert gases.

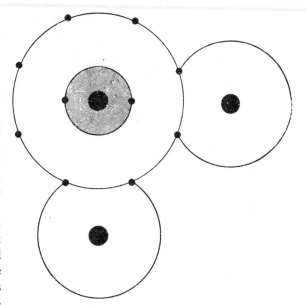

Fig. 8.7. By sharing electrons, each atom in the water molecule has achieved an inert gas structure.

Elements approaching the inert gas structure, in exerting their strong attraction for electrons, will even attract the electrons in the outer shell of another element. The annexing of extra electrons in this way leaves the receiving and donating atoms electrically charged. For example, in Fig. 8.6 the chlorine atom has attracted an extra electron from the sodium giving both atoms an inert gas structure. In addition the chlorine has an excess of negative charge and the soidum an excess of positive charge, and the atoms become bonded together by electrostatic attraction. What has been described is the chemical reaction of sodium and chlorine, which results in the formation of sodium chloride, or common salt. Figure 8.7 shows another way in which the inert gas structure can be achieved by a sharing of external electrons between atoms.

Atoms whose outer shells have either just begun or are almost full of electrons are chemically highly reactive. This is exemplified by potassium, a metal which is so reactive that it ignites spontaneously when in contact with water. It will even react with ice and so potassium must be immersed in an inert liquid for safe storage. Chlorine, with an almost completed shell, is a corrosive gas. The most reactive substance known is fluorine which

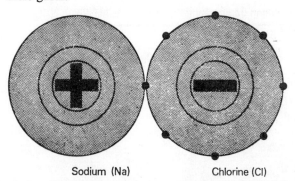

Sodium (Na)   Chlorine (Cl)

Fig. 8.6. An ionic bond between a sodium atom and a chlorine atom forms a molecule of sodium chloride.

has so great an affinity for electrons that it extracts electrons from such materials as glass. It therefore reacts with glass containers and for this reason fluorine is kept in containers of iron. A surface coating of a fluorine compound forms and prevents further corrosion of the underlying iron.

Subshells

In the simplest atom, hydrogen, which has only one electron, all the orbits in a main shell have the same energy. Where the atom of an element contains several electrons, they influence each other and several energies are possible within the same shell. Electrons in a shell having the same energy are said to belong to a *subshell*.

The number of subshells in a main shell depends on the size of the shell, i.e., on the principal quantum number n. The first shell, for which $n = 1$, has only one subshell, the second main shell has two and in general the nth main shell has n subshells.

Again each subshell has a fixed accommodation for electrons; the first subshell in a main shell holds two electrons, the next six, the next ten and the next fourteen. That is, each subshell holds four more electrons than the previous one. These subshells are given the letters s, p, d, and f as shown in Table 8.3.

The subshells are populated with electrons according to their energy; the subshells of lowest energy being filled first. If we represent the subshells on an energy diagram they fill up from bottom to top. (Fig. 8.8.)

Notice that the energy levels fall into sections which are in keeping with the peaks in the ioni-

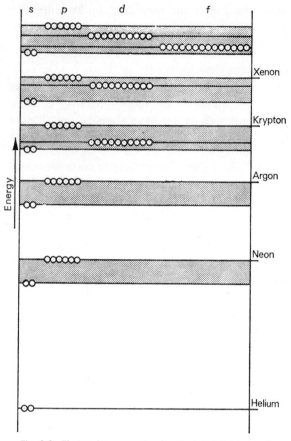

Fig. 8.8. Electronic energy levels. (Isolated light atom.)

zation potential. (Fig. 8.5.) These sections are referred to as *periods* and they are very important to the understanding of the properties of elements. Whereas the main shells arise from an arrangement of orbits according to size, the periods arise from

Table 8.3. Showing the number of electrons which can be accommodated in the subshells.

			Subshells					Total accommodation
	Designation	s	p	d	f	g		
		s	p	d	f	g		
	$n = 5$	O	2	6	10	14	18	50
	$n = 4$	N	2	6	10	14		32
MAIN-SHELLS	$n = 3$	M	2	6	10			18
	$n = 2$	L	2	6				8
	$n = 1$	K	2					2

an arrangement of orbits according to energy. The two arrangements do not coincide exactly as you can see from Fig. 8.8. Where a large orbit possesses less energy than a smaller one the larger orbit is filled first.

The atomic numbers of the elements having peak ionization potentials, which mark the end of the periods, can be calculated from the expression $2(1^2+2^2+2^2+3^2+3^2+4^2)$. This gives the atomic number of radon, the heaviest inert gas. The atomic numbers of the lighter ones may be obtained by cutting off the series earlier, i.e., at atomic numbers 54, 36, 18, 10, and 2.

The Periodic Table

If we arrange the elements in a table in order of atomic number or according to their ionization potentials, we can make useful generalizations about neighbouring elements. (Fig. 8.9.)

The inert gases helium, neon, argon, krypton, xenon, and radon have peak ionization potentials and they are arranged in a column on the extreme right. The very stable structure occurs when the first and second subshells are filled with their $2+6 = 8$ electrons.

The strongly metallic substances, lithium, sodium, potassium, etc., have one electron in excess of the inert gas and have the lowest ionization potential, and they are placed in a column on the extreme left.

A group of similar reactive elements called halogens—fluorine, chlorine, bromine, iodine, and astatine—are in the column before the inert gases. The semi-conductors carbon, silicon, and germanium are in group 4.

The subshell holding ten electrons (d subshell) is also a feature of the electron structure. All the elements in which this subshell is partly filled have low ionization potentials and are metals. The elements with one electron in excess of this complete subshell are the metals copper, silver, and gold which have high conductivities but which, being in the middle of the period, are rather unreactive chemically.

A group of fourteen rare metals of very similar properties follows lanthanum in the table. A further, but incomplete, group of fourteen follows actinum. In this last group only the elements as far as atomic No. 94, plutonium, have been found in nature. The remainder, as far as No. 103,

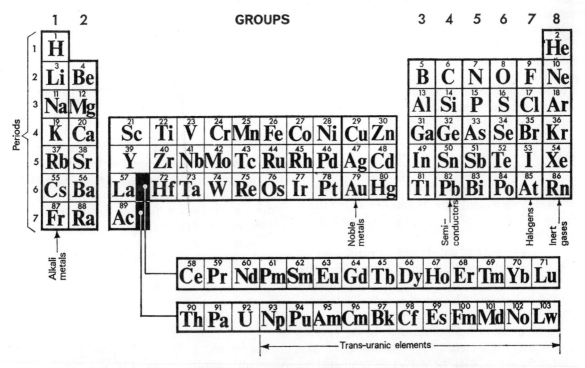

Fig. 8.9. The periodic table. Elements of similar properties are grouped in vertical columns.

lawrencium, have been produced artificially in particle accelerating machines. The heavier atoms above atomic number 83 are unstable, however, and each of them is in the process of reverting to one of the lighter elements by a process of radio-active decay. The importance of atomic structure in determining material properties is perhaps already obvious, but there are many more relations between the elements in this table which provide further convincing evidence.

Limitations of Orbit Model

The orbiting electron model of the atom has proved an important step in the history of the investigation of the atom. It is still an indispensable concept, because it is easy to communicate and gives an insight into atomic structure. The model is not, however, capable of accounting for many of the observed properties of elements such as the existence of the shells and subshells. We would expect electrons rotating in orbits to create an external electrical disturbance and thus lose energy and spiral into the nucleus. The fact that they do not do so shows that the model is inadequate or incomplete. Initially, we try to change a successful model slightly to make it fit new evidence. This may be possible at first but there comes a stage when it is necessary to make a reappraisal of the whole situation to seek a more suitable explanation. An improved model of the atom has been found but unfortunately, to appreciate it fully, we must have a command of mathematics of an abstract nature, beyond that required by the practical scientist or engineer.

A Modern View of the Atom

The modern quantum theory starts from an acceptance that the exact position and momentum of an electron cannot both be known but that there is always a degree of uncertainty in either or both quantities.

The uncertainty is not due to an inaccuracy of measuring instruments, which we can eventually look forward to correcting, but to a more funda-mental uncertainty which may never be corrected. The very act of measurement always interferes with the quantity being measured. In the case of large-scale phenomena, the interaction of the measuring device may be negligible compared to

experimental errors but, on a sub-atomic scale, the interaction becomes a more significant factor. This principle, the *Heisenberg's uncertainty principle*, surprisingly leads to a description of the atom which is more useful than the orbiting electron model.

It has been known for some time that a stream of electrons has some properties which are nor-mally associated with waves. Electrons can be reflected just as light-waves can and a further, and more revealing comparison, is that electrons

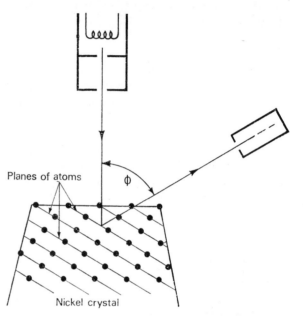

Fig. 8.10. Diffraction of electrons. The direction ϕ in which the electrons emerge from the crystal, depends on their wave-length $\lambda = h/mv$.

can be diffracted by the rows of atoms in a crystal just as X-rays would be, or as light is diffracted by the lines of a diffraction grating. (Fig. 8.10.) The conclusion is that electrons have a wave nature as well as a particle nature. Diffraction experiments with electrons show them to have a wave-length inversely proportional to their momentum (mass × velocity), i.e.,

$$\text{wave-length} \propto \frac{1}{\text{momentum}}$$

or

$$\lambda = h/mv$$

The factor h ($= 6\cdot625 \times 10^{-34}$ Js) is a universally constant quantity called *Planck's constant* after

Max Planck who, as a mathematical physicist, contributed greatly to atomic physics.

The dual nature of the electron is represented schematically in Fig. 8.11 which also conveys something of the significance of the uncertainty principle. The wave is associated with the momentum of the particle; it is not identical with an electromagnetic wave. The 'matter' wave has rather special properties in that it does not spread out in all directions like certain other waves.

Wave picture of an electron

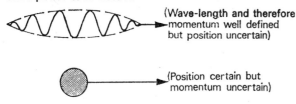

(Wave-length and therefore momentum well defined but position uncertain)

(Position certain but momentum uncertain)

Particle picture of an electron

Fig. 8.11. Alternative wave and particle pictures of an electron.

The application of the wave concept of matter to electrons in the atom leads to the model of the atom which is accepted at present. According to this 'wave mechanical' model of the atom, the electron sets up a standing wave in the space around a nucleus. The electron wave may be compared with the vibrations in a stretched string (Fig. 8.12) or, in two dimensions, by the vibration

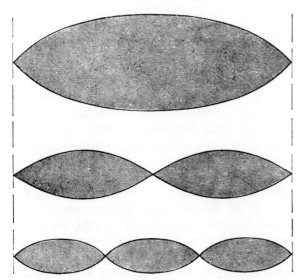

Fig. 8.12. Standing waves in a stretched string.

(a) Clamped at perimeter   (b) Clamped at centre

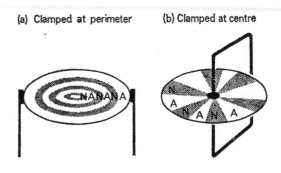

Dark areas represent nodes

Fig. 8.13. Standing waves patterns on a flat plate (Chladni figures).

in a metal plate (Fig. 8.13). The nodes and anti-nodes of electron standing waves extend in three dimensions about the nucleus. These standing waves called orbitals can assume a number of shapes and sizes. An orbital may be considered to represent a zone of charge and a typical orbital is shown in Fig. 8.14.

The size of the orbitals defines the main shells of the atom, and the shape of the orbitals defines the subshell structure.

The charge of the electron may now be imagined as being spread out in the orbital rather than concentrated at a point. More of the electron

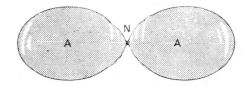

Fig. 8.14. Typical (p) orbital.

charge is located in the lobe of the orbital of Fig. 8.14 and none of it at the centre of the nucleus. Another way of looking at it is that at a certain instant the electron is more likely to be found near an antinode than near a node of the orbital. Just as only certain wave-lengths are present in the standing waves in a string, only certain orbitals are possible for an electron in an atom. The orbitals are related one to the other, in that electrons in them possess an integral multiple of a basic unit of angular momentum X, i.e., the angular momentum is quantized:

Angular momentum $= lX$

The shape and size of angular momentum of the first few orbitals are shown in Fig. 8.15. You can see from the diagram that l can have values 0, 1, 2, 3, etc., up to a maximum of n. Electrons in the orbitals for which $l = 0$ are spherical and possess no angular momentum, the vibration being directed into and out of the centre, symmetrically in all directions.

The number of electrons which can occupy the orbitals are those of the earlier theory (Table 8.2). Electrons in the same orbital have the same energy and the energies of the orbitals are as shown in Fig. 8.8. At ordinary temperatures, electrons do not remain in their basic orbitals but frequently

of subshells in the atom. A more complete theory takes into account the magnetic influence of the electron but enough has been described here to give some idea of the modern concept of the atom.

Dual Nature of Matter

The alternative ways of viewing an electron either as a particle or as a wave are not confined to the electron.

Other more massive particles may be diffracted and therefore be given a wave-length. However, the more momentum a particle has, the smaller its wave-length and the more difficult it becomes to demonstrate its wave nature.

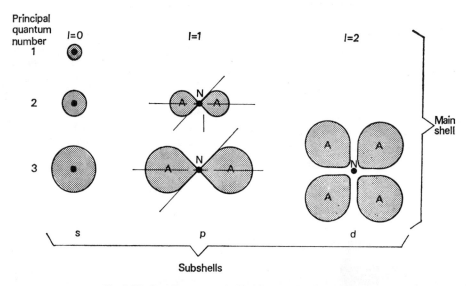

Fig. 8.15. Standing waves (orbitals) set up by electrons.

absorb energy and move to a higher energy orbital. On reverting from one of these orbitals (excited state) to the original orbital (ground state), the atom emits light of a definite energy. It is the analysis of the emitted energies on which much of our knowledge of the atom is based.

Any new theory must repeat the successes of the old, and the electron energy levels detected by experiment are also predicted by the wave theory of matter or *wave mechanics* as it is called. In fact, the two theories coincide in accounting for the simpler features of atomic structure, but wave mechanics also accounts for other behaviour of matter such as electron diffraction and the existence

What then of the waves which we recognize, such as light waves? Do they behave like particles and have momentum? Indeed they do! An intense beam of light radiation exerts a force on a surface on which it falls and, therefore, light has momentum. Furthermore, the light arrives as a number of separate amounts and not as a continuous flow of energy. (Fig. 15.6.) This modern concept of the nature of light revives to some extent the corpuscular theory of light, which was rejected in favour of the continuous wave theory.

The diffraction of electron-waves is used to produce magnification beyond the limit of optical microscopes which is set by the wave-length of

92

light. The very short wave-lengths, associated with electrons, have led to the development of electron microscopes which produce magnifications of about 200,000 as compared to the magnifications of about one thousand of optical microscopes.

Questions

1. How does the sodium atom resemble the hydrogen atom? And how is it different?

2. Suggest how we might define the size of an atom.

3. Why are metals good conductors of electricity?

4. Why will we never be able to see the structure of an atom?

5. How would the solar system be changed if the quantum theory applied to planets, too?

6. Heat is usually evolved when elements combine to form compounds. How can you explain this?

7. By what methods may electrons be removed from atoms?

8. What physical and chemical properties of elements vary periodically as the atomic number increases?

9. How was it possible to construct the periodic table of the elements before a theory of atomic structure was put forward?

10. Do you think it is legitimate to invent models such as the one of atomic structure, which, although they bear little relation to what an atom is really like, make it possible to explain how atoms behave?

11. Lithium and fluorine combine by the transference of an electron from lithium to fluorine. What other pairs of elements could form compounds in this way?

12. Describe the characteristic electron arrangement of
    (a) an alkali metal, like potassium or sodium;
    (b) an alkaline earth element, like calcium or magnesium;
    (c) an inert gas, like argon or krypton;
    (d) a gas like fluorine, chlorine, or bromine.

Problems

1. Rubidium has properties like sodium and potassium and an atomic number of 37. Estimate its ionization potential in electron-volts. (See Fig. 8.5.)
   Answer: 4·2 eV.

2. Krypton is an inert gas, with atomic number 36. What is its ionization potential in electron-volts? (See Fig. 8.5.)
   Answer: 14 eV.

3. If the periodic table was longer, where would you expect to find (a) the next heavier inert gas to radon, (b) the next after that?
   Answer: (a) 118th, (b) 168th.

9 Into the Nucleus

Compared with the orbiting electrons, the nucleus of an atom exists in a serene world. The electron shells screen the nucleus from external influences so that it is not affected by physical stresses or electrical disturbances, and is quite unaffected by any chemical reaction involving the atom as a whole.

Processes of change are often more revealing than the inert states before and after a change, and the investigation of something which changes little is not an easy task. Occasionally, certain radioactive nuclei undergo a very violent change, and the study of radioactivity has provided us with much information about the nucleus. By weighing the atoms, we can also tell a great deal about the nucleus, and hence all the atoms have been accurately weighed, and their nuclear charges measured.

The nucleus has been shown to have a structure which, in the first analysis, is a simple one. The nuclei of all the elements are composed of different combinations of two basic particles: the *proton* and the *neutron*. The proton and neutron have almost the same mass and are both described as *nucleons*. (Table 9.1.) The number of protons in a nucleus determines the positive charge on the nucleus, and hence the atomic number of the element to which it belongs. The number of neutrons follows no such rigid pattern. Very approximately, in elements of low atomic number, the number of neutrons is equal to the number of protons but the proportion of neutrons increases for heavier elements. (Fig. 9.1 and 9.2.)

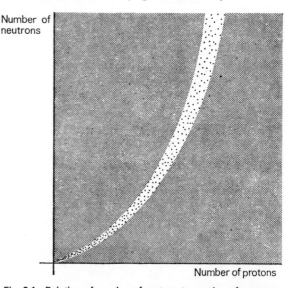

Fig. 9.1. Relation of number of protons to number of neutrons.

Isotopes

The number of protons in the nucleus of an element identifies the element and it is therefore constant, but the number of neutrons may vary for different nuclei of the same element. These different forms are called isotopes of the element.

Table 9.1. A comparison of the neutron, proton and electron

Particle	Symbol	Mass (kg)	Mass (u)	Charge
Proton	p	$1 \cdot 6725 \times 10^{-27}$	$1 \cdot 00727$	$+1$
Neutron	n	$1 \cdot 6748 \times 10^{-27}$	$1 \cdot 00867$	0
Electron	e	$9 \cdot 1091 \times 10^{-31}$	$5 \cdot 48597 \times 10^{-4}$	-1

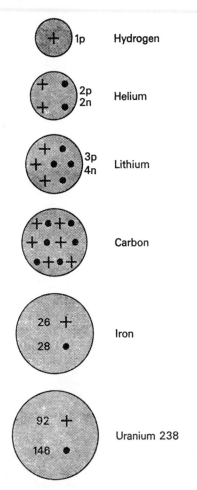

Fig. 9.2. Examples of the way protons and neutrons are combined in the nuclei of some atoms.

(Fig. 9.3.) The number of naturally occurring isotopes of an element varies from one, for the element gold, to ten, for the element tin. The average number per element is about three. A particular isotope is referred to by writing the total number of nucleons and the atomic number before the symbol for the element. For example, the nucleus of the main isotope of lithium contains three protons and four neutrons and is represented by $_3^7\text{Li}$. It is also referred to as lithium 7. The other isotopes of lithium which can exist are written

$$\begin{matrix} \text{no. of nucleons} \\ \text{nuclear charge} \end{matrix} \qquad _3^5\text{Li}, \qquad _3^6\text{Li}, \qquad _3^8\text{Li}.$$

As found in nature, one particular isotope of an element usually predominates, the other isotopes existing only in very small proportions, e.g., carbon consists of 98·89 per cent of isotope $_6^{12}\text{C}$, the remainder being the isotopes $_6^{13}\text{C}$ and $_6^{14}\text{C}$. For this reason, the atomic weights of elements are very near to whole numbers. (Table 9.2.)

Originally, the system of atomic weights was conceived on the basis of the hydrogen atom as the unit of mass. Later it proved more convenient to define the unit as exactly one-twelfth of the mass of the atom of the carbon isotope $_6^{12}\text{C}$. In this system the carbon 12 isotope has a mass of 12·000 u and the hydrogen atom has a mass of 1·00782 u.

Nuclear Stability and Radioactivity

Knowing, as we do, that like charges repel, how do we explain that protons in the nucleus in

Table 9.2. Atomic weights of the isotopes of some elements

Symbol	Element	Nuclear charge (atomic number Z)	Atomic mass (u)	Mass number (A)	Abundance when naturally occurring
$_1^1\text{H}$	Hydrogen	1	1·00782	1	99·985%
$_1^2\text{H}$	Hydrogen (deuterium)	1	2·01410	2	0·015%
$_1^3\text{H}$	Hydrogen (tritium)	1	3·01605	3	
$_2^3\text{He}$	Helium	2	3·01603	3	0·00013%
$_2^4\text{He}$	Helium	2	4·00260	4	$\simeq 100\%$
$_2^5\text{He}$	Helium	2	5·01229	5	
$_6^{12}\text{C}$	Carbon	6	12·0000	12	98·892%
$_6^{13}\text{C}$	Carbon	6	13·0033	13	1·108%
^{234}U	Uranium	92	234·0397	234	0·006%
^{235}U	Uranium	92	235·0428	235	0·714%
^{238}U	Uranium	92	238·0496	238	99·280%

Although the system was conceived with the hydrogen atom [$_1^1\text{H}$] having unit mass it is more convenient to take the carbon 12 atom to have a mass of exactly 12·000 which gives the hydrogen atom a mass slightly different from 1.

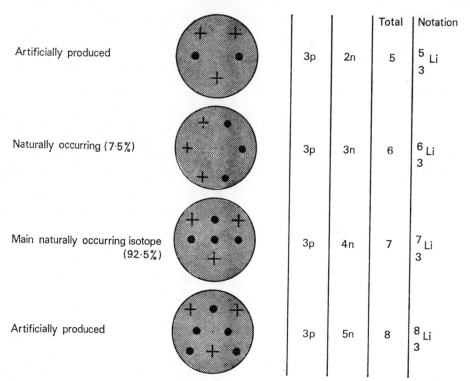

			Total	Notation
Artificially produced	3p	2n	5	$_{3}^{5}\text{Li}$
Naturally occurring (7·5%)	3p	3n	6	$_{3}^{6}\text{Li}$
Main naturally occurring isotope (92·5%)	3p	4n	7	$_{3}^{7}\text{Li}$
Artificially produced	3p	5n	8	$_{3}^{8}\text{Li}$

Fig. 9.3. The isotopes of lithium contain different numbers of neutrons. The one containing four neutrons is by far the most common.

such close proximity do not burst apart? There must be even greater forces of attraction operating at close quarters between both protons and neutrons. As the number of protons increases, so does the electrostatic repulsion and, therefore, to produce stability, more neutrons are needed, which add to the attraction but not to the repulsion.

The lighter nuclei contain approximately equal numbers of neutrons and protons but as the size increases a greater proportion of neutrons is needed for stability. In the heaviest nuclei the neutrons outnumber the protons one and a half times.

The forces in the nucleus which determine its stability are more complicated than we can describe here, but we can outline a few general trends. It is found that nuclei containing odd numbers of protons or odd numbers of neutrons tend to be less stable than those with even numbers. In reverting to a more stable state, nuclei emit charged particles and/or electromagnetic radiation, and we describe the process as *radioactive decay* or disintegration.

The electrostatic repulsion in the nuclei of elements of more than eighty-three protons cannot permanently be counteracted by the short-range attractive forces and the nuclei are unstable. Some of the elements of atomic number greater than eighty-three exist in nature, while others can be produced artificially, but they are all *radioactive* and in the process of changing to elements of lower atomic number.

The three most common types of emission from radioactive isotopes are named after the first three letters of the Greek alphabet: alpha (α)-particles, beta (β)-particles, and gamma (γ)-radiation. (Fig. 9.4.)

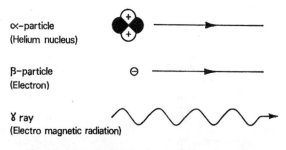

α–particle
(Helium nucleus)

β–particle
(Electron)

γ ray
(Electro magnetic radiation)

Fig. 9.4. The major types of radioactive emanation.

Alpha-Particles

Alpha-particles have a mass of 4 u and carry a charge of +2 elementary charges. In other words they are helium nuclei consisting of two neutrons and two protons. When an atom emits an alpha-particle its mass number reduces by four, and its atomic number (positive charge) reduces by two, i.e., it becomes a different element. For example, radium decays by emitting an alpha-particle and forms radon

$$^{226}_{88}Ra \longrightarrow {}^{222}_{86}Rn + {}^{4}_{2}\alpha$$

Alpha-particle decay is confined almost entirely to elements of atomic number greater than eighty-two. It has the effect of increasing the proportion of neutrons to protons in a nucleus. The penetrating powers of the three components of the radiation vary widely. Alpha-particles with typical energies of several MeV are absorbed by a few centimetres of air and they produce dense ionization of the air as they pass through it. Aluminium foil about 0·01 mm thick will eliminate them from radioactive emission. (Fig. 9.5.)

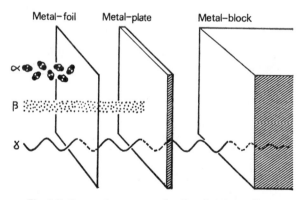

Fig. 9.5. Penetrating powers of radioactive emanation.

Beta-Particles

Beta-particles are simply fast moving electrons. A neutron in the nucleus emits the electron and becomes a proton. As a result of beta decay a nucleus increases its positive charge by one and thus changes into the element one higher in atomic number.

$$Thorium \longrightarrow Protoactinium + Beta$$

$$^{234}_{90}Th \longrightarrow {}^{234}_{91}Pa + {}_{-1}\beta$$

Beta-particles are emitted from a nucleus with a range of energies. The most energetic beta-particles from some reactions possess energies of several MeV and will penetrate a centimetre of aluminium. Normally, beta-particles have energies far less than this and about 3 mm of aluminium acts as an effective shield. It is usual to use plastic to shield against beta-particles since their absorption by a metal can cause the emission of harmful X-rays. Beta-emission is characteristic of nuclei which have an excessive proportion of neutrons. A nucleus which has emitted several alpha-particles might find itself in such a position and emit a beta-particle. Most elements have at least one isotope which emits beta-particles. Some of these beta-emitting isotopes occur in nature, while others can be artificially produced.

Gamma-radiation

Gamma-rays are electromagnetic rays of very short wave-length and they are generally the most penetrating of the radioactive emissions. The higher energy gamma-rays will penetrate up to a quarter of a metre of steel or a metre of concrete. (Fig. 9.5.) Gamma-radiation does not change the mass number or the atomic number of the emitting nucleus. It carries away the energy released by a rearrangement of the nucleus. Since this re-arrangement often follows an alpha- or a beta-emission, sources of alpha- and beta-radiation commonly, but not always, emit gamma-rays.

Positron Decay

Positrons are particles with the same mass as an electron but with a positive charge. Many nuclei decay by emitting a positron which converts a proton into a neutron. The process commonly occurs in light nuclei with an excessive proportion of protons.

$$Nitrogen \longrightarrow Carbon + Beta$$

$$^{13}_{7}N \longrightarrow {}^{13}_{6}C + {}_{1}\beta$$

Electron Capture

Another way in which a nucleus can reduce its proportion of protons is by capturing an electron. The electron is taken from an inner shell of the atom and converts a proton into a neutron. The process may be detected by the X-ray which is emitted as the vacancy in the lower shell is filled by an electron from a higher level in the atom.

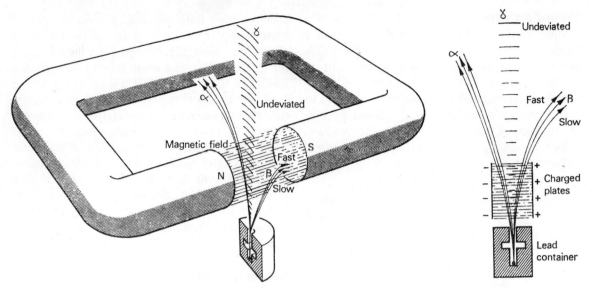

Fig. 9.6. Schematic diagrams showing the effect of electric and magnetic fields on α-, β-, and γ-radiations.

Cadmium + electron ⟶ silver

i.e., $^{107}_{48}\text{Cd} + _{-1}\text{e} \longrightarrow {}^{107}_{47}\text{Ag}$

The charge, mass, and velocity of radioactive particles can be determined by deflecting them in electric and magnetic fields. Where a source emits two or more types of radiation, fields can be used to separate them. (Fig. 9.6.) The diagram is very schematic because the ratio of charge to mass is several thousand times greater for the electrons than for the alpha-particles, and the difference in the deflections is very much greater than that shown.

Rate of Disintegration

The rate of disintegration of a radioactive nucleus is completely independent of its physical and chemical state. For example, one gramme of radium emits 3×10^{-10} alpha-particles per second, whether it is at the centre of the Earth at 4000°C and at a pressure of hundreds of times that of the atmosphere, or in a vacuum at the absolute zero of temperature. The rate of decay is directly proportional to the number, N, of radioactive atoms present.

Number of disintegrations per second = λN.

$$\frac{dN}{dt} = -\lambda N$$

where λ is the decay constant for a particular process, e.g., λ for radium 226 is $1·36 \times 10^{-10}$/s.

Figure 9.7 shows how the number of radium atoms reduces with time. An important quantity which helps us to describe radioactivity is the half-life. *The half-life is* the time taken for half the number of atoms to disintegrate. Thus after a period equal to the half-life has elapsed only half the original number of atoms remain unchanged.

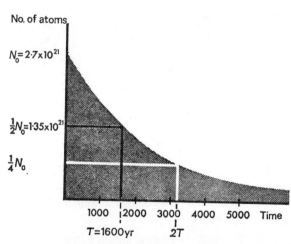

Fig. 9.7. The graph shows the way in which the number of atoms in one gramme of radium reduces with time. An important constant is the half-life or period, *T*, which is the time taken for half the number of radium atoms to disintegrate.

The half-life T is simply related to the decay constant for any particular decay process

$$T = \frac{0.693}{\lambda}$$

Radioactive Series

A nucleus may undergo a number of changes before it finally becomes stable. Table 9.3 shows the series of stages in the decay of uranium 238 into lead 206. All of these products are present in naturally occurring uranium. Two other major radioactive series exist, one starting with thorium 232 and the other with uranium 235 and both end in different isotopes of lead.

Detection of Radioactivity

The *Geiger counter* is one of the most rugged and versatile devices for detecting and counting any particles or radiation which produce ionization. (Fig. 9.8.) A potential of several hundred volts is applied between the central wire electrode and an outer cylinder. The pressure of the gas in the cylinder and the applied voltage are such that an electrical discharge is on the point of occurring. The ionization caused by a particle generates a pulse of electricity, which is suitably amplified and fed to a counter or made to produce an audible click in a speaker.

A *scintillation counter*, another method of detection, uses the flash of light emitted by some crystals when they are struck by an alpha-, beta-, or gamma-ray. The light releases electrons which are multiplied in stages by repeated acceleration and collision in a photo-multiplier. (Fig. 9.9.)

When an ionizing particle passes through a space which is super-saturated with water vapour,

Table 9.3. The uranium series

Uranium 238 changes into lead 206 by emitting eight alpha-particles and six beta-particles. Gamma-radiation is also emitted as a result of the energy change on rearrangement of the nucleons.

Element	At. no.	Mass no.	Particle ejected	Approx. half-life
Uranium	92	238		
			α	4.5×10^9 y
Thorium	90	234		
			β	25 days
Protoactinium	91	234		
			β	1.1 min
Uranium	92	234		
			α	300,000 yr
Thorium	90	230		
			α	83,000 yr
Radium	88	226		
			α	1600 yr
Radon	86	222		
			α	4 days
Polonium	84	218		
			α	3 min
Lead	82	214		
			β	27 min
Bismuth	83	214		
			β	20 min
Polonium	84	214		
			α	10^{-6} s
Lead	82	210		
			β	22 yr
Bismuth	83	210		
			β	5 days
Polonium	84	210		
			α	140 days
Lead	82	206		infinite

the water condenses on the ions, and makes the path of the particle clearly visible. This is the principle of the *cloud chamber*, in which the paths of individual particles can be photographed and studied. A more refined method of examining the paths of individual particles involves a volume

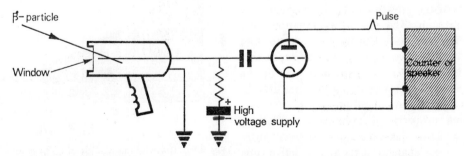

Fig. 9.8. A particle passing into the Geiger counter produces ionization which allows a pulse of charge to flow.

of photographic emulsion made up of many layers. After exposure to energetic particles, such as cosmic-rays, the emulsion is developed, and the particle paths can be reconstructed from a microscopic analysis of the traces in the various layers.

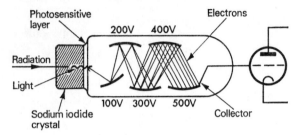

Fig. 9.9. A scintillation counter incorporates a photo-tube which multiplies the number of electrons in the pulse.

Uses of Radioactivity

When gamma-rays are absorbed by living matter they kill cells. This ability to destroy tissue can be used in the treatment of malignant growths in the body. The gamma-rays are kept directed at the tumour while the body is rotated round it. By this means, the malignant growth receives the largest exposure and a minimum of healthy tissue is destroyed.

Some elements which are not normally radioactive can be made artificially radioactive by subjecting them to bombardment by high energy particles from an atomic pile or a particle accelerator. These radioactive isotopes behave chemically exactly the same as a non-radioactive material, but their presence can be detected by their radioactive emission. Consider now how useful this detectable material can be. If a radioactive isotope of a material that can only be absorbed by a tumour, is injected into the blood stream, the exact limits of the growth can be determined by a radiation detector. The rate of assimilation of a substance into the body can be found by feeding a person a radioactive form of the substance and detecting its arrival at any particular part of the body. Many of these *tracer* techniques, are used in the study of plant and animal processes.

The same property of radioactive radiation, which can affect the human embryo so disastrously can also produce changes in the reproductive cells of, for example, a particular strain of wheat. These *mutations*, as they are called, are mostly inferior to the form which has evolved naturally, but certain mutations may be useful and lead to a hardier or more productive type of wheat.

The intensity of a beam of gamma-rays depends very precisely on the thickness of a particular material which it traverses. We can use this property to measure and control the thickness of continuously produced material, such as metal plate. Gamma-rays can be used to detect internal cracks or flaws in metal castings in a similar way.

Radioactive Dating

During their growth, plants absorb carbon from the carbon dioxide in the atmosphere. A certain proportion of the carbon in the atmosphere is formed by the conversion of nitrogen into carbon by the cosmic rays. The carbon formed in this way is radioactive with a half-life of 5600 years. Thus, the tissue of plants and animals (since they eat the plants) is slightly radioactive, and one gramme of the carbon from any living organism emits sixteen beta-particles per minute. Once dead, the organic matter absorbs no more carbon 14, and as time passes the amount present decays until after 5600 years only eight beta-particles are emitted per minute per gramme of carbon. (Fig. 9.10.) Thus, the age of a fragment of bone or wood can be dated by measuring the activity and the carbon content of the specimen.

A similar technique may be applied to dating rocks containing uranium. Uranium 238 decays by a number of stages to an isotope of lead (lead

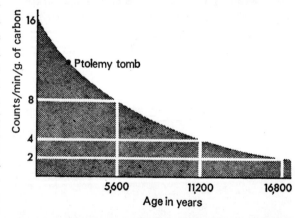

Fig. 9.10. Graph of the number of disintegrations per minute per gramme of carbon, derived from organic sources, plotted against the time since it ceased to function.

206) with a half-life of 4500 million years. By measuring the proportion of lead 206 to uranium in a particular stratum, we can deduce the time for which the rock has been in place. With the help of such measurements, the age of the Earth has been estimated at between 4 and 10 thousand million years.

Radiation Hazards

The ionization produced by radioactive emission is capable of killing living cells. Man has always been subject to ionizing radiation from the Earth and to the cosmic radiation from space, and his existence shows that he can survive a certain amount of radiation. However, he must proceed with caution.

Radiative sources are classified in terms of the number of disintegrations which they undergo in unit time. The unit of *activity* is the *curie* defined as $3 \cdot 7 \times 10^{10}$ disintegrations per second (d.p.s.).

$$1 \text{ curie (c)} = 3 \cdot 7 \times 10^{10} \text{ d.p.s.}$$
$$1 \text{ c} = 1000 \text{ mc} = 1,000,000 \text{ µc}$$

One gramme of radium has an activity of 1 c. Other materials are compared to radium and each other by the specific activity defined as the number of curies per gramme of the material.

Radiation, which passes unchanged through tissue, produces no damage. The damage is caused by the ionization produced when the radiation is absorbed by the living cell. The unit of exposure to X-radiation or gamma-radiation is the Roentgen; the radiation which will produce $2 \cdot 08 \times 10^9$ ion pair in a cubic centimetre of dry air at S.T.P. (i.e., $1 \cdot 293 \times 10^{-3}$ g of air).

$$1 \text{ Roentgen} = 1 \text{ r} = 1000 \text{ mr, etc.}$$

The radiation of any type actually absorbed, referred to as the dose, is measured in rads. The rad is the dose which imparts 10^{-5} joules of energy per gramme of matter.

Normal background levels of radiation are such that in a year each person receives about 0·1 rad. There is no evidence that this amount of radiation is harmless, but it is one of the natural hazards that the human race is subject to, and very little can be done about it. It may be that this background radiation is what causes mutations and allows natural selection to operate.

If received over a short period, an exposure to 100 rad would make a person seriously ill and a dose of about 400 rad would be fatal to 50 per cent of persons exposed. The question is where to set the limit to exposure compatible with human health. The effects of radiation may be very long term and they may not be easy to diagnose. For example, twenty years after the bombing of Hiroshima and Nagasaki hundreds of people still die as a result of the radiation received at that time. They may die prematurely of conventional diseases because their resistance to disease has been undermined by the radiation. Even a small increase in the background is thought to increase the number of malformed babies born, and the

Fig. 9.11. Radioactive materials warning sign.

incidence of certain diseases such as anaemia and cancer. As a result of our increasing understanding of the effects of radiation, our estimate of the amount of radiation that the human body can tolerate has been frequently revised, and with each revision the estimate has been reduced. At present, 0·2 rad/year is considered safe for the population at large and 5 rad/year is a maximum for those working with radioactive materials. To warn people of the presence of radioactive materials, a sign has been internationally adopted. (Fig. 9.11.)

Binding Energy

One reason for the deviation of the atomic weights of the elements from an exact multiple

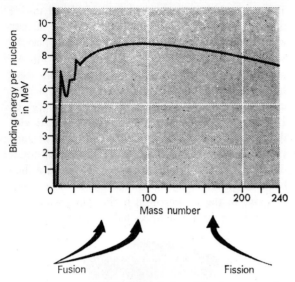

Fusion   Fission

Fig. 9.12. The binding energy per nucleon is greatest for medium sized nuclei.

of the weight of a nucleon is the binding energy of the protons and neutrons in the atom.

The binding energy is the difference between the total energy of the particles when separated and their total energy when combined in the nucleus. Since the energy of the nucleus is less than that of the separate particles, its mass is less than the sum of their masses. When the masses are known, the energy differences can be calculated from Einstein's equation

$$E = mc^2$$

where E is the energy in joules, m is the mass in kg, and c, the velocity of light, $= 3 \times 10^8$ m/s.

Certain arrangements of the nucleons have lower energy than others. In general, the change in mass due to the binding energy of the nucleons increases steadily with the number of nucleons, but the very large and very small molecules have more binding energy in relation to their size than the medium sized molecules. (Fig. 9.12.) If a very large atom splits into two smaller ones (fission), or several small atoms combine to form a larger atom (fusion), there is a net reduction in the total mass. The difference in mass appears as energy.

Since the energies of radioactive particles are usually measured electrically, it is convenient to express them in electrical rather than mechanical units of energy. The *electron-volt* is *the work done when the charge on one electron moves through a potential of 1 volt.*

$$1 \text{ MeV} = 1,000,000 \text{ eV} = 1\cdot6 \times 10^{-13} \text{ J}$$

Fusion

When hydrogen nuclei collide at high speed they combine to form a helium nucleus. The reaction also produces the positive electron or *positron*. It has the same mass as an electron and carries a charge of equal size but of opposite sign. (Fig. 9.13.)

$$4\,{}^1_1\text{H} \longrightarrow {}^4_2\text{He} + 2\,{}^0_1\beta$$

The process involves several stages but this is the result.

Looking at the graph of Fig. 8.5 you can see that the transition from hydrogen to helium involves a large energy change. This is confirmed when we compare the mass of the four hydrogen nuclei with the combined mass of the positron and the helium nucleus.

$4\,{}^1_1\text{H} = 4\cdot0314$ u ${}^4_2\text{H}$ $4\cdot0026$ u

                         $2_+\beta$ $0\cdot0011$ u

                                 $4\cdot0037$ u

Net loss in mass
= 0·0277 u

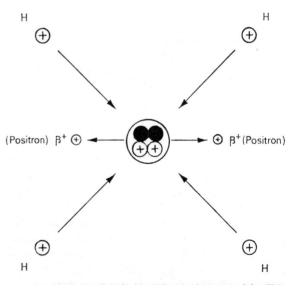

Fig. 9.13. Thermonuclear fusion. When hydrogen nuclei collide they combine to form a nucleus of helium and two positrons with the release of a great deal of energy. The reaction occurs in several stages.

Converting to kg
$$= 4.6 \times 10^{-29} \text{ kg}$$

Energy E
$$= mc^2$$
$$= 4.6 \times 10^{-29} (3 \times 10^8)^2 \text{ J/helium atom}$$
$$= 62 \times 10^{16} \text{ J/kg of helium produced.}$$

This process of fusion is called a *thermonuclear reaction* because, to have the necessary velocity of collision, the hydrogen must have a temperature of several million degrees. Such temperatures exist in the interior of stars which maintain their energy output by the conversion of hydrogen to helium. The Sun, a typical star, provides 3.3×10^{26} joules per second by this process. In consequence, the mass of the Sun reduces by 4.2×10^9 kg/s, but, have no fear, this amounts to only one millionth part of its total mass in 10 million years.

Fission

Fission is the splitting of a nucleus into two or more fragments. A slow neutron colliding with a nucleus of uranium 235 may cause it to split into smaller nuclei of krypton and barium, releasing two extra neutrons. (Fig. 9.14.)

$$^{235}_{92}\text{U} + ^{1}_{0}\text{n} \longrightarrow ^{141}_{56}\text{Ba} + ^{92}_{36}\text{Kr} + 3\,^{1}_{0}\text{n}$$

The total charge (lower prefix) and the total number of nucleons (upper prefix) remain unchanged by the reaction. The total mass of the particles produced is less than that of the uranium atom and the neutron. During the reaction, this mass has become associated with other forms of energy such as kinetic energy of the product particles and electromagnetic radiation. The process releases millions of times more energy than would the combustion of a similar mass of material.

The nucleus of uranium 235 does not always split into krypton 92 and barium 141; several other combinations are possible, e.g., silver 113 and rhodium 120; strontium 90 and xenon 143. In each case, neutrons make up the total of $235 + 1 = 236$ nucleons.

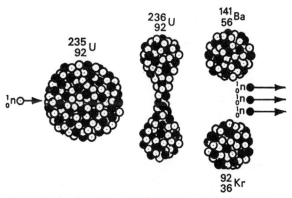

Fig. 9.14. One possible mode of splitting of uranium produces barium and krypton and three neutrons.

Note that the process of fission increases the number of free neutrons, some of which produce the fission of other uranium nuclei. Self-maintaining processes of this kind are called *chain reactions*. If every neutron released caused a further reaction, there would be a very rapid spread of fission to all the uranium nuclei present. Not all

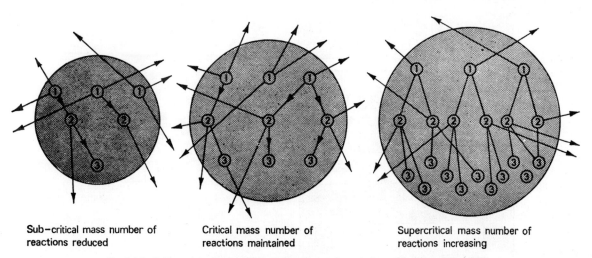

Sub-critical mass number of reactions reduced

Critical mass number of reactions maintained

Supercritical mass number of reactions increasing

Fig. 9.15. Schematic representation of three stages in a chain reaction in uranium 235.

the neutrons released succeed in producing fission. Most of them pass out through the boundary of the solid without making further collisions. In a large solid this escape is less likely and more of the neutrons produce fission. There is therefore a critical size above which the number of nuclei splitting grows in number. When the critical mass is only slightly exceeded, the material gets hotter and hotter; when the critical mass is grossly exceeded, it explodes. (Fig. 9.15.)

Atomic Pile

In an atomic reactor a mass of uranium is kept in a near critical condition by interspersing it with other materials. (Fig. 9.16.) Carbon slows down the product neutrons to thermal velocities which makes them more likely to initiate further fission. The boron rods on the other hand absorb neutrons and these reduce the rate of fission. Thus, by changing the position of the boron rods, engineers control the rate of heat output.

A flow of liquid or gas over the reactor carries away the heat to a heat exchanger where it produces steam. (Fig. 9.17.) This steam drives a turbine which either delivers the power on the spot, or is used to generate electrical energy for distribution.

Nuclear Explosives

In an atomic bomb, several sub-critical masses of uranium 235 are brought together to form one super-critical mass. (Fig. 9.18.) When the combined masses reach the critical quantity, the uranium explodes spontaneously in a fraction of a second. The explosion, in fact, begins as the masses approach each other, so that, in order to give as much time as possible for *fission* to occur,

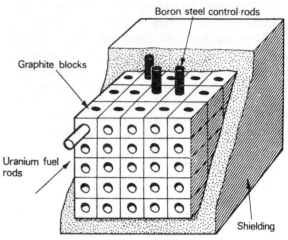

Fig. 9.16. In an atomic pile, the fission of uranium is controlled by retractable boron rods which absorb neutrons and slow down the chain reaction.

the separate masses of uranium 235 are shot together by charges of conventional explosive.

Much bigger explosions can be produced by the *fusion* of hydrogen nuclei. In this type of reaction, a temperature of several million degrees is produced by means of a fissional explosion, and, at this

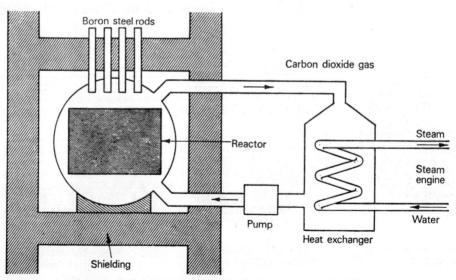

Fig. 9.17. Schematic diagram of one type of British nuclear reactor.

104

enormous temperature, the thermal velocities of atoms are sufficient to force hydrogen nuclei to combine to form atoms of helium. In fact, only heavy hydrogen isotopes (deuterium and tritium) have been made to produce explosions.

The heat from repeated underground nuclear explosions may prove, in the future, to be an effective means of deriving nuclear power, if a way can be found to extract this heat through remotely positioned heat exchangers. Attempts to control and harness thermonuclear energy have so far proved unsuccessful. The potentialities of nuclear explosions as weapons of war are obvious and terrible, as the bombings of Nagasaki and Hiroshima demonstrated.

Naturally occurring uranium consists mainly of uranium 238, the uranium 235 being less than 1 per cent. Fission of uranium 238 cannot be produced so readily as fission of uranium 235. After prolonged exposure to neutron bombardment however U 238 changes to a transuranic element plutonium which is more readily fissile. Plutonium may be used to produce an explosion or to enrich the uranium in a reactor in the same way as uranium 235. There are several stages in the reaction but it may be summarized as follows:

$$_{0}^{1}n + _{92}^{238}U \longrightarrow _{94}^{239}Pu + 2 \, _{-1}^{0}\beta$$

This plutonium is extracted from uranium which has been in an atomic pile. The first atomic piles were constructed for the purpose of making plutonium and not to generate power.

Since the neutron was identified less than 40 years ago, nuclear physics has undergone a phenomenal development. Many other elementary particles have been discovered, such as mesons, which are intermediate in mass between electrons and protons, and play a part in nuclear binding. Some *antiparticles* such as the positive electron or positron, the antiproton (negative proton) and even an anti-neutron have been observed in cosmic-rays, or produced by particle accelerating machines. Perhaps in space there exist worlds made of antimatter in which negatively charged nuclei are surrounded by positively charged electrons. If worlds of antimatter and matter were to meet they would annihilate each other in one great nuclear explosion.

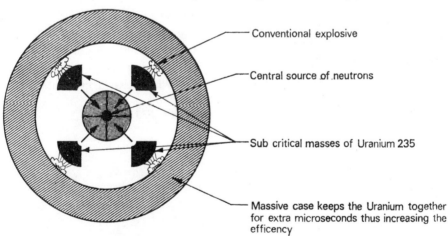

Fig. 9.18. A nuclear explosion is produced when several masses of uranium 235 are combined to produce a supercritical mass.

Questions

1. If the nucleus is screened by its electron shells, how is it we can tell one element from another by chemical tests?

2. Draw a diagram showing which way alpha- and beta-particles are deflected in an electric and a magnetic field, and showing the direction of the fields.

3. Why is the life of radioactive materials given in terms of the half-life rather than the whole life?

4. If you add the masses of two neutrons and two protons, the answer is slightly different from the mass of one alpha-particle. Why?

5. Can you think of any more uses of radioactive isotopes?

6. Why do sub-critical masses of uranium 235 not explode when separate, but do so when brought together?

7. Would a chemical or a physical process be necessary to separate different isotopes of the same element?

8. Why do we speak of alpha- and beta-particles, but gamma-radiation?

9. Why are free neutrons more difficult to detect than electrons or protons?

10. Why would you never find a pure sample of a radioactive element?

11. Before the first atomic bomb was exploded, some people believed that it would 'blow up the world'. Did they have any grounds for believing this?

12. Complete these equations:

$$_1^2H + {}_4^9Be = {}_0^1n + ?$$

$$_2^4He + {}_{13}^{27}Al = {}_0^1n + ?$$

Problems

1. In a nuclear disintegration, a mass of $8·2 \times 10^{-3}$ u is annihilated and 95 per cent of the energy produced is converted into the kinetic energy of an alpha-particle. What is its energy in MeV? ($1u = 1·66 \times 10^{-27}$ kg; one MeV $= 1·6 \times 10^{-13}$ J.)
Answer: 7·23 MeV.

2. How much energy, in joules, would be produced by the fission of 10 kg of uranium 235? (Energy per fission $= 200$ MeV; 1 MeV $= 1·6 \times 10^{-13}$ J; Avogadro's number $= 6·02 \times 10^{23}$ atoms/mole.)
Answer: $8·2 \times 10^{14}$ J.

3. 25 MeV of energy are released when four hydrogen atoms combine to produce a helium nucleus. How much energy would be produced if 10 kg of hydrogen forms helium? (1 MeV $= 1·6 \times 10^{-13}$ J; Avogadro's number $= 6·02 \times 10^{23}$ atoms/mole.)
Answer: $6·0 \times 10^{15}$ J.

4. Calculate the energy released in the following reactions and name each particle involved. ($1u = 1·66 \times 10^{-27}$ kg.)

$$_1^2H + {}_1^2H \longrightarrow {}_2^3He + {}_0^1n$$
$$_1^2H + {}_1^2H \longrightarrow {}_1^3H + {}_1^1H$$

(Mass of $_1^1H = 1·0078$ u; $_0^1n = 1·0087$ u; $_1^2H = 2·0141$ u; $_1^3H = 3·016$ u; $_2^3He = 3·016$ u.)
Answer: $5·2 \times 10^{-13}$ J; $6·6 \times 10^{-13}$ J.

5. If the Sun converts 6×10^{16} kg of hydrogen into helium per day, how much energy does this produce? (Mass of $_1^1H = 1·0078$ u; $_2^4He = 4·0039$ u; 1 u $= 1·66 \times 10^{-27}$ kg.)
Answer: $3·6 \times 10^{31}$ J.

6. Express in joules: 1 g; 1 kg; 1 u.
Answer: 9×10^{13} J; 9×10^{16} J; $1·49 \times 10^{-10}$ J.

7. The Earth radiates 3×10^{22} joules into space every day. What mass in kg would this be associated with?
Answer: $3·33 \times 10^5$ kg

10 Light Reflection

Geometrical optics is the study of the production of images and is based on the assumption that light travels in straight lines. This assumption is an approximation but it made possible a great deal of progress in optics when the more exact nature of light was unknown. We can see that the assumption is approximately true because point light sources cast sharp shadows and spotlights throw well defined beams. Geometrical optics is so called because geometrical construction is important in designing optical systems. Equations can sometimes be used when it is not convenient to construct scale drawings, but they are only useful when they describe correctly the geometrical construction on which they are based.

Reflection at Plane Surfaces

Light meeting a surface is only partly reflected, some is transmitted and some is absorbed. You will understand this better by thinking of cases where one or other process predominates, for example, a blackboard, a window, or a white painted wall or a mirror.

In considering the reflected component, we might pause to question the difference between the reflection at a matt white and at a mirror surface. The difference is not in the amount of light they reflect, it is in the way the light is scattered on reflection, as shown in Fig. 10.1.

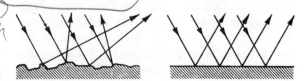

Fig. 10.1. Diffuse and specular reflection.

The matt surface reflects diffusely while the mirror reflects regularly. It is this latter type, called specular reflection, which we shall be concerned with in this chapter.

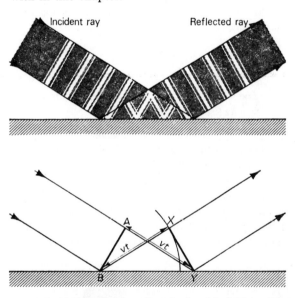

Fig. 10.2. Light waves are reflected symmetrically by a plane reflecting surface.

When a train of waves approaches a surface, one end of each wavefront meets the surface and is reflected before the other. (Fig. 10.2.) The velocity v of each part of a wave front remains constant before and after reflection. During a time t the end A of a particular wavefront travels to Y on the surface. The energy from B travels a similar distance vt away from the surface. The new position of the wavefront XY is tangential to the circle of radius vt centred on B. The reflected wave travels at right angles to the wavefront XY.

107

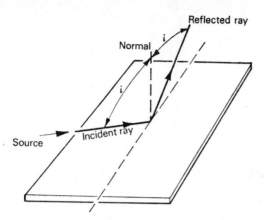

Fig. 10.3. Reflection at a plane surface.

The direction of a ray is always defined by the angle it makes with the normal to the surface and not with the surface itself. (Fig. 10.3.) The symmetry apparent in the reflection of a ray at a plane surface is summarized in the two laws of reflection:

1. *The angle of reflection is equal to the angle of incidence.*
2. *The reflected ray is in the same plane as the incident ray and the normal.*

The second law means simply that the reflected ray is not turned to left or right of the normal as viewed from the incident ray.

An important application of the laws of reflection is made in the design of some electrical instruments. The scale of a galvanometer is easier to read if the scale is enlarged and the pointer is made long to

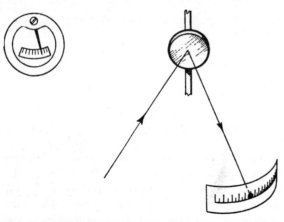

Fig. 10.4. The optical lever. A very long light beam may be used as a pointer without adding weight to the suspension.

match. A sensitive movement might be overloaded by a heavy pointer, but if the pointer is replaced by a minute mirror which moves with the mechanism, a ray reflected from it can be as long as required without increasing the inertia of the system. (Fig. 10.4.) As a bonus, the magnification is further increased by the fact that the total angle of deflection of the reflected beam is twice the angle of deflection of the suspended mirror. (Fig. 10.5.) The diagram shows that this is true when the light beam is initially normal to the mirror. You might like to show that it is valid for any initial angle of incidence.

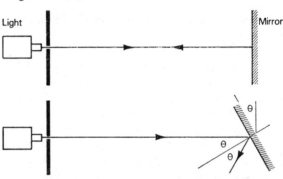

Fig. 10.5. The reflected ray turns through twice the angle of rotation of the mirror.

Image Formation in a Plane Mirror

When rays from the object obeying the laws of reflection are constructed, they diverge after reflection at the mirror. By comparison of Fig. 10.6a and 10.6b, it can be seen that the eye receives light as though from a point behind the mirror. The triangles *PBO* and *PBI* are congruent making *PO = PI*. Thus, the image is as far behind the mirror as the object is in front, a fact which is a matter of everyday observation.

Note also that the image in a plane mirror is inverted. (Fig. 10.7.) If you are not convinced by the diagram, try to read a book reflected in a mirror.

An important aspect of any image in optics is whether or not it can be received directly on a screen. The light rays from the plane mirror (Fig. 10.6) do not pass through the image, although they indicate its position. Such an image would not be visible on a screen placed at *I* and for this reason it is called a *virtual* image. The image viewed in a microscope is of this type.

Any image which can be seen on a screen placed in the position of the image is called a *real* image. Projected images such as those on a cinema or television screen are real images.

Reflection at Curved Surfaces

The giant radio telescope at Jodrell Bank and the small electric torch in your pocket, both employ curved reflectors. One is an enormous

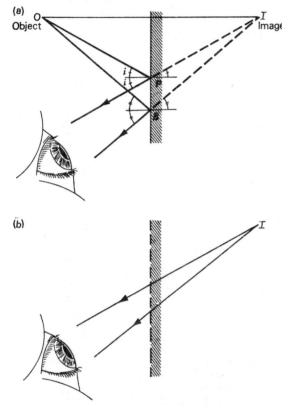

Fig. 10.6. The image is as far behind a plane mirror as the object is in front. The image exists at I in the sense that the eye receives a similar cone of light from I to that which it would receive from an object at I with the mirror removed.

bowl, 750,000 kg in weight, 76 m in diameter, which gathers radio waves from outer space and concentrates them on to a focus so that they can be studied and analysed. (Fig. 10.8.) The other is a small metal cup, only an inch or two across, which receives the light from a small bulb, and reflects it outwards to provide a convenient source of illumination. Between these two, curved reflectors of all shapes and sizes are used in a wide variety of applications, and in this chapter

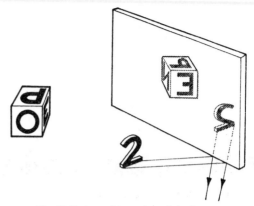

Fig. 10.7. Lateral inversion of the image.

we will consider the three basic types in common use: the concave spherical mirror, the convex spherical mirror, and the parabolic mirror.

A projectile fired upwards at an angle to the vertical describes a curve called a parabola. (Fig. 10.9.) The surface formed by rotating this curve about its axis of symmetry has the same shape as a parabolic reflector. The special feature of a parabolic reflector is that it concentrates a wide beam of light, travelling parallel to the principal axis of the reflector, on to a single focal point. Such reflectors are used in some types of telescope. (Fig. 10.10a.) But, more commonly, a source of light is placed at the focus and the reflector

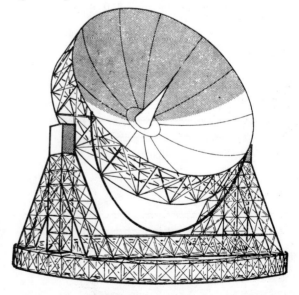

Fig. 10.8. The radio telescope at Jodrell Bank, which was built to detect radio waves from outer space, has a parabolic reflector 75 m in diameter.

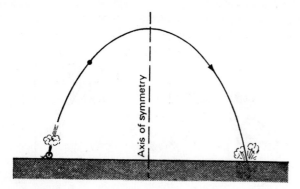

Fig. 10.9. A projectile describes a parabolic path.

produces a parallel beam as in a car headlight. To prevent any divergence of the direct light from the bulb, a shield is placed in front of the bulb, as in a spotlight. (Fig. 10.10b.)

A section of a spherical shell silvered on the inside can also produce a sharp focus from a parallel beam of light. (Fig. 10.11a.) If the beam of light is at an angle to the principal axis it still produces a focus. (Fig. 10.11b.) This is an important characteristic, because it makes possible the formation of an image of an object which subtends an appreciable angle at the mirror. A parabolic mirror can only produce an image if the light rays from the extremes of the object are almost parallel, as is the case with rays of light from distant objects like stars and satellites.

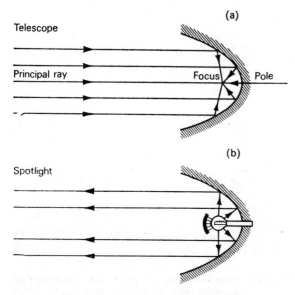

Fig. 10.10. Use of parabolic reflector.

Relation between *f* and *r*

In Fig. 10.12 a ray parallel to the principal axis is shown reflected through the focus. The normal at any position on a spherical surface passes through the centre of curvature so that QC is the normal at Q.

$\widehat{AQC} = \widehat{FQC}$ by 1st law of reflection.

$\qquad = \widehat{QCF}$ (alternate angles made with parallels AQ and CP).

Hence $\triangle FQC$ is isosceles and $CF = FQ$.

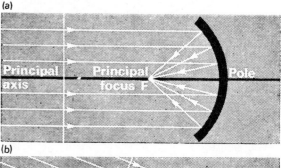

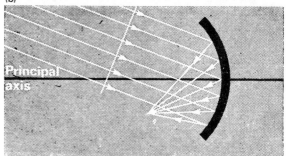

Fig. 10.11. A parallel beam of light in the direction of the principal axis passes after reflection through the principal focus. A parallel beam at an angle to the axis is brought to a focus off the axis.

For the sake of clarity, the shape is exaggerated in Fig. 10.12a more realistic proportions are illustrated in Fig. 10.12b. It can be seen that FQ is almost equal to FP, therefore $CF = FP = f$. When PQ is small, i.e., when the incident ray is near to the principal axis, the difference between CF and FP is very small and we may write:

$$r = CF + FP = 2f$$

When a beam of light, travelling parallel to the principal axis, strikes the surface of a concave mirror, the rays furthest away from the axis are focused at a point which is nearer the mirror than the point at which the rays travelling close

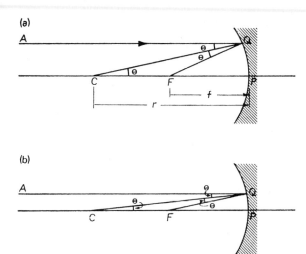

(a)

(b)

Fig. 10.12. Relation between f and r in a spherical mirror.

Formation of an Image in a Concave Mirror

Curved mirrors produce images just as plane ones do, but the position of the image is not quite so easy to predict. A diverging cone of light from a point on an object (situated outside the centre of curvature of a concave mirror) (Fig. 10.14a), is changed after reflection to a converging cone. The apex of this cone is a point on the image. Many such cones make up the complete image but its position can be located by tracing two particular rays from the top of the object. (Fig. 10.14b.)

1. The ray parallel to the principal axis passing through the focus after reflection.

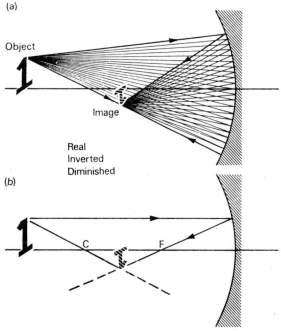

(a)

Object

Image

Real
Inverted
Diminished

(b)

Fig. 10.14. Formation of an image in a concave mirror.

to the principal axis are focused. The focus is, therefore, no longer a sharp point but spreads into a line along the axis. This blurring of the focus, called *spherical aberration*, imposes a severe restriction on the use of spherical surfaces. Figure 10.13 shows what happens when a wide aperture is used. The reflected rays do not all meet at F, but are tangents to a shape called a caustic curve. The extent of the deviation in any particular case can be determined by accurate scale drawing. Where it is necessary to use a wide aperture to collect sufficient light, parabolic mirrors are preferred. Thus, the larger instruments, such as the 5 m diameter telescope at Mount Palomar observatory in America, employ parabolic reflectors rather than lenses or spherical mirrors.

2. The ray directed through the centre of curvature meeting the mirror normally and returning along its own path.

At the point of intersection of these two rays is the image of the top of the object. The complete image extends from this point towards the principal axis.

Nature of the Image

Three facts are necessary to describe an image: whether it is (a) real or virtual, (b) magnified or diminished, (c) upright or inverted. Thus, the

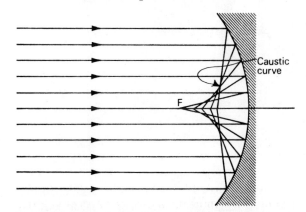

Caustic
curve

F

Fig. 10.13. Spherical aberration at a concave mirror. The outside rays are brought to a focus nearer the mirror than the central rays.

image (Fig. 10.14) is real because it would be projected on a screen placed at *I*, it is diminished being smaller than the object, and it is, of course, inverted.

As the object is moved towards the mirror, the

The Convex Mirror

If a spherical shell is silvered on the outside, the result is a convex mirror. Light incident on the mirror parallel to the axis is reflected away from a

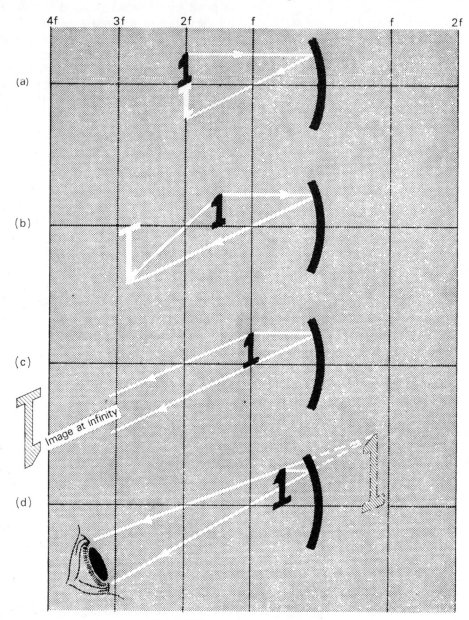

Fig. 10.15. Images in a concave mirror.

image position changes as shown in Fig. 10.15. The two construction rays can be used to locate the image, even though these particular rays would not in fact encounter the mirror.

focal point situated behind the mirror. (Fig. 10.16.) The focal length of the mirror is equal to half the radius of curvature. A convex mirror produces an image behind the mirror which is virtual,

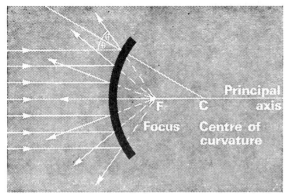

Fig. 10.16. Effect of a convex mirror on a parallel light beam.

diminished, and upright for all positions of the object. (Fig. 10.17.) An object at infinity has its image at the focal point of the mirror. As the object moves from infinity towards the mirror, its image moves from the focal point towards the mirror. Convex mirrors are popular as driving mirrors, because they give a wide angle of view.

(a)

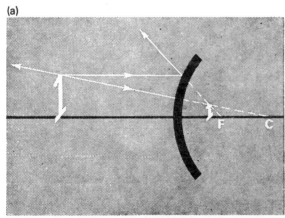

(b)

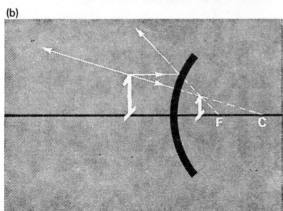

Fig. 10.17. The image in a convex mirror is virtual, diminished, and upright.

(Fig. 10.18.) However, because of the small movement of the image for a large movement of the object, it is rather difficult to estimate distances in convex mirrors.

Power of a Mirror

In the construction of ray diagrams the focal length is the important quantity, but when calculating the combined effect of several optical components, a more convenient quantity is the *power*, defined as *the reciprocal of the focal length, in metres*. The unit of power is the dioptre.

$$\text{Power in dioptres} = \frac{1}{\text{focal length in metres}}$$

For example a mirror having a focal length of

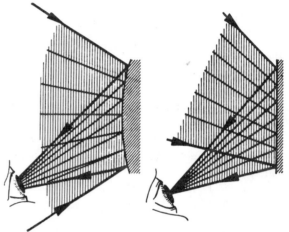

Fig. 10.18. A convex mirror gives a wider field of view than a plane mirror.

200 mm or 0·2 m has a power of $\frac{1}{0·2}$ = 5 dioptres. A 10 dioptre mirror has a focal length of $\frac{1}{10}$ m or 100 mm.

In order to distinguish between concave and convex mirrors, we give their powers positive and negative values. A concave mirror *converges* light to a real focus and has a *positive* power, while a convex mirror *diverges* light from a virtual focus and has a *negative* power. The focal length and radius of curvature of a mirror have the same sign as its power.

A similar convention is used to distinguish between real and virtual images. Distances are measured from the pole of the mirror to the image and are taken as *positive* if the image is a *real* one and *negative* if it is *virtual*. Most objects are real and therefore we reckon their distances from the mirror positive. Within more complex optical systems, virtual objects do arise, in which case we give them negative object distances.

Mirror Formulae

Consider a typical ray from an object at O forming an image at I. (Fig. 10.19.) The incident reflected rays make the same angle θ with the normal which passes through the centre of curvature C.

We make use of the geometrical relation that the external angle of a triangle is equal to the sum of the opposite interior angles.

Fig. 10.19*a*	Fig. 10.19*b*
$\beta = \alpha + \theta$	$2\theta = \alpha + \gamma$
also $\quad \gamma = \beta + \theta$	$\gamma = \beta + \theta$
Hence $2\beta = \alpha + \gamma$	therefore $2\beta = -\alpha + \gamma$

In practice, the angles of β and γ are quite small and the arc QP is little different from the arcs drawn from Q to the axis centred on I and O.

Writing the angles in radian measure, approximately

$$\alpha = \frac{QP}{OP}, \quad \beta = \frac{QP}{CP}, \quad \gamma = \frac{QP}{IP}$$

Substituting in equations above:

$\dfrac{2QP}{CP} = \dfrac{QP}{OP} + \dfrac{QP}{IP}$	$\dfrac{2QP}{CP} = -\dfrac{QP}{OP} + \dfrac{QP}{IP}$
applying the sign convention	applying the sign convention
$r = CP \quad u = +OP$	$r = -CP \quad u = +OP$
$v = +IP$	$v = -IP$
$\dfrac{2}{r} = \dfrac{1}{u} + \dfrac{1}{v}$	$\dfrac{2}{r} = \dfrac{1}{u} + \dfrac{1}{v}$

Since $r = 2f$, we may write this in the form

$$\frac{1}{u} + \frac{1}{v} = \frac{1}{f} = \frac{2}{r}$$

The equation applies to both concave and convex mirrors provided we observe the sign convention. It is most important that signs should be given to the quantities only when the numerical values are inserted.

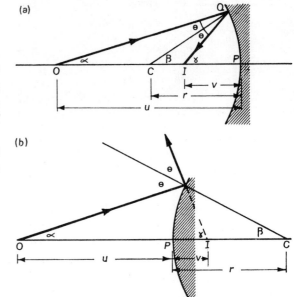

Fig. 10.19. The ray through the object and image obeys the laws of reflection.

Problem: (1) An object placed at 100 mm from a concave mirror produces a sharp image on a screen at 400 mm from the mirror. Calculate the focal length and power of the mirror.

Solution: $u = +100$ mm
$$v = +400 \text{ mm}$$
$$f = ?$$
$$\frac{1}{u} + \frac{1}{v} = \frac{1}{f} = \text{power}$$

i.e., $\quad \dfrac{1}{100} + \dfrac{1}{400} = \dfrac{5}{400} = \dfrac{1}{f}$

$$f = \frac{400}{5} = 80 \text{ mm}$$

Power $(P) = \dfrac{1}{f \text{ (metres)}} = \dfrac{1}{0 \cdot 08} = +12 \cdot 5$ dioptres

Problem: (2) An object is placed at 150 mm from a concave mirror of focal length 200 mm, where is the image?

114

Solution: $u = +150$ mm

$$f = -200 \text{ mm}$$
$$v = ?$$
$$\frac{1}{u} + \frac{1}{v} = \frac{1}{f}$$
$$\frac{1}{150} + \frac{1}{v} = \frac{1}{-200}$$
$$\frac{1}{v} = \frac{1}{-200} - \frac{1}{150} = \frac{-7}{600}$$
$$\therefore \qquad v = -86 \text{ mm}$$

i.e. the image in 86 mm behind the mirror.

Linear Magnification

The linear magnification m produced by an optical element such as a mirror or lens is defined by the ratio of image size to object size. (Fig. 10.20.)

$$m = \frac{\text{image size}}{\text{object size}} = \frac{H_I}{H_o}$$

The ray from the top of the object makes equal angles of incidence and reflection at the pole of the mirror. The shaded triangles are similar and, therefore,

$$m = \frac{H_I}{H_o} = \frac{v}{u}$$

This ratio gives the magnification for all positions of the image, but positive and negative signs are ignored when calculating the magnification. Diminished images are represented by magnification less than one.

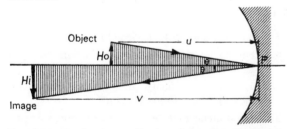

Fig. 10.20. The linear magnification of the mirror is the ratio H_I/H_o.

Problem: Calculate the magnification for Problems 1 and 2 above.

Solution: In Problem 1, $u = +100 \qquad v = +400$

$$m = \frac{v}{u} = \frac{400}{100} = 4$$

In Problem 2, $u = +150 \qquad v = -86$

$$m = \frac{v}{u} = \frac{-86}{150} = -0 \cdot 57$$

and neglecting the sign, $m = 0 \cdot 57$.

Measurement of Mirror Constants

The focal length of a concave mirror may be quickly estimated by focusing on a screen a sharp image of a distant object such as a window frame. The image is produced approximately at the principal focus. (Fig. 10.21.)

A more accurate value may be obtained by locating several corresponding object and image

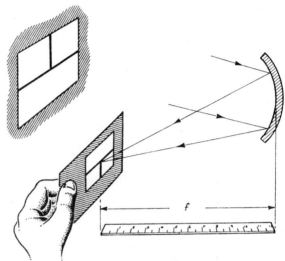

Fig. 10.21. The quickest method of estimating the focal length of a concave mirror is to focus an image or a distant object on to a screen.

distances, u and v, and substituting them in the mirror formula. Alternatively, the particular distance at which object and image coincide gives the radius of curvature directly. (Fig. 10.22.)

The constants of convex mirrors are not easily measured by optical methods, but the radius of curvature of both convex and concave mirrors can be measured quickly and accurately by means of a *spherometer*.

The instrument is based on the property of a

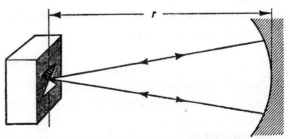

Fig. 10.22. Object and image coincide at the centre of curvature of a concave mirror.

circle whereby the product of the intercepts of any two intersecting chords are equal. This is best understood by reference to Fig. 10.23 where two chords AB and CD intersect at O

$$AO \times OB = CO \times OD$$

In this symmetrical case where $AO = OB$
$$x^2 = h(2r-h) = 2rh - h^2$$

Since h is small h^2 can be neglected
$$r = x^2/2h$$

A micrometer measures h the vertical displacement of the centre pin from the plane of the other three pins. The horizontal distance x from the centre to an outer pin is fixed for the instrument. Spherometers may be calibrated directly in radii, focal lengths, or powers as required.

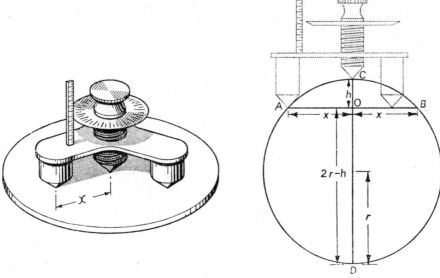

Fig. 10.23. The spherometer measures the radius of curvature of the sphere of which the mirror is a part.

Questions

1. What are the advantages and disadvantages of parabolic and spherical reflectors used in optical systems?

2. What is meant by spherical aberration of a curved mirror?

3. Draw ray diagrams showing how the same concave mirror can produce a real image and a virtual image.

4. Show that it is impossible for a convex mirror to form a real image of a real object.

5. What do we mean by a virtual object?

6. What do we mean by a magnification less than one?

7. How does your image in a plane mirror differ from how other people see you?

8. Do you prefer a plane, concave, or convex driving mirror. Why?

9. Where do object and image coincide for a concave mirror?

10. What do we mean by 'an image at infinity'?

Problems

1. What length of vertical plane mirror is needed to enable a 1·8 m tall man to see his complete reflected image?

   Answer: 0·9 m.

2. The mirror of a galvanometer deflects through 5 degrees. What is the displacement of the reflected ray on a scale 1 m away which was originally at right angles to the ray?

   Answer: 0·176 m.

3. Complete the following table.

p	f (mm)	r (mm)	type
$+8$	$+125$	$+250$	converging
—	—	$+600$	—
—	-160	—	diverging
-4	—	—	—
—	—	-150	—
—	$+400$	—	—
$+20$	—	—	—
—	-100	—	diverging

Answer:

p	f (mm)	r (mm)	type
$+8$	$+125$	$+250$	converging
$+3\frac{1}{3}$	$+300$	$+600$	converging
$-6\frac{1}{4}$	-160	-320	diverging
-4	-250	-500	diverging
$-13\frac{1}{3}$	-75	-150	diverging
$+2\frac{1}{2}$	$+400$	$+800$	converging
$+20$	$+50$	$+100$	converging
-10	-100	-200	diverging

4. A real image of twice the linear size of an object is thrown on a screen by a concave mirror. Screen and object are both moved until the image is three times as big as the object. If the screen has to be moved 250 mm, how far does the object move and what is the mirror's focal length?
Answer: 41·6 mm; 50 mm.

5. What is the diameter of the image of the Sun formed by the mirror of the Mount Palomar reflecting telescope, with a focal length of 18 metres? The Sun has a diameter of $1·4 \times 10^9$ m and is $1·5 \times 10^{11}$ m away.
Answer: 168 mm.

6. The radius of curvature of a concave mirror is 200 mm. What object positions give (a) a real image three times the object height and (b) a virtual image twice its height?
Answer: 133 mm and 50 mm from mirror.

7. A piece of wire 50 mm long lies along the axis of a converging mirror which has a radius of curvature of 200 mm. The centre of the wire is 250 mm from the mirror. Find the length of the image of the wire.
Answer: 23 mm.

8. What is the length of the image of a pole lying along the axis of a convex mirror of focal length 1 m, if one end of it is 4 m and the other 9m from the mirror?
Answer: 0·1 m.

9. A driving mirror is made from a cylindrical mirror a radius 120 mm and length (measured round the curve) of 120 mm. Assuming the eye of the driver is a long way from the mirror, what is his angle of view?
Answer: 2 radians.

10. Calculate from first principles the position and size of the image formed by a converging mirror of focal length 80 mm when an object 5 mm high is placed 200 mm from the mirror.
Answer: 133 mm; 3·3 mm.

11. An object is located at 250 mm from a mirror of focal length $+200$ mm. Find the position of the image graphically and by formula.
Answer: 1 m from mirror.

12. An object is placed at 500 mm from a mirror of power $-12·5$ dioptres. Determine the position and nature of the image.
Answer: 69 mm behind mirror, virtual.

13. Calculate the position of the image of a car in a convex driving mirror of focal length 1 m when the car is at (a) 10 m, (b) 4 m.
Answer: (a) 0·91 m behind mirror, (b) 0·8 m behind mirror.

14. A shaving mirror 50 mm from a man's face gives a magnification of 2. Find the focal length of the mirror.
Answer: 100 mm.

15. A spherometer with legs 40 mm apart reads 1·5 mm on a convex mirror. Calculate the distance from the outer legs to the centre leg and, hence, determine the focal length of the mirror.
Answer: -890 mm.

16. A convex mirror has a radius of curvature of 160 mm. What is the position and size of the image when an object 5 mm high is placed 200 mm from the mirror?
Answer: 57 mm behind mirror, 1·4 mm high.

17. An image 3·3 mm high is produced 133 mm in front of a concave mirror by a real object 5 mm high. What is the position of the object and the focal length of the mirror?
Answer: 200 mm in front of mirror, $+80$ mm.

18. A dentist uses a concave mirror of 40 mm radius of curvature 10 mm away from a tooth. Where is the image formed and what is the magnification?
Answer: 20 mm behind mirror, magnification 2.

11 Refraction

When a ray of light passes from a vacuum into a material it slows down. Except in the case of normal incidence, the reduction in velocity causes the transmitted ray to deviate at the surface. This bending, called refraction, is responsible for such natural phenomena as mirages and rainbows, and it makes possible a wide range of optical instruments from a simple magnifying glass to a complex wide screen projector.

Wave Explanation

We can explain refraction at a surface in terms of the wave nature of light. Figure 11.1 shows

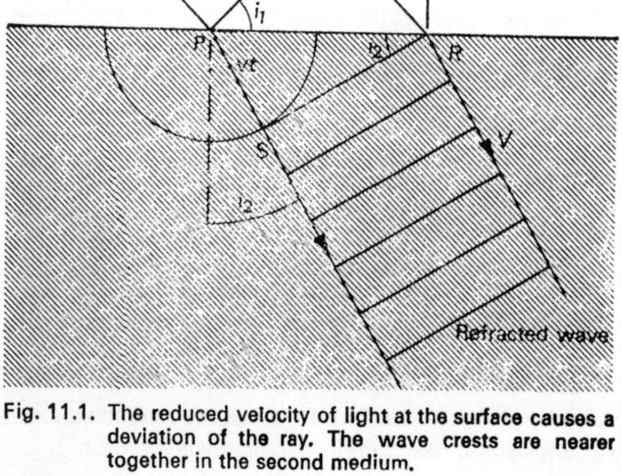

Fig. 11.1. The reduced velocity of light at the surface causes a deviation of the ray. The wave crests are nearer together in the second medium.

light waves approaching the surface of a transparent material with a velocity c. At a certain instant the wavefront PQ has one end P touching the surface. During the time that the end Q travels towards the surface, the end P travels on into the materials with a reduced velocity v, where v is the velocity of light in the material. The end of the wavefront Q takes a time t to reach the surface at R, a distance of ct. The other end of the wave will then have moved a distance vt from P, that is, it will be somewhere on the circle centred on P and of radius vt. The new wavefront extends from R and is a tangent to the circle. The ray travels on into the material perpendicular to this wavefront.

Laws of Refraction

The behaviour of the ray at the surface can be described by two simple laws.

1. *The ratio of the sine of the angle of incidence to the sine of the angle of refraction is constant.*
2. *The incident ray, the refracted ray, and the normal at the point of incidence lie in one plane.*

The first law follows directly from the wave diagram Fig. 11.1.

$$PR \sin i_1 = ct$$
$$PR \sin i_2 = vt$$

$$\therefore \qquad \frac{\sin i_1}{\sin i_2} = \frac{c}{v} = \text{a constant} \qquad (1)$$

The second law simply means that the refracted ray does not deviate to left or right of the plane of incidence.

Refractive Index

The ratio of the velocity of light in a vacuum, c, to that in a particular medium, v, is called the *refractive index* of the medium μ.

$$\mu = \frac{c}{v}$$

Alternatively, from equation (1),

$$\mu = \frac{\sin i_1}{\sin i_2}$$

Since c is the maximum velocity at which energy can travel in the universe, this ratio is greater than one.

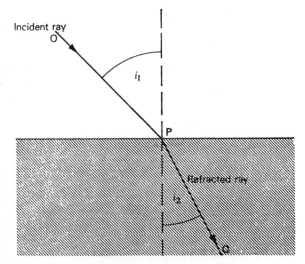

Fig 11.2. A light ray is bent towards the normal as it enters an optically denser medium.

Light is reversible, i.e., a reversal in direction of a light ray at any point causes a retracing of the original path. For example, if the ray OPQ in Fig. 11.2 were to be reversed so as to be incident along QP, then it would be refracted along PO. The refractive index in this case could be expressed as the ratio v/c but, generally, the refractive index for either direction of incidence is quoted in the form greater than one, i.e., c/v. Note that the refractive index correlates with the density of the material to some extent, though not entirely. (Table 11.1.) For this reason, refractive index is sometimes called *optical density*.

Table 11.1. A comparison of refractive index and density
($\lambda = 5\cdot893 \times 10^{-7}$ m)

Substance	Density (kg/m³)	Refractive index
Water	$1\cdot0 \times 10^3$	$1\cdot33$
Vitreous silica	$2\cdot2 \times 10^3$	$1\cdot46$
Quartz	$2\cdot7 \times 10^3$	$1\cdot54$
Glass—crown	$2\cdot5 \times 10^3$	$1\cdot48$
flint	$3\cdot0 \times 10^3$	$1\cdot56$
denser crown	$3\cdot6 \times 10^3$	$1\cdot61$
denser flint	$4\cdot76 \times 10^3$	$1\cdot74$
Diamond*	$3\cdot52 \times 10^3$	$2\cdot42$

* Diamond has the greatest refractive index of these substances but not the greatest density.

Problem: The velocity of light *in vacuo* is 300,000 km/s. What is its velocity in sea water of refractive index 1·4?

Solution: Refractive index $\mu = \dfrac{c}{v}$

$$\text{velocity } v = \frac{c}{\mu}$$

$$= \frac{300,000}{1\cdot4}$$

$$= 214,000 \text{ km/s}$$

When light passes across a surface between two materials it is deviated towards the normal in the optically denser medium. In this case

$$\frac{v_1}{v_2} = \frac{\sin i_1}{\sin i_2}$$

Since

$$\mu = \frac{c}{v}$$

$$v_1 = c/\mu_1 \text{ and } v_2 = c/\mu_2.$$

Hence

$$\frac{\sin i_1}{\sin i_2} = \frac{c/\mu_1}{c/\mu_2} = \frac{\mu_2}{\mu_1}$$

i.e.,

$$\mu_1 \sin i_1 = \mu_2 \sin i_2$$

$$\mu \sin i = \text{a constant}$$

This relation, called Snell's law, applies either to a single surface or to a series of parallel surfaces (Fig. 11.3):

$$\mu_1 \sin i_1 = \mu_2 \sin i_2 = \mu_3 \sin i_3 = \mu_1 \sin i_1$$

In this case, the ray emerges into the air parallel to its original direction.

119

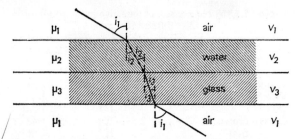

Fig. 11.3. A ray passing through several parallel sided media leaves parallel to its original direction.

One effect of refraction is to make submerged objects appear nearer to the surface than they really are. (Fig. 11.4.) Thus, a partially submerged object appears bent at the surface and an object viewed through a slab of material appears to be displaced towards the slab. (Fig. 11.5.)

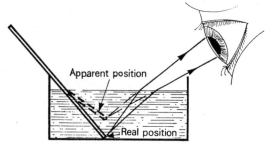

Fig. 11.4. A partly submerged object appears to be bent at the surface, due to refraction of the light rays.

Total Internal Reflection

Consider a ray of light being reflected and refracted at a surface, as it enters a less optically dense material. (Fig. 11.6a.) An increase in the angle of incidence causes the refracted ray to approach the surface until eventually it skims the surface. (Fig. 11.6b.) A further increase in i and the refracted ray disappears. (Fig. 11.6c.) The reflected ray shows a rapid increase in power as the refracted ray approaches the surfaces, the transfer being complete as the incident angle exceeds a critical value, i_c.

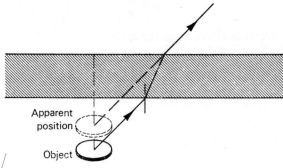

Fig. 11.5. An object below a slab of material appears to be displaced from its real position.

The laws of refraction still apply to the critical ray

$$\mu = \frac{\sin 90}{\sin i_1}$$

$$\mu = \frac{1}{\sin i_c}$$

Problem: What is the maximum angle of incidence of light which emerges from the surface of glass of refractive index 1·5?

Solution: Light emerges for angles of incidence from zero to the critical angle i_c

$$\sin i_c = \frac{1}{\mu} = \frac{1}{1·5}$$

$$i_c = 42°$$

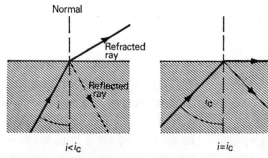

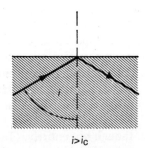

Fig. 11.6. The refracted ray disappears as the angle of incidence in the denser medium exceeds the critical angle, i_c. The ray is then totally internally reflected.

120

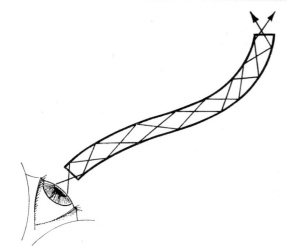

Fig. 11.7. A light probe directs light to inaccessible places by repeated internal reflections, in this case in a rod of Perspex.

Total internal reflection can be used to direct light into otherwise inaccessible places. Light directed into a rod of pliable material is confined to the rod by repeated total internal reflections and emerges only at the end of the rod where it meets the surface almost normally. (Fig. 11.7.)

Refraction has a very distorting effect on the view of the above-surface world by a submerged skin-diver or fish. The vertical arc from horizon to horizon extends through 180 degrees but this is seen from below the surface within a cone of semi-vertical angle i_c. (Fig. 11.8). Submerged objects are seen directly and also seen reflected in the water surface outside this cone.

Prism Reflectors

Total internal reflection has two distinct advantages:

1. It is a very efficient form of reflection.
2. All the reflection occurs at a single surface.

The second advantage is better appreciated by comparing total internal reflection with the reflection from the more common back-silvered mirror. Multiple reflections from the front and back glass surfaces can cause a reduction in the definition of an image. (Fig. 11.9.) Front-silvered mirrors can be used to eliminate these secondary reflections but such mirrors tend to be vulnerable to tarnishing and scratching.

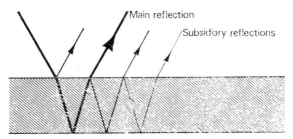

Fig. 11.9. Multiple reflections at a back-silvered mirror.

In order to use total internal reflection, the light must be introduced into the denser medium. This is achieved by the use of right-angled prisms as in Fig. 11.10.

Such reflecting prisms are used in binoculars to extend the optical length while keeping the physical

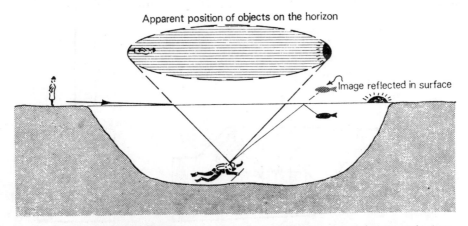

Fig. 11.8. A skin-diver's view of the outside world is confined to a cone of vertex angle about 100 degrees.

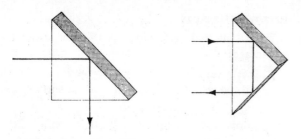

Fig. 11.10. A 45 degree right-angled prism may be used as a single or double reflector.

length as short as possible. Another example is the periscope, used in submarines to view the surface when submerged. (Fig. 11.11.)

Dispersion

The velocity of light in a medium varies with the frequency of the light, the higher frequency blue light travelling more slowly than the low-frequency red light. This gives light of each colour a slightly different refractive index, so that a ray of white light is dispersed into its colours after refraction at a single surface. (Fig. 11.12a.) The dispersion is small compared to the deviation of a ray and it is cancelled out by a second parallel surface. (Fig. 11.12b.) If the second surface is at an angle to the first, as in the case of a triangular prism, the dispersion can be further increased.

(Fig. 11.12c.) Such prisms are used in a spectrometer to analyse the frequencies which are emitted by a light source.

Mirages

The gradual change in density of air due to a difference in temperature produces the deviation of a ray passing through it. This can cause a *mirage* to be formed under certain conditions. These conditions are often realized on a road which has been heated by the sun and which establishes a vertical temperature gradient in the air above it. (Fig. 11.13.)

The rays from the sky entering the layers of air of decreasing density are refracted away from the normal until eventually they are totally internally reflected upwards before reaching the road. The blue colour of the light from the sky gives the mirage the appearance of puddles on the road.

Measurement of Refractive Index

There are many applications of a knowledge of refractive index apart from its obvious importance for geometrical optics. The design of optical components, such as camera lenses, calls for a precise knowledge and control of the refractive index of the materials used, but this application is rather specialized and concerns only the manufacturers of optical equipment.

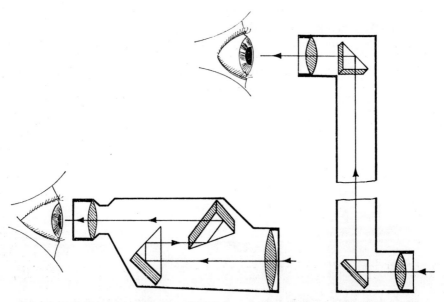

Fig. 11.11. Prisms are employed as reflectors in periscopes and some types of binoculars.

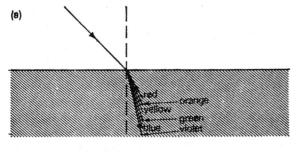

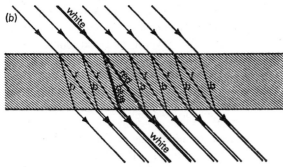

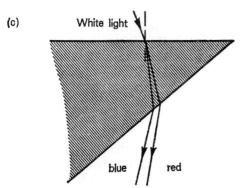

Fig. 11.12. (a) White light is dispersed into its coloured components by refraction at a single surface. (b) A second parallel surface restores it to its original direction so that adjacent rays combine to give white light. (c) The dispersion of light is increased by a second surface at an angle to the first, as in the prism.

The electrical properties of a material are related to its refractive index and, in particular, the relative permittivity ϵ_r and the refractive index μ are connected by the equation

$$\mu = \sqrt{\epsilon_r} = \frac{c}{v}$$

Both ϵ_r and μ vary with frequency. The relative permittivity is most important up to radio frequencies, whereas the refractive index is important at the higher light wave frequencies.

Impurity in a substance may cause its refractive index to differ from that of the pure products The difference in index is a sensitive measure or the amount of impurity present, and so the measurement of refractive index serves as a powerful tool for chemical analysis.

In forensic science, the science of crime detection, the measurement of refractive index can provide important evidence. Glass, being a mixture of substances, exhibits a variation of index from pane to pane. Minute fragments of glass found, perhaps, in a suspect's turnups or embedded in the fabric of a sleeve, may be identified with that of a broken window. The chance of two pieces of glass having the same refractive index to an accuracy of one part in 10,000 is remote unless they are from the same pane of glass.

The measurement of the refractive index of small irregular pieces of a transparent solid

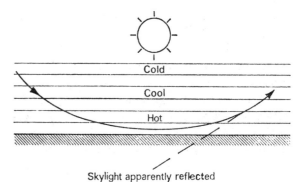

Skylight apparently reflected

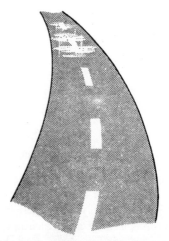

Fig. 11.13. Mirages are formed when a temperature gradient is established in still air. The light from the sky is deflected upwards and appears to come from the surface of the ground.

presents a difficult problem. It is solved by the use of a number of solutions of known refractive indexes in a range near to that of the test material. When the specimen is immersed in a solution of identical refractive index its surfaces do not reflect and it becomes invisible. Very fine control of the refractive index of a solution is possible by using mixtures of liquids in different proportions.

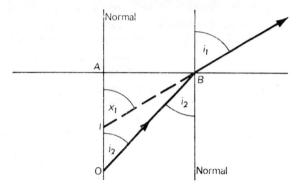

Fig. 11.14. Rays from O are refracted at the surface and appear to come from I vertically above O.

Real and Apparent Depth Method

Consider a ray OB from an object (Fig. 11.14) which is refracted away from the normal at the surface and appears to come from a point I above the object. Normals to the surface are drawn through the object and through the point of incidence.

$$i_1 = x_1 = A\hat{I}B, \qquad i_2 = A\hat{O}B$$

$$\mu = \frac{\sin i_1}{\sin i_2} = \frac{AB/BI}{AB/BO} = \frac{BO}{BI}$$

If the object is viewed from almost vertically above it, then

$$\frac{BO}{BI} \doteq \frac{AO}{AI}$$

$$\mu = \frac{\text{real depth}}{\text{apparent depth}}$$

From this relation, the refractive index of a material in the form of a block can be determined with the aid of a travelling microscope. We read the microscope scale after focusing it in each of the positions of Fig. 11.15 and hence we can calculate the real and apparent depths of the block.

We could apply this method equally well to measure the refractive index of a liquid placed in a suitable container.

The Air-Cell Refractometer

The most accurate methods of measuring the refractive index of a liquid are those which depend on the measurement of the critical angle. The least expensive, and therefore the most widely available in schools and colleges, is the air-cell refractometer. We use it to measure the indices of liquids of which at least several hundred cubic centimetres are available. The air-cell consists of a thin layer of air sandwiched between two glass plates sealed around the perimeter. It is immersed in the liquid under test and rotates about a vertical axis parallel to the plates. (Fig. 11.16.) At a certain angle of incidence i_c, the light from the source is *totally internally reflected* at the first glass–air surface and does not emerge. As this critical angle is approached the cell is crossed by a vertically edged shadow which is set in line with the source and viewing slit.

$$\mu_{\text{liquid}} \sin i_{\text{liquid}} = \mu_{\text{glass}} \sin i_g = \mu_{\text{air}} \sin 90°$$
$$= 1 \times 1$$

i.e.,

$$\mu_{\text{liquid}} = \frac{1}{\sin i_{\text{liquid}}}$$

We determine i_c by halving the angle between the extinction position on each side of normal incidence.

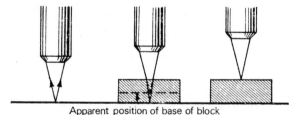

Apparent position of base of block

Fig. 11.15. The real depth and the apparent depth of a block of material may be measured by a travelling microscope.

Abbé Refractometers

A more accurate instrument than the air-cell, and one requiring only a minute quantity of liquid, is the Abbé refractometer. The light is arranged to strike a liquid–glass interface at a range of

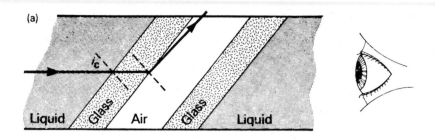

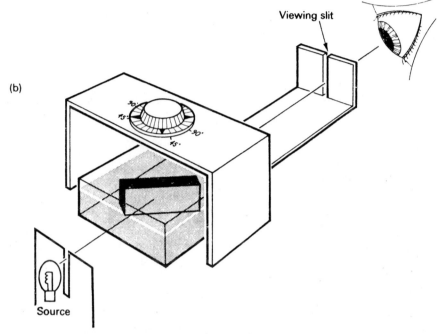

Fig. 11.16. Air-cell refractometer. *(a)* The ray just fails to emerge from the cell when it is incident at the critical angle, i_c. for the liquid. *(b)* The refractometer gives a direct reading of the critical angle of a liquid.

angles, including grazing incidence. (Fig. 11.17). The light transmitted into the second prism makes a range of angles up to but not beyond the critical angle for the surface. The emergent rays from the prism are picked up by a microscope which is set on the division between light and shade. The angular setting is dependent on the refractive index, and instruments are calibrated directly in refractive index.

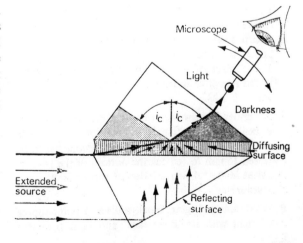

Fig. 11.17. The Abbé refractometer measures the critical angle of a liquid.

125

Questions

1. What would happen to a light ray in a material in which the optical density increased with depth?

2. Why would you be suspicious if you measured a refractive index and found it to be less than 1?

3. Why do we sometimes use light rays, and sometimes waves, in considering the behaviour of light?

4. Explain how light can reach us from the Sun when the Sun is below the horizon?

5. Why are diamonds, rather than glass, used for jewellery?

6. How would you prove the second law of refraction? (Incident and refracted ray and normal are in the same plane.)

7. As well as the common mirages seen on hot roads, reports have been made of mirages of objects seen apparently in the sky. Can you account for this?

8. What are the advantages and disadvantages of front-and back-silvered mirrors?

9. How would you show that the colours produced by a prism were caused by refraction and not absorption?

Problems

1. A light ray strikes a 200 mm thick glass block at 60° to the normal. Calculate the lateral displacement of the ray. (($\mu_g = 1.5$.)
Answer: 103 mm.

2. If a skin-diver sees an object high in the air at 30° to the vertical, what is its real angle to the vertical ($\mu_w = 1.5$)?
Answer: 56°.

3. What is the wave-length of light in glass of refractive index 1·5 if its wave-length in air is 5.88×10^{-4} mm?
Answer: 3.92×10^{-4} mm.

4. A light ray strikes one face of an equilateral glass prism at 50° to the normal. At what angle does it emerge, and what is the deviation produced? ($\mu_g = 1.5$).
Answer: 47°, 37°.

5. A light ray strikes a glass block at 45° to the normal. What is the thickness of the block if a lateral displacement of 10 mm is produced? ($\mu_g = 1.5$).
Answer: 30 mm.

6. A cup is held 135 mm·below the surface of a liquid and a ball is suspended 110 mm above the surface. If the image of the ball appears in the cup, what is the refractive index of the liquid?
Answer: 1·23.

7. A vernier microscope is focused on the bottom of a beaker. Turpentine is poured into the beaker until it is 50 mm deep and the microscope has to be raised 16 mm to refocus the bottom of the beaker. What is the refractive index of turpentine?
Answer: 1·47.

8. A 40 mm thick glass block touches a point source of light with its lower face, and light from the source is totally reflected outside a circle 30 mm radius on the upper face. What is the refractive index of the glass?
Answer: 1·67.

9. The centre of the Sun seems to be at an angle of 30° with the horizon. What is its true angle? (vacuum $\mu_{air} = 1.0003$).
Answer: 29° 58′.

10. A flaw in a glass block seems to be 40 mm below the surface. What is its real distance below the surface, if the refractive index of the glass is 1·52?
Answer: 60 mm.

11. What is the critical angle between carbon disulphide and water? ($\mu_{water} = 1.33$, $\mu_{cs2} = 1.64$).
Answer: 54·4°.

12. A light ray strikes a rectangular, thin walled glass jar full of liquid at 60° to the normal. If the ray is displaced by 40 mm in passing through the liquid, and the thickness of the liquid is 74 mm what is the refractive index of the liquid?
Answer: 1·6.

13. A jar of depth d is half-filled with liquid of refractive index μ_1 and the other half is filled with liquid of refractive index μ_2. Prove that the apparent depth of the jar, seen from above, is $\frac{d}{2}\left(\frac{1}{\mu_1} + \frac{1}{\mu_2}\right)$.

14. A block 80 mm thick made of glass with a refractive index of 1·6 lies at the bottom of a jar, which is then filled to a depth of 125 mm with liquid of refraction index 1·5. 60 mm of water of refractive index 1·33 is then floated on top. If a mark on the underside of the block is viewed from above, where does it appear to be?
Answer: 92·5 mm above the bottom of the jar.

15. A glass block is supported horizontally in a jar of water. A light ray strikes the water surface at 60° to the normal. At what angle does it strike the top surface of the glass, and the bottom surface? ($\mu_{water} = 1\cdot33$, $\mu_{glass} = 1\cdot50$).
    Answer: 40·6°, 35·2°.

16. The edge of a pond shelves from 1 m to 8 m deep over 10·5 m. What is the apparent slope? ($\mu_{water} = 1\cdot33$).
    Answer: 1 in 2.

17. A glass block 100 mm thick and with a refractive index 1·52 has its lower surface 60 mm above a bulb. Where does the bulb appear to be when viewed from above through the block?
    Answer: 25·8 mm below lower surface of block.

12 Lenses

In most industrialized countries, the manufacture of optical instruments is booming. Movie cameras and slide projectors, once considered the equipment of the specialist, are becoming commonplace in our homes. The application of optical instruments to problems in engineering, from time and motion study to rapid accurate measurement, is increasing. The assessment of the value of an optical aid often boils down to an understanding of the optics of the lens, which is the basic element of most optical instruments.

A lens is usually bounded by two spherical surfaces and may have a variety of shapes. Basically, lenses fall into two categories, convex lenses which are thicker at the centre than at the perimeter, and concave lenses which are thicker at the perimeter. Both convex and concave lenses may be bent into several shapes which although they look different have essentially the same power. (Fig. 12.1.)

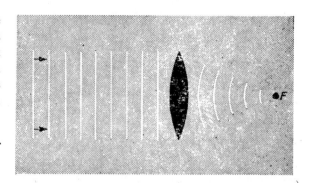

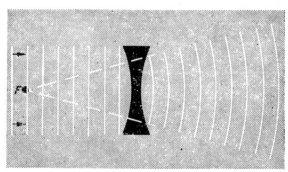

Fig. 12.2. A series of plane light waves is made to converge to a point by a convex lens and to diverge from a point by a concave lens.

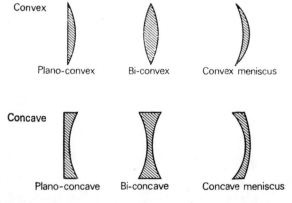

Fig. 12.1. Convex and concave lenses bent into different shapes.

Effect of a Lens on Light Waves

You can appreciate the action of the two types of lenses by considering their effect on light waves. A series of plane light waves passing through a lens is slowed down in the lens material. In a convex lens, the centre of the waves spends more time in the lens and is therefore retarded, allowing the perimeter of the waves to overtake on the outside. (Fig. 12.2a.) After leaving the lens, the waves converge to a point on the principal axis. This point is the principal focus of the lens.

A concave lens retards the waves most at the perimeter. The waves then travel outwards and diverge as though from a point on the incident side of the lens. (Fig. 12.2b.) Because the waves do not originate at this point, we call it a virtual focus.

The focal length of a lens is the distance between the pole of the lens, P, and the focal point, F. A lens has the same focal length for either direction of incident light. (Fig. 12.3.)

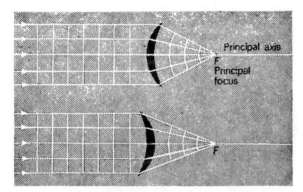

Fig. 12.3. The focal length of a lens is the same for either direction of incidence.

Formation of an Image by a Convex Lens

An illuminated object scatters light in all directions and so we can consider each point on the object to be a source of light.

A cone of light from a point on the object is converged by the lens to a point, which forms part of the image. (Fig. 12.4a.) The exact position of the image may be obtained by tracing only two rays from a point on the object. One ray parallel to the axis is refracted through the focus. A second ray in the direction of the pole, where the sides of the lens are virtually parallel passes through the lens undeviated. These two rays intersect at a point on the image. (Fig. 12.4b.)

When the object is outside the focal length, the image is real and inverted. (Fig. 12.5a.) When the object is within the focal length, the rays leaving the lens are still divergent. They appear to diverge from an upright virtual but magnified image on the same side of the lens as the object. (Fig. 12.5e.)

When the object is at the focal distance, the emergent light is parallel. The image is said to be formed at infinity, it is magnified and regarded as real. (Fig. 12.5d.) At an object distance of 2f the lens produces an image of the same size as the object. (Fig. 12.5b.) The diagram also shows that the minimum distance between a real object and image is 4f, a fact well worth remembering in experimental work.

Formation of an Image by a Concave Lens

A ray from the object to the pole of a concave lens passes through undeviated. A ray parallel to the axis after refraction diverges from the focus. (Fig. 12.5f.) The image formed at the intersection of these two rays is diminished, virtual, and upright. This description applies to all the images of a real object produced in a concave lens, although the magnification does vary with the object position. You can see the extent of this variation if you construct separate ray diagrams for a distant object and for an object almost in contact with the lens.

Linear Magnification

We define the linear magnification produced by a lens as *the ratio of the image size to the object size.*

$$m = \frac{\text{image size}}{\text{object size}}$$

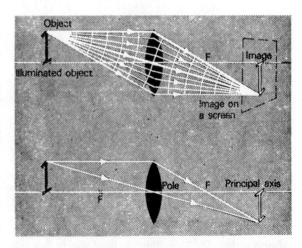

Fig. 12.4. The light waves can be more conveniently represented by rays. Two rays are required to locate an image. (a) A ray parallel to axis passing through F. (b) a ray passing undeviated through the pole of the lens.

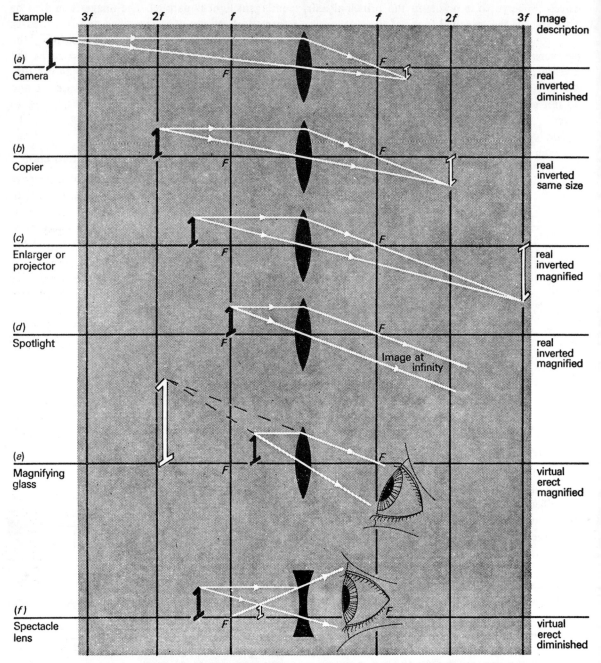

Fig. 12.5. The image produced by a convex lens *(a)–(e)* varies in nature and magnification with the position of the object. The image produced by a concave lens *(f)* is virtual, erect, and diminished for all positions of a real object.

A typical object and image linked by a ray through the pole is shown in Fig. 12.6. The shaded triangles bounded by the ray, the axis, the object, and the image are similar, and therefore

$$\frac{H_i}{H_o} = \frac{\text{image distance}}{\text{object distance}} \quad \text{i.e.,} \quad m = \frac{v}{u}$$

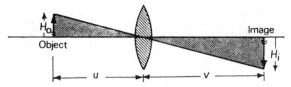

Fig. 12.6. The linear magnification of a lens is given by the ratio H_i/H_o or v/u.

Lens Equation

To predict the position of an image in a lens we use a simple formula connecting the object distance u, the image distance v, and the focal length f

$$\frac{1}{u} + \frac{1}{v} = \frac{1}{f}$$

The sign convention adopted for curved mirrors also applies to lenses.

The values of u and v are taken as positive if measured from a real object or image, and negative if measured from a virtual object or image. The focal length of a lens is positive when it converges light (convex lens) and negative when it diverges light (concave lens).

The equation applies to all object and image positions in both concave and convex lenses if the sign convention is observed. It is important that the sign be introduced only when a numerical value is inserted.

Lens designers, interested in the quality of an image, sometimes construct large-scale detailed diagrams. Many simple lens problems may be solved conveniently by a scale drawing, but in any case a sketch of a ray diagram gives a useful check on a calculation.

Problem: A concave lens of focal length 110 mm forms an image of an object 220 mm away from the lens. Where is the image and what linear magnification is produced?

Solution: $\dfrac{1}{u} + \dfrac{1}{v} = \dfrac{1}{f}$

$$\frac{1}{220} + \frac{1}{v} = \frac{1}{-110}$$

$$\frac{1}{v} = -\frac{1}{110} - \frac{1}{220} = -\frac{3}{220}$$

$$v = \frac{-220}{3} = -73 \text{ mm}$$

∴ The virtual image is 73 mm from the lens.

$$\text{Magnification} = \frac{v}{u} = \frac{73}{220}\text{(numerically)} = \tfrac{1}{3}.$$

Power of a Lens

The power of a lens we define as the reciprocal of the focal length

$$p = \frac{1}{f}$$

The power is given by this equation in dioptres, if f is expressed in metres. The sign of the power is the same as the focal length, i.e., positive for a converging lens and negative for a diverging lens.

The total power of a lens is the sum of the powers of its two surfaces

$$p = p_1 + p_2$$

The power of each surface depends on the difference in refractive index on either side of the surface,

$$(\mu_{glass} - \mu_{air}), \text{ i.e., } (\mu_{glass} - 1)$$

and on the radius of curvature of the surface r

$$p_1 = (\mu - 1)\frac{1}{r_1}$$

The radius of curvature is expressed in metres and follows the sign convention. For the second surface of radius r_2

$$p_2 = (\mu - 1)\frac{1}{r_2}$$

Adding the surface powers, we get an expression for the total power, sometimes called the *lens makers equation*

$$p = (\mu - 1)\left(\frac{1}{r_1} + \frac{1}{r_2}\right)$$

A lens designer would use this equation to produce a lens of a required power from a material whose refractive index is known.

When two or more thin lenses are placed in contact the combined power is the sum of the separate powers

$$p_{(combination)} = p_a + p_b + \text{etc.}$$

This can be expressed in focal lengths as

$$\frac{1}{f} = \frac{1}{f_a} + \frac{1}{f_b} + \text{etc.}$$

These equations are derived from basic assumptions at the end of the chapter.

131

Problem: What radius of curvature would be needed for a plano-convex lens made of glass, refractive index 1·5, to have a power of 2 dioptres?

Solution:

$$\text{Power} = (\mu - 1)\left(\frac{1}{r_1} + \frac{1}{r_2}\right)$$

$$= (1\cdot5 - 1)\left(\frac{1}{r_1} + \frac{1}{\infty}\right)$$

$$= 0\cdot5\left(\frac{1}{r_1} + 0\right)$$

$$\therefore \quad 2 = \frac{0\cdot5}{r_1}$$

$$r_1 = 0\cdot25$$

∴ Radius of curvature required $= 0\cdot25$ m
$$= 250 \text{ mm}$$

Measurement of Lens Constants

You can obtain an approximate value of the focal length of a convex lens by focusing a sharp image of a distant object on a screen. (Fig. 12.7.)

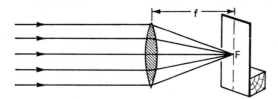

Fig. 12.7. We may determine the position of the principal focus for convex lens by focusing the image of a distant object on to a screen.

The position of the principal focus can be more accurately determined if you place a plane mirror behind the lens and find the point where object and image coincide. (Fig. 12.8.)

By far the most accurate and convenient instrument is the 'lens measurer' used by opticians. Basically, the instrument is a spherometer which

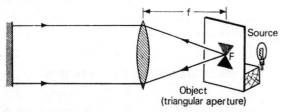

Fig. 12.8. When a plane mirror is placed behind the lens, object and image coincide at the principal focus. The rays are reflected normally and return along their original path.

measures the curvature of spherical surfaces. It has three pins in line, the centre pin being movable, spring loaded and geared to a pointer. (Fig. 12.9.) The scale may be calibrated directly in power, when it will refer specifically to lenses made from a material of a given refractive index. The instrument can be used for lenses made of other materials or for curved mirrors if we use it in conjunction with a scale of refractive indices.

Fig. 12.9. A lens measurer is a spherometer which gives a direct reading of the power or the radius of curvature of a spherical surface.

Lens Defects

If the light coming from the object were un-limited, then a quite simple spherical lens would produce a sharp image. This would be achieved by using only the centre of the lens near to the principal axis. In practice, light from the object is limited so that to produce an image of adequate illumination, a large area of lens, i.e., a wide aperture is required. Now a spherical refracting surface does not produce a sharp focus for wide apertures, therefore the image becomes blurred.

This blurring may be attributed to the specific shortcomings of lenses—called aberrations. You may ask why we persevere with spherical surfaces since they are subject to these aberrations. One answer is that for many purposes the aberration is not appreciable. Another reason is the com-parative ease with which high quality spherical surfaces can be manufactured. It is therefore easier to use several spherical surfaces designed to minimize aberrations than to use a single non-spherical shape.

A spherical surface is easy to manufacture because it has the same curvature in all directions and at all points. It makes no exacting demands on the positioning of the grinding equipment. (Fig. 12.10.) Any other shape of surface would require equipment capable of precise positioning and vibration free operation.

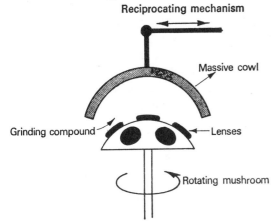

Fig. 12.10. Grinding of spherical surfaces. In the production of lenses, grinding compound is introduced between a reciprocating cowl and the lenses which are mounted on a rotating block.

Chromatic Aberration

The shorter the wave-length of a light-wave, the more it will deviate towards the normal when it strikes the surface of a material of higher optical density, so that violet light will deviate more than light from the red end of the spectrum, which has a longer wave-length. (Fig. 12.11.) Each particular colour of light gives rise to an image which is

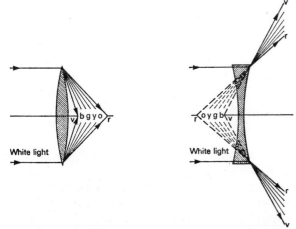

Fig. 12.11. Chromatic aberration is caused by the variation of refractive index with wave-length. The colours are brought to a focus in different positions.

slightly displaced from the images cast by other colours. Lines of contrast in the final image appear coloured and the image as a whole loses definition. This, the most troublesome of all lens defects, is called *chromatic aberration*. Note that the concave lens produces colour separation in the opposite direction to the convex lens.

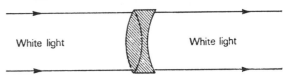

Fig. 12.12. When convex and concave lenses of the same material are combined, cancellation of the dispersion also results in zero deviation.

If a convex lens is placed in contact with a concave lens of the same power and material, the dispersion of the colours disappears, but so does the deviation. This fact was known to Newton, who applied himself to the problem but failed to solve it, and concluded that it was impossible to produce deviation of light without dispersion. So, indeed, it was in the seventeenth century, when scientists were restricted by the limited range of glasses available to them, but, in modern times, glass manufacturers have developed a wide variety of different types of glass, and can produce a glass with a high refractive index and low colour dispersion, or vice versa.

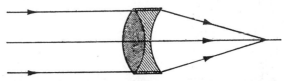

Fig. 12.13. When lenses of different materials are suitably combined, deviation can be produced without dispersion.

In designing an achromatic positive lens, we combine a powerful convex lens of low colour dispersion, with a less powerful concave lens of high colour dispersion. We select the lens powers so that their dispersions are equal in magnitude and opposite in direction, leaving a combination of net positive power but no colour dispersion. (Fig. 12.13.)

Spherical Aberration

A point focus only exists for a lens for small angles of deviation of rays through the lens. This is emphasized in the various approximations

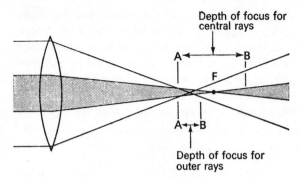

Fig. 12.14. Spherical aberration is a result of the peripheral rays meeting at a shorter focal distance than the central rays.

which are made in deriving the lens formula. When larger angles of deviation are allowed, images rapidly become blurred as the more deviated rays come to a shorter focus. (Fig. 12.14.) We frequently eliminate the external rays by a circular screen or stop, as it is called. Unfortunately, although image definition is improved by this, the amount of light entering the lens is reduced. Where the amount of light is critical, definition is sacrificed for greater illumination. In this case, the best image is produced in the plane of the circle of least confusion: this is the smallest circle through which all the rays from the lens pass. When designing a lens system, we minimize spherical aberration by sharing the deviation equally between the lens surfaces as shown in Fig. 12.15.

Distortion. When a stop is placed in front of the lens to control the aperture it cuts off the

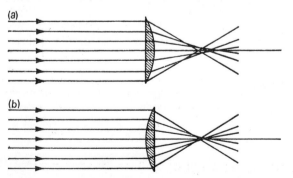

Fig. 12.15. To minimize spherical aberration, the deviation should be shared more equally between the surfaces, as in *(b)*, rather than in *(a)* where all the deviation occurs at the second surface.

shorter rays from off-axis points on the object. This has the effect of increasing the object distance *u*. The linear magnification *v/u* is less for the points furthest from the principal axis. The image of a regular pattern of squares has the shape shown in Fig. 12.16. This shape gives the name of *barrel distortion* to the defect.

A stop placed behind the lens causes the effective image distance to be increased and the *pin cushion* distortion of Fig. 12.17 is produced.

An important effect of the use of wider apertures is also illustrated by Fig. 12.14. If the image produced is acceptable, using the full aperture, then an equally or better defined image is obtained

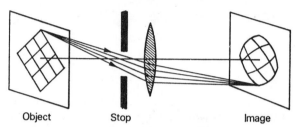

Fig. 12.16. A stop before the lens effectively increases the object distance for the extremity of the object, hereby reducing the magnification in this region. The result is barrel distortion.

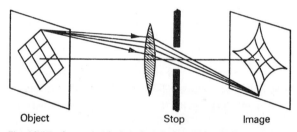

Fig. 12.17. A stop behind the lens increases the image distance for the extremities of the image, thus increasing the magnification and producing pin cushion distortion.

anywhere within the region *AB*. The distance from *A* to *B* is called the *depth of focus* and it is usually expressed in terms of the object positions corresponding to image positions *A* and *B*. The depth of focus increases as the aperture decreases.

The Camera Lens

The modern camera lens system is an example of design which minimizes the lens aberrations. (Fig. 12.18.) We place the stop between the lenses so that the pin cushion and barrel distortions cancel each other out. Each of the two component lenses is an achromatic doublet. We choose the separation of the lenses to equalize the deviations among the surfaces and thus minimize spherical aberration.

There are other aberrations of lenses in addition to the ones described. They can be minimized by adding more lens elements to the system but the cost soars while the improvement gets smaller and smaller.

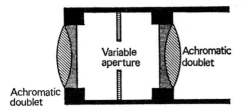

Fig. 12.18. A camera objective designed to minimize aberrations.

Derivation of Lens Equations

We have introduced the lens equations without derivation to streamline a first reading of this chapter. You will obtain a better understanding of the value of the equations and the limitation of spherical surfaces by following the derivations in detail.

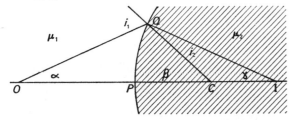

Fig. 12.19. Refraction at a single spherical surface.

Figure 12.19 shows a ray from an object on the principal axis making an angle i_1 with the normal to the surface at Q. The normal passes through the centre of curvature C. The refracted ray makes an angle i_2 with the normal and meets the surface at I where the image is formed. Then, from Snell's law

$$\mu_1 \sin i_1 = \mu_2 \sin i_2$$

If the rays make very small angles, i_1 and i_2 with the normal and if these angles are expressed in radians, then approximately

$$\mu_1 i_1 = \mu_2 i_2$$

Also

$$i_1 = \alpha + \beta$$
$$\beta = i_2 + \gamma$$

} The external angle of a triangle equals the sum of the opposite interior angles.

Combining these three equations to eliminate i_1 and i_2

$$\mu_1(\alpha + \beta) = \mu_2(\beta - \gamma)$$

or

$$\mu_1\alpha + \mu_2\gamma = (\mu_2 - \mu_1)\beta$$

If angles α, β, and γ are small, then the radian measure of the angles is equal to their tangents, i.e.,

$$\alpha = \frac{QP}{OP} \qquad \beta = \frac{QP}{CP} \qquad \gamma = \frac{QP}{IP}$$

Substituting these ratios in the above equation

$$\mu_1 \frac{QP}{OP} + \mu_2 \frac{QP}{IP} = (\mu_2 - \mu_1)\frac{QP}{CP}$$

Dividing through by QP and applying the sign convention to this case of real object and image and a converging surface

$$u = +OP \qquad v = +IP \qquad r = +CP$$

$$\frac{\mu_1}{u} + \frac{\mu_2}{v} = (\mu_2 - \mu_1)\frac{1}{r}$$

In order to preserve the sign convention, $(\mu_2 - \mu_1)$ is always reckoned a positive quantity.

Thin Lens Equation

The first surface of a lens refracts a ray from the object in the direction of I'. (Fig. 12.20.) Now, I' is a real image for the first surface but it becomes a virtual object for the second surface.

This is the first time that we have encountered a virtual object and it needs some explanation. Virtual objects only occur within optical systems and they can be recognized by the fact that they are associated with converging light, whereas light always diverges *from* a real object.

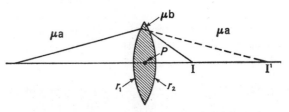

Fig. 12.20. Refraction at two spherical surfaces.

Assuming the two surfaces are approximately coincident at P, then for the first surface

$$\frac{\mu_a}{OP} + \frac{\mu_b}{I'P} = (\mu_a - \mu_b)\frac{1}{r_1}$$

and for the second surface

$$\frac{\mu_b}{-I'P} + \frac{\mu_a}{IP} = (\mu_a - \mu_b)\frac{1}{r_2}$$

Adding these equations to eliminate $I'P$ which does not interest us because no image is formed there,

$$\frac{\mu_a}{OP} + \frac{\mu_a}{IP} = (\mu_a - \mu_b)\left\{\frac{1}{r_1} + \frac{1}{r_2}\right\}$$

In general dealing with a lens of refractive index μ in air of refractive index $1 \cdot 0$

$$\frac{1}{u} + \frac{1}{v} = (\mu - 1)\left(\frac{1}{r_1} + \frac{1}{r_2}\right)$$

The r.h.s. of this equation is a constant for a given lens and is called the power of the lens. The relation of this power to the focal length can be understood by considering the extreme case of an object at a large distance from the lens which produces an image at the focal distance, i.e., $\mu = \infty$, $v = f$, hence

$$(\mu - 1)\left(\frac{1}{r_1} + \frac{1}{r_2}\right) = \frac{1}{\infty} + \frac{1}{f} = \frac{1}{f}$$

Thus
$$\frac{1}{u} + \frac{1}{v} = \frac{1}{f}$$

Combination of Thin Lenses in Contact

The first lens of Fig. 12.21 directs the rays towards an image at I', and the second lens deviates

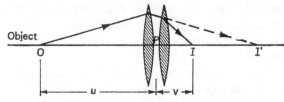

Fig. 12.21. A combination of two convex lenses.

the ray further to the final image at I. Writing the lens equation for both lenses, and remembering that I', a real image for the first lens becomes a virtual object for the second lens,

$$\frac{1}{u} + \frac{1}{PI'} = \frac{1}{f_1}$$

$$-\frac{1}{PI'} + \frac{1}{v} = \frac{1}{f_2}$$

adding

$$\frac{1}{u} + \frac{1}{v} = \frac{1}{f_1} + \frac{1}{f_2}$$

By comparing this with the equation of the previous section, we see that the combination behaves like a single lens of focal length f, such that

$$\frac{1}{f} = \frac{1}{f_1} + \frac{1}{f_2}$$

or written in terms of powers

$$p = p_1 + p_2$$

If you want to check on your understanding of the principles underlying the derivations of these lens equations, try to repeat them for diverging surfaces.

Questions

1. How would a parallel beam of light be affected by an air bubble shaped like a biconvex lens enclosed in a glass block?

2. If a spectacle lens is a diverging one, objects seen through it appear to move in the same direction as the lens when the lens moves from side to side, while through a converging lens they move the opposite way. Explain this.

3. What is a virtual object?

4. Why does the equation $\frac{1}{f} = \frac{1}{u} + \frac{1}{v}$ apply only to thin lenses?

5. What factors have to be considered when deciding which lens aperture to use when taking a photograph?

6. Under what circumstances can a diverging lens produce a real image?

7. If an object moves from infinity towards a converging lens, which way will the image move? Which way if the lens is a diverging one?

8. Why do we persevere with spherical lenses despite their aberrations?

9. Can a lens have more than one focal length?

10. In what two different ways can a convex lens produce a magnified image?

Problems

1. An object 20 mm high, 60 mm away from a convex lens and on its principal axis, produces an image 120 mm from the lens. What is the size of the image and the focal length of the lens?
   Answer: 40 mm, 40 mm.

2. An approximate way of finding the focal length of a converging lens is to measure the distance from the lens to the image produced by the lens of a distant object. If the lens has a focal length of 100 mm what percentage error is produced in the estimated focal length if the object is 500 mm, then 3·5 m away?
   Answer: 25 per cent, 3 per cent.

3. If a biconvex lens whose faces have radii of curvature of 100 and 150 mm is used in water, what is its focal length? ($\mu_{water} = 1\cdot33$, $\mu_{glass} = 1\cdot5$).
   Answer: 470 mm.

4. A lens of refractive index 1·5 has a convex surface of radius 200 mm and a concave one of radius 300 mm. What is its focal length?
   Answer: 1·2 m.

5. What radius of curvature would you give a plano-convex lens made from glass of refractive index 1·5, if you wanted a power of 2 dioptres?
   Answer: 250 mm.

6. A projector is used to throw an image of a 50 mm square colour slide on a screen 2 m away. If the image is 1 m square, how far is the slide from the lens?
   Answer: 100 mm.

7. A thin transparent globe, 2 m diameter is filled with water. Where does it focus a parallel beam of light? ($\mu_{water} = 1\cdot33$).
   Answer: 1·2 m beyond sphere.

8. Two lenses are in contact, a converging one of focal length 300 mm and a diverging one of focal length −100 mm. What is the focal length and the power of the combination?
   Answer: −150 mm, −6·7 dioptres.

9. A light beam is converging to a point 120 mm behind a lens before refraction and, after passing through the lens, converges to a point 200 mm behind the lens. What is the focal length of the lens?
   Answer: −300 mm.

10. A convex lens of focal length 60 mm is used to form an image twice as big as an object. How far is the object from the lens if the image is real and how far if it is virtual?
    Answer: 90 mm, 30 mm.

11. Moonlight passes through a converging lens of focal length 190 mm, which is 205 mm from a second converging lens of focal length 20 mm. Where is the image of the Moon produced by the lens combination?
    Answer: 145 mm from the first lens, 60 mm from the second.

12. A converging lens of focal length 150 mm and a diverging lens are mounted 90 mm apart, and a real image of the object 400 mm from the first lens is formed 300 mm beyond the second. What is the focal length of the diverging lens?
    Answer: −300 mm.

13. A thin biconvex lens is placed on a flat sheet of glass and the space between the two filled with water. The focal length of the whole is 216 mm. If the biconvex lens is turned over, and the space again filled with water, the focal length is 213 mm. If the focal length of the glass lens is 158 mm, what is the refractive index of the glass? ($\mu_{water} = 1\cdot33$).
    Answer: 1·63.

14. A plano-convex lens with a radius of curvature of 400 mm has a refractive index of 1·51 for red light and 1·53 for blue. What are the focal lengths of the lens for red and blue light? If the lens is 50 mm in diameter, what is the diameter of the red image of a distant light source on a screen when the blue image is focused on it?
    Answer: 785 mm, 755 mm, 1·91 mm.

15. A convex lens is used to form an image of a light filament on a screen with a linear magnification of 2½. If the lens is moved 300 mm nearer the screen, a sharp image is also formed on the screen. What is the focal length of the lens?
    Answer: 143 mm.

16. A symmetrical biconvex lens has a focal length of 150 mm. An object 80 mm from the lens coincides with its own image formed by refraction at the front of the lens and reflection at the back face. What is the refractive index of the lens?
    Answer: 1·57.

17. A camera telephoto lens is made up of a converging lens of focal length 50 mm mounted 30 mm in front of a diverging lens of focal length 25 mm. How far must the film be behind the diverging lens to receive a sharp image of a distant object?
    Answer: 100 mm.

18. A light bulb is 1 m from a screen and a converging lens is moved between the bulb and the screen. In moving from bulb to screen, two clear images are

focused on the screen, with the lens in two different positions. If the ratio of the lengths of the images is 1 : 5, what is the focal length of the lens?

Answer: 214 mm.

19. A camera is fitted with a plano-convex lens, of focal length 20 mm convex side outwards. What is the position and size of the image of an object 10 mm high placed 30 mm from the lens? What is its position and size if the camera is filled with water?

Answer: 60 mm from lens, 20 mm high; 80 mm from lens, 26·7 mm high.

20. A parallel light beam is diverged by a concave lens of focal length −125 mm and then made parallel once more by a convex lens of focal length 500 mm. How far are the two lenses apart?

Answer: 375 mm.

21. A small object is placed on the axis and 100 mm from one of the principal foci of a thin converging lens; the lens produces a real image of the object 400 mm from the other principal focus. Calculate the focal length of the lens and the linear magnification of the image. Derive any formulae used. Sketch the path of a pencil of rays from a point on the object, not on the axis, to the corresponding image point.

(I.E.R.E.)

Answer: 200 mm, 2.

13 Optical Instruments

The purpose of optical instruments is to extend human vision. This chapter shows how the geometrical optics of lenses, mirrors, and prisms is applied in the design of optical instruments, which play an essential part in every branch of science and engineering. Some of the instruments described in this chapter you will have used already, others you may use later in your work or leisure. The optical systems described here are basic ones which will help you to appreciate quickly the system of any instrument you meet.

The Eye

The optical instrument with which we are most familiar is the eye. We usually think of the eye as the organ with which we see the world around us, but, in fact, the eye cannot see at all. It is the brain that actually sees, using the eye as its primary optical instrument. Because the eye, like all human sense organs, is imperfect and capable of error, we have to invent other optical instruments to help it to convey accurate information to our brains. Some of these, the camera, for instance, imitate the workings of the eye very closely indeed; conversely, we can consider the eye as a type of camera, and describe it as such.

Basically, the eye consists of a convex lens, which produces a real, inverted, and diminished image on the screen formed by the curved back of the eye-ball. (Fig. 13.1.) This surface, called the *retina*, is covered with millions of nerve-endings, which are sensitive to light, and which transmit messages to the brain about the shape and colour of the image. The brain sorts out these messages, and from the small, upside-down image on the

retina interprets the information it receives about the world outside. The eye, of course, like the camera, has to alter its focus according to the distance of the object it is looking at, the power of its lens being controlled by the *ciliary* muscles.

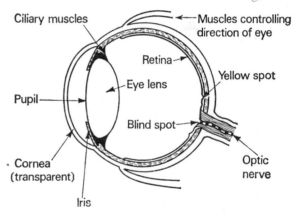

Fig. 13.1. This is a cross-sectional plan view of the right eye.

The eye is only sensitive to fine detail over a very small area, called the *yellow spot*, at the centre of the retina. This spot, which corresponds to a visual angle of only 1°, is rich in *cones*, nerve-endings which record the detail of an image. You will have noticed when you are reading, how your eyes move jerkily over the page, jumping from one phrase to the next, because outside your direct line of vision you cannot clearly distinguish the outline of a word.

The second type of light-sensitive nerves are the *rods*, which predominate in the rest of the retina. These rods are sensitive to a lower level of illumination than the cones, and we rely on them

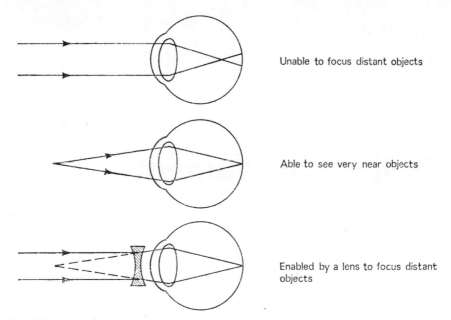

Unable to focus distant objects

Able to see very near objects

Enabled by a lens to focus distant objects

Fig. 13.2. In myopia, or short sight, the eye lens does not relax sufficiently to focus distant objects on the retina.

to see in poor lighting. We can, in fact, detect dimly-lit objects more clearly when we are not looking directly at them. The rods are also more sensitive to movement than the cones, and this is why you can catch a moving ball an instant after you have seen it out of the corner of your eye.

At the point where the optic nerve passes through the retina, the absence of nerve endings causes an area of blindness, the *blind spot*. You are not normally conscious of this gap in your vision but you can detect it as follows. Make two large dots about 8 cm apart. Cover the right eye

and look at the right-hand dot with your left eye. Vary the distance between your face and the paper, and the left hand dot will disappear as its image falls on the blind spot.

The retina is protected from over-illumination by the iris, an opaque coloured membrane at the front of the eye. It responds to strong light by contracting the pupil, which is the aperture at the centre of the iris. Both the iris and the pupil are protected by a transparent layer of tissue, called the cornea, and the whole eye is kept clean by the eyelids which wipe it clean every few seconds.

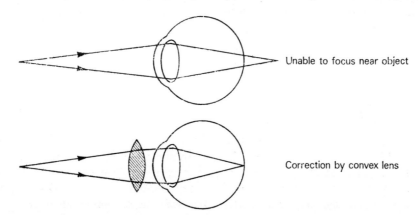

Unable to focus near object

Correction by convex lens

Fig. 13.3. In hypermetropia, or far sight, the eye lens is not powerful enough to focus near objects on to the retina. The condition is corrected by a convex lens.

140

The brain, of course, does not rely only on the information it receives from one eye, but considers the images formed simultaneously on the retinas of two eyes; and, because the two eyes are in different positions, the image received by one is slightly different from the image received by the other. By this means the degree of parallax occurring between objects at different distances is measured by the brain, which enables it to conceive the objects in three dimensions, and to estimate the distance of the objects. The binocular nature of our vision has been imitated in the stereoscopic camera, and has been given a more practical application in the range-finder.

Defects of the Eye

Myopia (*Short Sight*). This defect arises because the eye lens is not matched to the depth of the eye ball. The lens is unable to relax sufficiently to focus parallel light. (Fig. 13.2a.)

Even when fully relaxed the eye lens is too powerful and the image is focused in front of the retina. On the other hand, when the ciliary muscles are tensed, the eye can usually see objects much closer to the eye than normal, (Fig. 13.2b), hence the name of the defect, short sight.

A concave lens enables the eye to see distant objects because it makes the light diverge as though from a less distant object. (Fig. 13.2c).

Hypermetropia (*Far Sight*). An eye subject to the defect of *hypermetropia* is unable to focus on objects close at hand. The condition is sometimes called far sight or long sight which means that distant objects are seen more clearly than closer ones. The ciliary muscles cannot contract sufficiently to bring the image of near objects to a focus on the retina. (Fig. 13.3a.) A convex correcting lens converges light from the near object and makes it appear to come from a more distant position which the eye can cope with. (Fig. 13.3b.)

The *near point* of the eye is the nearest point at which it can see distinctly. It varies considerably from person to person. The exact distance of the near point at which we consider an eye to be defective and, therefore, to need correction is a matter of choice. If we choose the average value of the near point, then 50 per cent of people require spectacles. We choose the value of 0·25 m which is

a few cm outside the average value. Any person who cannot see clearly objects closer than 0·25 m is prescribed spectacles which enable him to do so. We regard this distance as the standard near point in the design and evaluation of optical instruments.

Accommodation in optics is the range of adjustment of the eye between the furthest and nearest distances of clear vision. In the normal eye, this extends from infinity to at least 0·25 m. With advancing years, the range of accommodation reduces until myopia or hypermetropia, or even both, are present. This may necessitate two pairs of spectacles or, alternatively, a single pair with bifocal lenses. (Fig. 13.4.) This defect of reduced accommodation is called *presbiopia*.

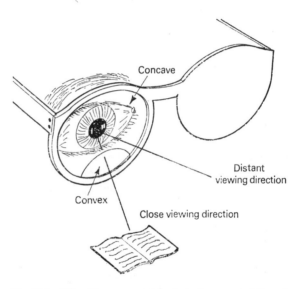

Fig. 13.4. Bifocal lenses correct for lack of accommodation of the eye at both extremes of the range of vision.

Astigmatism is a defect caused by the eye lens having different curvatures along different axes through the lens. It is corrected by fitting a lens which is itself asymmetric, i.e., strong in the direction in which the eye is weak, and weak where the eye is strong. The simplest case would be that of a lens curved only in one axis, i.e., a section from a cylinder. (Fig. 13.5.) In practice, astigmatism may be combined with other eye defects and require a corrective lens which is curved in two directions.

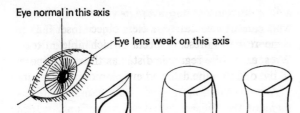

Eye normal in this axis

Eye lens weak on this axis

Fig. 13.5. A cylindrical lens is used to correct simple astigmatism. Where it is combined with other defects, the corrective lens has a more complex shape.

Magnification of Optical Instruments

In order to see an object in greater detail, the size of the image on the retina must be increased. The retinal image size depends not so much on the size of the object but rather on the angle it subtends at the eye. So far we have found the notion of linear magnification a useful one, but its limitation can be seen if we consider the case of an image produced at infinity. (Fig. 13.6.) The linear magnification is infinite, but can we see the object in infinite detail? Of course we cannot, because there is insufficient light coming from the image and we cannot get near the image to view it.

A better measure of the improvement in vision produced by an instrument is the angular magnification defined as follows:

Angular magnification

$$= \frac{\text{angle subtended by the image in the instrument}}{\substack{\text{angle subtended to the naked eye by the object} \\ \text{in its optimum position}}}$$

More briefly:

$$m = \frac{\text{angle of image}}{\text{angle of object}}$$

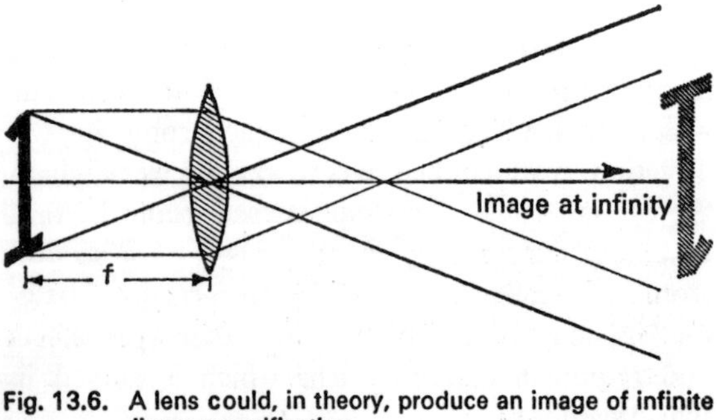

Fig. 13.6. A lens could, in theory, produce an image of infinite linear magnification.

142

Note: In the evaluation of the angular magnification of a telescope, the optimum position of the object—the Moon, for example, or a mountain—is beyond our control, and is, therefore, where it happens to be. In the calculation of the magnification of a microscope, on the other hand, the optimum position is taken to be the standard near-point distance of 0·25 m.

The Magnifying Glass

An object placed within the focal length of a convex lens gives rise to an erect and magnified image further from the lens than the object. This enables the object to be viewed when it is much nearer the eye than would otherwise be possible.

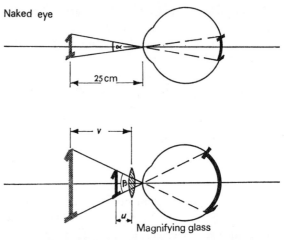

Fig. 13.7. The magnifying glass produces angular magnification by allowing the object to be viewed clearly much closer than with the naked eye. Angular magnification = β/α.

In this position the object subtends a greater angle at the eye and therefore produces a larger image on the retina.

The eye and the lens are approximately in the same position, and the best position of the virtual image is at the standard near point distance of 0·25 m. As usual the scale of the diagram has been exaggerated, and in practice the angles are small enough to be replaced by their tangents.

Angular magnification:

$$m = \beta/\alpha = \frac{\tan \beta}{\tan \alpha} = \frac{h_2/0\cdot25}{h_1/0\cdot25}$$

$$m = h_2/h_1$$

Thus, in the particular case of the simple magnifying glass, the linear and angular magnifications are equal. You can see from Fig. 13.7 that the image on the retina is greatest when the object is as near as possible to the eye. With the image at 0·25 m, the minimum distance of the object, distance u depends on the focal length of the lens.

Using the lens equation $\dfrac{1}{u} + \dfrac{1}{v} = \dfrac{1}{f}$, for a virtual image at the near point $\dfrac{1}{u} + \dfrac{1}{-0.25} = \dfrac{1}{f}$

This equation shows that the smaller the focal length f, then the smaller the value of the object distance u. The lower limit to the value of f is set by the distortion which occurs when the curvature of the surfaces is very great. To obtain greater magnification the deviation is shared between two lenses as in the compound microscope.

The Compound Microscope

The compound microscope consists basically of two lenses of very short focal length. A minute object placed just outside the focal length of the objective lens produces a magnified real and inverted image. (Fig. 13.8.) This image falls inside

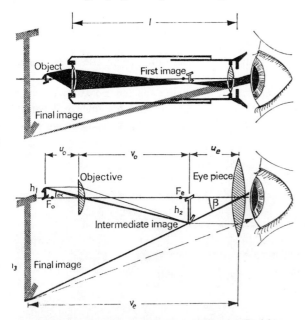

Fig. 13.8. The compound microscope produces a final image which is inverted virtual and magnified.

the focal length of the eyepiece and hence produces a final image which is further magnified and remains inverted. Being virtual, this image could not be received on a screen at I and it is viewed by the eye which is placed near to the eyepiece. The magnification of the instrument is the ratio of the visual angles subtended by the object with and without the instrument

$$m = \frac{\beta}{\alpha} = \frac{\text{angle subtended by final image}}{\text{angle subtended by the object at 0·25 m}}$$

If the final image is at a distance v_e from the eyepiece and all distances are measured in metres

$$m = \frac{h_3/v_e}{h_1/0.25}$$
$$= \frac{h_3}{h_1}\frac{0.25}{v_e} = \frac{h_3}{h_2}\frac{h_2}{h_1}\frac{0.25}{v_e}$$
$$= \frac{v_e}{u_e}\frac{v_o}{u_o}\frac{0.25}{v_e} = \frac{v_o}{u_o}\frac{0.25}{u_e}$$

The specified magnification is obtained by placing the final image at 0·25 m from the eye. Viewing at that distance is tiring for long periods and for a small sacrifice in magnification the image can be viewed at infinity. To achieve this, the eyepiece is moved back slightly until $u_e = f_e$.

Problem: A compound microscope has an objective with a focal length of 10 mm and a tube 100 mm long. An image is produced 0·25 m from the eyepiece when the object is 12 mm from the objective. What is the angular magnification produced?

Solution: $\dfrac{1}{u_o} + \dfrac{1}{v_o} = \dfrac{1}{f_o}$

$$\frac{1}{0.012} + \frac{1}{v_o} = \frac{1}{f_o}$$

$$\frac{1}{v_o} = \frac{1}{0.01} - \frac{1}{0.012} = \frac{1}{0.06}$$

$$v_o = 0.06 \text{ m} \quad (60 \text{ mm})$$

therefore $u_e = 0.10 - 0.06 = 0.04$ m

and magnification $= \dfrac{v_o}{u_o}\dfrac{0.25}{u_e} = \dfrac{0.06}{0.012}\dfrac{0.25}{0.04} = 31$

An approximate value for the magnification of a microscope can be calculated from the equation

$$m = \frac{v_o}{u_o}\frac{0.25}{u_e}$$

143

Since the image distance v_o occupies almost all the length of the main tube, l, and the object is nearly at the focal length of the objective, i.e., $u_o \simeq f_o$. (Fig. 13.8b.)

thus
$$m \simeq \frac{l}{f_o}\frac{0 \cdot 25}{f_e} \ (f_o, f_e \text{ in metres})$$

This is useful when the focal length of the lenses are known. Frequently, the magnifications are marked on the objectives and eyepiece, in which case we calculate the overall magnification from $m = m_o \times m_e$. To increase the magnification of a microscope, we reduce f_o or f_e or increase the length of the tube. Cheaper microscopes have a variable tube length, while more expensive instruments may have a selection of alternative objectives or eyepieces. Undesirable effects may accompany an increase in magnification. For example, at larger magnifications, more light is required, and larger angles of light must be received by the lenses. Thus, they are more likely to have image defects due to aberration than less powerful lenses. The optimum magnification of a microscope is not the greatest one possible but the one which effects the best compromise between these factors. The *endoscope* used to examine internal organs of the body is a very specialized form of microscope which has a small magnification to maintain a larger field of view. (Fig. 13.9.)

Resolving Power

The resolving power of an optical instrument is a measure of its ability to produce separate images of objects which are very close together. This ability is associated with the diffraction of light and it improves as the aperture of the lenses increases. The resolving power is just as important a feature of an instrument's design as its magnification. For example, it may be useless to further magnify an image which is basically indistinct.

The image of an object being viewed must be big enough and bright enough to be seen and, in addition, it must be well resolved. In some cases, these requirements are conflicting. Large magnifications demand high resolving powers, which together are provided by powerful lenses and wide angle apertures. These are just the circumstances under which lens aberrations are exaggerated. When an object emits insufficient light, the remedy is not simply to illuminate the object more strongly. The heat from too intense a concentration of light may cause damage to a biological specimen, or cause convection currents in a liquid specimen.

For greater resolving power the oil-immersion objective satisfies some of these conflicting requirements, by using a property of a spherical surface not yet mentioned. For a given single spherical surface there exists one object and image position for which no spherical aberration occurs, and a very wide angle of rays from the object produces a sharp image. (Fig. 13.10.a) The two points are called aplanatic points of the surface. One problem remains; since the aplanatic points exist only for a single surface the object must be placed inside the material of the lens. This is achieved by filling the space between the object and the lens with an oil which has the same refractive index as the lens itself. (Fig. 13.10b.)

The light rays are admitted to the second lens without deviation because they meet the surface at right angles. Leaving the second surface under aplanatic conditions the light becomes sufficiently converged to be dealt with by a third conventional lens.

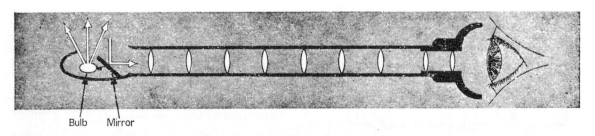

Bulb   Mirror

Fig. 13.9. Endoscopes have a train of lenses accurately located within a narrow tube and are used to view internal organs such as the throat or the stomach.

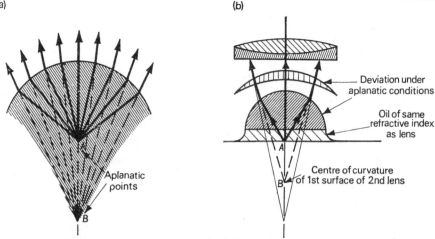

(a)   (b)

Deviation under
aplanatic conditions

Oil of same
refractive index
as lens

Aplanatic
points

Centre of curvature
of 1st surface of 2nd lens

Fig. 13.10. A spherical surface has two aplanatic points *A* and *B* such that a wide angle of rays from *A* diverges after refraction as though from *B*, without any spherical aberration (a). In the oil-immersion objective, two surfaces refract in this way (b).

Telescopes

The astronomical telescope has a basic optical system similar to the compound microscope. (Fig. 13.11.) An important difference, however, is that the objective lens has a long focal length. This produces a large intermediate image of a distant object at the focal length of the objective.

The magnification of a telescope is always quoted for the case of normal adjustment, i.e., with the final image at infinity (eye relaxed).

$$m = \frac{\text{angle subtended by image}}{\text{angle subtended by object}}$$

$$= \frac{\beta}{\alpha} = \frac{h/f_e}{h/f_o}$$

$$m = \frac{f_o}{f_e}$$

The magnification may be increased slightly by producing the final image at the near point distance of 250 mm. The final image of the telescope is laterally inverted and upside down which makes it nonetheless useful for astronomical use. We can modify it for general use as shown in Fig. 13.12 when we call it a *terrestrial telescope*.

Binoculars are a modification of the astronomical telescope whereby an erect image is produced and the tube length of the instrument shortened. The light is totally internally reflected four times by two 45 degree prisms. (Fig. 13.13.) The larger rectangular surfaces of the prisms are parallel and their triangular surfaces are at right angles to each other.

Galileo, the first man to direct a telescope towards the stars, used a concave lens, as the eyepiece of his telescope. The system of the Galilean telescope is still used in opera glasses. The concave lens must have a shorter focal length than the convex objective and the lenses are situated so that their focal points coincide. (Fig. 13.14.) Parallel light from a distant object is converged by the objective and diverged by the eyepiece, to produce a virtual image at infinity, which subtends a greater angle than the object.

$$\text{Magnification } m = \frac{\beta}{\alpha} = \frac{f_o}{f_e}$$

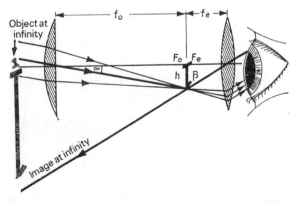

Fig. 13.11. The astronomical telescope produces an inverted magnified image.

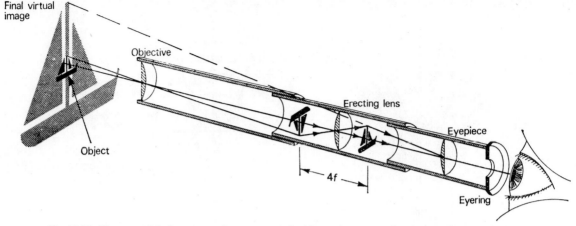

Fig. 13.12. The terrestrial telescope produces an erect final image by means of an intermediate erecting lens. This lens increases the length of the telescope by at least four times its focal length.

The instrument is conveniently short $(f_o - f_e)$ but, because of its small field of view, it is used only for magnifications of about two or three.

Telescopes with magnifications less than one are sometimes used in camera viewfinders or range-finders. (Fig. 13.15.)

Reflecting Telescopes

All refracting surfaces suffer from chromatic aberration, which can be reduced by combining several optical elements. The grinding of several large surfaces for use in large instruments is costly, however, and to mount heavy elements in

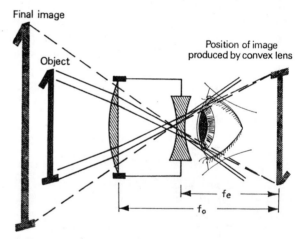

Fig. 13.14. Galilean telescope. The instrument produces an upright final image; its tube length is short but its field of view is small.

a large telescope in such a way that they are both stable and well-balanced requires huge supports and a massive control mechanism. Almost all large modern astronomical telescopes, therefore, have reflecting objectives, because these are free from chromatic aberration and because the balance of the telescopes is improved when their heaviest elements are placed at the bottom. (Fig. 13.16.)

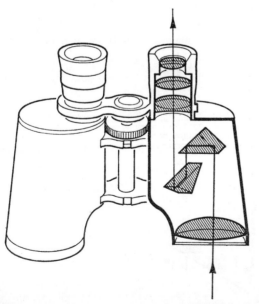

Fig. 13.13. The prisms in binoculars produce a final upright image and reduce the physical length of the tube.

146

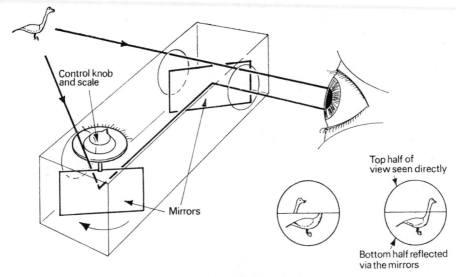

Fig. 13.15. The range-finder superimposes the views from two horizontally displaced positions. The images of an object are made to coincide by rotating one mirror, the position of which correlates with the range of the object.

Control knob and scale

Mirrors

Top half of view seen directly

Bottom half reflected via the mirrors

The Eye Ring

The rays of light which build up the final image in an optical instrument must naturally pass through every lens in that instrument. Each lens

Pole star

F

F

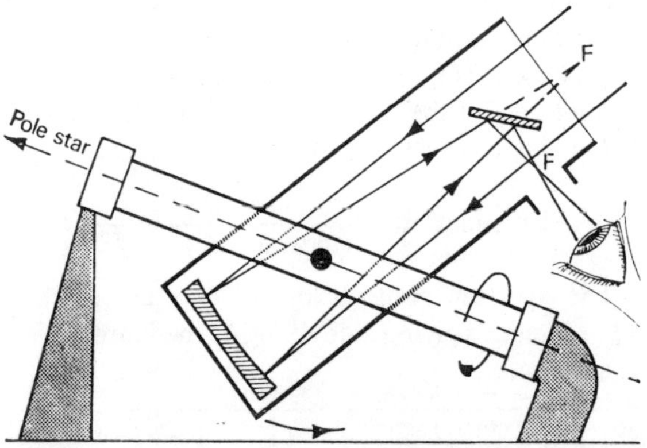

Fig. 13.16. In the reflecting telescope, the main mirror is parabolic. The subsidiary plane mirror which diverts the image to the side where there is more room for recording instruments obscures only a small fraction of the total aperture.

in turn occupies an aperture which sets a limit on the amount of light passing through it. The pupil of the eye is also an aperture, and its position is, therefore, an important feature of the optical system. To ensure that the eye, like all the other lens-apertures, adopts the best position for admitting all the light that has travelled through the

instrument, the casing of the instrument is made to extend beyond the eye-piece, to form the *eye ring*. (Fig. 13.17.)

Projectors

A projector has two distinct parts; the system of illumination and the projection lens. The large magnification produced by projectors demands a very high level of illumination which is usually provided by a tungsten filament or carbon arc source. A large fraction of the total light from

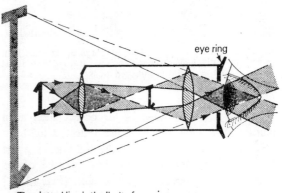

eye ring

The dotted line is the limit of eye piece
The full line is the limit of objective

Fig. 13.17. The eye ring locates the eye where it receives most light from the object. The dotted rays pass through the limit of the eyepiece and the full rays through the limit of the objective.

the source is directed on to the film by a curved mirror and condensing lens system. (Fig. 13.18). This particular arrangement of the condenser lenses minimizes spherical and chromatic aberrations, giving an even white illumination of the film. This film lies just outside the focus of a lens which produces a real magnified image on the screen. The film itself is inverted and gives rise to an upright image.

A liquid filter, which absorbs the infra-red component of the radiation, or a fan protects the film from the intense heat of the source.

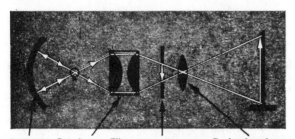

Reflector Condenser Film or transparency Projection lens

Fig. 13.18. The projector produces high magnifications and requires a very intensely illuminated object.

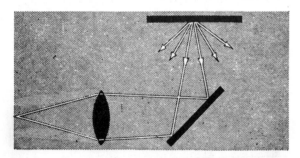

Fig. 13.19. The episcope projects an image by reflected light for pictures of strong contrast. It gives best results when used in a darkened room.

To project the image of an object such as a picture in a book we must use reflected light. In this case only a fraction of the light leaving the surface reaches the projection lens because of the diffusion which occurs at the surface. (Fig. 13.19.) The low illumination of the final image makes this instrument, called the *episcope*, more suitable for use in a darkened room. In special cases the Schmidt optical system is used to project an image of a surface diffusing light. (Fig. 13.20.)

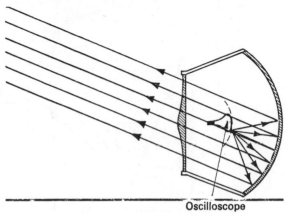

Oscilloscope

Fig. 13.20. The Schmidt camera or projector can be used for very wide angles and apertures. The spherical aberration of a concave spherical mirror is eliminated by a non-spherical correction plate or lens. This optical system is used to project television pictures.

The Camera

The simplest form of camera is a box with a pinhole at one end. (Fig. 13.21.) The image is made up of light from points on the object defined into narrow beams by the pinhole. If the pinhole is increased in area, the image becomes brighter but more diffuse. In order to obtain enough light to expose a photographic film adequately, a convex lens is used. (Fig. 13.22.) The light energy falling on unit area of the film increases with the diameter of the lens but decreases with its focal length.

$$\text{Illumination} \propto \frac{(\text{diameter})^2}{(\text{focal length})^2} = \frac{d^2}{f^2}$$

The aperture controls of cameras are marked off at intervals giving a doubling of the illumination in each case.

$\frac{d^2}{f^2} \propto$ illumination $\propto$	$\frac{1}{500}$	$\frac{1}{250}$	$\frac{1}{125}$	$\frac{1}{63}$	$\frac{1}{32}$	$\frac{1}{16}$
f numbers (f/d)	22	16	11	8	5·6	4

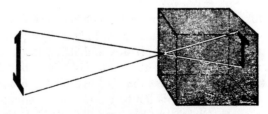

Fig. 13.21. The pinhole camera.

148

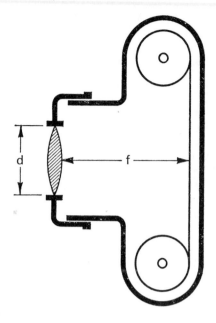

The values of f/d, called f numbers, are marked alongside each of these divisions, called stops.

Moving objects must be snapped in a short interval of time to prevent a blurred effect due to the movement of the image. Thus, the speed of opening and closing of a shutter over the aperture must be short. This requires an increased size of aperture to provide adequate illumination of the film.

The lens can be moved to focus objects from about a metre distance to infinity. In general, we use as small an aperture as possible in order to increase the depth of focus of the lens.

Fig. 13.22. The illumination of the film increases with the area of the lens and reduces with the lens to screen separation.

Questions

1. In what ways is the eye like a camera and in what ways is it different?
2. The lenses in our eyes are convex and produce real, inverted images on our retinas. Why then do things appear the right way up?
3. Suggest reasons why very powerful binoculars are not used for watching horse-races.
4. By using an anamorphic lens system, it is possible to compress a Cinemascope image on the 35 mm wide film. Suggest how this can be projected to give a normal Cinemascope image.
5. Why do children who suffer from miopia often grow up with normal sight?
6. Suggest factors which limit the amount of detail which can be seen by the unaided eye.

7. To what extent, when considering optical systems, do we worry about the focal length of the lens of our eye which, after all, forms part of the system?
8. Can a telescope be used with a camera to take enlarged pictures without modifying either instrument? What are the difficulties?
9. How is the f number of a lens affected (a) by an increase in its focal length and (b) by an increase in its aperture?
10. In enlarging films, some of the defects of the camera lens can be cancelled out by using the same lens backwards in the enlarger. Which defects can be cancelled and which cannot?

Problems

1. The objective of an astronomical telescope has a focal length of 800 mm and the eyepiece has a focal length of 50 mm. How far apart should the lenses be situated when both object and image are at a great distance?
   Answer: 850 mm.
2. A portrait camera lens has an aperture of 18 mm. If its f number is 2·8, what is its focal length?
   Answer: +50·4 mm.
3. The lens of a camera has an aperture of 40 mm. If its focal length is +112 mm, what is its f number?
   Answer: 2·8.

4. A long-sighted person has a least distance of distinct vision of 1 m. What is the power of lens required to restore normal sight?
   Answer: 3 dioptres.
5. A short-sighted person has a least distance of distinct vision of 200 mm and a greatest distance of distinct vision of 2 m. If he wishes to see distant objects, what power of lens does he need and what is his least distance of distinct vision with the lens?
   Answer: ½ dioptre, 222 mm.
6. A compound microscope has a 12 mm focal length objective and a 75 mm focal length eyepiece, and the

two lenses are mounted 200 mm apart. If the final image is 225 mm from the eyepiece, what is the magnification produced?

Answer: 49.

7. A refracting astronomical telescope of angular magnification 1000 has an objective of 15 m focal length. What is the focal length of the eyepiece?

Answer: 15 mm.

8. If the Moon subtends an angle of $\frac{1}{2}$ degree, what is the diameter of the Moon's image produced by the objective of a telescope of focal length 9·14 m?

Answer: 79·6 mm.

9. Opera glasses are made with objectives of 100 mm focal length and with the eyepiece lenses 80 mm away from the objectives. What is the focal length of the objectives and what angular magnification is produced?

Answer: 20 mm, 5.

10. What is the diameter of the image of the Sun formed by the mirror of the 5 m reflecting telescope at Mount Palomar, which has a focal length of 18 m? (Distance of Sun $= 1·5 \times 10^{11}$ m, diameter $1·4 \times 10^9$ m.)

Answer: 168 mm.

11. A Galilean telescope has an objective of 120 mm focal length and an eyepiece of 50 mm focal length. If the image seen by the eye is 300 mm from the eyepiece, what is the angular magnification?

Answer: 2·8.

12. A photograph of primitive earthworks is taken from an aircraft flying at 1500 m using a camera of focal length 250 mm and the negative is enlarged ten times. The earthworks are 100 mm long on the enlargement. What is their actual size?

Answer: 60 m.

13. A refracting astronomical telescope is made up with two converging lenses of focal length 300 mm and 50 mm and focused on the Moon. How far must the eyepiece lens be moved to focus on an object 6 m away?

Answer: 16 mm.

14. A Galilean telescope is designed to consist of two lenses of focal lengths 150 mm and −50 mm. How much movement must the eyepiece be allowed if the instrument is to focus down to 5 m?

Answer: 4·7 mm.

15. A pair of binoculars is designated 11 × 60. If its eyepieces have a focal length of 25 mm, what are the focal lengths and diameters of its objectives?

Answer: 275 mm, 60 mm.

16. A person whose least distance of distinct vision is 250 mm uses a convex lens of focal length 50 mm to form a virtual magnified image. What is the maximum angular magnification if the lens is close to the eye?

Answer: 6.

17. If the eye lens becomes opaque, it can be removed by an operation, and the eye can then be considered as filled with fluid of refractive index 1·33. If the diameter of the eyeball is 20 mm and the radius of curvature of the front of the eye is 10 mm, what power of spectacle lens is needed to focus distant objects on the retina?

Answer: 16·7 dioptres.

18. A microscope has a 30 mm focal length objective and a 60 mm focal length eyepiece set 260 mm apart. If it is used to project an image on a screen 1·5 m from the eyepiece, how far must the object be from the objective?

Answer: 35·7 mm.

19. What accuracy in range is possible using a range-finder of 2 m base to measure a range of 100 m if the movable mirror angle can be measured to $\pm 0·005$ degree?

Answer: Max. error is 11·6 per cent.

20. An astronomical refracting telescope, with an objective of focal length 1 m and eyepiece of focal length 25 mm, is adjusted to project a real image of the Sun, 96 mm in diameter, on a screen 300 mm behind the eyepiece. What angle does the Sun subtend at the objective?

Answer: $\frac{1}{2}$ degree.

21. Draw a ray diagram to illustrate the action of a reflecting telescope. Write a short essay comparing the action and capabilities of an optical and a radio telescope.

(I.E.R.E.)

22. Explain what is meant by the magnifying power of an optical instrument. Give ray diagrams of (i) a simple microscope and (ii) a refracting telescope to illustrate your answer.

A distant object subtends an angle of 0·1 degree at the objective of an astronomical telescope. If the objective lens has a focal length of 1 m, what is the diameter of the image formed by the objective? How far from the eyepiece, which has a focal length of 100 mm, should this image be formed, if the final image is to be formed 250 mm from the eyepiece?

(I.E.R.E.)

Answer: 1·75 mm, 71·4 mm.

14 Illumination

The comfort, speed and precision with which we can do a job depends very largely on how well we can see to do it. If we have normal eyesight, we still need adequate lighting to be able to use it, and architects and interior designers, when planning new offices, factories and other buildings, have to give very careful consideration to their illumination. In this, they are helped by modern methods of building, which enable the exteriors of buildings to be composed almost entirely of glass, and by modern techniques of artificial lighting, which illuminate interiors to daylight standards, efficiently and economically. An excellent example of the skill of today's lighting engineers is the bowling-alley, in which a high standard of illumination is produced without the discomfort of glare.

Lighting engineers, of course, do more than merely provide adequate illumination; they also use lighting to create atmosphere and to add variety to our surroundings. In the theatre, for example, artistic use is made of lighting to enhance scenic effects and to suggest mood, and the restrained lighting in clubs and coffee-bars induces an intimate atmosphere, in which people can take pleasure in meeting and talking to their friends. The photographer and television engineer, too, are particularly concerned with illumination, and make the most exacting demands on its control. To meet this need for the precise control of illumination in our homes and public buildings, on film sets, in the theatre, in the television tube, and in thousands of other applications, engineers require two things—accurate methods of measurement, and a convenient system of units.

The Candela

The establishment of the modern unit of light source power has an interesting story of development and it illustrates the way in which many quantities have been internationally standardized. Very often the most obvious standard is not the one best suited to the ultimate requirements of science or industry, and early mistakes can be very costly. When the demand for a new unit emerges, we recognize it to be of great importance, and an international committee considers the problem. Such a committee at the right time might have avoided the irrationalities of the British systems of weights, measures and currency, and we should not now be faced with the difficult and costly task of changing them.

The earliest standards of light source power were candles. Although they were of specified material and size, scientists could not depend on their being identical. Lamps burning pentane and other fuels replaced them, and were better in this respect. The adoption of different lamps as national standards by different countries caused some difficulty, and the increasing demand for greater accuracy eventually made even the better designs of lamp inadequate. Meanwhile engineers had developed the electric filament lamp whose dimensions and operating conditions they could more accurately specify and control. In 1909, America, Britain, and France agreed to a standard defined in terms of carbon filament lamps, which was a great step forward. Gradually more countries accepted this standard and it became the basis of the 'international candle'.

Even filament lamps change significantly with

use, however, and it became obvious that a standard independent of the performance of particular lamps was needed. In 1948, such a standard was internationally adopted. Its name is the *candela* and it is about the same size as the candle power. The candela is defined as the luminous intensity of 1/600,000 of a square metre of a radiating cavity at the temperature of freezing platinum (2042K).

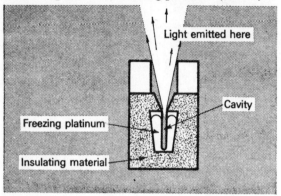

Fig. 14.1. Apparatus to determine the standard candela

The experiment to realize the standard is not an easy one and is performed only once every few years. On these occasions, filament lamp sub-standards are calibrated and used for the more routine standardizations.

The Solid Angle

In order to appreciate certain aspects of light measurement, we must understand the way in which the space around a point can be divided into solid angles. The solid angle or *steradian*, as we call it, may be considered as the three-dimensional equivalent of a radian. A radian is the angle subtended at the centre of a circle by a length of arc equal to the radius at the circumference. The three-dimensional equivalent of a radian divides the sphere around a point into areas each equal to r^2. (Fig. 14.2b.) *A unit solid angle is the angle subtended at the centre of a sphere by an area r^2 on its surface.* The total number of unit solid angles surrounding a point is equal to

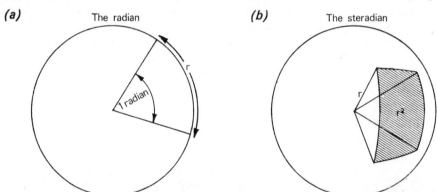

Fig. 14.2. The steradian in three dimensions may be compared with the radian in two dimensions.

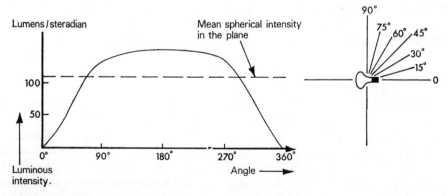

Fig. 14.3. The graph shows the variation of luminous intensity with angle for the 100 watt light source on the right.

the number of areas r^2 on the surface of the sphere i.e.,

$$\frac{\text{surface area of sphere}}{r^2} = \frac{4\pi r^2}{r^2} = 4\pi$$

Thus there are $4\pi = 12\cdot57$ solid angles surrounding a point.

The Lumen ✕

If a one candela source radiates uniformly in all directions, the amount falling within a unit solid angle is called a lumen. The lumen is a subdivision of the candela such that

$$1 \text{ candela} = 4\pi \text{ lumens} = 12\cdot57 \text{ lm}$$

Luminous Intensity

In practice sources are never symmetrical. A one candela source will have a power greater than unity in some directions, and correspondingly less than unity in others. We call the effective candle power in a certain direction *luminous intensity* and we measure it by *the number of lumens per unit solid angle in that particular direction*. The variation of the luminous intensity with angle in one plane through a light bulb is shown in the graph of Fig. 14.3.

Problem: Fifty per cent of the light from a source of 80 candelas is evenly distributed through a solid angle of 3 steradians. What is the luminous intensity in this direction?

Solution:

$$\text{Luminous intensity} = \frac{\text{No. of lumens}}{\text{solid angle}}$$

$$= \frac{80 \times 4\pi}{3} \cdot \frac{50}{100}$$

$$= 168 \text{ lumens/steradian}$$

Polar Diagram

We can express the same results in the form of a polar diagram. (Fig. 14.4.)

The luminous intensities are set off directly as radii along the directions in which the measurements are made. The average value of the luminous intensity in the plane is shown as a dotted circle in Fig. 14.4. We could draw polar diagrams for many planes through the source and find a grand

(a)

(b)

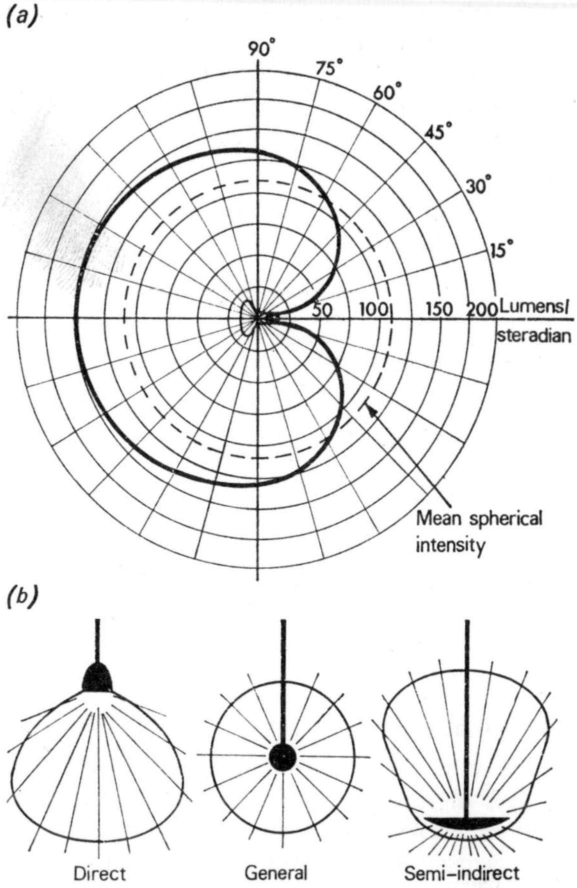

Fig. 14.4. (a) is the polar diagram of the source shown in Fig. 14.3. and (b) shows how polar diagrams give the light distribution at a glance.

average for all of them. This value, called the *mean spherical intensity* acts only as a guide to the effectiveness of the source and, for precise control, knowledge of the polar diagrams is essential. Such diagrams are used extensively to express the light distribution of sources or of complete light fittings. (Fig. 14.4*b*.)

Integrating Sphere

In the mass production of light bulbs, samples are tested periodically to check the quality. The determination of the mean spherical intensity for these specimens would be a tedious job.

This averaging can be done practically by placing the source at the centre of a sphere having a white diffusing surface. (Fig. 14.5.) Multiple reflections produce equal illumination on each

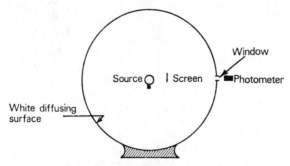

Fig. 14.5. An integrating sphere is used to measure the mean spherical intensity.

part of the sphere irrespective of any asymmetry of the source. The photometer receives light from a window in the surface and is screened from direct light from the source. In this integrating sphere, a single reading gives a measure of the mean spherical intensity of a source.

Illumination ✕

We now come to consider light energy as it arrives at its destination. The illumination of a surface denoted by the letter E is simply the light flux arriving per unit area of surface. The unit is called the lux.

The lux is the illumination produced on a surface by one lumen of light flux per square metre.

One lux of illumination is produced on the inside surface of a sphere of radius 1 m when a 1 cd source is situated at the centre. (Fig. 14.6.)

When we know the total number of lumens of

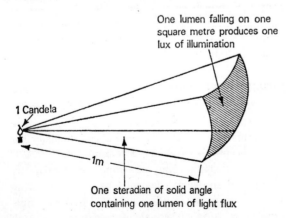

One lumen falling on one square metre produces one lux of illumination

1 Candela

1m

One steradian of solid angle containing one lumen of light flux

Fig. 14.6. The definition of the lux.

light falling on a surface, we calculate the illumination from the equation.

$$E = \frac{\text{number of lumens}}{\text{area}}$$

More often, however, the information given concerns the power of the source and the position of the receiving surface. In this case, the illumination can be calculated more conveniently from the illumination equation which is arrived at in the following sections.

An illumination of 50 lux is sufficient for general interior lighting. The required illumination increases for special purposes to 100 lux for reading, and to 300 lux for fine drawing, while an operating table might require 1000 lux. The light reflected from the surrounding surfaces, walls and floor, etc., contributes as much to this illumination as the power of the source.

Problem: Three-quarters of the light from a 150 cd source fall on a floor measuring $4\,\text{m} \times 3\,\text{m}$. What is the average illumination?

Solution:

Number of incident lumens $= 150 \times 4\pi \times \dfrac{3}{4}$

$$\text{Illumination} = \frac{\text{no. of lumens}}{\text{area}}$$

$$= \frac{150 \times 4 \times \pi}{4 \times 3} \times \frac{3}{4}$$

$$= 118 \text{ lumens/m}^2$$

Inverse Square Law ✕

Assuming that no absorption of light occurs, the illumination produced on a surface varies according to an inverse square law.

$$E \propto \frac{1}{d^2}$$

where d is the distance of the surface from the source. The law only holds true for a point source, i.e., one which is small compared to the distance d.

We can deduce the law by considering a divergent beam from a point source falling on each of three screens. (Fig. 14.7.) The total number of lumens is the same for each screen. The screen distances are in the ratio 1:2:3 but the areas are in the ratio 1:4:9, i.e., $1^2:2^2:3^2$. Hence the illuminations are proportional to $\dfrac{1}{1^2}$, $\dfrac{1}{2^2}$, and $\dfrac{1}{3^2}$, i.e., to $\dfrac{1}{d^2}$.

Now, assuming that the illumination is directly proportional to the luminous intensity of the source, we have:

$$E \propto \frac{I}{d^2}$$

This may be written $E = \dfrac{kI}{d^2}$

where k is the constant of proportionality.

Consider a source of I candelas at the centre of a sphere of radius d. By the inverse square law,

$$\text{Illumination } E = \frac{kI}{d^2}$$

But from the definition of illumination

$$E = \frac{\text{number of lumens}}{\text{area}}$$

$$= \frac{4\pi I}{4\pi d^2} = \frac{I}{d^2}$$

Comparing this with the above expression for E, $k = 1$ and therefore $E = \dfrac{I}{d^2}$

Inclined Surface Illumination

If light falls at an angle on to a surface, the original definition of illumination is quite valid, i.e.,

$$E = \frac{\text{number of lumens}}{\text{area of surface}}$$

To allow for the inclination, we must introduce a factor in the inverse square law equation.

Consider the two surfaces A and B. (Fig. 14.8.) A is perpendicular to the source of incident light and B is inclined to A at an angle θ. If A were removed, the amount of light falling on A would then fall on B. Since B is greater in area, its illumination will be less than that of A.

$$\text{illumination of } B, \quad E_B \propto \frac{1}{xy}$$

$$\text{illumination of } A, \quad E_A \propto \frac{1}{xy \cos \theta}$$

$$\therefore \qquad\qquad E_B = E_A \cos \theta$$

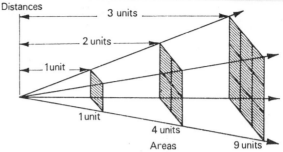

Fig. 14.7. The diagram demonstrates the inverse square law. Screens at distances of one, two, and three units have areas of one, four, and nine units.

and since $\qquad E_A = \dfrac{I}{d^2}$

then $\qquad\qquad E_B = \dfrac{I \cos \theta}{d^2}$

Thus for an inclined surface

$$E = \frac{I \cos \theta}{d^2}$$

The units are again lumens/unit area.

Problem: A light source of 200 cd is placed 3 m vertically above the centre of a table. What is the illumination at the centre when the table top is (a) horizontal, (b) inclined at 15 degrees to the horizontal?

Solution: We use equation $E = \dfrac{I \cos \theta}{d^2}$

(a) Horizontal case, illumination

$$E = \frac{200 \times 1}{3^2} = 22 \cdot 2 \text{ lumens/m}^2$$

(b) Inclined case, illumination

$$E = \frac{200 \cos 15°}{3^2} = 21 \cdot 4 \text{ lumens/m}^2 \text{ or lux}$$

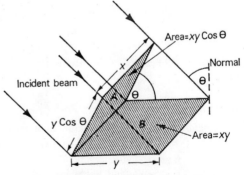

Fig. 14.8. The inclined areas A and B are related by the equation $A = B \cos \theta$.

When equation $E = I \cos \theta / d^2$ is used, the units of illumination are sometimes called metre-candles. It is preferable to use the name lux or lumens per square metre which is dimensionally correct, although area may not be directly involved in the calculation.

Luminance or Brightness

When a surface emits light we say that it has a brightness or *luminance*. The light may result from reflection or transmission or it may actually be generated at the surface. The term 'luminance' is preferable to brightness, which is used in everyday speech in a less precise way to describe such effects as brilliance and dazzle.

The unit of luminance is the candela per square metre (cd/m²)

$$\text{Luminance} = \frac{\text{Total candelas emitted}}{\text{Area}}$$

Just as a source has different strengths in different directions, so the luminance of a surface can vary directionally according to its shape and nature.

The luminance of a surface may be due to light produced at the surface, such as with an incandescent object. Luminance may also be a result of reflection, e.g., the light reflected from a sheet of paper, or it may be a result of light being transmitted through a diffusing surface such as a lampshade.

Luminance may be expressed in terms of the number of lumens per square metre in which case since

$$1 \text{ cd} = 4\pi \text{ lm}.$$
$$1 \text{ cd/m}^2 = 4\pi \text{ lm/m}^2.$$

The luminance of the tungsten filament of an electric lamp is about 10^6 cd/m², while a carbon arc may reach 20×10^6 cd/m². The Moon's luminance is about 2500 cd/m², and a paper suitably lit for drawing would have a luminance of about 12.000 cd/m².

Reflection and Transmission Factors

The *reflectance* or *reflection factor* of a surface is the ratio of the reflected light to the incident light.

$$\rho = \frac{\text{reflected light}}{\text{incident light}}$$

Similarly the *transmittance* or *transmission factor* of a slab of material is defined as the ratio of the transmitted light to the incident light energy.

$$\tau = \frac{\text{transmitted light}}{\text{incident light}}$$

When a slab of material is placed in the path of light from a source it reduces the effective luminous intensity in the ratio of the transmission factor. Transmission and reflection factors can be defined whether the emitted light is directional or generally diffused.

Problem: Sixty lumens per unit area are incident on a glass surface from a 240 cd source, 45 lumens are transmitted, and 9 lumens are reflected, the remainder being absorbed. Calculate the reflection and transmission factors for the surface and the effective power of the source through the surface.

Solution:

Reflection factor $= \dfrac{9}{60}$ or 15 per cent.

Transmission factor $= \dfrac{45}{60}$ or 75 per cent.

Effective power of source through the surface

$$= \frac{75}{100} \times 240 \text{ cd}$$
$$= 180 \text{ cd}$$

Visual Photometers

Just as the skin is a poor judge of temperature, the eye is a poor judge of absolute brightness. In fact, it is worse, partly because of the iris which responds to varying illumination but mostly because of the adjustment of the response of the light sensitive nerves in the eye. Objects under a clear starlit sky enjoy only one ten-millionth part of the illumination of full sunlight, yet the eye adjusts to both conditions. It is this adaptation which makes the eye useless for direct measurement. What the eye can do quite well is to detect small differences in the brightness of adjacent surfaces. Visual photometers make use of this ability to measure light quantities.

A visual photometer is an arrangement whereby two identical surfaces are illuminated by two separate sources. The sources are placed normal

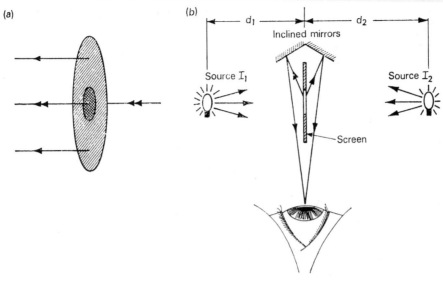

Fig. 14.9. In the grease spot photometer, the light from one source is reflected by the screen and is compared with the light from the other source transmitted through the screen.

to the surfaces at such distances that they produce equal illuminations. Then applying equation

$$E = \frac{I \cos \theta}{d^2}$$

where $E_1 = E_2$ and $\cos \theta_1 = \cos \theta_2 = 1$.

$$\frac{I_1}{d_1^2} = \frac{I_2}{d_2^2}$$

If one of the sources is a known standard, the power of the other can be calculated. Several types of visual photometers have been developed, differing in the way in which equal brightness of the surfaces is recognized.

Grease Spot Photometer ✕

A grease spot on a piece of white absorbent paper acts as an effective photometer. The grease renders the paper translucent so that the reflected light from one source can be compared with the transmitted light from the other source. (Fig. 14.9a.) In practice the grease spot never quite disappears because the grease spot reflects and absorbs some of the light. The best photometric balance is obtained when both sides of the paper appear identical. A pair of inclined mirrors makes the exact comparison an easier task. (Fig. 14.9b.)

Lummer-Brodhun Photometer

By means of total internal reflection, as shown in the diagram of Fig. 14.10, the light from the two surfaces traverses equivalent optical paths before being brought into adjacent positions at the focus of the eye-piece. The lower double

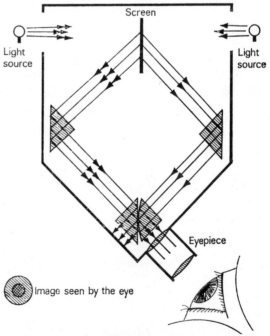

Fig. 14.10. The Lummer-Brodhun photometer allows us to view both sides of the screen at once.

prism is responsible for bringing the surface images together. It consists of two 45° prisms, one of which has a convex spherical surface pressed into optical contact with the other. Thus, the central rays from one source pass through undeviated, whilst the peripheral rays from the other source are totally internally reflected.

Flicker Photometer

When two illuminated surfaces are presented alternately to the eye several times a second, the eye detects a flicker. If, however, the surfaces are equally illuminated, the flicker disappears or reduces to a minimum. The *flicker photometer* uses the eye's sensitivity to this flicker to judge equality of illumination. Photometric balance is obtained by moving the sources until the minimum flicker occurs, under which conditions the photometer equation can be applied.

This instrument makes it easier to compare illuminations of different colours, since colour fusion (i.e., the point where the flicker caused by the difference in colour disappears) occurs before brightness fusion (i.e., the point where the flicker caused by the difference of illumination disappears).

In the commonest arrangement, the eye-piece is directed at the edge of a disc, which spins between two light-sources. The edge of the disc consists of two oblique bevels, cut so that the base of one is the apex of the other, and so that the broadest part of the surface of each bevel faces the eye-piece once in each revolution of the disc. By this means, the light from each source is reflected alternately into the eye-piece. A glance at Fig. 14.11 will clear up any confusion about the shape of the disc, which can be regarded as two obliquely truncated cones joined at their bases. The speed at which the eye is most sensitive to the alternations, that is, to the rapid presentation first of one bevel-edge and then the other, is about twelve alternations per second. At above twenty alternations per second, no flicker can be detected.

Problem: When an unknown source is placed at a distance of 1·5 m from a photometer screen, it produces photometric balance with a standard source of 90 cd at a distance of 2 m.

What is the luminous intensity of the source under test.

Solution:

$$\frac{I_1}{d_1^2} = \frac{I_2}{d_2^2}$$

$$\frac{I_1}{1\cdot5^2} = \frac{90}{2^2}$$

$$I_1 = \frac{1\cdot5^2 \times 90}{2^2} = 50\cdot6 \text{ cd}$$

Photoelectric Photometer

When light falls on to a metal surface, it causes electrons to shoot off, the number of electrons being greater or smaller according to the strength of the light and to the nature of the surface. A potential of 20 volts applied to an anode will

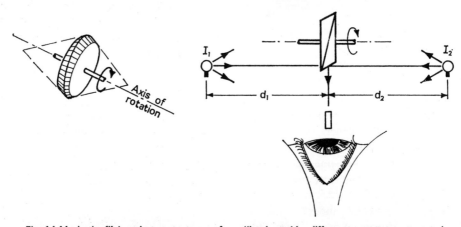

Fig. 14.11. In the flicker photometer two surfaces illuminated by different sources are presented to the eye in rapid succession.

sweep up these electrons and produce a current of electricity proportional to the illumination of the light falling on the metal surface. The current can be used, therefore, to measure the strength of the light.

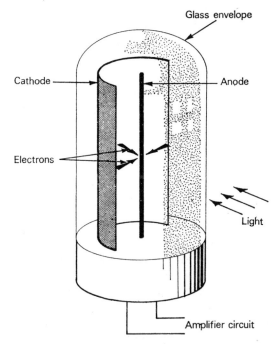

Fig. 14.12. Photoelectric cell. Electrons ejected by the light falling on the shaped cathode are collected by the anode which is at a small positive potential.

The photoelectric photometer makes use of this principle. Naturally, the more sensitive the response of the metal cathode, the more accurate will be the measurement. A surface which gives a high sensitivity over the visible part of the spectrum can be made by depositing a thin layer of caesium on a base of antimony or bismuth.

Sometimes a gas-filled photocell is used. The photoelectrons collide with the gas molecules, which then split into positive ions and negative electrons. These drift with the applied voltage and add considerably to the photocurrent. It is, however, more unstable than the vacuum cell, as it is sensitive to variations in the potential and in the pressure of the gas.

Emission cells can be used as switching devices to operate burglar alarms and to automatically open doors. The interruption of a light beam directed on to the cell changes its conductivity,

which triggers off a secondary mechanism. Because the response of these cells can be conveniently amplified, they are used in conjunction with spectrometers to measure the intensity of spectral lines.

The Photo-Voltaic Cell

A photographic exposure meter is basically a photo-voltaic cell. It needs no amplification or electrical supplies and gives a direct meter reading of light intensity. This makes for compactness and portability while its accuracy, though less than that of the vacuum cell, falls well within the tolerances of photographic emulsions.

The cell is made up of a thin transparent layer of gold deposited on the surface of a slab of grey crystalline selenium which is itself in contact with an iron base plate. (Fig. 14.13.) Light falling on the gold layer reaches the surface of the semiconducting selenium. This light at the boundary induces electrons to flow into the gold from the selenium, creating a difference of potential across the junction. Externally a conventional current flows from the iron base contact via a microammeter to the gold surface. The instrument requires frequent recalibration, as it is affected by temperature and as it suffers from both long and short term fatigue with exposure.

We can use other light sensitive properties to measure illumination. For example, some semiconducting materials change their electrical resistance when light falls on them. The light energy weakens the attachment of electrons to atoms within the material. (Fig. 14.14.) The greater the incident light energy, the greater the number of charge carriers and the lower the electrical resistance becomes. This photoconductive effect is sometimes used as a control device, for example

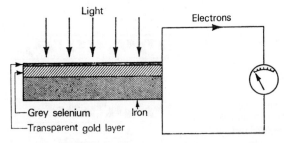

Fig. 14.13. The photo-voltaic light meter does not require any electrical supplies. Light causes electrons to flow from the selenium into the gold.

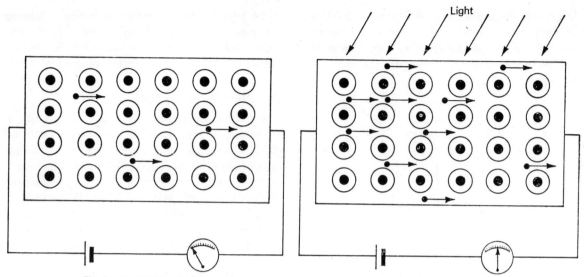

Fig. 14.14. The light increases the number of mobile electrons and reduces the resistance of a photoconductive material. The meter reading correlates with the light intensity.

in television receivers to adjust the screen brightness automatically to suit the changing illumination in a room.

Photographic Light Recording

If we wish to record the pattern of illumination, or measure the total incident light energy over a period of time, we can use the photographic process. This is an example of the *photochemical effect*, in which a permanent chemical change in a substance is produced by exposure to light. Microscopically fine particles of a photosensitive substance, such as silver bromide, suspended in a thin layer of gelatin form a photographic emulsion. The light ejects electrons from the molecules of silver bromide, which separates the silver metal from the bromine. The number of grains of silver bromide, partly reduced to silver in this way, increases with the amount of incident light. During *development* those particles which are affected by

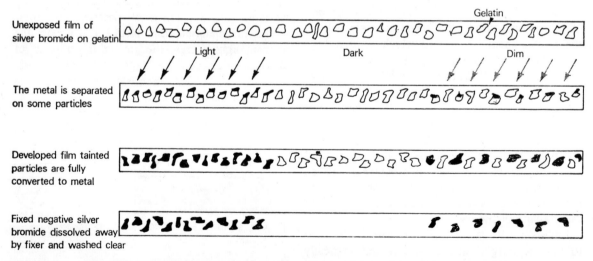

Fig. 14.15. A photographic film undergoes the processes of exposure development and fixing to produce a negative.

the light are completely reduced to metal by chemical means. The remaining particles of silver bromide are not changed by the developer and they are dissolved away by a liquid called a *fixer*. (Fig. 14.15.)

At this stage we have made a *negative*, which grades from being opaque, where the greatest exposure occurred, to being completely trans-parent, where no exposure occurred. Such a negative can be calibrated and used to measure light intensities. To produce a picture, or positive as we call it, we shine light through the negative on to a paper coated with a photographic emulsion. After developing and fixing we obtain the final positive with which we are more familiar. (Fig 14.16.)

Fig. 14.16. Light shone through the negative exposes an emulsion coated paper after which development and fixing produce the final print.

Questions

1. What is the relation between the candela and the lambert?

2. Why is it so much colder at the poles than at the equator when they are only slightly further away from the Sun, compared with the distance of the Sun from the Earth?

3. Why is the eye a poor judge of illumination?

4. Why is it difficult to compare the intensities of lights of different colours?

5. How could you roughly determine the efficiency of an electric bulb in converting electrical energy to light?

6. The inverse square law is not obeyed by a searchlight. How do you account for this?

7. What is the difference between luminous intensity and illumination?

8. How would you use a visual photometer to measure the transmission factor of a glass block?

9. How does a diffusing shade prevent glare from a lamp without very much affecting the illumination produced?

10. What kind of polar diagram would you expect from a car fog-lamp? (*a*) in a vertical plane, (*b*) in a horizontal plane.

Problems

1. A source of light has a mean spherical intensity of 5 cd. How many lumens does it emit?
Answer: 62·8 lm.

2. A source has a luminous intensity of 150 cd in a certain direction. How many lumens are emitted per unit solid angle in this direction?
Answer: 150 lm.

3. A lamp emits 200 lumens equally in all directions. What is its power?
Answer: 15·9 cd.

4. A point source of 100 candela is hung 6 m above a horizontal road. What is the illumination at the point directly below the source and at 9 m from this point?
Answer: 2·8 lx; 0·47 lx.

5. A photometer measuring head is placed between two lamps, one of 160 cd. If the lamps are 1 m apart and produce equal illuminations on the photometer when it is at 800 mm from the 160 cd source, what is the intensity of the other source?
Answer: 10 cd.

161

6. If it takes 4 s to get a satisfactory print from a negative held 1 m from a 32 candela lamp, what exposure will be needed 500 mm from a 16 candela lamp?
Answer: 2 s.

7. Lights falls normally on to a screen at 3 m from a source. If it is moved to a distance of 2 m, at what angle must the screen be inclined to keep its illumination the same?
Answer: 63·5 degrees to its original position.

8. Equal illuminations are measured on a photometer head from two lamps, 600 and 700 mm away. When a sheet of glass is placed between the head and the nearer lamp, the other lamp has to be moved 30 mm further away so that the illuminations are again equal. What percentage of light is transmitted by the glass?
Answer: 92 per cent.

9. A 60 watt electric lamp has an efficiency of 1 candela/watt. How far above a table must the lamp be hung to produce an illumination of 20 lx directly below it?
Answer: 1·73 m.

10. Two lamps, one of 8 and one of 16 cd are 6 m apart. Where are the two positions along the line joining the lamps where a screen would receive equal illumination from each lamp?
Answer: 2·5 m and 14·5 m from the 8 cd lamp.

11. The full Moon produces the same illumination on a screen as a 1 candela source at a distance of 1·22 m. What is the luminous intensity of the Moon, treating it as a point source? (Distance of Moon = 240,000 miles.)
Answer: 10^{17} cd.

12. A 40 candela lamp illuminates a screen 4 m away. The intensity of illumination of the screen can be doubled either by moving the lamp, or by changing the lamp for one of a different power. What is required in each case?
Answer: 2·8 m from screen, 80 cd lamp.

13. Two lamps produce equal illumination at a photometer at distances of 400 mm and 600 mm. A plane mirror is placed 50 mm behind the weaker lamp, and the other lamp has to be moved 110 mm nearer the photometer to equalize the illuminations again. What percentage of light is reflected by the mirror?
Answer: 78 per cent.

14. Two lamps give equal illuminations at a photometer when their distances away are in the ratio 4:5. When a sheet of glass is put in front of the stronger lamp, the distances are in the ratio 16:19. What percentage of light is transmitted by the glass?
Answer: 90·3 per cent.

15. A 100 candela lamp illuminates a screen 1 m away. If a filter is put in front of the lamp, the lamp has to move 0·5 m nearer the screen to restore the same illumination. What percentage of light is absorbed by the filter?
Answer: 75 per cent.

16. A 100,000 candela lamp at a distance of 0·75 m produces an illumination equal to the Sun. What is the luminous intensity of the Sun? (Distance of the Sun = 15×10^{10} m.)
Answer: 4×10^{27} cd.

17. The polar diagram of a light source is given by the following table:

Angle (°)	0	20	40	60	80	100
Intensity (cd)	31	32	34	35	34	33
Angle (°)	120	140	160	180	200	220
Intensity (cd)	27	20	10	0	20	20
Angle (°)	240	260	280	200	320	340
Intensity (cd)	27	33	34	35	34	32

Assuming this distribution applies to the other planes through the same pole, what is the mean spherical intensity of the source?
Answer: 28·5 cd.

18. A road is lit by a row of 300 candela lamps 6 m above its surface at intervals of 30 m. What is the approximate maximum and minimum illumination of the road?
Answer: 8·3 and 0·85 lx.

19. How many 100 watt lamps are required to produce a minimum average illumination of 140 lx on an operating table, if 15 per cent of the light from the lamps is concentrated on to an area of 0·37 m² and the efficiency of the lamps is 1·25 cd/W?
Answer: 2.

20. A parabolic reflector of 500 mm diameter subtends a solid angle of 5 steradians at a point source of 200 cd placed at the focus. Assuming that the reflection factor of the mirror is 0·9, what is the illumination in the path of the parallel beam from the lamp?
Answer: $1·15 \times 10^3$ lx.

21. Define the unit of luminous intensity and explain the relationship between this unit and the lumen.

A lamp is placed 2·0 m above the centre of a horizontal circular table of diameter 1·5 m and produces on the table at its perimeter, an illumination of 20 lx. Assuming the lamp to emit light equally in all directions and that 50 per cent of the light reaching the table is indirect light due to reflection, calculate the luminous intensity of the lamp.

(I.E.R.E.)

Answer: 48·8 candela.

15 Physical Optics

Physical optics is the study of the nature of light itself. Much of the behaviour of light can be explained on the assumption that it travels in straight lines, but in some cases we must consider the detail of its wave nature. In this chapter, we explain the patterns formed by the interaction of light waves. We describe how they can be used to investigate spectra and to make the most accurate measurements of length man has ever made.

There are several reasons why the wave nature of light was not readily recognized by early scientists and why most people are not aware of it in normal seeing. Unless special precautions are taken, the pattern is not visible because it is either too minute, or too faint compared to the background illumination, or too short-lived for the eye to record it. In some cases, phenomena directly caused by the wave nature of light are attributed to other causes. For example, the colours apparent in thin films such as oil films on water, are produced by interference, but they might be considered to be caused by the absorption of light by the oil itself.

Theories of the Nature of Light

The earliest accepted theory of the nature of light was that light is a stream of tiny particles or corpuscles travelling so fast that they are hardly affected by gravity. Like projectiles, on meeting an obstacle, they could either rebound elastically from its surface, pass right through it, or be stopped in the material. The theory seemed to fit the facts of reflection, transmission, and absorption of light.

Newton in particular supported the corpuscular theory of light. He explained refraction by assuming that the denser material attracted the light corpuscles, causing a deviation towards the normal. (Fig. 15.1.)

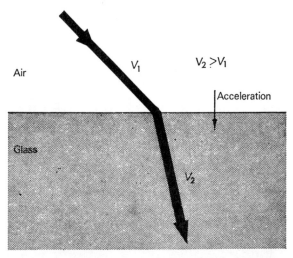

Fig. 15.1. According to the corpuscular theory of light, the corpuscles of a light beam were attracted by the molecules of a denser medium which increased their velocity and changed their direction at the surface.

Huygens, on the other hand (1678), thought that light was more akin to the ripples on the surface of water than to a stream of corpuscles. He put forward a wave theory, which explained refraction in terms of a slowing down of the waves as they enter a denser medium. (Fig. 15.2.) Two considerations discouraged Newton and others from accepting Huygen's theory. First, sound and liquid waves could bend round obstacles whereas light appeared not to do so, since it produced sharp shadows. Second, sound and liquid waves require a medium for their propagation. How, therefore, could a wave travel through empty space as light

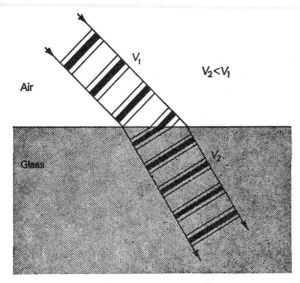

Air

V_1

$V_2 < V_1$

Glass

V_2

Fig. 15.2. Huygens proposed that light waves were slowed down as they entered a denser medium and the retardation caused the waves to slew around at the surface.

velocity of light could not at that time be measured in a material, and the decision between the two theories was made on different evidence.

The crucial experiment was made by Thomas Young an English scientist. He added light to light and produced darkness, which could never happen with corpuscles. The light radiating from two slits was superimposed on a screen and instead of even illumination a series of light and dark bands appeared. (Fig. 15.3.) He explained this on the wave theory as follows. Where the dark bands occur on the screen, the waves from the two sources always arrive out of step and the crests of one wave cancel out the troughs from the other. At the light bands, the waves arrive exactly in step, crest adding to crest and trough to trough to produce a greater illumination.

Had he been alive at the time, Newton would have been the first to appreciate the significance of Young's experiment. Unfortunately, Newton's name had become associated with the corpuscular theory, and admirers of Newton blindly supported the corpuscular theory and ignored the new evidence for many years. Eventually, the wave theory became widely accepted, and in 1880 the first measurements of the velocity of light in a medium confirmed that the velocity of light is less in a material than in air.

One useful idea first put forward by Huygens was that each point on a wavefront may be regarded as itself a source of light. Now, if a

must do to come from the Sun and stars? The idea of a wave without matter was unacceptable and equally difficult was the idea of a medium, the ether, which filled all space and had fantastic properties such as no mass and no viscosity. One important difference between the theories was that the corpuscular theory of refraction predicted that light would travel faster in a material than in air, (Fig. 15.1), whereas the wave theory predicts a slower velocity in a material (Fig. 15.2). The

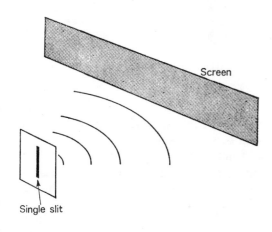

Screen

Single slit

One source overall illumination

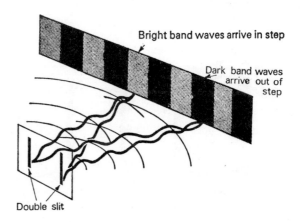

Bright band waves arrive in step

Dark band waves arrive out of step

Double slit

Two sources bright and dark lines

Fig. 15.3. Schematic diagram showing the way in which light waves may supplement each other and cancel.

wave travels with velocity v for a time t it will move a distance vt. To find the future position of a wavefront, we construct circles of radius vt on each part of the wavefront and the new wave position is the tangent to these circles.

The construction does not work in all situations but where it does it is very helpful. (Fig. 15.4.)

Diffraction and Interference

When light waves are restricted by an aperture or by the edge of an obstacle, some of the light spreads into the region not directly in line with the source. This bending of the light is called *diffraction*, and it increases as the aperture becomes narrower. (Fig. 15.5.) The light waves appear to diverge from the slit as predicted by Huygens' construction, regarding each point on a wavefront as a source itself.

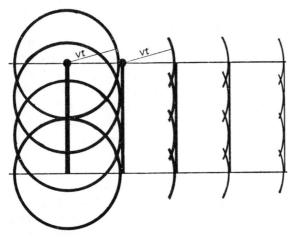

Parallel beam

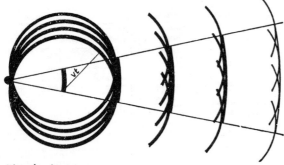

Diverging beam

Fig. 15.4. Huygens' construction. Circles are drawn with their centres on one wavefront and the tangent to these circles in the direction of the wave is the new wavefront.

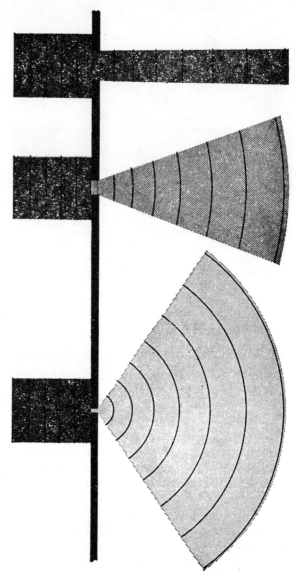

Fig. 15.5. Diffraction by a slit. As the slit is narrowed the spreading of the light into the geometrical shadow increases.

Young's experiment, which superimposes the light from two sources, is an example of the *interference* of light waves. The interference pattern is visible only under special conditions. The demonstration requires two coherent sources of light, i.e., sources having the same frequency (colour) and exhibiting the same changes in phase. A light source sends out its waves in very many short bursts, each of which starts abruptly at a different stage or phase. An impression of this may be

(a)

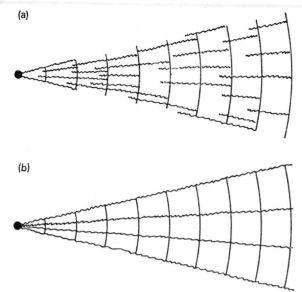

(b)

Fig. 15.6. The light from a source shows many changes of phase represented by (a) and is not continuous as shown by (b).

obtained from Fig. 15.6 but this picture should not be taken as representing the full reality of a source of waves. The reason for this intermittent emission will be understood when we realize that the electron transition within an excited atom, which is the source of the light, lasts for only 10^{-8} s. Thus the 'wavelet' or *photon* as it is called only extends over about 3 m. The radiation then ceases until a further electron transition takes place. A light beam consists of many such short pulses Although non-coherent sources do interfere with each other the interference pattern changes its

position every time the phase changes, i.e., at intervals of 10^{-8} s or less.

The only way to produce coherent sources is to derive two sources from a single source. Young did this by illuminating two identical slits. (Fig. 15.7.) Note that the lines are equally spaced and the position of the lines depends on the wave-length. When the source emits white light, which consists of many wave-lengths (colours), only the first few lines are visible and these have coloured edges. Further out, the lines of the different colours overlap completely and the pattern disappears.

The Two-Slit Interference Pattern

The position of the maximum and minimum illumination produced on a screen by two coherent sources is easily calculated. At the point on the screen equidistant from the two sources, the two light wave trains always arrive in phase and produce a maximum. (Fig. 15.8.) At any other point, such as P on the screen at an angle θ to the bisector of the sources, there is a path difference between the light from the two sources. This is shown on Fig. 15.8 by completing an isosceles triangle SPQ isolating the path difference $S_2 - Q$.

When S_2Q is exactly one wave-length the waves arrive at P in phase and produce a peak of illumination. When S_2Q is exactly an odd number of half wave-lengths, the waves arrive at P out of phase, cancel each other out, and produce zero illumination. By assuming that $x \gg d \gg \lambda$, which in practice is always the case, we can obtain a simple expression for the position of these bright and dark lines on the screen.

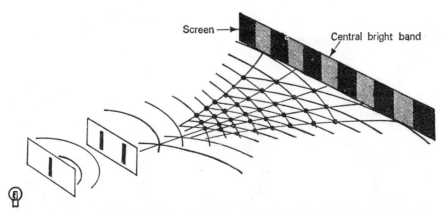

Screen → 　　　　　Central bright band

Fig. 15.7. Young's two-slit interference pattern.

167

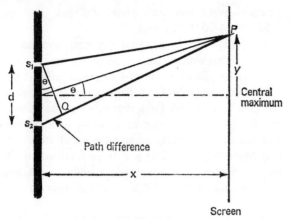

Fig. 15.8. Geometry of the two-slit interference pattern.

$$\theta = \frac{\text{path difference}}{d} = \frac{y}{x}$$

$$y = \text{path difference} \times \frac{x}{d}$$

Bright lines occur where

$\quad y = 0$ central maximum

$\quad y = \lambda\dfrac{x}{d}$ first order maximum

$\quad y = 2\lambda\dfrac{x}{d}$ second order maximum

$\quad y = 3\lambda\dfrac{x}{d}$ third order maximum, etc.

Dark lines occur where

$\quad y = \tfrac{1}{2}\lambda\dfrac{x}{d}$ first order minimum

$\quad y = 1\tfrac{1}{2}\lambda\dfrac{x}{d}$ second order minimum

$\quad y = 2\tfrac{1}{2}\lambda\dfrac{x}{d}$ third order minimum, etc.

Problem: Two slits $2\cdot0 \times 10^{-4}$ m apart produce interference fringes on a screen 5 m away, when illuminated by light of wave-length $6\cdot0 \times 10^{-7}$ m. How far is the third order minimum from the central maximum?

Solution: For third order minimum

$$y = 2\tfrac{1}{2}\lambda\,\frac{x}{d}$$

$$= \frac{5}{2} \times 6 \times 10^{-7} \times \frac{5}{2 \times 10^{-4}}$$

$$= 3\cdot75 \text{ m} \times 10^{-2}$$

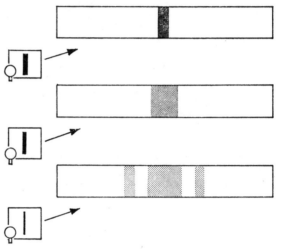

Fig. 15.9. Diffraction pattern of a slit showing the effect of reducing the width of the slit.

Diffraction in a Single Aperture

If light is shone through a single slit, which is progressively narrowed, it diverges increasingly into the region of geometrical shadow. The light not only diverges from the slit but it also produces a pattern of light and shade on a screen placed at a comparatively large distance away. (Fig. 15.9.)

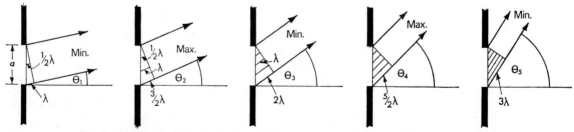

Fig. 15.10. We can obtain the directions of the maxima and minima in a diffraction pattern by dividing up the slit and considering it as a case of interference.

This is a diffraction pattern and it can be considered as being due to the interference of light from the different parts of the aperture. The centre of the pattern is bright since the light from all parts of the aperture arrives in phase.

Consider the light from the aperture travelling in the direction shown in Fig. 15.10a, so that the difference between light from the edges of the aperture is one wave-length. The path difference between the light from the centre of the aperture p and from its upper edge p' is $\frac{1}{2}\lambda$, which corresponds to a phase difference of 180 degrees. Thus, the rays of light from p and p' are out of phase and they cancel each other out. The same path difference occurs between corresponding points q, q', r, r', etc., on the lower and upper halves of the aperture and so they cancel in pairs, and produce zero intensity in this particular direction.

If the angle increases, so that the path difference between the edges of the slit is $\frac{3}{2}\lambda$, a peak in intensity occurs. This is best understood if we imagine the slit divided into three sections. (Fig. 15.10b.) The light from the upper and centre sections interferes destructively, as we have just described, because of the phase difference of 180 degrees between corresponding points. Light from the lowest third of the aperture is transmitted uncancelled. Figure 15.10c, d, and e, attempts to show how the peaks and zeros of intensity can be explained by dividing up the aperture and treating it as a special case of interference. Thus

$a \sin \theta = 0, \frac{3}{2}\lambda, \frac{5}{2}\lambda, \frac{7}{2}\lambda, \ldots$ for a maximum
$a \sin \theta = \lambda, 2\lambda, 3\lambda, 4\lambda, \ldots$ for a minimum

The Diffraction Grating

The double slit interference pattern can be used to measure the wave-length of the light, but it is not convenient because the lines are rather diffused and of low intensity. By using a large number of slits, the intensity and the sharpness of the lines can be increased, enabling the wave-length of the light to be accurately measured. (Fig. 15.11.) In a diffraction grating, these slits are defined by drawing a large number of grooves, commonly 600 per mm, on a surface.

For the central maximum, there is no path difference, so we call it the zero order. The first order maximum occurs for a given wave-length

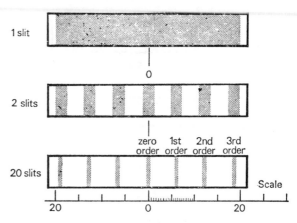

Fig. 15.11. Showing the effect of increasing the number of slits of constant apertures 0·1 mm.

in a direction for which there is a path difference of a complete wave-length between corresponding points on neighbouring slits. (Fig. 15.12.)

The first order maximum occurs where
$$(a+b) \sin \theta = \lambda$$

The second order where
$$(a+b) \sin \theta = 2\lambda$$

and the nth order where
$$(a+b) \sin \theta = n\lambda$$

Each wave-length present produces a maximum in a different position and the overall pattern we call a spectrum. (Fig. 15.13.) The dispersion of the lines of different wave-length is greater in the higher orders of the spectrum. Gratings are used in conjunction with spectrometers to analyse the

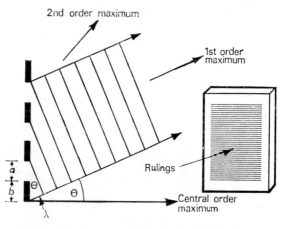

Fig. 15.12. Magnified schematic diagram of the grating ruling.

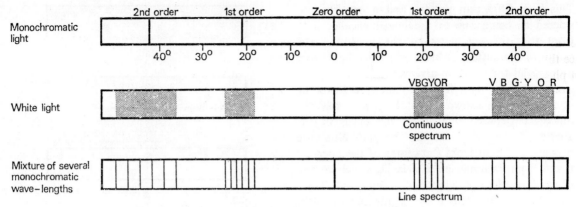

Fig. 15.13. Pattern produced by a diffraction grating of 600 lines/mm.

wave-lengths present in the spectra of light sources. The optical system of a spectrometer employing the diffraction grating is shown in Fig. 15.14.

Diffraction and Resolving Power

Quite apart from its converging or diverging power, a lens of an optical instrument is a circular aperture, and consequently it gives rise to diffraction. Thus, a point on the object produces a diffraction pattern rather than a point on the image. This effect may not normally be obvious but in high magnification it sets a limit to the resolution, i.e., to the smallest separation of points on the object that we can distinguish clearly. Two points are said to be resolved when the first dark ring of one image falls on the central maximum of the other. (Fig. 15.15.) The smallest

angle subtended by two points on the object, which are just resolved, is dependent on the wave-length and the aperture as follows:

$$\theta \propto \lambda/a$$

When the object is at infinity, the constant of proportionality in this expression which satisfies the above criterion of resolution for a circular aperture is 1·22, i.e.,

$$\theta = 1\cdot 22 \frac{\lambda}{a} \text{ radians}$$

The limit of resolution of the eye set by diffraction at its 3 mm diameter aperture is 47 seconds of arc. But other shortcomings of the eye restrict its actual resolution to about a minute of arc. The objective for a telescope of diameter 1 metre will just resolve points which subtend an angle of about 0·14 seconds.

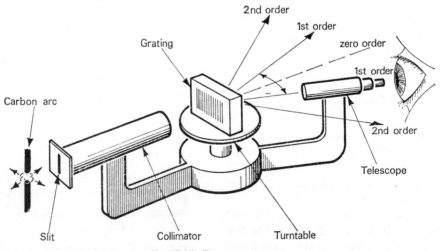

Fig. 15.14. The spectrometer.

The resolving power of a microscope is not so simple to determine, since it depends on the object distance as well as the wave-length of the light and the aperture of the lens.

Problem: The headlights of a car are one metre apart. At what distance could they be resolved by a telescope having a 50 mm diameter objective? The effective wave-length of white light is $5 \cdot 6 \times 10^{-7}$ m.

Solution: Let the maximum distance at which the headlights can be resolved be x metres.

$$\frac{1}{x} = 1 \cdot 22 \frac{\lambda}{a}$$

$$\frac{1}{x} = \frac{1 \cdot 22 \times 5 \cdot 6 \times 10^{-7}}{5 \times 10^{-2}}$$

$$x = 73,200 \text{ m}$$

This could not be realized in practice because of imperfections in the lenses and the fact that the Earth's curvature would obscure the line of sight.

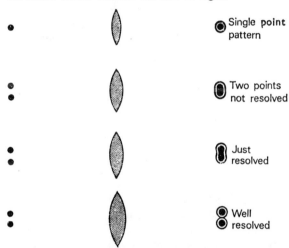

Fig. 15.15. Each point on the object gives rise to a diffraction pattern image which gets smaller as the lens aperture increases.

Interference Effects in Thin Films

Some of the most easily observed interference phenomena are those associated with thin films. The colours in soap bubbles and in the oil on puddles of water are examples of this. The colours which flit across the surface of steel during tempering are a result of the formation of a semi-transparent oxide coating on its surface. These interference effects can be put to use in the measurement of the wave-lengths of light and other small distances.

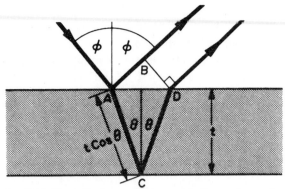

Fig.15.16. The reflection at the top and bottom surfaces of a film introduces a path difference $2\mu t$ cos θ before the rays emerge parallel.

When light is reflected at the upper and lower surfaces of a parallel sided film, such as the oil film shown in Fig. 15.16, a path difference is introduced between adjacent rays. Light of a single wave-length (monochromatic light), incident at all angles on to the film, produces a pattern of bright and dark bands.

Path difference $= \dfrac{2\mu t}{\text{Cos } \theta} - 2t \tan \theta \sin \Phi$

The μ in the first term allows for the fact that the waves are shortened in the ratio $1 : \mu$ in the material.

$$\text{pd} = \frac{2\mu t}{\cos \theta} \left(1 - \tan \theta \sin \Phi \frac{\text{Cos } \theta}{\mu} \right)$$

substituting $\mu = \dfrac{\sin \Phi}{\sin \theta}$ and $\tan \theta = \dfrac{\sin \theta}{\cos \theta}$

$$\text{pd} = \frac{2\mu t}{\cos \theta} \left(1 - \frac{\sin \theta \sin \Phi \cos \theta \sin \theta}{\cos \theta} \frac{}{\sin \Phi} \right)$$

$$= \frac{2\mu t}{\cos \theta} (1 - \sin^2 \theta)$$

but $1 - \sin^2 \theta = \cos^2 \theta$

$$\text{pd} = \frac{2\mu t \cos^2 \theta}{\cos \theta} = 2\mu t \cos \theta$$

Thus for a maximum $2\mu t \cos \theta = \mu\lambda$
and for a minimum $2\mu t \cos \theta = (n - \frac{1}{2}) \lambda$

When white light is used, the film causes the rays of a certain colour to be absent in some directions and to predominate in other directions. This is the case for daylight diffusing on to an oil film of uniform thickness and explains why such films appear coloured. (Fig. 15.17.)

When light is incident at zero degrees a certain wave-length given by

$$n\lambda = 2\mu t$$

will tend to be absent from the reflected light. This wave-length will be transmitted through the film. This principle is used in the blooming of lenses which is the application of an anti-reflection

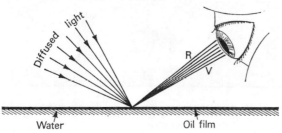

Fig. 15.17. The colours seen in an oil film on water are a result of interference.

coating. The thickness of the coating is designed to produce destructive interference between the light reflected from the glass surface and that reflected from the coating surface. This can only be complete for one wave-length of light which we usually choose to be near the middle of the spectrum. The small amounts of red and blue light from the ends of the spectrum which are reflected give the blooming its characteristic purple colour.

Wedge Films

When light is incident on a film of varying thickness, a series of dark and light bands is seen in the reflected light even at normal incidence. These bands are caused by the interference of light reflected from the top and bottom surfaces of the film. (Fig. 15.18.) The film introduces a path difference at any point of twice the film thickness since the light reflected at the lower surface crosses the film twice. For a particular band, assuming both reflections to be external.

$$2t = n\lambda$$
$$t = \tfrac{1}{2}n\lambda$$

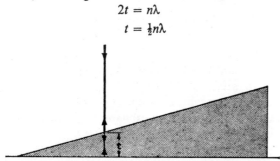

Fig. 15.18. Showing the path difference of 2t introduced in the light reflected at the top and bottom surfaces of a wedge film.

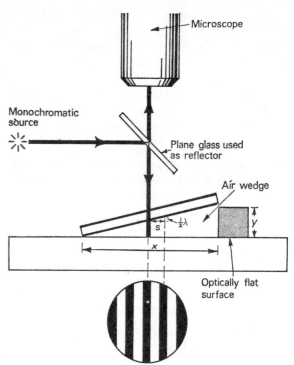

Fig. 15.19. Apparatus used to observe the interference bands produced by an air wedge.

where n is a whole number. Thus the film thickness t changes by half a wave-length from one band to the next, as n increases by unity.

In some important applications, an air film is formed by two inclined solid surfaces. The interference bands produced by this air wedge can be observed with the apparatus of Fig. 15.19. The vernier microscope serves also to measure the horizontal distance s between the bands. The bands are always at right angles to the direction of the gradient which is given by

$$\text{gradient} = \frac{y}{x} = \frac{\lambda/2}{s}$$

The apparatus can be used to measure the wave-length, but more commonly it is used to measure accurately the thickness y of the separator, when λ is known. Even small changes in y due, for example, to thermal expansion can be measured, and hence the method can be used to determine the coefficients of the expansion of materials available only in small quantities.

The principle may also be used to estimate the flatness of surfaces. If the surfaces confining the air wedge were perfectly flat, the interference bands would be straight and regular. Any departures from flatness in either surface shows up as an irregularity in the interference pattern. Standard optically flat quartz blocks are available and these are used to check the flatness of other surfaces. Deviations from flatness of the order of 10^{-7} m, can be detected by this method.

Note that, in the case of the air wedge, one reflection is internal and the other is external. The internal reflection produces no phase change in the reflected light, whereas the external reflection does. Consequently, in addition to the changing phase produced by a path difference, there is a 180 degree phase change introduced by the reflection. The expression:

$$2t = (n - \tfrac{1}{2})\lambda$$

becomes the condition for a maximum and the expression:

$$2t = n\lambda$$

becomes the condition for a minimum. Where the two surfaces meet, there is zero path difference but a minimum occurs due to this phase change in the externally reflected light.

Problem: A microscope slide 50 mm long, rests with one edge in contact with an optically flat, horizontal surface and the opposite edge is propped up by a piece of wire. The air wedge so formed is illuminated normally by light of wave-length 5.89×10^{-7} m, and it is found that the distance between the 11th dark fringe and the 21st is 0.1 mm. How thick is the wire?

Solution:

Distance between fringes $= s = \dfrac{0.1}{10}$ mm

$$= 0.01 \text{ mm}$$

$$\frac{y}{x} = \frac{\lambda/2}{s}$$

$$\frac{y}{50} = \frac{5.89 \times 10^{-4}/2}{0.01}$$

Therefore thickness of wire, $y = 1.47$ mm.

Newton's Rings

An air wedge may be formed between the curved surface of a lens and the plane surface of another piece of glass. (Fig. 15.20.) This produces an interference pattern consisting of a number of rings centred on the point of contact between the lens and the surface. The point of contact gives rise to a dark circle, there being zero path difference at this point, but 180 degrees change in phase in the light externally reflected at the lower surface. The geometry of this wedge is different from that of the wedge bounded by plane surfaces. Using the geometrical theorem that the product of the intercepts of intersecting chords are equal, we have

$$r^2 = AB \times BC$$
$$= t(2R - t) = 2Rt - t^2$$

or approximately, since t^2 is small:

$$r^2 = 2Rt$$

Now the path difference for a bright ring (allowing for the phase change on external reflection) is given by:

for the first ring, path difference
$$= 2t_1 = \tfrac{1}{2}\lambda$$

for the second ring, path difference
$$= 2t_2 = 1\tfrac{1}{2}\lambda$$

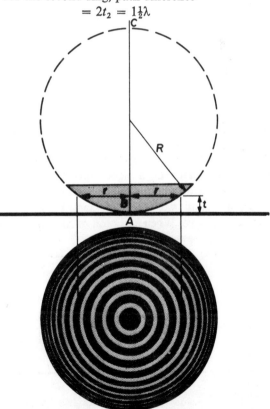

Fig. 15.20. Newton's rings, produced by interference at the air wedge formed by the lower urface of the lens and a plane glass surface.

for the third ring, path difference
$$= 2t_3 = 2\tfrac{1}{2}\lambda$$

for the nth ring, path difference
$$= 2t_n = (n - \tfrac{1}{2})\lambda$$

Putting this expression for $2t_n$ in the above equation for r^2

$$r_n{}^2 = 2Rt_n = R(n - \tfrac{1}{2})\lambda$$

This circular pattern referred to as Newton's rings may be used for any of the purposes for which the air wedge is used. Additionally, the circular pattern may be used to determine the radius of curvature of a lens or to detect any deviations from a spherical shape in the lens surface.

Problem: If the radius of the 14th Newton's ring is 1 mm, when light of wave-length $5 \cdot 89 \times 10^{-7}$ m is used, what is the radius of curvature of the lower surface of the lens used?

Solution:
$$r_n{}^2 = R(n - \tfrac{1}{2})\lambda$$
Substituting values in millimetres
$$1^2 = R(14 - \tfrac{1}{2}) \times 5 \cdot 89 \times 10^{-4}$$
$$R = 1^2 \times \frac{2}{27} \times \frac{1}{5 \cdot 89 \times 10^{-4}}$$
$$R = 126 \text{ mm.}$$

Polarized Light

The phenomena of physical optics show that light has essentially a wave nature. There is a periodic fluctuation in electric and magnetic fields along the length of a light wave. These fields vary at right angles to the direction of motion of the wave, and we therefore classify light as a transverse wave. When a photon of light is emitted

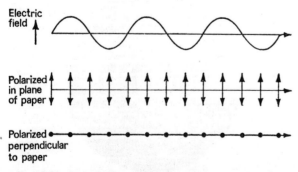

Fig. 15.21. Representing polarized light. The magnetic field at right angles to the electric one is present at every stage but for simplicity it is not represented.

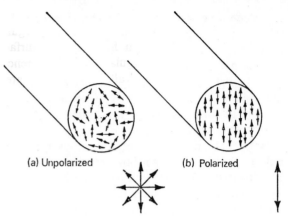

Fig. 15.22. Schematic representation of an unpolarized and a polarized beam of light.

by an atom, its electric field is confined to one plane and we say that it is a plane polarized wave, representing it as in Fig. 15.21.

A ray of light from a normal source contains millions of photons of light, the direction of whose vibration is completely random. This is shown schematically in Fig. 15.22a. The ray as a whole is said to be unpolarized. The ray may be rendered plane polarized as represented by Fig. 15.22b in several ways which we now describe.

Polarizing Sheet. Polarizing sheet produces polarized light and allows us to use large apertures. It depends for its action on a parallel arrangement of crystals which has two effects on the light.

1. It resolves the direction of vibration of the photons of light into only two directions mutually at right angles.

2. It absorbs one of these components of the light and transmits the other. (Fig. 15.23.)

In the polarizing sheet known as 'Polaroid', crystals of iodosulphate of quinine are embedded in the plastic cellulose acetate which, when stretched, lines up all its crystals in the same direction. In a more recent product, the plastic polyvinyl alcohol is first stretched to line up its

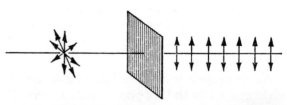

Fig. 15.23. The polarizing effect of polaroid sheet.

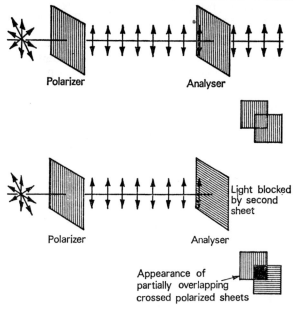

Fig. 15.24. Showing the effect of parallel and crossed polarizing sheet.

long chain-molecules and then it is dipped into a solution of iodine in alcohol. The iodine crystals attach themselves to the plastic chains, all in the same direction. Both materials have a grid structure which, although it is not in fact visible, is shown in the diagrams for convenience of reference.

The effect of a second sheet of polarizer on a light beam depends on its orientation relative to the first polarizing sheet. Its effect changes from being negligible when the polarizing sheets are lined up to completely obscuring the light when they are at right angles. (Fig. 15.24.) For this reason we call the second sheet the analyser and the first sheet the polarizer.

Polarization by Reflection and Scattering

When light meets a surface, both the reflected and refracted components are partially polarized. (Fig. 15.25.) At a certain angle of incidence, however, the reflected light is plane polarized and an analyser can block it completely. This occurs at the angle of incidence (the polarizing angle), for which the reflected and refracted rays are perpendicular. It is left as an exercise for the reader to show that the polarizing angle i_p and the refractive index are related as follows.

$$\mu = \tan i_p$$

This can be used as a basis of measuring the refractive index of non-transparent materials.

The fact that reflected light is partly polarized in general makes polarized sun glasses particularly effective. They will reduce the light from other sources to less than 50 per cent, but by having their polarizing direction vertical they cut down the dazzling reflections from horizontal surfaces by a much bigger factor. Polarizing filters are used by photographers to avoid reflections when they are taking pictures of objects on the other side of glass or water surfaces.

As you may have observed light is scattered by fine particles, shorter wave-length blue light being the most strongly scattered. Thus direct sunlight, contains more of the longer wave-lengths and appears yellowish white, while the sunlight, scattered by dust particles from all parts of the sky, contains a preponderance of shorter wave-lengths, and appears blue. The scattering also tends to polarize the light at right angles to the incident direction, and this can be detected by observing the effect of polarizing sheet on the blue light from the sky. (Fig. 15.26.)

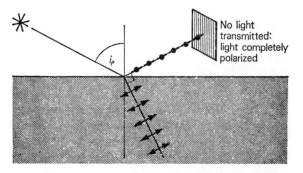

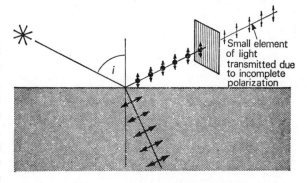

Fig. 15.25. Polarization of the reflected light is only complete when the reflected and refracted rays are perpendicular.

175

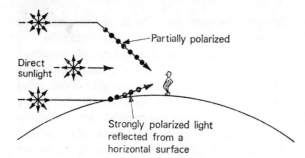

Fig. 15.26. Polarization of sunlight by reflection from horizontal surfaces and by atmospheric scattering.

Double Refraction

In many crystals, such as quartz and calcite, the direction of vibration of the incident light affects the velocity at which it travels through the material. These materials transmit the perpendicular components of the light vibration at different speeds, and therefore the two components are refracted at different angles. (Fig. 15.27.) One of these components (the ordinary ray) has the same velocity for all directions through the crystal, whereas the velocity of the other component (the extra-ordinary ray) varies with the direction. In some crystals, such as tourmaline, one of the rays is heavily absorbed while the other is transmitted, and so the crystal acts as a polarizer. The minute crystals used in 'Polaroid' polarizing sheets are of this type. In other materials, such as calcite, both the ordinary (o) and the extraordinary (e) rays are transmitted.

A polarizer called a Nicol prism can be made from a calcite crystal by eliminating one of the two rays. A calcite crystal is cut into two at a certain angle and then stuck together again by a thin layer of Canada Balsam, which has a refractive index between that of the e and o rays in calcite. Now the e ray is meeting an optically denser material at the surface and it passes into the Canada Balsam. (Fig. 15.28.) The o ray on the other hand is meeting a less optically dense material and it is totally internally reflected to be absorbed by the blackened surface of the crystal. Although the apertures possible with a Nicol prism are limited, they are used in many optical instruments.

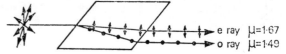

Fig. 15.27. Double refraction by a calcite crystal.

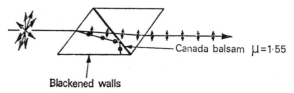

Fig. 15.28. The Nicol prism.

Photoelastic Stress Analysis

When a doubly refracting material is placed between a crossed polarizer and analyser, it causes light to be transmitted through the analyser. (Fig. 15.29.) Now, some materials, such as glass and perspex, become doubly refracting only when they are under physical stress. The effect is called *photoelasticity*.

If a model of a structure is stressed and placed between crossed polaroids, the distribution of the stress in the structure is revealed as a pattern of

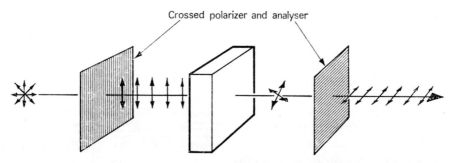

Fig. 15.29. The incident plane polarized light is resolved in two perpendicular directions by the doubly refracting material. A component of both of these now passes through the analyser.

light and shade visible through the analyser. (Fig. 15.30.) The method can be applied to estimate the stress in structures, such as gear teeth, and it is specially useful in cases where calculation is difficult.

Optical Rotation

Certain materials, such as sugar and cellophane, rotate the plane of polarization of light which passes through them. The rotation produced depends on the thickness of the materials traversed and, in the case of sugar, on the strength of the solution. The angle of rotation can be measured

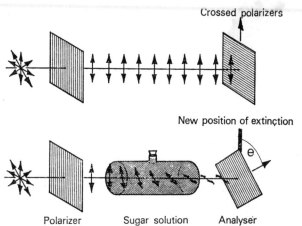

Fig. 15.31. The angle of rotation θ of the plane of polarized light by a sugar solution is measured on a form of polarimeter, the principle of which is shown here.

by placing the materials between crossed polarizer and analyser, when the optical rotation produced enables some light to emerge from the analyser. (Fig. 15.31.) The analyser is then rotated through a measured angle until the light is again extinguished. The instrument used to measure optical rotation is a *polarimeter* and, when it is applied to the measurement of the strength of sugar solutions, it is called a *saccharimeter*.

Polarized light, which was once relegated to the category of amusing but useless phenomena, has found many important applications in science, in engineering, and in our everyday lives.

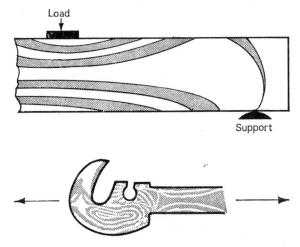

Fig. 15.30. Photoelastic stress patterns in a beam and a hook.

Questions

1. If you squint at a bright point of light it appears to radiate horizontal and vertical shafts of light. How can this be explained in terms of diffraction?

2. What factor decides whether light changes its phase on reflection?

3. What is the difference between diffraction and interference?

4. Why is it difficult to see the interference pattern produced by two slits?

5. Why is it that the two headlamps of a car are seen as one when the car is far away, yet may be seen as two through a telescope?

6. Why is a diffraction grating more effective than a single slit in producing diffraction patterns?

7. Can a significant increase in the resolving power of a microscope be made by using ultra-violet light?

8. What are the advantages of a diffraction grating over a prism for use in a spectrometer?

9. Can a Nicol prism transmit more than half the light it receives?

10. There is a theory that homing pigeons use the direction of polarization of light diffused from the sky to navigate. Would this be a possibility under cloudy conditions?

Problems

1. Two glass plates are separated by an air wedge and light of wave-length 5.88×10^{-7} m falls on them from above. How far is the upper one lifted if five fringes pass a fixed point on the plate?
Answer: 1.46×10^{-6} m.

2. Interference fringes were produced by two slits 0.25 mm apart, on a screen 150 mm from the slits. If eight fringes occupy 2.62 mm, what is the wave-length of the light producing the fringes?
Answer: 5.46×10^{-7} m.

3. Two flat rectangular glass plates touch along one edge and are separated at the opposite edges by a piece of wire. Sixty-four bright fringes are produced under sodium illumination. What is the diameter of the wire? (Wave-length of sodium light = 5.89×10^{-7} m.)
Answer: 1.88×10^{-5} m.

4. Light of wave-length 6×10^{-7} m falls normally on a diffraction grating with 400 lines per mm. At what angles to the normal are the first, second and third order spectra produced?
Answer: $13.9°$, $28.7°$, $46.1°$.

5. What is the smallest separation of objects at a range of 400 m which can be resolved by binoculars with 40 mm diameter objective lenses?
Answer: 73 mm.

6. If a diffraction grating produces a first order spectrum of light of wave-length 6×10^{-7} m at an angle of 20° from the normal, what is its spacing?
Answer: 5.7×10^2 lines/mm.

7. A slit 0.3 mm wide produces a diffraction pattern from a parallel light beam on a screen 100 mm away. If the wave-length of the light is 6×10^{-7} m, how wide is the central bright band?
Answer: 0.4 mm.

8. A tube 100 mm long is filled with a solution of dextrose at a concentration of 0.2 kg/litre. Through what angle will the solution rotate the plane of polarization of polarized light? (Dextrose solution at 1 kg/l rotates the plane through 0.525°/mm.)
Answer: $10.5°$.

9. What is the critical angle at which the ordinary ray is totally internally reflected at the layer of Canada balsam in a Nicol prism? (Refractive index of calcite for o ray is 1.658, refractive index of Canada balsam for o ray is 1.530.)
Answer: $68.5°$.

10. A plano-convex lens is in contact with a flat glass plate, and the space between the two is filled with transparent oil. Newton's rings are produced by illuminating the system normally with light of wave-length 5.9×10^{-7} m and the diameter of the fifth dark ring is 3.86 mm. What is the radius of curvature of the lens? (Refractive index of oil = 1.58.)
Answer: 2m.

11. Newton's rings are formed between a lens and a flat glass surface of wave-length 5.88×10^{-7} m. If the light passes through the gaps at 30° to the vertical and the diameter of the fifth dark ring is 9 mm, what is the radius of curvature of the lens?
Answer: 23.8 m.

12. A receiving station 80 km from a transmitter receives radio waves both directly and indirectly by reflection from the ionosphere, which can be assumed to be 80 km up. What will happen to the signal if the wave-length transmitted is changed gradually from 395 to 405 m?
Answer: Six points of maximum signal will be heard (assuming no phase-change on reflection).

13. A beam of monochromatic light is diffracted by a grating with 400 lines/m. The sines of the angles of diffraction for first, second, and third order spectra are 0.252, 0.501, and 0.755. What is the average wave-length of the light?
Answer: 6.285×10^{-7} m.

14. What thickness of quartz is required to retard the ordinary ray half a wave-length more than the extraordinary ray of light of wave-length 5.89×10^{-7} m? (Refractive index of quartz (o ray) = 1.544; refractive index of quartz (e ray) = 1.553.)
Answer: 3.27×10^{-5} m.

15. What is the least thickness of calcite which will produce destructive interference of light of wave-length 5.89×10^{-7} m if the calcite is placed between crossed Nicol prisms? (Refractive index of calcite (o ray) = 1.658; refractive index of calcite (e ray) = 1.486.)
Answer: 1.71×10^{-6} m.

16. A film of oil is floating on a water surface and is illuminated normally with light of wave-length 5.89×10^{-7} m. How thick is it at the tenth bright band from a point of zero thickness? (Refractive index of oil = 1.48.)
Answer: 1.9×10^{-3} mm.

17. If the opening in the iris diaphragm in someone's eye is equivalent to 3 mm, what is the angle subtended by objects which can just be resolved in light of wave-length 6×10^{-7} m.
Answer: $0.0115°$.

18. Show how the wave theory of light can be used to explain (i) reflection and (ii) refraction at a plane boundary. At what velocity would red light travel in a medium whose refractive index for red light is 1·60? If the refractive index of the medium varies by 2 per cent over the visible spectrum, what (approximately) would be the velocity of blue light in the same medium? (Velocity of light in free space = 3×10^8 m/s.)

(I.E.R.E.)

Answer: $1·875 \times 10^8$ m/s, $1·84 \times 10^8$ m/s.

19. What are the conditions that have to be satisfied if two sources of light are to give rise to a visible optical interference pattern? Describe one method of producing such a pattern. Two line sources of light 0·5 mm apart give rise to a series of fringes on a screen 1 m away. If the wave-length of the light from the sources is $5·89 \times 10^{-7}$ m, what is the separation of the fringes in the interference pattern?

(I.E.R.E.)

Answer: 1·18 mm.

16 Electromagnetic Waves

Light is a form of energy on the move. Its speed is 300,000 km/s, and nothing can travel faster than this. Light has a wave nature, its energy residing in the fluctuating electric and magnetic fields along its path. In this respect, light is like radio and radar waves, infra-red, and X-rays which collectively are called electromagnetic waves. (Fig. 16.1.) They all have the same velocity *in vacuo* and differ from light and from each other only in their wave-lengths (and, therefore, in their frequency since frequency = velocity/wave-length). This variation in wave-length causes the radiations to behave quite differently when they react with matter.

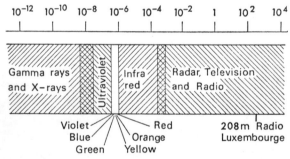

Fig. 16.1. The electromagnetic spectrum. (Wavelengths shown in metres.)

In this chapter we first examine the mechanism of propagation of electromagnetic waves, and then describe some of their properties and applications.

Electromagnetic Forces

A stationary charge of electricity exerts an influence on its surroundings which we call an electric field. This field can be detected by the deflection it produces in a light, suspended, charged particle placed near the charge. (Fig. 16.2a.)

When a charge moves, its electric field moves with it and produces a second type of influence which we call a magnetic field. An example of this is the magnetic field associated with an

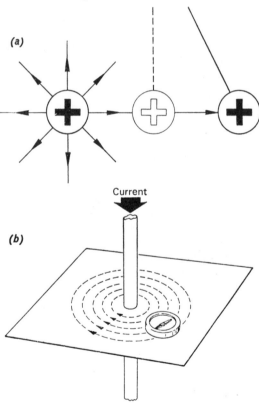

Fig. 16.2. Electromagnetic fields. *(a)* A light charged object is deflected by an electric field. *(b)* A compass needle sets in the direction of the magnetic field.

electric current. (Fig. 16.2b.) The individual charges moving in the current carry the electric field with them and they may be thought of as producing a changing electric field. *Thus any change in an electric field produces a magnetic field.*

Now, as you will know, the movement of a magnet near a wire induces a flow of charge in the wire. We can further analyse this process into two stages. First, *the changing magnetic field produces an electric field* in the wire and then the electrons in the wire move under the influence of this field.

Thus, a change in an electric field gives rise to a magnetic field and a change in a magnetic field gives rise to an electric field. This interdependence suggests the possibility of a repeated transfer of energy between an electric and a magnetic field.

Electromagnetic Waves

Imagine a vibrating charge, which produces a changing electric field around it. This produces a changing magnetic field beyond that, which produces a changing electric field beyond that, and so on, one field following the other in leap-frog fashion. (Fig. 16.3.) In this way, energy travels away from the source as an electromagnetic wave.

The pattern of fields in an electromagnetic wave is shown in Fig. 16.4, the electric and magnetic components being perpendicular to each other and to the direction of travel. Near the source, the electric and magnetic fields are out of step (90 degrees phase difference) but further from the source the two fields get in step and remain so.

Since both electric and magnetic fields can exist in a vacuum, electromagnetic waves do not require any medium for their propagation and they can travel through empty space. The waves travel at a speed of 300,000 km/s (3×10^8 m/s) in a vacuum, but within a material they have a slower speed which depends on the properties of the material.

James Clark Maxwell (1856) first proposed the existence of electromagnetic waves and expressed the results of his theoretical investigation in four fundamental equations, the now famous Maxwell's

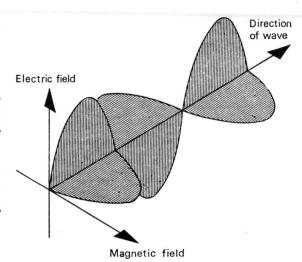

Fig. 16.4. Field variations along an electromagnetic wave.

equations. The velocity of an electromagnetic wave, calculated by Maxwell, agreed so exactly with the velocity of light, which had been measured earlier, that he was convinced that light was an example of an electromagnetic wave. He predicted that an electric charge, in speeding up or slowing down, would emit electromagnetic (e.m.) waves but he did not suggest how such a source could be realized in practice.

The Discovery of Radio Waves

It was about thirty years after Maxwell published his work that Hertz, a young German scientist, successfully produced and detected e.m. waves. He used an induction coil to produce an intermittent high-voltage discharge between two spheres which were connected to short metal rods and fixed about 3 mm apart. (Fig. 16.5.) An e.m. wave was generated by the rapid acceleration of charge in the spark gap. In one of his experiments, a pair of metal parabolic reflectors focused the rays onto a receiver formed by two straight wires and a spark gap. Every spark produced at the transmitter produced a similar though smaller spark at the receiver some 20 m away. As the e.m. wave arrives at the receiver, it exerts an alternating electric field on the electrons in the receiving dipole and thereby produces an alternating current which jumps across the spark gap.

Even today, waves of the wave-length Hertz produced (radiowaves) are sometimes called

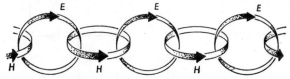

Fig. 16.3. Propagation of electric and magnetic fields in an electromagnetic wave.

181

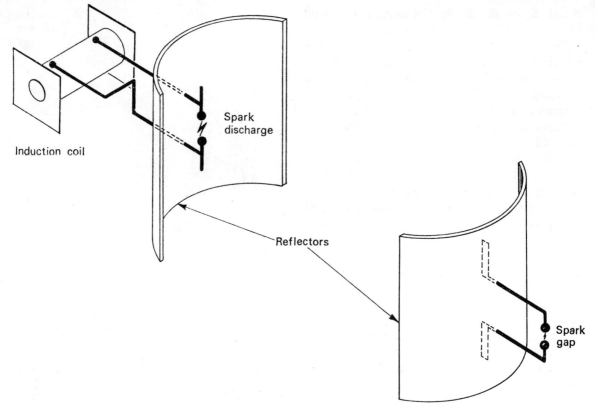

Fig. 16.5. Early experiment to demonstrate the transmission of electromagnetic waves.

Hertzian waves. He reflected the waves from metal surfaces and refracted them by means of a prism made from half a ton of asphalt, thus confirming that the radio waves behave in a similar way to heat and light radiation, differing from them only in wave-length.

A greater degree of control over the trans-mission and detection of e.m. waves is made possible by the use of tuned circuits in both transmitter and receiver. Each of these circuits contains a solenoid of wire, which produces a magnetic field when a current flows through it, and a capacity which produces an electric field when charged. (Fig. 16.6.)

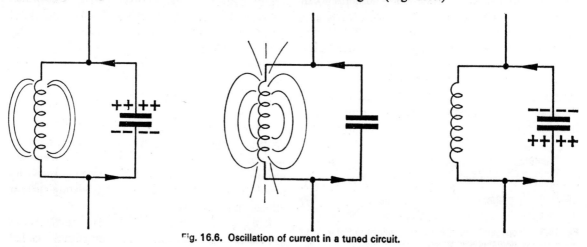

Fig. 16.6. Oscillation of current in a tuned circuit.

1. The starting capacity is charged, and current flows around the circuit producing a magnetic field near the coil.
2. As the current begins to diminish, the changing magnetic field in the coil makes the current continue in the same direction beyond the point where the capacity is discharged.
3. As the magnetic field reaches zero, the capacity is charged opposite to its original one.

The sequence is repeated as the charge transfers back and forth between the plates. This produces an alternating current at a certain frequency, which depends on the capacity and the induction of the solenoid. Because of the resistance in the circuit, energy must be supplied to maintain the oscillation and this is provided by an auxiliary circuit not shown.

The transfer of energy between an oscillating circuit and an e.m. wave is made more efficient by the use of an aerial or antenna. This is a conductor which extends the physical dimensions of a circuit to a size which is related to the wave-length of the transmitted waves. A simple example of this is the Hertzian aerial. (Fig. 16.7.)

Applications of Radio Waves

The term radio waves covers the range of e.m. radiation from wave-lengths of 100 km to 1 mm. Although basically they have the same nature, some of the various wave-lengths of radiation are more suitable for certain purposes than others.

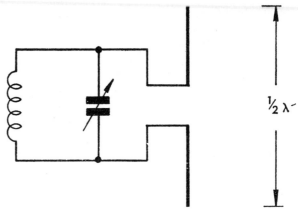

Fig. 16.7. Hertzian aerial.

We divide radio waves into a number of wave-length ranges, giving each range a particular name as shown in Table 16.1.

As with other types of wave, the frequency f and wave-length λ are related to the velocity v of the wave by the equation

$$v = f\lambda$$

One use of radio waves of the shortest wave-length is in the treatment of conditions such as rheumatism and arthritis. They can be focused on to a region within the body, where they are absorbed and produce local heating. The major application of radio waves is in the field of communication. All radio waves can be transmitted between aerials which are directly in line with each other. The curving Earth's surface restricts the range of radar, television, and v.h.f.

Table 16.1. Radio Wave Bands

Abbreviation	Description	Frequency	Wave-length	Application
v.l.f.	very low frequency	3 kHz	100 km	Marine
l.f.	low frequency	30 kHz	10 km	} Long wave broadcast
m.f.	medium frequency	300 kHz	1 km	Medium wave broadcast
h.f.	high frequency	3000 kHz	100 m	
v.h.f.	very high frequency	30 MHz	10 m	} Short wave
u.h.f.	ultra high frequency	300 MHz	1 m	T.V. and F.M.
s.h.f.	super high frequency	3000 MHz	100 mm	Radar and radio astronomy
e.h.f.	extremely high frequency	{ 30,000 MHz	10 mm	{ micro waves } Radiotherapy
		300,000 MHz	1 mm	

waves to line-of-sight distances of about forty kilometres. The range can be extended by the use of very high aerials, such as that on the 190 m Post Office tower in London which transmits programmes to a range of about 70 kilometres.

The rectilinear propagation of microwaves is utilized in radar to plot the position of objects within a few miles of a transmitter. The aerial transmits a narrow beam of radiation as it rotates through a complete circle and also acts as a receiver of the radiation reflected back from any obstacles.

The Earth's atmosphere absorbs most frequencies of electromagnetic waves but it transmits light and microwaves. These act as our windows on the universe. By means of giant radio telescopes, radio astronomers are studying the microwaves from astronomical sources. They have produced interesting new information and discovered the existence of radio stars which are not emitting visible light.

Radio waves of low and medium frequency are refracted by changes in the density of the atmosphere and, being deviated by obstacles, they are able to follow the curvature of the Earth. These waves will give good reception up to about a hundred and fifty km, and a powerful transmitter and favourable geographical position will extend this range several times over.

Long range radio communication is made possible by the ability of the ionosphere to reflect radio waves. The waves may be reflected back and forth several times between the Earth and the ionosphere before arriving at the receiving aerial. The several layers of ionized particles in the ionosphere which reflect the waves vary with the time of day, the season of the year and outbursts of enormous turbulence on the surface of the Sun (sunspots). You may at times have noticed the fading and instability of some radio stations caused by these fluctuations in the ionosphere.

With the development of artificial satellites, we may soon be able to dispense with the ionosphere as a reflector of radio waves and use satellites instead to transmit television and radio waves around the Earth.

X-rays

X-rays are so penetrating that, at the time of their discovery, scientists did not realize they were

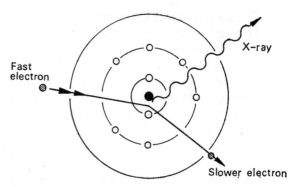

Fig. 16.8. When an electron is slowed down by collision with the nucleus, the energy lost is radiated as an X-ray.

electromagnetic radiations and they called the rays X-rays, meaning unknown rays.

X-rays are produced by the rapid deceleration of electrons as they strike the atoms of a substance. (Fig. 16.8.) Electrons (cathode rays) having acquired their speed by falling through a large potential difference in a high vacuum tube, then collide with a metal target which emits the X-rays. The X-ray tube was developed by W. D. Coolidge to permit the independent control of the intensity and the penetrating power of the X-rays. (Fig. 16.9.)

The intensity of the X-rays, i.e., the energy flowing per unit area per second, increases with the number of electrons in the cathode-ray beam. Thus, the X-ray intensity can be increased by increasing the filament current, raising its temperature, and causing it to emit more electrons.

The ability of X-rays to penetrate matter is related to their wave-length, the shorter wave-lengths generally (but not always) having the greater penetrating power. To shorten the wave-length, we must increase the energy of the individual electrons in the cathode-ray beam. This is achieved

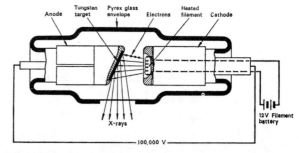

Fig. 16.9. The Coolidge X-ray tube shown here is used in medicine to diagnose disease or damage in the body.

by increasing the potential across the tube. The most penetrating X-rays have wave-lengths down to about 10^{-15} m and can penetrate several centimetres of steel or half a metre of concrete.

Only about 1 per cent of the electrons in the cathode rays produce X-rays, the energy of the remaining electrons being absorbed by the target and changed to heat. For this reason, targets are sometimes air or oil cooled.

The X-rays from a typical target are not evenly distributed among the wave-lengths but are more concentrated near certain wave-lengths. These concentrations appear as peaks on a continuous X-ray spectrum. (Fig. 16.10.) We account for the features of the X-ray spectrum in terms of two X-ray producing mechanisms.

The deceleration of electrons by collisions with atoms of the target produces the continuous spectrum. The frequency of the X-rays is related to the energy lost in a collision by the equation

$$\text{Energy} = hf$$

where the constant, h, is called Planck's constant. Only a few electrons are stopped dead by a single collision. Most of them are stopped by a series of collisions, so that the X-rays have a range of frequencies up to the limit set by the potential applied to the X-ray tube.

The peaks in the X-ray spectrum are caused by the ejection of electrons from orbits near to the nuclei of the target atoms. An excited electron creates a vacancy which is quickly filled by an electron from an outer orbit of the atom. The

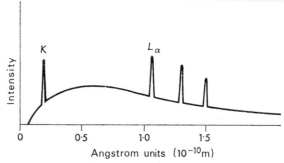

Fig. 16.10. The X-ray spectrum from a typical target shows a continuous band of wave-lengths on which are superimposed peaks at certain wave-lengths.

filling of this vacancy is accompanied by the emission of an X-ray whose wave-length is characteristic of the atoms of the target. (Fig. 16.11.)

Problem: Calculate the wave-length and frequency of the most energetic X-rays produced by a tube operating at 100,000 V (Planck's constant = $6 \cdot 6 \times 10^{-34}$ Js).

Solution: The energy acquired by the electrons in falling through a potential of V volts is given by

$$E = QV$$
$$= (1 \cdot 6 \times 10^{-19})(10^5)$$
$$= 1 \cdot 6 \times 10^{-14} \text{ J}$$

Now
$$E = hf$$

Therefore frequency, $f = \dfrac{E}{h} = \dfrac{1 \cdot 6 \times 10^{-14}}{6 \cdot 6 \times 10^{-34}}$
$$= 2 \cdot 4 \times 10^{19} \text{ Hz}$$

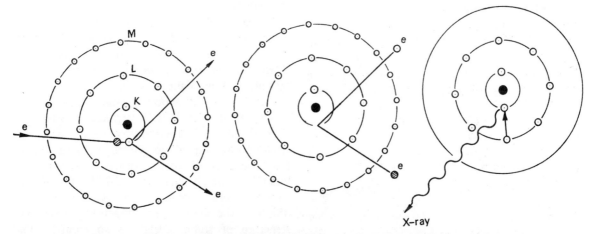

Fig. 16.11. When a fast electron ejects an electron from the lowest, or K shell, it is immediately replaced by an electron from an upper orbit and an X-ray is emitted.

Also $c = f\lambda$ where c, the velocity of e.m. waves =
3×10^8 m/s.

Therefore $\lambda = \dfrac{c}{f} = \dfrac{3 \times 10^8}{2 \cdot 4 \times 10^{19}}$

$$= 1 \cdot 25 \times 10^{-11} \text{ m}$$

Gamma-rays

Gamma-rays were so named to distinguish them
from the other emissions from radioactive substances, i.e., the α(alpha)- and β(beta)- particles.

Gamma-rays are indistinguishable from X-rays,
differing only in the way they are produced. In
general, the range of wave-lengths emitted by
radioactive nuclei (down to 10^{-13} m) is contained
within the range of wave-length that can be
produced in X-ray tubes (down to 10^{-15} m).
Gamma-rays are emitted from some radioactive
substances as a result of the rearrangement of the
nuclei of their atoms. The nuclei revert to a lower
energy state, at the same time emiting the excess
energy as a quantum of gamma-radiation.

One most interesting property of high energy
e.m. radiation is its ability on striking a nucleus
to change itself into a pair of particles. The
radiation disappears and both a normal negatively
charged electron and a positive electron are
created in its place. A positive electron or *positron*
produced by this or any other reaction, is very
short lived, combining immediately with an electron to produce further e.m. radiation. (Fig. 16.12.)
Radiation derived in this way is called annihilation
radiation.

Uses of X-rays and Gamma-rays

Within weeks of the discovery of X-rays by
Roentgen in 1895, they were being used to aid
surgeons in carrying out operations. Nowadays,
most of us are X-rayed regularly as a matter of
routine. The most common medical application

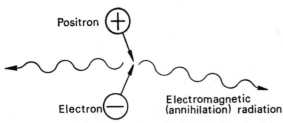

Fig. 16.12. A positron and an electron annihilate each other
and give rise to e.m. radiation.

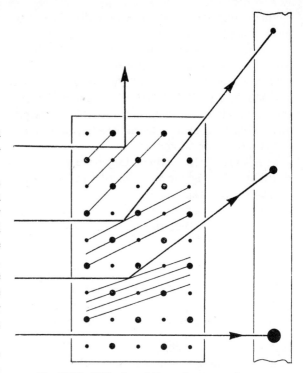

Fig. 16.13. Diffraction of X-rays by planes of atoms.

of X-rays makes use of the different absorbing
powers of the various types of body tissue. The
body acts like a photographic negative and any
unusual features, such as bone fractures or
malignant growths, are made visible on a sensitized
plate. A second medical use of X-rays and gamma-
rays is in the treatment of cancerous growths,
which are arrested in their development by the
irradiation.

The study of X-rays is almost inseparable from
the science of crystallography. Originally, X-rays
were identified as e.m. radiation by diffracting
them with the regular planes of atoms within a
crystal, just as light is diffracted by the lines
drawn on a diffraction grating. (Fig. 16.13.)
Having used crystals with well-known structures
to establish the nature and wave-length of X-rays,
scientists were quick to use them to investigate
the structures of other crystals. X-ray crystallography, which may be called 'microscopy
without lenses', involves the recognition of an
object by the shape of its diffraction pattern. The
structure of some crystals is so complex that
their X-ray diffraction patterns take years to

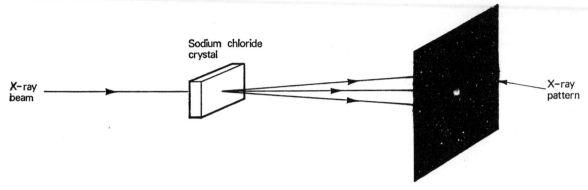

Fig. 16.14. An X-ray diffraction pattern.

analyse. (Fig. 16.14.) This is a field in which computers can be used with great advantage.

The compactness of radioactive sources of e.m. radiation favours the use of gamma-rays in many cases. Some of the applications of gamma-rays are described in chapter 9.

Optical Radiations

The optical section of the complete e.m. spectra includes the infra-red, the visible and the ultra-violet wave-lengths. All three of these radiations can be reflected and refracted by optical instruments to produce images. Since glass absorbs some ultra-violet and infra-red radiation, however, instruments designed for use with these wave-lengths must have lenses of materials which are transparent to these radiations, such as quartz (u.v.) and rocksalt (i.r.). Alternatively, mirrors instead of lenses are used.

If the temperature of a solid is raised, it begins to glow dull red at about 1000K. As the temperature rises further, the solid emits more light, and the colour changes to orange, then yellow, and eventually, at about 6000K, to white. The graph of Fig. 16.15 shows how the energy radiated from a hot solid is distributed among the wave-lengths at various temperatures, and it can be seen that the visible light is only a part of the total radiant energy.

With increasing temperature, the energy peak moves to shorter wave-lengths until at 6000K, the Sun's temperature, the peak occurs in the visible region. This is no coincidence, but a result of the evolution of the eye to be sensitive to the most predominant wave-lengths in daylight. About 48

per cent of the Sun's total radiant energy is infra-red radiation, 40 per cent is visible light, and 12 per cent is ultra-violet light.

All three optical radiations affect the human body. The skin absorbs infra-red, visible, and ultra-violet radiation, all of which contribute to a rise in temperature which is detected by the nerves in the skin. The retina of the eye is sensitive not only to the presence of light but also to the actual pattern of light and shade.

The ultra-violet light affects the skin in a different way. It produces a chemical change which results in darker pigmentation, i.e., a suntan. The u.v. component of sunshine helps the body to make vitamin D which is essential for the healthy growth of teeth and bones. Excessive amounts of u.v. radiation can cause damage to the retina and can cause temporary or even permanent blind-

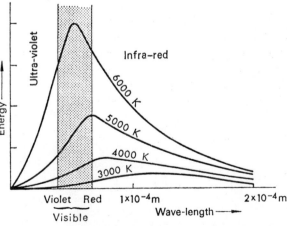

Fig. 16.15. Distribution of the electromagnetic radiation from a hot object up to the Sun's surface temperature (6000K).

ness. Dangerous levels of u.v. radiation are to be found at high altitude and where the Sun's rays are strongly reflected from snow or sand surfaces. In these settings, sun goggles or glasses are worn for protection rather than for comfort or adornment.

Ultra-violet radiation kills germs and is used in hospitals to sterilize instruments and room interiors. Food keeps longer in a fresh condition if it is radiated with u.v. rays to kill the germs which cause decay.

Infra-red radiation penetrates fog and haze, and, by using suitable sensitive photographic plates, we can take clear photographs under conditions which would make ordinary photography impossible.

Infra-red radiation may penetrate deeply into a substance before being absorbed and it can thus be used to produce more even heating. This property finds an application in the quick drying of paints on cars and in the dehydration of foods.

Some of the sources, detectors, and applications of e.m. radiation are shown in Table 16.2.

The Spectrometer

The distribution of energy among the radiated wave-lengths from a particular light source is measured by means of a spectrometer. The essential function of the instrument is to disperse the radiation into its different wave-lengths. This is achieved either by a diffraction grating or by a triangular prism. (Fig. 16.16.) The collimator

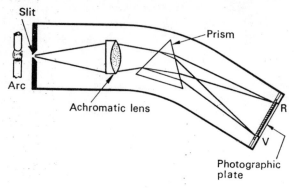

Fig. 16.17. Prism spectrometer.

projects a parallel beam of light through an illuminated slit and, after passing through the grating or prism, this light is focused onto the crosswires of an eyepiece or a photographic plate. (Fig. 16.17.) Each wave-length produces an image of the slit in a different position on the photographic plate. The overall pattern is a spectrum of the source.

Emission Spectra

When the atoms of a gas or vapour are excited, as for example by heating or by an electrical discharge, they emit light. As a result of the excitation, electrons transfer from their normal low energy orbits into higher energy orbits further from the nucleus. The light is emitted every time an electron returns to an orbit of lower energy. In each transition, the difference in energy between two orbits, represented by energy states E_1 and E_2, is radiated as a photon of light of a definite frequency

$$E_1 - E_2 = hf$$

Since the number of possible electron orbits in an atom is limited, the transitions are also limited, so that the light emitted contains a limited number of frequencies. (Fig. 16.18.) Such a source produces a line spectrum extending beyond the visible spectrum and characteristic of the atoms of the source. (Fig. 16.19.)

Sometimes molecules, each consisting of several atoms, can be excited to act as a source of light. In this case, the effect of the closely packed atoms on each other is to allow slight variations of the single energy states of individual atoms. (Fig. 16.20.) This multiplies the number of possible

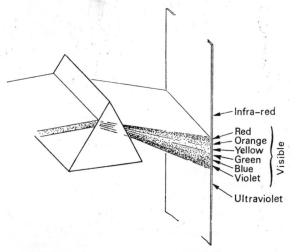

Fig. 16.16. Dispersion of optical radiations by a prism.

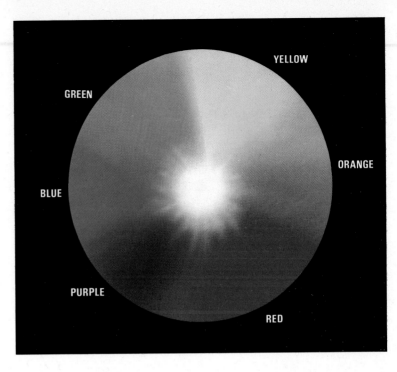

Fig. 16.19 Emission spectra, absorption spectra, and Fraunhofer absorption lines in the light from the Sun.

Fig. 16.24 Range of spectral and non-spectral colours.

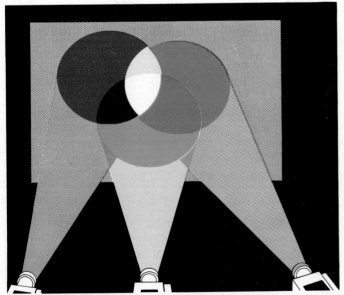

Fig. 16.27 Additive primary colours.

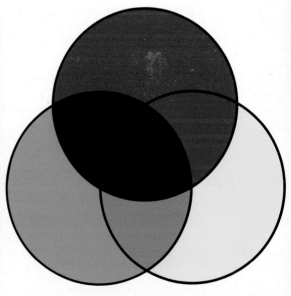

Fig. 16.28 Subtractive primary colours.

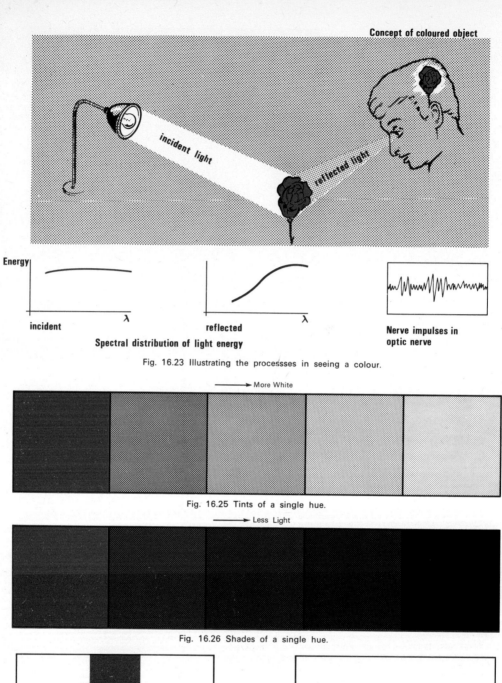

Concept of coloured object

incident light

reflected light

Energy

incident

reflected

λ

λ

Spectral distribution of light energy

Nerve impulses in optic nerve

Fig. 16.23 Illustrating the processses in seeing a colour.

More White →

Fig. 16.25 Tints of a single hue.

Less Light →

Fig. 16.26 Shades of a single hue.

Fig. 16.29 If the gaze is fixed on this picture and then transferred to a plain white sheet, the image will be seen momentarily in complementary colours.

Table 16.2.

	γ-rays and X-rays	Ultra-violet	Light	Infra-red	s.h.f.	u.h.f.	v.h.f.	h.f.	m.f.	l.f.	v.l.f.
Frequency (Hz)		3×10^{16}	7.5×10^{14}	4×10^{14} ; 3×10^{14} ; 3×10^{11}	3×10^{9}	3×10^{8}	3×10^{7}	3×10^{6}	3×10^{5}	3×10^{4}	
λ (m)	10^{-15} ; 10^{-11}	10^{-8}	4×10^{-7}	7×10^{-7} ; 10^{-3}	10^{-1}	1	10	10^{2}	10^{3}	10^{4}	
SOURCES	Deceleration of high energy particles; Radioactive nuclei	Electron transitions in atoms →	Incandescent objects →	Molecules during rotational transitions	Electrons resonating magnetically	Inter-stellar hydrogen	*Aerials carrying oscillating currents* →	Nuclei resonating magnetically			
DETECTORS	Geiger Counters or Fluorescent Materials; Scintillation Counters; Photographic emulsions →		Eyes	Thermometers, thermopiles, photoelectric cells, the skin	*Aerials and Tuned Electronic circuits* →						
APPLICATIONS	Radiation therapy; Medical examination; Inspection of materials; Investigation of crystal structure and of nuclear and atomic structure	Germicide generator of vitamins in the body; Chemical analysis and investigation of atomic structure photography →		Radiant heating	Radar	Television →		International and amateur	Radio Broadcasting →	Mobile radio; Navigation →	

189

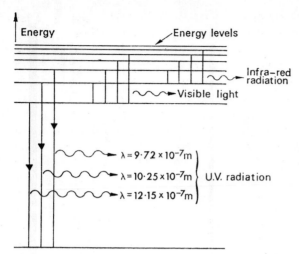

Fig. 16.18. Energy levels in the hydrogen atom. The transitions of an electron between energy states of an atom are limited. Each transition is accompanied by the emission of light of a certain frequency.

transitions between states. Each line in the spectrum from separate atoms becomes a series of lines when molecules are the source. These lines are grouped so close together that they appear to merge into bands. (Fig. 16.19.)

When the source of light is an incandescent solid, liquid, or highly compressed gas, the interaction of the atoms increases to such an extent that the light emitted contains a continuous range of frequencies and produces a continuous spectrum.

Absorption Spectra

We have seen that, when an electron in the atom transfers to a lower energy orbit, it emits light, but the reverse process is also possible, i.e., an electron may absorb light and transfer to a

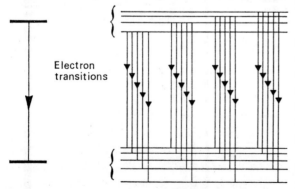

Fig. 16.20. Single levels in the isolated atom are multiplied into a band of levels in the molecules because a larger number of transitions become possible.

190

higher energy orbit. Any photon of light which has sufficient energy can produce the transfer, but the most effective frequency is that which provides exactly the right amount of energy. Consequently, an atom absorbs most strongly those frequencies of light which it emits when excited. This effect is shown in Fig. 16.19 where an emission spectrum of mercury is compared with an absorption spectrum of mercury produced by passing the light from an incandescent solid through mercury vapour.

Applications of Spectroscopy

No two elements have the same spectrum and, therefore, the light from the vapour of an element identifies the element precisely. Where a mixture of several elements is emitting light, we can not only identify the elements, but also deduce the

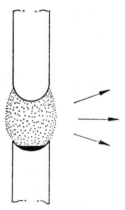

Fig. 16.21. Light from the vapour of a substance is produced by placing it in the crater of a carbon arc.

percentage composition by measuring the relative brightness of the spectrum of each element. Spectrum analysis is especially important where non-destructive testing is essential or where extremely rapid results are required. A minute quantity of a substance acts as an adequate source when placed in the crater of a carbon arc. (Fig. 16.21.) Alternatively, the absorption spectrum may be used for the analysis of some transparent solids, liquids, and vapours.

The interior of the Sun emits a continuous spectrum of light, but certain frequencies are absorbed as the light passes through the cooler exterior of the Sun and the atmosphere of the Earth. (Fig. 16.19.)

The black lines which appear in the spectrum of sunlight (called Fraunhofer lines) give information about the elements present in the Sun. In the early investigation of the Fraunhofer lines, one series of lines did not correspond to any element then known on Earth. It was some twenty-five years before the element helium, which produces these lines, was discovered on Earth.

A great deal of the information we have about the atom was, in fact, gained from a detailed study of spectra. Historically, it was the simplicity of the hydrogen spectrum which encouraged scientists to develop more sophisticated models of the electronic structure of the atom. (Fig. 16.22.)

The wave-lengths of these lines follow the empirical formula

$$\frac{1}{\lambda} = R\left\{\frac{1}{n^2} - \frac{1}{m^2}\right\}$$

where R is a constant and n and m are small whole numbers such that $m > n$. The lines in the

4×10^{-7}m $\qquad\qquad\qquad$ 7×10^{-7}m

Fig. 16.22. Lines in the visible spectrum of hydrogen.

visible part of the spectrum have $n = 2$ and $m = 3, 4, 5, 6$, etc. Other series exist, one in the ultra-violet, for which $n = 1$, and two in the infra-red, for which $n = 3$ and $n = 4$.

This equation, which relates the frequency of the emitted light to the difference between two terms, was an important stepping stone towards the idea of electron transitions between energy states and towards the orbital model of the atom.

Colour

Colour has always played an important part in the life of man but not until recent years has the value of colour been widely realized. Skilful use of colour has been found to increase efficiency in the factory and promote sales in the supermarket. More important, colour can be used to create a pleasant atmosphere in man's home and environment.

Colour is one of the most familiar yet least understood feature of our everyday lives. The root of this lack of understanding lies in our subjective appreciation of colour. (Fig. 16.23.) Colour, like beauty, exists essentially in the eye of the beholder. In the perception of colour, as in the case of sound, the human senses are better able to compare than they are to judge absolute values. The eye can distinguish very finely between adjacent colours in the spectrum but it cannot be relied upon to give an objective evaluation of a single colour.

The basic stimulus for colour vision lies in a narrow range of wave-lengths in the electro-magnetic spectrum which we call light (4×10^{-7}–7×10^{-7} m). The way in which the light energy is shared among the wave-lengths of the spectrum gives rise to the sensation of colour. For example, a light containing a predominance of energy in the longer wave-lengths is red, while an energy predominance in the shorter wave-lengths produces a blue colour. It is common to identify six colours in the complete spectrum, namely, red, orange, yellow, green, blue, violet. The number of colours we identify and the boundaries between them are matters of pure choice, since there are no sudden changes in wave-length as we go across the spectrum.

Each line in a line spectrum has its own distinct colour, but the colours we see in the world around us are rarely so well defined. The nearest approach to monochromatic light we commonly see is the light from the yellow sodium vapour street lamps. Most lights are composed of a wider range of wave-lengths of varying intensity. Such mixtures give rise to a colour sensation which cannot be reproduced by any single spectral colour. White light is a mixture of all the wave-lengths of the visible spectrum in approximately equal intensities. Purple does not exist in the spectrum but is obtained by combining the red and blue light from the extremes of the spectrum.

Colour Description

The English language is rich in words describing colour. Apart from colours which have their own names, (how many names can you think of which refer to a type of red?) there are many qualifying words such as vivid, bright, clean, pale, light—to mention only a few. In a particular context, such words may be useful and apt but they are rather imprecise. For objective description, we require words which describe well defined colour variables. In general, a colour may differ in three respects, described as hue, saturation, and lightness.

Hue. Hue is the colour of the predominant wave-length present in the light. It defines the position of a colour in the spectrum. (Fig. 16.24.) Although purple has no position in the continuous spectrum, it is included as a principal hue between red and blue. (Fig. 16.24.)

Saturation. The degree to which light energy is concentrated into a range of wave-lengths determines the saturation of a colour. When most of the wave-lengths present in a colour are near the predominant wave-length, the colour is highly saturated. Adding white to a colour reduces the saturation. The ultimate in saturation is the light in a single spectral line. Even the most saturated colours we commonly see are far less saturated than a spectral line. Variations of saturation produced by adding white to a colour are called tints. (Fig. 16.25.)

Lightness. The lightness of a colour is the most difficult feature to specify. The eye tends to equalize the lightness of colours viewed independently by opening or closing the iris. The eye can only compare the levels of light being emitted from different surfaces. Lightness is therefore measured for a surface colour by its reflectance factor, i.e., by the ratio of the light intensity reflected from the colour to the light reflected from a standard white surface under the same illumination. Colours which differ only in lightness are called shades. (Fig. 16.26.)

Colour Vision

The detection of colour on the retina is thought to be a photochemical process but at present there is no adequate theory which is supported by anatomical evidence. There are two types of light receptors, the rods and the cones. The cones are associated with colour vision, whereas the rods respond to all colours of light but give only the sensations of grey, black, and white. At low levels of illumination the cones are not stimulated. Thus, in poor light, such as moonlight, we see no colour, and everything appears grey.

The eye is not a reliable indicator of colour in the absence of a reference colour. It is primarily sensitive to the presence and distribution of longer and shorter wave-lengths of light. A remarkably wide range of colour sensation is stimulated if lights of only two different wave-lengths are combined in different proportions. For example, a picture projected using only green and orange light would appear to have a range of colour variation. The scene is first photographed through two different coloured filters and two black and white transparencies made. One transparency is illuminated with the green and the other with the orange, and the projected images are accurately superimposed.

When we cannot see *any* red or blue light we are hardly aware of their absence, and the picture appears vivid. It is not until we see a picture made up of a wider range of visible wave-lengths that the deficiencies of the two-component picture becomes obvious. You may have noticed a similar effect when wearing tinted sun glasses. After you have worn them for some time, things appear to have their normal colours, despite the fact that your eye may be receiving a reduced range of wave-lengths.

Another interesting subjective phenomenon is the inversion of colour sensation which occurs when a particular colour is viewed fixedly for some time. On transferring the gaze to a plain white sheet, the complementary colour is seen for a short time. (Fig. 16.29.)

Defective Colour Vision

Dalton was the first person to report colour deficiency. He was himself colour blind, as he discovered when flowers appearing the same colour to him were declared to be different by his friends.

In one common form of colour blindness, the sensitivity to the longer wave-lengths of light stops short at $6 \cdot 8 \times 10^{-7}$ m, instead of the normal $7 \cdot 5 \times 10^{-7}$ m. This gives a reduced sensitivity to red light, and the person sees a restricted range of hues. In a second type of colour deficiency, red and green light produces the same sensation which a person with normal vision would describe as yellow. Thus, when two colours differ only in a region of the spectrum of reduced sensitivity, they appear the same to a person with defective colour vision.

About 8 per cent of men and about 1 per cent of women have some degree of colour blindness, although they may not be aware of it. Under poor lighting conditions, a person with mildly defective colour vision could confuse colour coded wires, etc. Effective tests do exist for detecting colour blindness and these are used to advise people against entering occupations in which colour deficiency is a disadvantage, or even a danger, such as that of a pilot. An engineer would not normally find colour defective vision a disadvantage, but knowledge of the defect would enable him to avoid working in poor light with colour coded components.

Addition of Coloured Lights

When coloured lights are combined, the resulting colour contains all the wave-lengths present in the components, and the colour sensation they produce is intermediate between the two on the continuous spectrum, e.g., red plus green gives yellow. If these colours are too far apart, they produce a new non-spectral colour sensation, e.g., blue plus red equals purple (not green).

Control of the light of all the visible wave-lengths is not essential to produce a certain colour sensation. It is found by experiment that any given colour can be matched to the eye's satisfaction by combining together in the right proportion, light from only three parts of the spectrum. The three colours of light which are most effective in producing a match, when added together, are red, green, and blue and, for this reason, they are called primary colours. (Fig. 16.27.)

If two particular colours produce white when they are added together, e.g., yellow and blue, magenta and green, they are said to be complementary colours.

Subtractive Processes

Paints, dyes, and inks produce colour by the selective absorption of certain wave-lengths from the radiation which is incident upon them. Red opaque substances reflect red light and absorb green and blue light. In the same way, green substances absorb red and blue light, while blue substances absorb green and red light. Most substances do not absorb in so well defined a way as this. A substance appears yellow if it absorbs the complementary colour, blue. Thus, a magenta substance absorbs green light and a turquoise substance absorbs red light. In a similar way the production of colour by passing light through coloured filters is a subtractive process. The primary colours for subtractive processes are red, yellow, and blue. (Fig. 16.28.)

Specification of a Colour

The specification of a colour is a quantitative measurement, as distinct from a description which is qualitative. A colour is specified most precisely by its spectral distribution curve. (Fig. 16.30.) This is obtained in two stages:

1. Separation of the wave-lengths present by prism diffraction grating or colour filter.

2. Measurement of the light intensity in each range of wave-lengths by photometer.

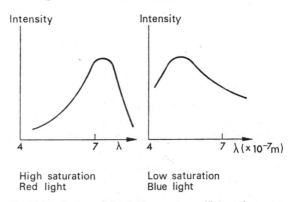

High saturation
Red light

Low saturation
Blue light

Fig. 16.30. A spectral distribution curve specifies a colour more exactly than matching techniques.

It is not necessary to know the complete spectral distribution to specify a colour to the satisfaction of the eye. If the colour is first matched by a combination of the three primary colours, and the intensity of each primary recorded, the colour can then be specified, and it can be reproduced at any time. This is the basis of the Commission Internationale de l'Eclairage (C.I.E.) system of colour specification.

An alternative system is to match a colour by comparison with a series of standard coloured cards. These are divided first into the major hues, which may number as many as forty-eight, including non-spectral colours. Within each hue, the saturation and lightness of the cards are varied in a systematic way. The final match is specified by the reference number of the matching card. The illumination used in judging the colour match is critical, and checks must be made to detect any change which the passage of time may bring about in the colour of the cards.

Questions

1. Why was Maxwell's discovery that light was an electromagnetic wave so important?

2. How did we receive T.V. programmes from Europe before artificial satellites?

3. Why are X-rays rather than light rays used to investigate crystal structure?

4. An absorption spectrum is produced by an electron absorbing light of a particular wave-length and being raised to a higher energy stage. Since it will emit light of the same wave-length when it reverts to its original state, why do the two effects not cancel out?

5. If the sensation produced in your brain by the colour red is the same as that produced in someone else's brain by the colour green, could you detect this? Does the question mean anything?

6. Why do women, when matching accessories, often carry them to the shop door to compare them?

7. Explain why shorter wave-length X-rays are more penetrating, while infra-red rays are better at penetrating fog than shorter wave-length visible light.

8. How could you use the Doppler effect to measure the rotation of the Sun?

9. Explain rainbows.

10. Why does mixing coloured lights have a different effect from mixing paints of the same colours?

11. Could you see a light beam travelling through space?

12. Why do you think some spectra show bands with one edge sharply defined, while the other edge tails off gradually?

13. What are the advantages and disadvantages of recording a spectrum photographically, and scanning it with a photoelectric instrument?

14. Explain how some dyes (often put in anti-freeze solutions) appear green by reflected light, but red by transmitted light.

15. From what kind of source can one obtain a line emission spectrum?

16. How can (a) radio waves and (b) X-rays, be used in medicine?

17. In what way is the human body sensitive to ultra-violet, infra-red, and light radiations?

18. How do we explain the peaks of the X-ray spectrum?

19. Why do we need to control independently the penetrating power and the intensity of X-rays?

Problems

1. Find the frequency of light of wave-length $4 \cdot 2 \times 10^{-7}$ m. ($c = 3 \times 10^8$ ms^{-1}).
   Answer: $7 \cdot 14 \times 10^{14}$ Hz.

2. Calculate the energy of a quantum of the following radiations:
   (a) A radio wave, frequency $1 \cdot 0 \times 10^6$ Hz.
   (b) An infra-red wave, frequency $3 \cdot 0 \times 10^{14}$ Hz.
   (c) An X-ray, frequency $3 \cdot 0 \times 10^{17}$ Hz.
   (Planck's constant $= 6 \cdot 6 \times 10^{-34}$ Js.)

Answer: (a) $6 \cdot 6 \times 10^{-28}$ J; (b) $2 \cdot 0 \times 10^{-19}$ J; (c) $2 \cdot 0 \times 10^{-16}$ J.

3. What is the energy of an electron striking the face of a television set after travelling through a potential difference of 750 volts? (Charge of electron $= 1 \cdot 6 \times 10^{-19}$C; Planck's constant $= 6 \cdot 6 \times 10^{-34}$ Js.)
   Answer: $1 \cdot 2 \times 10^{-16}$ J.

17 Sound Waves

The source of all compressional waves is vibration. The essential requirement for the propagation of these waves is a medium in which the particles are close enough to react on each other. This is provided by solids, liquids, and gases at normal and higher pressure, but not by a vacuum or a highly rarified gas. The fluctuating quantity in a compressional wave is the position of the particles in its path, which, in turn, gives rise to periodic variations in the pressure. Some vibrations you can see or feel, as is the case with a drum or a plucked guitar string, but a much wider range of energies and frequencies of compressional waves can be detected by the ear as sound. Vibrations of frequencies which the ear cannot detect are the *infrasonic* frequencies below about 20 vibrations per second and the *ultrasonic* frequencies of above about 20,000 vibrations per second.

The ear is sensitive to three properties of sound: the energy concentration in the sound wave, which determines the loudness of the sound; the frequency of the sound wave, which determines the pitch of the note; and the complexity of the sound wave, which determines the tone or quality of the note. Sound is, however, a subjective sensation and, although this may be our ultimate interest, we will first consider compression waves independently of the sensation they produce.

Compression Waves

Compression waves are longitudinal, that is, the particles in the path of the wave move to and fro in the direction the wave travels. A longitudinal wave can be represented graphically by plotting the displacement of each particle from its equilibrium position against its distance along the wave. Alternatively, the wave can be represented by a graph of pressure against distance along the wave. (Fig. 17.1.) The molecules in gases do not keep fixed equilibrium positions but maintain an

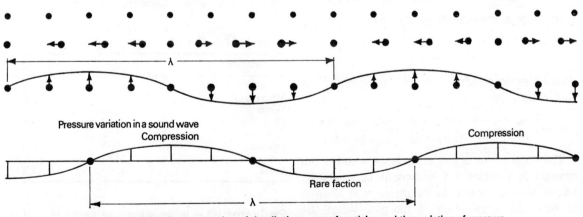

Fig. 17.1 Graphical representation of the displacement of particles and the variation of pressure in a compression wave. Note that momentarily undisturbed particles are at the centre of rarefactions and compressions.

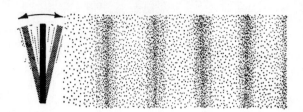

Fig. 17.2. Pressure variations in a sound wave.

average distribution so that it is easier to visualize a sound wave in a gas as a pressure variation. (Fig. 17.2.)

The velocity of a compression wave depends on the rate with which the displaced particles in its path return towards their undisturbed positions. The restoring force which determines this speed increases with the elasticity of the medium. The return is retarded by the inertia of the medium, which is effectively represented by its density. The velocity depends on these two factors in the following way, which can be verified by direct measurement.

$$\text{Velocity} = \sqrt{\frac{\text{elasticity}}{\text{density}}}$$

In a solid rod, the equation for the velocity of sound in a medium of density ρ becomes

$$v = \sqrt{\frac{E}{\rho}}$$

where E is Young's modulus defined as

$$E = \frac{\text{stress}}{\text{strain}} = \frac{\text{force/cross-sectional area}}{\text{fractional change in length}}$$

In a liquid, the velocity is given by

$$v = \sqrt{\frac{K}{\rho}}$$

where K is the bulk modulus of the liquid defined by the equation

$$K = \frac{\text{bulk stress}}{\text{bulk strain}} = \frac{\text{compressive force/unit area}}{\text{fractional change in volume}}$$

The elasticity of a gas depends on whether the changes in pressure are isothermal or adiabatic, i.e., on whether or not the compression is allowed to raise the temperature of the gas. When the change occurs slowly, there is time for any excess heat to be conducted away and thus the temperature remains constant. The change is then isothermal and it follows the relation

$$pV = \text{a constant}$$

The bulk modulus in this case is equal to its pressure p.

In a sound wave, the changes in pressure along a wave are rapid. There is not time for the heat to flow to equalize the temperature. Momentarily the compressions are warmer and the rarefactions cooler than the average temperature. (Fig. 17.3.) The changes in a sound wave are thus adiabatic and they are governed by the relation

$$pV^{\gamma} = \text{a constant}$$

where γ is a constant for a particular gas as explained previously. The bulk modulus in an adiabatic is equal to the product γp, and the equation for the velocity of sound in a gas becomes

$$v = \sqrt{\frac{\gamma p}{\rho}}$$

The velocity of sound waves in different media are given in Table 17.1.

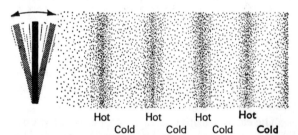

| Hot | Hot | Hot | **Hot** |
| Cold | Cold | Cold | **Cold** |

Fig. 17.3. The pressure changes in a sound wave instantaneously produce temperature variations.

Table 17.1. Velocity of sound in different media

Medium	m/s	km/h
Air at 0°C	331	1190
Hydrogen	1270	4570
Water	1440	5170
Pine	3320	12000
Oak	3850	13800
Granite	6000	21600
Iron	5130	18400
Brass	3500	12600

Problem: What is the velocity of sound in steel of density 7.8×10^3 kg/m³ and modulus of elasticity 2×10^{11} N/m².

Solution:

$$\text{Velocity} = \sqrt{\frac{\text{Elasticity}}{\text{density}}} = \sqrt{\frac{2 \times 10^{11}}{7 \cdot 8 \times 10^3}}$$

$$= 5 \cdot 1 \times 10^3 \text{ m/s}$$

Variation of Velocity with Temperature

We have seen that the velocity of sound waves in any medium is determined by its elasticity and density. In the case of solids and liquids, these quantities do not always change regularly with temperature, but they do in the case of gases.

$$\text{Velocity} = \sqrt{\frac{\gamma p}{\rho}}$$

For a given mass of gas in a volume V we know that

$$pV = mRT \text{ and } \rho = m/V$$

$$\therefore \quad \text{Velocity} = \sqrt{\frac{\gamma mRT/V}{m/V}} = \sqrt{(\gamma RT)}$$

Since γ and R are constants, the expression shows that the velocity of sound in a gas is directly proportional to the square root of the absolute temperature. It also shows that a change in pressure affects the density in such a way that the velocity of sound remains constant.

Problem: Calculate the velocity of sound in air at 0°C and 20°C if the density of air at S.T.P. is $1 \cdot 3 \text{ kg/m}^3$, and γ for air equals $1 \cdot 4$.

Solution: Standard atmospheric pressure is equal to $101 \times 10^3 \text{ N/m}^2$

$$\text{Velocity at } 0°C = \sqrt{\frac{\gamma P}{\rho}} = \sqrt{\frac{1 \cdot 4}{1 \cdot 3} \times 101 \times 10^3}$$

$$= 330 \text{ m/s}$$

Since velocity $\propto \sqrt{(\text{absolute temp})}$

$$\text{velocity at } 20°C = 330 \sqrt{\frac{293}{273}} = 353 \text{ m/s}$$

Reflection and Refraction of Sound Waves

When a sound wave meets a boundary at which its velocity changes, some of its energy is reflected. (Fig. 17.4.) The reflection may be regular, as for

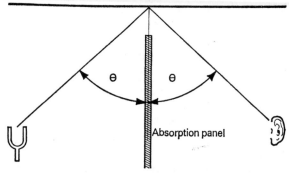

Fig. 17.4. Sound is reflected regularly at a smooth hard surface; the maximum intensity being detected in the direction which makes angles of incidence and reflection equal.

a light wave, but in the case of sound, this is not so apparent because it is strongly scattered by obstacles in its path. The amount of sound energy reflected at a boundary increases with the angle of incidence and with the abruptness of the change in its velocity. (Fig. 17.5.)

When sound waves are changed in velocity by entering a different medium or by changes in the properties within one medium, their direction may be changed. This refraction is occurring constantly to sound waves travelling through the air due to temperature gradients in the air. Thus, sounds

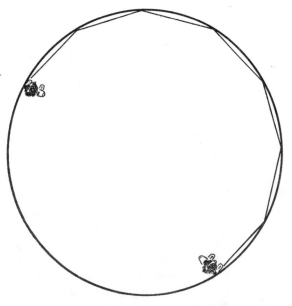

Fig. 17.5. In the whispering gallery of St. Paul's, repeated total internal reflection of sound at grazing incidence confines the sound, near the surface and makes even a whisper audible.

197

carry further at night than during the day because of the different temperature distributions which exist at these times. (Fig. 17.6.)

A similar effect is produced by a wind blowing between source and observer. The velocity of the wind increases with the distance from the ground, and this gradient slews the waves round, thus changing their direction. (Fig. 17.7.)

Doppler Effect

Everyone has heard the Doppler effect at some time, though perhaps without realizing it. The Doppler effect is the drop in the observed frequency of a source of sound as it passes and recedes from the observer. It is most evident

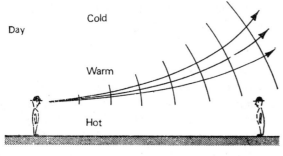

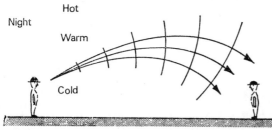

Fig. 17.6. The typical daytime temperature gradient refracts the sound waves up into the air over the head of the listener. At night, the sounds are refracted down onto the ground and they are heard at a greater distance.

when trains blowing their whistles are observed from the platform of a station through which they pass at speed. An observer of a car or motor cycle race can hardly fail to be aware of the changes in the notes of the engines as they pass.

The effect is caused by a shortening of the wave-length of the sound in front of the moving source and a lengthening of the wave-length behind it. (Fig. 17.8.)

The Doppler effect is also apparent to a moving observer who is passing a stationary source. This

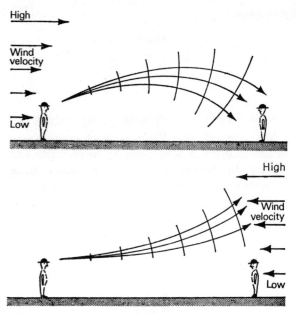

Fig. 17.7. Sounds are heard better down wind of a source, not because the wind 'carries' the sound but because it brings the sound down onto the surface.

effect is due to the change of the relative velocity of the sound waves as they appear to the observer, the observed frequency being proportional to the relative velocity.

We will derive a general expression to predict the observed frequency for the general case when both observer and source are in motion. We will regard the velocity of the source, v, and that of the observer, u, as positive when they are directed towards each other. (Fig. 17.9.) Suppose that the

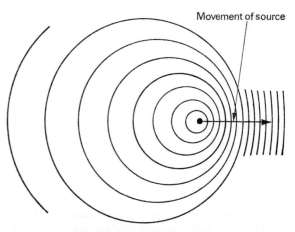

Fig. 17.8. Shortening of wave-length before, and lengthening behind, a moving source.

198

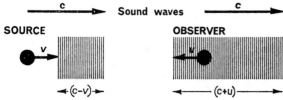

Fig. 17.9. During 1 s the source emits f_0 vibrations which are spread over a distance $(c-v)$ and the source encounters a length of $(c+u)$ of the wave train.

velocity of sound in the medium is c and the source is emitting a frequency of f_0 vibrations per second. The first vibration emitted at the beginning of a particular second travels a distance c during this second, while the source travels a distance v. Thus, f_0 vibrations are spread over a distance $c-v$, and each wave occupies a wave-length

$$\lambda = \frac{c-v}{f_0}$$

The observer encounters the waves at a relative speed of $c+u$, i.e., in one second he encounters a length $c+u$ of waves.
Thus the observed frequency

$$f = \frac{\text{length of waves encountered in 1 s}}{\text{length of each wave}}$$

$$= \frac{c+u}{\lambda} = \frac{c+u}{(c-v)/f_0}$$

$$f = f_0\frac{(c+u)}{(c-v)}$$

If the velocity of either source or observer is directed away from the other, the sign of its velocity is reversed in this equation. If either the source or the observer is not moving along the direct line joining the two, the observed frequency is calculated by using the resolved components of their velocities in this direction. (Fig. 17.10.)

$$f = f_0\frac{c+u\cos\beta}{c-v\cos\alpha}$$

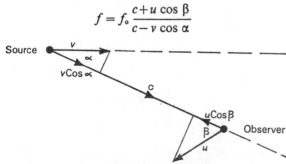

Fig. 17.10. It is the components of the velocities of the source and observer in the direction joining them that is significant in the Doppler effect.

The Doppler effect also applies to light waves, producing, for example, a change in the colour of the light emitted from receding stars. The change in wave-length is towards longer wave-lengths, that is, the red end of the spectrum, and this red 'shift' is used to estimate the velocity of stars. The effect is also used with radar waves to estimate the velocity of aircraft.

Interference of Sound Waves

When two compression waves are passing through the same region, they interact with each other. The resulting pattern of particle movements and pressure variations is simply the sum

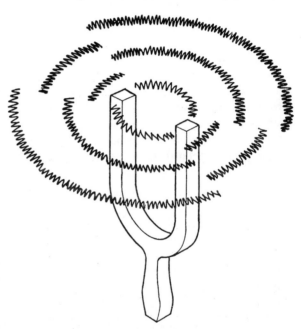

Fig. 17.11. Vibrating tuning fork.

of the disturbances produced by each separate wave. As is the case with other types of wave, the interference of compression waves can only be observed under certain conditions. One particularly simple example of the interference of sound waves can be demonstrated with a tuning fork. (Fig. 17.11.) The vibrating prongs act as two coherent sources of sound, i.e., they have the same frequency, amplitude, and phase relation. At the same time as compression is produced between the prongs, a rarefaction is produced outside the prongs and vice versa. Thus, two waves are generated by the

199

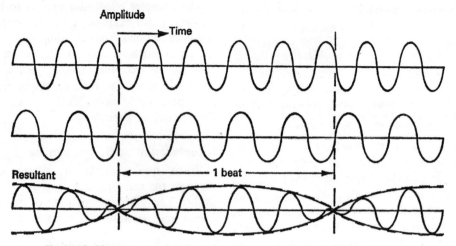

Fig. 17.12. The two waves interfere to produce a periodic rise and fall in loudness.

prongs, radiating from different positions and overlapping in some directions. In these directions, the waves are exactly out of phase, and the compression of one wave is annulled by the rarefaction from the other, thus producing a minimum of sound. These minima can be heard if a sounding tuning fork is rotated about an axis through its stem.

Beats

The interference of two sound waves is also apparent when the frequency of one wave is near to that of the other. The interaction of the waves causes a periodic change in intensity (loudness) of the sound. This can be explained by adding graphically the amplitude of the two waves at every instant in time. (Fig. 17.12.) The resultant amplitude is a maximum when the waves are in step and a minimum when they are out of step. If these frequencies differ by (say) five vibrations

per second then the waves get in and out of step five times per second, and a number of pulses or beats heard per second is five. (Fig. 17.13.) In general,

$$\text{beat frequency} = f_1 - f_2$$

Up to a beat frequency of 16 hertz, we hear a note of frequency intermediate between that of the two sources, waxing and waning in loudness. At beat frequencies above this, we hear the two notes separately, but they produce a disagreeable sound, which gets more dissonant as the beat frequency rises. Eventually, the beat frequency itself is heard as a separate note. This plays an important part

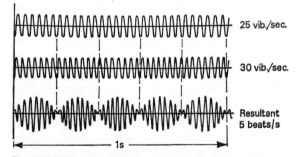

Fig. 17.13. The beat frequency is equal to the difference between the two frequencies sounding.

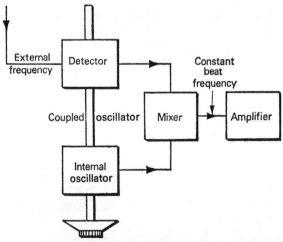

Fig. 17.14. In a superheterodyne, the frequency of the internal oscillator is coupled to the frequency of the incoming signal to produce a constant beat frequency.

200

in harmony, as we shall see later. The effect is used to tune a piano string to the same frequency as the tuning fork, and to tune one string of a guitar with another. The tension of the string is varied until the beat frequency reduces to zero.

The superheterodyne radio receiver employs the phenomenon of beats to derive a low frequency electric current by combining the high frequency oscillations from two tuned circuits. The incoming signal provides one frequency while an internal oscillator provides the other, both of the controls being coupled together. The stations broadcast at different frequencies, but the internal oscillator is coupled to the incoming signal in such a way that the beat frequency remains constant. Thus further amplifying stages can be simplified to deal with the constant frequency. (Fig. 17.14.)

Stationary Waves

A sound wave which is reflected at right angles to a boundary travels back along its own path and produces an interference effect, which we call a

stationary or *standing wave*. This wave has the same frequency and wave-length as the reflected progressive wave, but the particles in its path move in a different way.

The condition imposed on the wave is that the reflected and incident waves must sum to zero at the rigid boundary. At the instant $T=0$ in Fig. 17.15 the incident wave has zero amplitude at the boundary and, therefore, so has the reflected wave. At this instant, they seem to produce an increased amplitude in some positions. We can predict their subsequent positions by moving the waves equal distances in their respective directions of travel as shown in Fig. 17.15.

There are several important features of stationary waves.

1. There are particles in certain positions which we call nodes, which do not themselves move (hence the name stationary wave) but which are at the centre of the compressions and rarefactions.

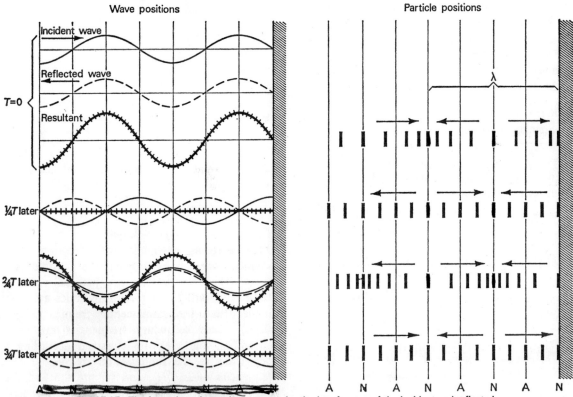

Fig. 17.15. The formation of a stationary wave by the interference of the incident and reflected waves.

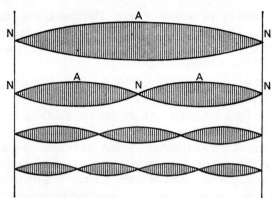

Fig. 17.16. Modes of vibration of a string under tension.

2. The other particles appear to bounce back and forth between the nodes.

3. The particles between any two successive nodes are in phase.

4. The amplitude of the particles between successive nodes varies from zero at the nodes to a maximum at points midway between the nodes called *antinodes*.

Stationary waves are formed when waves confined to one direction are efficiently reflected as in a pipe or a rod or string. The formation of a standing wave is closely connected with resonance of vibrating objects. An object resonates at those frequencies for which the standing waves fit exactly into the dimensions of the object.

Vibration in Strings

Strings vibrating transversely often act as a source of sound. The velocity of a progressive wave in a string is the same for all wave-lengths and it varies with the tension and the mass per unit length as follows:

$$\text{Velocity, } v = \sqrt{\frac{\text{Tension}}{\text{mass/unit length}}} = \sqrt{\frac{T}{m}}$$

A stationary wave is formed when the progressive wave is reflected at the fixed ends of the string,

Fig. 17.17. Several waves may be present in a string at the same time.

which act as nodes. The simplest mode of vibration, and the one which accounts for the greatest part of the energy in a string, has a single antinode between two nodes. In this case, the wave vibrates at its fundamental frequency f_1, and the length of the string is equal to half the fundamental wavelength λ_1 of the stationary wave. (Fig. 17.16.) (Remember a complete wave-length contains two loops.)

$$l = \lambda_1/2$$
$$\therefore \quad \lambda_1 = 2l$$

and

$$f_1 = \frac{v}{\lambda_1} = \frac{v}{2l}$$

substituting the above expression for v

$$f_1 = \frac{1}{2l}\sqrt{\frac{T}{m}}$$

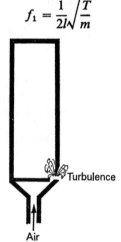

Fig. 17.18. The air in a pipe is set into vibration by the turbulence produced as a jet of air meets a sharp edge.

This equation summarizes what are sometimes called the laws of vibration of a stretched string, i.e.,

(a) $f_1 \propto 1/l$
(b) $f_1 \propto \sqrt{T}$
(c) $f_1 \propto 1/\sqrt{m}$

Other patterns or modes of vibration which produce nodes at the supports are possible. (Fig. 17.16.) These frequencies are present when the string is vibrating, but their amplitudes are much smaller than the fundamental frequency. (Fig. 17.17.) These secondary frequencies are called harmonics, and they are classified according to their ratio to the fundamental frequency. Thus frequencies of $2f_1$, $3f_1$, and $4f_1$ are the 2nd, 3rd, and 4th harmonics respectively of the frequency f_1, which is itself the 1st harmonic. Plucking the string in the middle tends to favour the odd harmonics, which have an antinode in the middle of the string. A higher proportion of the energy is contained in the higher harmonics when the string is plucked nearer to the support. The difference in the sound of the string plucked in these two positions can be clearly heard. It is possible to emphasize one particular harmonic by touching the string at a point between the supports and thereby imposing a node at the right place for the selected frequency.

Stationary Waves in Air Columns

A column of air may be made to vibrate by means of a jet of air blowing against a sharp edge at one end of the pipe. (Fig. 17.18.) The disturbance acts as an antinode, sending waves up the column, where they are reflected, producing a stationary wave with a node at the rigid end. Only those waves that fit into the tube with an antinode at one end and a node at the other resonate and produce audible sound. The fundamental frequency and other frequencies emitted by the pipe are shown in Fig. 17.19.

When the end of the pipe is open, sound waves are still reflected. A compression reaching the open end is suddenly released producing a large

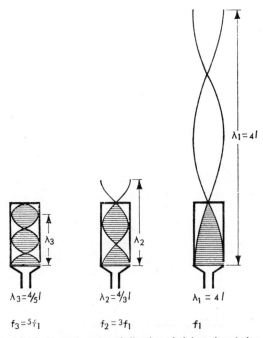

$\lambda_3 = \frac{4}{5}l$ $\lambda_2 = \frac{4}{3}l$ $\lambda_1 = 4l$

$f_3 = 5f_1$ $f_2 = 3f_1$ f_1

$\lambda_1 = 4l$

Fig. 17.19. Normal modes of vibration of air in a closed pipe.

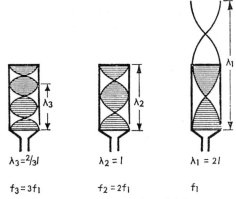

$\lambda_3 = \frac{2}{3}l$ $\lambda_2 = l$ $\lambda_1 = 2l$

$f_3 = 3f_1$ $f_2 = 2f_1$ f_1

Fig. 17.20. Normal modes of vibration of air in an open-ended pipe.

particle amplitude or antinode at the end. The frequencies which resonate in an open-ended tube are shown in Fig. 17.20.

Longitudinal and Transverse Vibrations in Rods

When a rod is struck or rubbed, stationary waves are formed by reflection at its ends. A rod will resonate to longitudinal vibrations which have a node where the rod is supported and an antinode at any free end. (Fig. 17.21.) The length of the rod and the way it is supported determine the wave-length and therefore the frequency of the sound emitted.

If the rod is flexible, it can be made to vibrate transversely, in which case it becomes a reed. The nodal pattern of Fig. 17.21 can represent equally well the modes of transverse vibrations in a rod, although the velocities of longitudinal and transverse waves in the same rod are different, and the frequencies of the sounds they emit, therefore, will also be different.

Musical Instruments

Wind instruments, such as organs and whistles, depend on the resonance of air columns. The pitch of a note emitted by a column is generally controlled by changing the length of the resonating column. In woodwind instruments, the physical length is fixed, but their effective length is varied by opening and closing holes and valves. The organ has a large number of pipes, which can be separately selected. In brass instruments, we increase their length by opening valves which introduce new

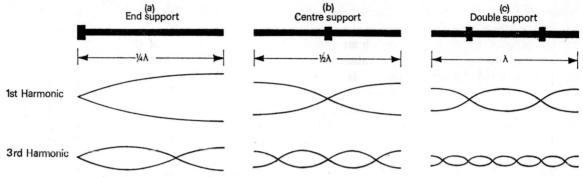

(a)
End support

(b)
Centre support

(c)
Double support

$\frac{1}{4}\lambda$

$\frac{1}{2}\lambda$

λ

1st Harmonic

3rd Harmonic

Fig. 17.21. Modes of vibration of a rod showing the absence of the even harmonics.

sections of tube, and the trombone has a telescopic u-shaped tube which can slide in and out.

The resonance in some instruments, such as clarinets and saxophones, is controlled by reeds, while in others such as the trumpet, the vibration of the player's lips controls the resonance.

The Sonometer

We can measure the frequency of a source of sound by using a stretched wire whose length l and tension T, can be varied. (Fig. 17.22.)

$$\text{frequency } f_0 = \frac{v}{\lambda_0} = \frac{1}{2l}\sqrt{\frac{T}{m}}$$

where m is the mass per unit length of the wire.

The tension of the wire is set by a screw and measured by a calibrated spring balance. The length of the wire is varied by means of a movable bridge, until it emits a note of the same frequency as the source of sound under test. The frequency can thus be calculated if the mass per unit length of the wire is known. The method requires some skill and is not a very accurate one because of the errors in the measurement of the tension, which is different on either side of the bridge.

Resonance Tubes

A tube of variable length can be used to deter-mine the frequency of a source of sound. (Fig. 17.23.) The source of unknown frequency, in this case a tuning fork, is sounded at the open end of the tube. The length of the tube is varied by means of the movable reservoir, until an increase in the loudness of the source signifies that the column is resonating. The antinode actually occurs a little way beyond the end of the tube, and usually about a third of the diameter should be added to the physical length when calculating frequencies. This end correction can be eliminated by measuring the distance between the positions of two major resonances, which is exactly half a wave-length. Hence, if the velocity of sound is known, the frequency can be calculated from the equation

$$v = f\lambda$$

A variant of the resonance tube is the Kundt tube, an apparatus used to measure the velocity of sound in a gas. In this apparatus, a frequency is imposed on an air column by the longitudinal vibrations of a rod. The length of the column is adjusted by means of a plunger, and resonance is detected visually by the vigorous movement of very fine dust in the tube. A resined or wetted cloth drawn along the rod makes it vibrate, while at the same time the plunger is moved to a position which produces resonance. If the vibration is

Sounding board   Movable bridge   Calibrated spring balance

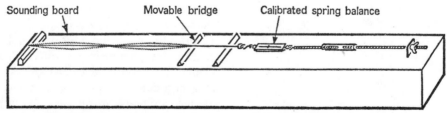

Fig. 17.22. The sonometer is used to measure the frequency of sound sources.

204

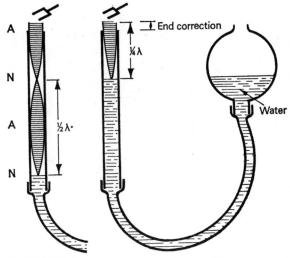

Fig. 17.23. The resonance tube showing two different resonant positions of the liquid surface.

continued, after the tube has been set to resonance, it throws the powder into piles at the nodes.

At the resonance, the frequency of the rod and column are the same and, if the velocity of sound in the rod is known, its velocity in the gas can be calculated

$$f = \frac{v_r}{\lambda_r} = \frac{v_g}{\lambda_g}$$

The instrument is used to determine the atomicity of gases from the relation

$$v = \sqrt{\frac{\gamma p}{\rho}} \text{ where} \begin{cases} \gamma = 1 \cdot 66 \text{ monatomic gases} \\ \gamma = 1 \cdot 4 \quad \text{some diatomic gases} \\ \gamma < 1 \cdot 4 \quad \text{polyatomic gases} \end{cases}$$

If the velocity of sound in the rod is not known, it can be obtained by measuring the quantities in the equation

$$\text{velocity} = \sqrt{\frac{\text{elasticity}}{\text{density}}}$$

Calibrated Instruments

Modern methods of frequency measurement involve the use of calibrated electrical instruments.

If the source of sound is visible, we can measure its frequency by a *stroboscope*. This provides a means of viewing the source intermittently. When the frequency of viewing coincides with the frequency of the source, the source is seen every time at the same stage in its vibration, and it therefore appears stationary. A stroboscope can operate either by interrupting the light falling on the source (Fig. 17.25a) or by interrupting the line of sight of the observer. (Fig. 17.25b.)

The stroboscope can be used to measure the frequency of rotating or reciprocating machinery. It is important to find the highest frequency of the stroboscope which 'stops' the vibration, since stroboscope frequencies, which are exact fractions of the source frequency, e.g., $\frac{1}{2}$, $\frac{1}{3}$, $\frac{1}{4}$, etc., produce the same visual effect.

If the vibrating source is not visible but is emitting a sound, we can measure its frequency by means of a signal generator. This is a device which produces an alternating current whose frequency can be controlled. The output from the signal generator is fed to a loudspeaker, and its frequency is tuned by ear to unison with the sound under test. The frequency may be read directly from the scale of the instrument, which can be checked if necessary against tuning forks emitting a standard frequency.

Lissajous Figures

A further method of frequency measurement employs the cathode-ray oscilloscope (CRO). A microphone converts the sound to an alternating potential, which is connected across the Y plates of the CRO. This controls the vertical deflection

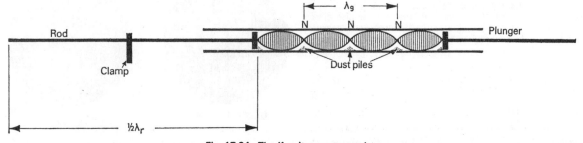

Fig. 17.24. The Kundt resonance tube.

205

of the cathode-ray beam. A horizontal deflection is imposed on the beam by a sweeping potential generated within the instrument and applied to the X plates. The frequency of the source can be deduced from the resulting pattern on the cathode-ray tube. (Fig. 17.26.)

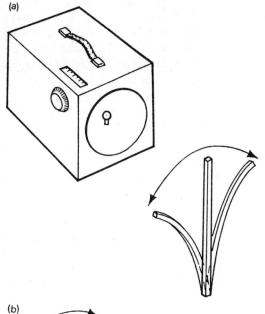

(a)

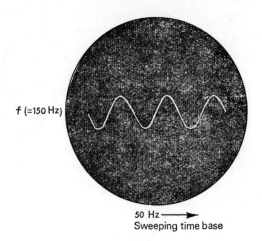

f (=150 Hz)

50 Hz ⟶
Sweeping time base

Fig. 17.26. Cathode-ray tube pattern.

resulting cathode-ray patterns are called Lissajous figures. The ratio of the frequencies applied to X and Y plates can be deduced from these figures. (Fig. 17.28.)

By means of the CRO, we can not only measure the frequency but also investigate the complexity of the waveform. (See chapter 18, Fig. 18.10.)

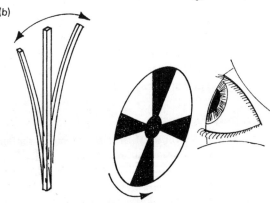

(b)

Fig. 17.25. The stroboscope. When the frequencies coincide, the object is seen only in one position. *(a)* The flashing xenon light stroboscope gives a direct reading of frequency. *(b)* The sectored disc 'chops' the light from the source at a frequency measured by a rev-counter.

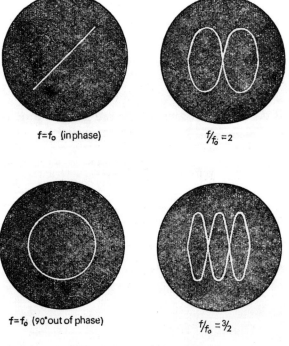

$f=f_o$ (in phase)

$f/f_o = 2$

$f=f_o$ (90° out of phase)

$f/f_o = 3/2$

Fig. 17.27. Lissajous' figures.

Using the internal time base, the horizontal deflection of the cathode-ray beam increases gradually from left to right and then returns instantaneously to zero. If a sinusoidal alternating potential is applied to the horizontal plates, the

Questions

1. How can a bugler sound different notes?

2. If you clap your hands near a long corrugated iron fence, you may produce a high-pitched squeak. Can you account for this?

3. What is the effect of pressure on the velocity of sound in a gas?

4. If an aircraft is travelling at the speed of sound, what effect on the apparent frequency of its engine note is noticed by a stationary observer in front of it, a stationary observer behind it, and the pilot?

5. How would you construct a lens to focus sound waves?

6. Why is it that a man up a ladder can hear one on the ground, but the one on the ground has difficulty in hearing the one up the ladder?

7. Why is it that light is said to travel in straight lines but sound can be heard round corners?

8. Why does a wet sheet form a much more effective sound barrier than a dry one?

9. How do you think you could set about finding how fast a distant star was receding from the Earth?

10. What is the effect produced by the Doppler effect on the apparent frequency of a note heard by a stationary observer, when the source moves along a line not directly towards or away from him?

11. If someone shouted at you, could you create silence by shouting back, using interference?

12. If you push one end of a metal bar, does the whole bar move immediately? If not, what determines the time lag before the far end moves?

13. Why are waves of various sorts so useful in conveying information from one place to another?

14. A sound wave is a series of regions of pressure above and below the normal. Why does the air not flow from high pressure to low pressure regions and destroy the wave?

15. What is the 'sound barrier'?

16. It is required to check the calibration of a variable frequency sound source. Assuming that the only *measuring* apparatus available consists of a metre scale, a (weighing) balance, a thermometer and a clock, explain how you would use some or all of this apparatus to carry out the required calibration. (Tables of physical constants and materials normally available in a physics laboratory could be used if required, in conjunction with the experiment.) (I.E.R.E.)

17. Distinguish between transverse and longitudinal waves and explain why these two types of waves are propagated at different velocities along a steel wire. (I.E.R.E.)

Problems

1. Find the frequencies of the fundamental note and second harmonic of a 2 m organ pipe with its end open and closed (neglect end-corrections). (Velocity of sound = 330 m/s.)
Answer: Open, 82·5, 165. Closed 41·3, 123·9 Hz.

2. A wire 1 m long has a fundamental note of 200 Hz when a 2 kg weight is hung from it. What length of the same wire would give a fundamental note of 400 Hz at the same tension, and what would the fundamental frequency be, if the 1 m wire had 8 kg hanging on it?
Answer: 50 cm, 400 Hz.

3. A steel wire of length 239 mm and diameter 0·8 mm vibrates with a fundamental frequency of 256 Hz. What is the tension in the wire? (Density of steel = 7800 kg/m³.)
Answer: 58·8 N.

4. Someone on a station platform notices that the apparent frequency of a train's whistle drops from 900 to 800 Hz as the train passes through. How fast is the train going? (Speed of sound = 330 m/s.)
Answer: 19·4 m/s.

5. A stationary source emits a note of 500 Hz. What frequency does an observer hear if he approaches it at 30 m/s and then goes away from it at the same speed? (Speed of sound = 330 m/s.)
Answer: 545 Hz, 455 Hz.

6. What is the fundamental and third harmonic frequency produced by blowing across the edge of a closed tube 10 mm long? (Speed of sound = 330 m/s.)
Answer: 8250 Hz, 24,750 Hz.

7. What are the wave-lengths in air of the piano's lowest note (frequency 27·5 Hz) and its highest (frequency 4186 Hz)? (Speed of sound = 330 m/s.)
Answer: 12 m, 79 mm.

8. What length would an open organ pipe have to be to give a frequency of 500 Hz? (Speed of sound = 330 m/s.)
Answer: 330 mm.

9. Two pieces of the same wire are cut, one piece ⅞ as long as the other. In what ratio must the tensions of the wires be for the shorter wire to give twice the frequency of the longer?
Answer: 16/9.

10. If a stretched string 600 mm long is plucked at its centre, what is the wave-length and frequency of the fundamental note? (Velocity of waves in string = 840 m/s.)
Answer: 120 cm, 700 Hz.

11. Two closed organ pipes are 785 and 800 mm long. What is the frequency of the beats produced between their fundamental tones? (Speed of sound = 330 m/s.)
Answer: 2 beats/s.

12. A 600 mm long pipe, closed at one end, has a third harmonic in tune with the fundamental of another pipe, open at both ends. What is the length of the second pipe? What is its fundamental frequency? (Speed of sound = 330 m/s.)

Answer: 800 mm, 206 Hz.

13. Compare the tensions of a brass wire (density 8400 kg/m^3) and a steel wire (density 7800 kg/m^3) if the second harmonic of the brass wire has the same frequency sa the fundamental tone of the steel one, both wires having the same dimensions.
Answer: The tensions are in the ratio 7:26.

14. In experimenting with Kundt's tube, using a brass rod, and filling the glass tube with carbon dioxide, the following was found: length of brass rod = 600 mm; frequency of rod = 2920 Hz; distance between nodes in CO_2 = 45 mm. What is the velocity of sound in brass and CO_2?
Answer: 3504 m/s, 263 m/s.

15. At 20°C, a closed organ pipe 500 mm long is in tune with a tuning fork. At a lower temperature, four beats/sec are produced. What is the temperature, approximately, assuming the frequency of the fork is constant? (Speed of sound at 20°C = 340 m/s.)
Answer: −3°C.

16. How long is a closed tube which emits a fundamental frequency of 250 Hz at 27°C? At what temperature would it emit 125 Hz? (Speed of sound = 350 m/s at 27°C.)
Answer: 350 mm, −198°C.

17. A car, sounding its horn at a frequency of 256 Hz, approaches a wall and the echo from the wall has a frequency of 288 Hz. How fast is the car moving? (Speed of sound = 330 m/s.)
Answer: 19·4 m/s.

18. A radar beam of frequency 3×10^{10} Hz is reflected from a satellite approaching the transmitter. If the frequency received is $\frac{900,009}{299,997} \times 10^{10}$ Hz, what is the satellite's speed relative to the station? (Velocity of radar waves = 3×10^8 m/s.)
Answer: 3×10^3 m/s.

19. Assuming that the equations for the Doppler effect in sound apply to light waves, what deductions could be made from a change in wave-length from a star from its normal wave-length of $6562 \cdot 784 \times 10^{-10}$ m to $6562 \cdot 912 \times 10^{-10}$ m?
Answer: velocity = $5 \cdot 9 \times 10^3$ m/s away from Earth.

20. Discuss the difference between natural and forced vibrations of a body, and indicate how the response of a system to the application of a periodic force varies with the frequency of the applied force.

The air in a cylindrical tube is at a temperature of 20°C and is set in vibration by a diaphragm actuated by a 100 Hz generator.

If the far end of the tube is closed, what is the minimum length of the air column which will resonate with the vibration of the diaphragm? (Velocity of sound in air at 0°C = 330 m/s.)

(I.E.R.E.)

Answer: 0·825 m.

21. (i) A steel wire 0·5 m long and weighing 4·0 g is stretched with a tension of 500 newtons. What is the frequency of the fundamental note emitted by the wire?
(ii) Determine the change in frequency of the note produced by an organ pipe when the temperature changes from 10°C to 20°C, if the frequency at 10°C is 384 Hz.
(iii) A source emitting sound of frequency 1000 Hz is moving at a velocity of 33 m/s. What is the wave-length of the sound waves noted by a stationary observer when the source is travelling (a) directly towards, (b) directly away, from the observer? (Velocity of sound = 330 m/s.)

(I.E.R.E.)

Answer: (i) 2·50 Hz; (ii) 6·5 Hz; (iii) (a) 1100 Hz, (b) 917 Hz.

22. Write down an expression for the velocity of sound in a medium in terms of the elastic modulus and density of the medium. From the definition of modulus of elasticity derive an expression for the appropriate modulus to be used in the case of

sound propagation through a gas, stating any assumptions made. Hence show that the velocity of sound in a gas is:

(i) independent of changes of pressure;

(ii) proportional to the square root of the absolute temperature. (I.E.R.E.)

23. Describe a method for determining the velocity of sound along a metal rod. Explain the theory upon which the method is based and show how the result would be calculated.

(I.E.R.E.)

18 Sound Perception

The sound of a grasshopper can be clearly heard at a range of many metres, at which distance the displacement the sound causes in the air is no bigger than the diameter of a molecule. At the other end of the scale, the ear can tolerate a thunderclap, which is about 10^{10} times more energetic than the sound of the grasshopper. In addition to this wide range of energies, the ear is astonishingly sensitive to the complexity of sound waves and it can separately detect, for example, the different instruments of an orchestra playing simultaneously. Hearing is the last of our senses to become dormant when we sleep and the first one to function on waking. This very highly developed sense of hearing has played an important part in animal survival by enabling animals to catch their prey and avoid their enemies.

Sound waves themselves are objective phenomena, but man's perception of them is strictly subjective and varies from person to person. Because of man's dependence on sound perception, it is the subjective aspect of sound which interests him most. In this chapter we will examine the process of hearing and the way in which it is stimulated by sound waves.

The Ear

The ear has three sections—the outer, the middle and the inner ear. (Fig. 18.1.) The outer ear funnels the sound waves to a membrane called the ear drum, which is made to vibrate. In the middle ear, the vibrations of the ear drum are transmitted to a smaller membrane at the entrance to the inner ear. At the same time, the pressure variation is increased about sixty times. This amplification is achieved partly by means of three bones in the middle ear, which act as levers, and partly because of the difference in area between the ear drum and the inner membrane.

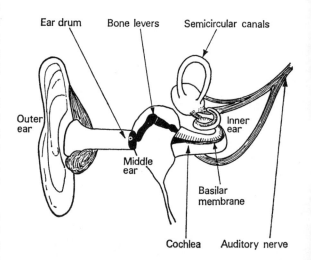

Fig. 18.1. The ear.

The inner ear converts the mechanical vibrations to nerve impulses. The conversion takes place in a tapering spiral resonator, filled with a liquid and called the *cochlea*. The cochlea is divided longitudinally by the basilar membrane. This membrane is covered with nerve endings which transmit responses to the brain, the place where perception really occurs.

The ear is situated near an organ which, by being sensitive to fluid pressure, gives animals a sense of balance. The organ consists of three semicircular canals and probably developed with the ear from a common, more primitive, organ.

Sound Energy

The energy in a sound wave is the basic stimulus for the sensation of loudness. The rate at which sound energy is given out by a source is measured in joules per second, i.e., watts. A small radio receiver emits sound at an average power of about 10^{-7} W $= 0.1\mu$ W, while an amplifier suitable for a small auditorium will deliver an average of about 1 µW.

The *intensity* of a sound at a certain place in the path of a sound wave is *the number of watts passing at right angles through a unit area of intercepted surface*. As the sound energy travels away from the source, it spreads out and is attenuated, i.e., its intensity reduces. If there is no frictional loss of energy, and no obstacles or reflecting surfaces, the sound intensity for a point source of sound is attenuated according to an inverse square law. In this case, the intensity E at a radius r from the source is given by:

$$\text{Intensity } E = \frac{\text{power of source}}{\text{area of sphere}} = \frac{P}{4\pi r^2}$$

In practice, these conditions are rarely satisfied, but the law serves as a rough guide.

Problem: What are the intensities at distances of 5 and 10 m from a loudspeaker emitting sound at a power of 3 µW uniformly in all directions?

Solution:

$$\text{Intensity} = \frac{\text{power}}{4\pi r^2}$$

At 5 m
$$E = \frac{3}{4\pi \, 5^2} \simeq 10^{-2}\ \mu\text{W/m}^2$$

At 10 m
$$E = \frac{3}{4\pi \, 10^2} \simeq \tfrac{1}{4} 10^{-2}\ \mu\text{W/m}^2$$

If an amplifier increases the intensity of a sound from 4 µW/m² to 5 µW/m², we can express this either by a change of 1 µW/m² or as a change in the ratio of 4 : 5. The latter method of expressing the change as a ratio tells us far more about the amplification than the change expressed as a difference. Therefore, in acoustics, we express amplifications and attenuations, not as differences, but as ratios

$$\text{Intensity ratio} = \frac{E_1}{E_2}$$

In fact, we go further than this by defining a unit of ratio or *relative intensity*. The unit is called the Bel and it is equal to a ten-fold increase in intensity.

Now, 1 Bel corresponds to a ratio of one to 10 or 10^1

    2 Bel corresponds to a ratio of one to 10×10 or 10^2

    3 Bel corresponds to a ratio of one to $10 \times 10 \times 10$ or 10^3

and n Bel corresponds to a ratio of one to 10^n

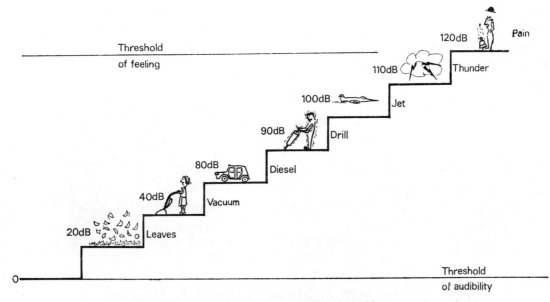

Fig. 18.2. Some examples of sound relative intensities.

Thus, the relative intensity n of two intensities is given by the equation

$$\frac{E_1}{E_2} = 10^n$$

taking logarithms,

$$\log_{10} \frac{E_1}{E_2} = n \log_{10} 10 = n \times 1 = n$$

Hence,

$$\text{R.I.} = \log_{10} \frac{E_1}{E_2} \text{ Bel}$$

i.e., the relative intensity in Bels is the log of the intensity ratios.

The Bel is a very large unit and so we divide it into ten equal ratios called decibels. One decibel corresponds to a ratio of $1:1.26$ or an increase of 26 per cent. We can show this as follows:

Let r be the ratio represented by 1 dB

$$10 \text{ dB} = 1 \text{ Bel}$$

i.e.,

10 r–fold increases = 1 ten-fold increase

$$\therefore \qquad r^{10} = 10$$

and $\qquad r = \sqrt[10]{10} = 1.26$

To calculate a relative intensity in dB, use the equation

$$\text{R.I.} = 10 \log_{10} \frac{E_1}{E_2}$$

This may be regarded as a definition of the decibel. Note that negative relative intensities denote attenuation. (Table 18.1.)

This method of dealing in units of ratio does not come easily to anyone without practice. Why,

Table 18.1. Intensity ratios compared with their expressions in decibels

Intensity Ratio E_1/E_2	Relative Intensity (dB)
0·001	−30
0·01	−20
0·1	−10
1	0
1·26	1
1·58	2
2·00	3
2·51	4
3·16	5
3·98	6
5·01	7
6·31	8
7·94	9
10·00	10
100	20
1000	30
10,000	40

then, do we use it? Well, there are several reasons which make it worth while to persevere with these units. First of all, the human sense of hearing grades loudness in a way which broadly approximates to the decibel scale. (Fig. 18.3.) Next, the decibel happens to be a convenient size, because it is about the smallest change in intensity which the ear can detect. A further advantage is that relative intensities are directly additive and subtractive. Thus, when an amplifier contains three stages of amplification, that is, stages producing amplifications, A_1, A_2, and A_3 dB, the total amplification A is given by

$$A = A_1 + A_2 + A_3$$

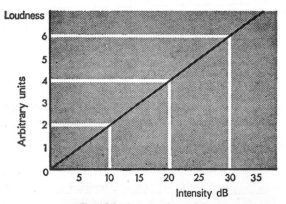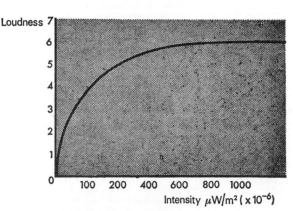

Fig. 18.3. A comparison of the loudness response of the ear and the intensity measured *(a)* in dB, *(b)* in μW/m^2 ($\times 10^{-6}$).

If a certain type of wall causes a loss of x dB in reflecting a sound, then two such reflections will cause a loss of $2x$ dB, etc.

Because of the convenience of the dB system of expressing relative intensities, the system has been adapted so that it can indicate absolute values in intensity. This is done by defining a standard intensity and then expressing any other intensity in decibels above this standard level. The intensity chosen is that of 10^{-6} μW/m², a sound which is very near to the lowest intensity of sound audible to the human ear.

Problem: The intensities of a sound are amplified from 10μW/m² to 150 μW/m². Calculate the amplification produced in dB.

Solution: Relative intensity $= 10 \log \dfrac{E_1}{E_2}$

$$= 10 \log \frac{150}{10}$$

$$= 11 \cdot 76 \text{ dB}$$

Problem: An acoustic panel reduces the intensity of a sound from 60 μW/m² to 8·0 μW/m². Express the attenuation in dB.

Solution: R.I. $= 10 \log \dfrac{E_1}{E_2} = 10 \log \dfrac{8}{60}$

$$= 10 \, (\log 8 - \log 60)$$

$$= 10 \, (\bar{1} \cdot 1249)$$

$$= -8 \cdot 8 \text{ dB}$$

Problem: The intensity of the noise from the engine of a jet plane is 0·4 W/m² (cf. Table 18.2) at a distance of 10 m. What is the noise level when the plane is directly overhead at an altitude of 200 m?

Solution: We know $E \propto \dfrac{1}{d^2}$

$$\frac{E_a}{E_b} = \frac{1/d_a^2}{1/d_b^2}$$

$$E = \frac{0 \cdot 4 \times 10^2}{200^2} = \frac{40}{40,000}$$

$$= 10^{-3} \text{ W/m}^2$$

Expressing this in dB above the standard 10^{-12} W/m²

noise level $= 10 \log \dfrac{E_1}{E_2} = 10 \log \dfrac{10^{-3}}{10^{-12}}$

$$= 10 \log 10^9 = 90 \text{ dB}$$

Problem: Express the noise of intensity 2×10^{-6} W/m² in decibels. Above the standard (10^{-12} W/m²).

Solution: Relative intensity $= 10 \log \dfrac{2 \times 10^{-6}}{10^{-12}}$

$$= 10 \log 2 \times 10^6$$

$$= 63 \cdot 0 \text{ dB}$$

Loudness

For a given frequency, the more intense the note, the greater the stimulus to the cochlea and the louder the note is. In order to appreciate the conception of loudness, we must face three problems:

1. Loudness is a matter of personal judgement, which may vary from one person to another.

2. The human response to sound energy is not directly proportional to the energy content.

3. The loudness of a sound is dependent on its frequency as well as its intensity.

Although the ear is not able to judge the loudness ratio of two sounds objectively, it is able to judge equality of loudness. Using this ability, we can solve the first problem by having a large number of people make a variety of sound comparisons and can, thus, arrive at an average response to intensity. We are then able to define the response of an average ear, in the same way as illumination engineers define the response to colour of an average eye. Such statistical methods can act as very useful aids to greater precision of measurement.

When a sound is doubled in intensity, an observer will by no means judge it to have doubled in loudness. In fact, about a tenfold increase in intensity is needed to double the loudness. The response of the average ear to intensity is much nearer to the decibel system of intensity measurement than it is to the absolute intensity. For this reason, we use the decibel of relative intensity as a measure of loudness. The zero on this scale is the threshold of audibility for a note of 1000 Hz (10^{-6} μW/m²). The loudness of some common sounds ranging from the audibility threshold to the pain threshold, at which a sound imparts physical pain, is given in Table 18.2.

Table 18.2. Absolute intensities compared with the noise level expressed in relative intensities above the threshold of audibility

	$\mu W/m^2$	dB
Threshold of feeling	10^6	120
Thunder	10^5	110
Jet engine	10^4	100
Pneumatic drill	10^3	90
Diesel engine	10^2	80
Vacuum cleaner	1	60
Conversation	10^{-2}	40
Rustling leaves	10^{-4}	20
Threshold of audibility at 1000 Hz	10^{-6}	0

There remains the problem that equally intense sounds of different frequencies are not judged equally loud by an observer. The relative intensity of a note in dB is a good measure of loudness for frequencies near to 1000 Hz, but the ear is less sensitive to sounds of high and low frequency. The extremes of frequency are not so loud as their relative intensities would indicate. The curves shown in Fig. 18.4 are drawn through those intensities which sound equally loud. Note that the curves are approximately horizontal at very high intensities.

We can express the loudness of a sound in a unit, *the phon*, which is independent of the frequency. *The loudness of a sound in phons is equal to the intensity, in decibels above threshold, of the* 1000 Hz *note which sounds equally loud.* The loudness of a note of a single frequency may be obtained by plotting its position on the graph of Fig. 18.4 and thus determining which curve of equal loudness it lies on.

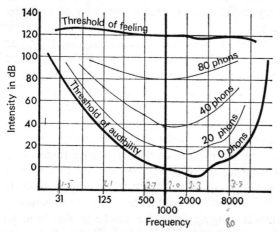

Fig. 18.4. Variation of intensity with frequency of notes of equal loudness.

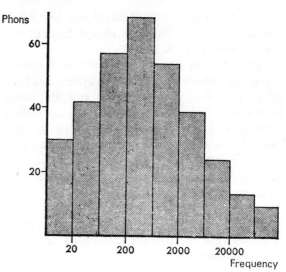

Fig. 18.5. A noise profile is obtained by measuring the loudness of each frequency band.

Noise Measurement

Noise is the name we give to unwanted sound and the level of noise is an important feature of human environment. It can cause effects ranging from minor irritation to permanent deafness, sometimes without the knowledge of the people who are subject to it. Thousands of people in this country willingly work, and are allowed to work, under noisy conditions which specialists agree will cause some degree of permanent deafness. It costs money, however, to suppress noise and, in the case of engines, it may result in a loss of power. Inevitably, there is a conflict between economic necessity and the need to limit noise levels, whether it be the problem of supersonic booms from aircraft or the protection of industrial workers from noise acceptable to themselves and their employers. What government will pass legislation which will render jet aircraft or the majority of its railway rolling stock illegal?

If standards are to be set up and become accepted, it is necessary that convenient methods of measurement are developed. A noise meter is basically an amplifier whose input is a non-directional microphone and whose output is recorded on a meter, which has been standardized and calibrated in decibels of intensity. The best instruments incorporate a series of filters, which allow the loudness of the different frequency bands present to be measured separately. These

214

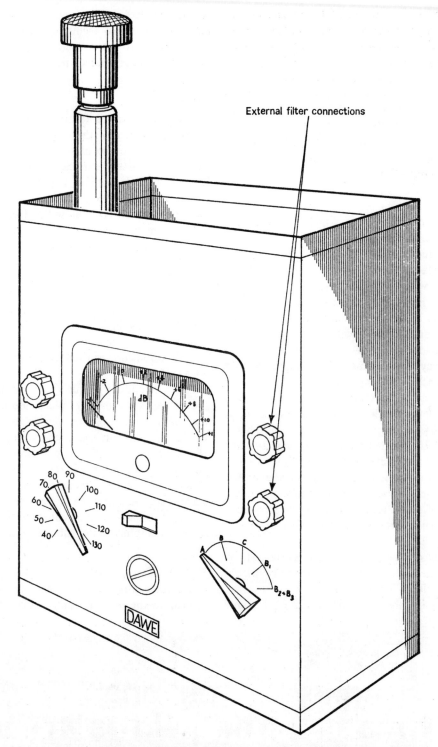

External filter connections

Fig. 18.6. The sound level meter measures the combined intensity of all frequencies on the *C* weighting but its response is made nearer to that of the ear by the *B* and *A* weightings for medium and low intensities.

are then converted to phons of loudness with the help of the equal loudness curves and plotted as a noise profile. (Fig. 18.5.) For safety, the loudness of all the frequency ranges should be below the level at which aural damage is possible.

For a less exact measurement of general noise level, noise meters are available which, by the use of filters, attenuate the intensity at low frequencies so as to make the response of the instrument approximate to the response of the average ear. (Fig. 18.6.)

Deafness

An infection or accident which damages the middle ear can affect the sound transmission mechanism and result in deafness. The sufferer from this defect will hear some sounds by bone conduction to the cochlea through the head. If, on the other hand, the nerves in the cochlea are damaged and not functioning, no sound will be heard at all, and deafness will be complete.

As we get older, the sensitivity of our ears to high frequency sound reduces. This can cause mild deafness, which is first apparent as a difficulty in hearing speech clearly. Our identification of words depends far more on the consonants such as b, p, t, f, etc., than on the vowels a, e, i, o, u. This is also true of the written word, and some systems of shorthand completely omit the vowels. The consonants are formed by sounds of the higher audible frequencies and are the first to become indistinct with the reduction in high frequency sensitivity. An impression of the effect of this is given in Fig. 18.7.

This type of deafness can be corrected by amplifying the higher frequency sounds by means of a hearing aid. With only one ear aided, however, the wearer loses the sense of direction of sound which two ears can convey. The use of a hearing aid in one ear also seems to reduce the ability of an observer to listen selectively to one sound against a background of noise.

Pitch

The human ear is far more sensitive to differences in frequency than it is to differences in intensity of a source of sound. In some frequency ranges, a trained ear can detect differences in frequency of less than 1 per cent. The lowest frequency note which produces a perception of pitch is about 20 Hz. Below this frequency, we are only aware of the individual pulses. The human ear loses its sense of pitch and, indeed, its sensitivity to any sound above a frequency of about 20,000 Hz. The sensitivity of the ear of an adult to high frequencies reduces regularly with advancing years. Dogs are sensitive to sounds at frequencies as high as 40,000 Hz, while the bat, which relies on sound much in the same way as we rely on vision, can detect vibrations of around 50,000 Hz.

Each individual frequency of sound stimulates the nerves in a number of places along the cochlea, the main centres of stimulation being nearer to the open end for the higher frequencies. (Fig. 18.8.) An increase in sound intensity causes both an increase in response and a spreading of the area of the nerves affected. This may render the ear less sensitive to pitch or even cause a change in the pitch of a source of constant frequency. This serves to emphasize the subjective nature of pitch.

Tone or Complexity

We have already mentioned the sensitivity of the ear to the intensity and frequency of a sound

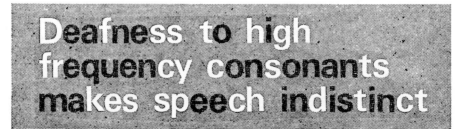

Fig. 18.7. An impression of the effect of partial deafness. Deafness to high frequency consonants makes speech indistinct.

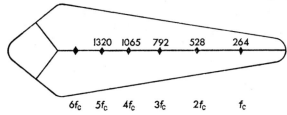

$$\text{Musical interval} = \frac{f_2}{f_1}$$

The basic unit of musical interval is the *octave* which denotes a frequency ratio of 2:1. Thus, there is an octave interval between notes of 264 and 528 Hz and between notes of 220 and 440 Hz. The octave may be sub-divided into twelve equal ratios r such that

$$r^{12} = 2$$

i.e., $$r = 1\cdot06$$

Thus, we can construct a scale, the scale of *equal temperament*, composed of particular frequencies separated by this interval. (Fig. 18.11.) Each of these intervals is called a half tone, or semitone, two half tones making a tone, and there being six complete tones to an octave.

Rarely are all the twelve notes within an octave involved in any one short tune or section of a piece of music and, commonly, only seven notes are used. (Fig. 18.12a.) We letter the seven notes A, B, C, D, E, F, and G, using the same letters for notes an octave apart. If the sequence of notes from C to C is sounded, we hear the tune associated with the names of the notes doh, ray, me, fah, soh, la, te, doh.

The intermediate frequencies between the notes A, B, C, etc., are referred to either as sharps (♯) of the lower note or as flats (♭) of the upper note.

wave, but perhaps more amazing is its ability to detect differences in the complexity of a sound vibration. The various kinds of instruments in an orchestra can be identified even when they are playing simultaneously, and instruments of different kinds playing the same note can be distinguished easily. The sound energy emitted by every instrument is divided differently between its fundamental frequency and the higher harmonics. (Fig. 18.9.) Each harmonic produces subtle differences in the pattern of responses in the cochlea, and the brain interprets these as differences in tonal quality. (Fig. 18.10.)

Musical Scales

As in the case of intensity, the ear is sensitive to the ratio of the frequencies of notes rather than the differences between them. The ratio of the frequency of two notes is called the musical interval between the notes.

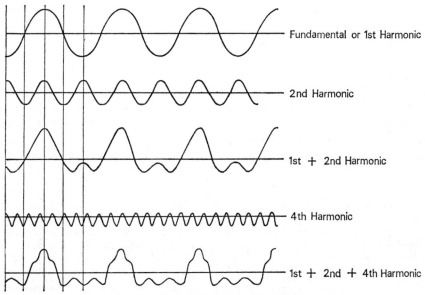

Fig. 18.9. Fundamental and higher harmonics.

217

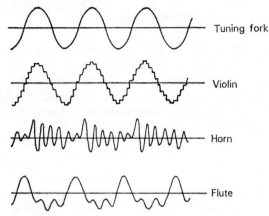

Fig. 18.10. The ear can distinguish between different instruments playing the same note from their waveform.

Table 18.3. Consonance and dissonance between notes is dependent on the ratio of their frequencies.

More consonant ratios	2:1
	3:2
	4:3
	5:4
↕	6:5
	5:3
	8:5
	9:8
	15:8
More dissonant ratios	16:9
	16:15

Thus, on this notation a frequency of 277 can be referred to either as C♯ or as D♭. (Fig. 18.12a.)

Several notes played together form a chord. When the frequencies of the notes in these chords are in one of the simple ratios, 1:2, 2:3, 3:4, 4:5, 5:6, they produce a high degree of consonance, the actual degree we recognize being a matter of convention and, ultimately, of personal taste.

(Table 18.3.) The notes of the most harmonious chord made up of notes on the scale of equal temperament only approximate to the simple ratios which produce the greatest consonance, e.g.,

$$\frac{f_E}{f_A} = \frac{329 \cdot 2}{440} \simeq \frac{330}{440} = \frac{3}{4}$$

$$\frac{f_C}{f_A} = \frac{261 \cdot 6}{440} \simeq \frac{264}{440} = \frac{3}{5}$$

A scale of frequencies, *a diatonic scale*, which allows these ratios to be more exact, can be constructed. (Fig. 18.12b.) The intervals on this

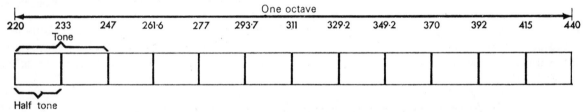

Fig. 18.11. Frequencies on the scale of equal temperament.

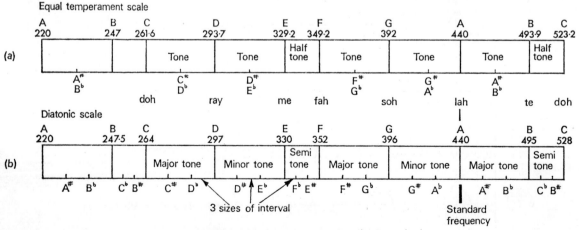

Fig. 18.12. *(a)* Equal temperament scale. *(b)* Diatonic scale.

218

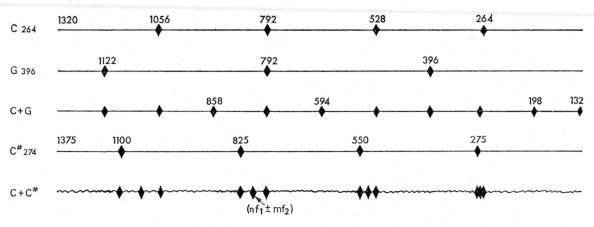

Fig. 18.13. Tone patterns of stimulation in the cochlea.

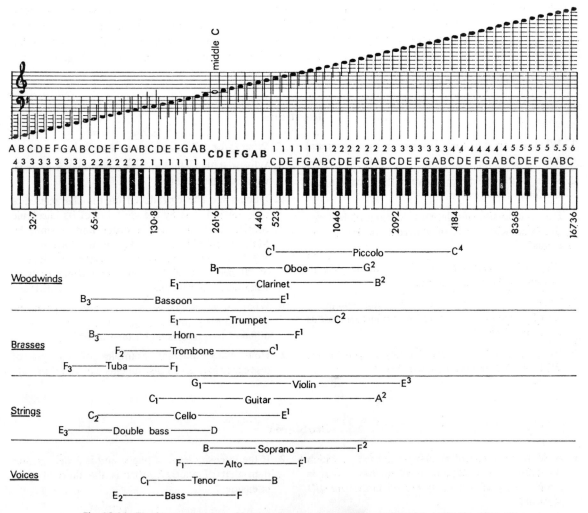

Fig. 18.14. The frequency range of instruments and the musical notation of these frequencies.

scale are of several sizes, none of which corresponds exactly to either the tone or a half tone of the equal temperament scale. The frequencies of the notes A, B, C, D, E, F, and G are approximately equal on the two scales. The notes available on the equal temperament scale allow the same tune to be played starting on any of the twelve notes. Any tune or pattern of intervals played on a diatonic scale can only be repeated exactly, starting on different notes, if more frequencies are used. Thus, a number of frequencies between the notes A, B, C, D, E, F, and G are required to accommodate diatonic scales, commencing on any of these notes. Many of these are provided by allowing the sharps and flats to represent different frequencies. (Fig. 18.12b.)

Where an instrument can be made to emit any frequency which is judged suitable by the ear, e.g., a violin, the diatonic intervals are preferred. If, however, the frequencies of the instrument are set, as in the case of a piano, and we can only select the notes, they are tuned to the scale of equal temperament. Thus, a tune sounds the same when commenced on any note on the piano, though it sounds slightly different than it would if played on the diatonic scale of a violin. If the piano were tuned to the diatonic scale, a tune would only sound 'right' if it were played commencing on a particular note, or an exact number of octaves from this note.

The sounding of a single frequency stimulates the nerves at points in the cochlea corresponding to the harmonics of this frequency. (Fig. 18.13.) When two notes are sounded together the points corresponding to the sum or difference of any of their harmonics are also stimulated, i.e., $nf_1 \pm mf_2$ where n and m are any small whole numbers. The combined pattern of stimulation is a simple one for the more consonant chords and a complex one for the more dissonant chords. (Fig. 18.13.)

Questions

1. What is the difference between a musical sound and a noise?

2. What is the difference between the loudness and the intensity of a note?

3. How is it possible for the ear to distinguish between the same note played on different musical instruments?

4. Why is it necessary to use a logarithmic scale to measure differences in sound intensity?

5. What factor is important in deciding whether a chord is harmonious or not? Can a non-harmonious chord be musical?

6. How many different musical scales do you know? What is the difference between them?

7. What is the difference between a decibel and a phon?

8. Why is it that children can sometimes hear bats, while adults cannot?

9. Discuss the effect produced on the characteristics of a musical note by the variation of its harmonic content both as regards order and magnitude. Make a suitable scale diagram to illustrate the effect on a sinusoidal waveform of the introduction of 20 per cent of 2nd and 3rd harmonics both separately and together.   (I.E.R.E.)

10. What do you think would be the main problems in composing music, using pure sine waves of different frequencies and a tape recorder?

11. How many different examples of the use of resonance in musical instruments can you think of?

Problems

1. A 45 rev/min record is playing a tune in which A=440 Hz but is turning at 44 rev/min. What is the frequency of A actually heard? Is the tune still musical?
   Answer: 430·2 Hz. Yes.

2. If the intensity level of one sound is 3 Bels greater than that of another, what is the ratio of their intensities?

   Answer: 1000:1.

3. Noise coming through an open window at 70 dB is reduced to 50 dB when the window is closed. What percentage of the sound is excluded?
Answer: 99 per cent.

4. An ear can just hear a sound of intensity 10^{-12} W/m², and just stand a sound of 10^2 W/m². What is the difference in these levels in decibels?
Answer: 140 dB.

5. A 32 Hz sound is just audible at an intensity of 10^{-5} W/m², while a 1000 Hz sound is just audible at 10^{-12} W/m². What difference in intensity does this represent, as a ratio and in decibels?
Answer: 10^7, 70 dB.

6. What is the musical interval between F and G?
Answer: 1·12.

7. Machines *a*, *b*, and *c*, when operating alone produce sound levels of 70 dB, 80 dB, and 85 dB respectively. Calculate the noise levels that would be possible for all combinations of machine operation.
Answer: 86·3 dB, 80·4 dB, 86·2 dB, 85·1 dB.

19 Applications of Sound

Sound is essential to mankind. It is the basis of speech, by which we communicate ideas and information to one another. It provides us with a ready awareness of events which we could not detect so quickly with any of the other senses. In the form of music, it contributes to our enjoyment of life. The study of this type of energy is nothing new; twenty-five centuries ago, for example, men knew something of the mathematical ratios underlying the musical scales. But, whereas in the past men were chiefly interested in sound as a means of communicating ideas or for creating melody, in modern times, scientists have investigated it more thoroughly and objectively, and many new applications of sound have been discovered. This chapter describes some of these applications.

Acoustics of Buildings

The study and design of building interiors to produce specific listening conditions is called acoustics. W. C. Sabine, a professor at Harvard University founded the study of acoustics as recently as the beginning of this century but, already, acoustics ranks in importance with lighting, ventilating, and sanitation in building design.

The acoustics of a building are closely linked with *reverberation*, that is, the persistence of a sound due to its repeated reflection from the boundaries of an interior. The time interval between the making of a sound and the moment when its reverberation just becomes inaudible is the *reverberation time*. It is usually defined as the time in which a note of 512 Hz falls to 1 millionth part of its initial intensity. The reverberation time

is almost zero in the open air where there is no reflection. It is several seconds in a large swimming pool and, thus, sounds are indistinct because of the overlapping of reverberations. The optimum reverberation time increases with the size of the auditorium, and it is greater for orchestral music than it is for light music and speech. The ideal reverberation time thus might range from half a second for speech in a small school hall to $2\frac{1}{2}$ seconds for orchestral music in a concert hall.

Each time a sound wave is reflected, a fraction of the incident energy is absorbed by the surface. This fraction is the absorption coefficient α of the surface.

$$\alpha = \frac{\text{absorbed energy}}{\text{incident energy}}$$

The combined absorption, called the Sabine absorption a, of a number of surfaces is computed by adding the product of the surface areas S_1, S_2, S_3, etc., and their individual absorption coefficients α_1, α_2, α_3, etc.

$$a = S_1\alpha_1 + S_2\alpha_2 + S_3\alpha_3$$

Sound is absorbed quickly in small rooms where it undergoes many reflections in a short time. The reverberation time t in seconds is given by the equation:

$$t = 0{\cdot}16\,\frac{\text{room volume}}{\text{Sabine absorption}}$$
$$= 0{\cdot}16\,\frac{V}{a}$$

The equation holds when metres are used in the calculation of V and a (the equation is not dimensionally consistent as it stands because the factor 0·16 is inversely proportional to the velocity of sound).

The reverberation time of a room can be reduced by lining the walls with cellular material, such as cork or fibre or polystyrene, which responds to sound vibration converting it to heat energy. (Table 19.1.) These coverings are used to prevent resonances in alcoves or sound concentrations due to focusing by large curved surfaces. The acoustics of a room change according to the number of people present because of the absorption of sound which the people produce. This is corrected by padding the seats to make their absorption coefficient about the same when empty as when occupied.

Table 19.1. Examples of absorption coefficient of some common surfaces

Surface	α
Open window	1·0
Cellulose fibre tiles	0·8
Felt	0·6
Heavy carpet	0·4
Heavy curtains draped	0·5
Acoustic plaster	0·25
Wood	0·03
Brickwork	0·025
Concrete	0·02
Plaster	0·02
Glazed tiles	0·01

In some auditoriums, moveable baffles and draperies are employed to reduce the reverberation time for speech and to lengthen it for orchestral music. Many successful experiments have recently been made with electronic amplification systems which relay the sound with a controlled delay to different parts of the auditorium. This diminishes any reliance on reflection of the sound and gives a wider control of the acoustic properties of a room.

In the design of houses and flats, sound insulation is very important. Sound insulation problems are of two kinds: the reduction in sound transmitted through the air of one room through a wall to the air of the next room, and the reduction of the sound transmitted by the structure of the building itself. The sound insulating effect expressed in decibels provided by a partition wall to airborne sound, increases uniformly with its weight. The insulating effect of light partition walls can be improved to some extent by the use of double layers separated by felt or by a wider layer (>100 mm) of air.

Structure-borne sounds such as those travelling along water pipes are reduced by the introduction of sound absorbing sections. Both air-borne and structure borne sounds are minimized by the covering of surfaces with materials which absorb reflected sound.

Geophysical Prospecting

An earthquake or major explosion generates vibrational waves which may travel very large distances through the Earth. When these vibrations are recorded on seismographs at different places on the Earth's surface, they can be used to detect and locate and classify the disturbances or to give information about the structure of the Earth.

The reflection of such waves through rock strata is used by geologists, prospecting for oil, to detect the structures likely to contain oil deposits. (Fig. 19.1.)

Depth sounding of the ocean employs a similar technique. An instrument records the time between the sound and the return of its echo from the ocean bed. From a knowledge of this time and the velocity of sound in sea water, the depth can be deduced.

Ultrasonics

When a piece of quartz cut along a certain axis is compressed, positive and negative charges are exhibited on its opposite faces, and the polarity of the charges reverses when the crystal is under tension. This is the *piezo-electric* effect. The alternate compressions and stretchings of a quartz crystal, when under the influence of a compressional wave, generate a small alternating potential across the crystal, which provides an effective means of detecting and measuring the wave.

Conversely, if we apply an alternating electrical potential to the quartz, it expands and contracts at the same frequency by an amount which increases with the potential. The amplitude of vibration of the quartz becomes large when the frequency of the alternating potential coincides with one of the natural modes of vibration of the crystal. The quartz crystal is an efficient *transducer*, i.e., a device for converting electrical impulses to mechanical vibrations and vice versa.

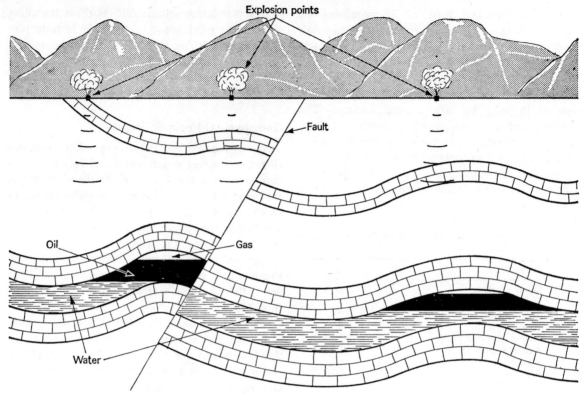

Fig. 19.1. Oil prospectors plot the structure of the rock strata by timing the echoes of surface explosions.

The fundamental frequency of a vibrating crystal depends on its dimensions and on the velocity of sound in the crystal

$$f = \frac{\text{velocity}}{2 \times \text{length}} = \frac{v}{2l}$$

Thus, a 0·1 m long quartz crystal has a fundamental frequency of:

$$f = \frac{5 \times 10^3}{0·2} = 2·5 \times 10^4 = 25{,}000 \text{ Hz}$$

This frequency is well above the range of audibility of the ear but near to the bottom of the range of ultrasonic frequencies. A very thin slice of quartz can be made to emit frequencies as high as 500 MHz, and other transducers have reached 10,000 MHz.

Square or other shaped holes can be bored into a surface if a hardened rod, in contact with the surface, is subject to ultrasonic vibrations. The cutting head does not rotate, it vibrates and, with the help of an abrasive, produces holes the same shape as the cutting head. Plastic components can be welded together by ultrasonic vibrations which produce heat through friction at the points of contact.

Ultrasonic waves in liquids produce cavitation. That is, they produce tiny spaces in the liquid. The partial vacuum in these spaces exerts a strong pull on exposed solid surfaces, detaching any particles of dust which may be adhering to them. Even the insides of hypodermic needles can be cleaned in this way.

Ultrasonic vibrations in liquids may be used to emulsify immiscible liquids or to destroy bacteria by bursting their cells. These vibrations also have the effect (rather like an increase in temperature) of decomposing some liquids and of speeding up chemical reactions in others. The waves can be used to remove the air bubbles from liquids such as the molten metal used for castings.

The slice of quartz is sandwiched between electrodes in the grid circuit of a valve oscillator

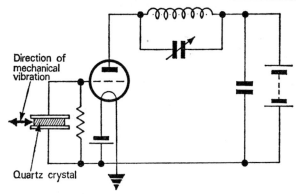

Direction of mechanical vibration

Quartz crystal

Fig. 19.2. Circuit used to stimulate resonances in a quartz crystal.

$$x = \frac{n\lambda_1}{2} = (n+1)\frac{\lambda_2}{2}$$

Also the velocity

$$v = f\lambda$$

$$\therefore$$

$$x = \frac{n\,v}{2f_1} = \frac{(n+1)}{2}\frac{v}{f_2}$$

which gives on eliminating n

$$x = v/2(f_2 - f_1)$$

The method allows us to check the thickness of plates, pipes, or sheathing, which are subject to corrosion, and it has even been used to measure the thickness of the fat layer on pigs.

These are only some of the applications of the ultrasonic waves produced either by piezo-electric transducers, such as quartz, or else by magneto-strictive transducers, such as nickel or cobalt. Transducers of the latter type change their lengths when they are magnetized and thus, in alternating magnetic fields, they vibrate in a similar way to quartz.

as shown in Fig. 19.2. The resonant frequency of the quartz is very sharply defined and, when coupled with the oscillator circuit, it vibrates at a very stable frequency. This stability makes the device ideal for controlling electric clocks and the frequency of radio transmitters.

Originally piezo-electric transducers were cut from single crystals but more recently poly-crystalline ceramic materials, such as barium titanate, have been used. The minute piezo-electric regions in the ceramic are normally randomly orientated but they can be lined up by the application of an electric field of about 3×10^6 V/m.

Ultrasonic waves have found many applications. One of the earliest ones was to improve depth sounding methods used by ships. The high frequency waves can be emitted in narrow beams and they are not absorbed by the water so strongly as the lower frequency waves. This makes it possible to obtain a continuous record of the profile of the ocean floor. The waves can be used to transmit messages between submarines, and they serve in a similar way to radar in tracking underwater craft and objects such as icebergs.

Another application of the echo sounding principle is the use of ultrasonic waves to detect flaws in large metal castings. Even invisible cracks in the metal can be detected by the waves they reflect back to the detector.

The thickness of a metal plate at any point can be measured even when we have access to only one side. We measure the successive frequencies f_1 and f_2 of the transducer, which produce resonance in the plate thickness x. (Fig. 19.3.)

Sound Reproduction

The last 100 years have seen a rapid growth in the importance in our daily lives of sound reproduction. Listening to sound recordings and broadcasts now occupies a major place in our leisure activities, and large sections of the entertainment and electronic industries are devoted to it.

The reproduction of sound relies on the conversion of sound vibrations into exactly corresponding vibrations of another quantity. The most convenient quantity into which sound can be

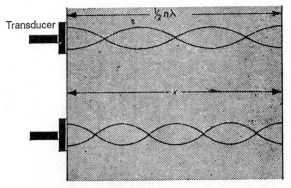

Transducer

Fig. 19.3. Measuring the thickness of a layer by setting up ultrasonic standing waves.

225

converted is that of oscillating electrical current. We will describe separately three stages of the reproduction of sound, its conversion to an alternating current, the methods of regenerating these currents into sound and the methods of recording and storing the sounds.

Microphones

Microphones convert mechanical sound waves into electrical impulses. The qualities we require in a microphone are:

(*a*) A large electrical output.
(*b*) The faithful reproduction of audible frequencies.
(*c*) An absence of background noise.

We will describe three types of microphone in use which fulfil these conditions to varying degrees.

In the moving coil microphone, the pressure variation of the sound wave causes an identical vibration in a corrugated paper cone. (Fig. 19.4.) The fine wire coil wound round the neck of the cone and moved to and fro in the field of a magnet generates a minute alternating current. At certain frequencies, the cone may resonate and produce an unduly large output, while at high frequencies its output falls because of certain electrical effects. By skilful design, however, the resonant frequencies of the cone can be made high and thus compensate for the reduced response at these high frequencies. The output of the moving coil microphone is weak but it matches closely the pattern of sound vibration.

In the crystal microphone, the vibrations of the

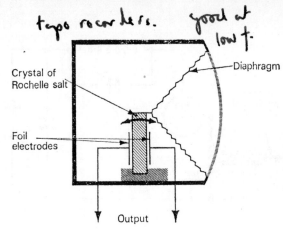

tape recorders. *good at low f.*

Fig. 19.5. The crystal microphone.

cone are transferred to a piezo-electric crystal or to a ceramic material. The bending of the crystal produces a potential difference between its opposite faces, which fluctuates with the movement of the cone. (Fig. 19.5.) The varying potential is picked up by metal foil electrodes.

The electrical impulses produced by the crystal microphone do not correspond closely with the sound vibrations. The cone and the crystal resonate at certain frequencies producing some distortion, while at higher frequencies the output falls rapidly. The output at low frequencies is high, however, and needs minimal amplification which is one reason why these microphones are so widely used.

The carbon granule microphone acts as a variable resistance which responds to sound waves and modulates any current flowing through it. The pressure variation in the sound wave is communicated by a diaphragm to a volume of fine carbon grains. (Fig. 19.6.) The improved electrical contact between the grains at high pressures reduces the electrical resistance and allows a higher current to flow. The energy for the vibration comes from an externally applied e.m.f. This type of microphone is standard in telephones, the electrical energy being supplied from a battery at the telephone exchange.

The frequency response of the carbon microphone is uniform, and its output is high. It cannot be used for quality reproduction, however, because of the background hiss, which is caused by minute arcing of the current between the granules.

The electrostatic microphone is used by professional recording engineers because of its very uniform sensitivity to a wide range of frequencies.

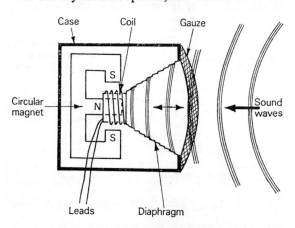

Fig. 19.4. Moving coil microphone.

Good quality.

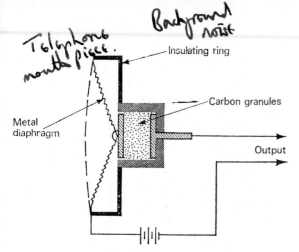

Telephone mouthpiece. *Background noise*

Fig. 19.6. The carbon granule microphone.

(Fig. 19.7.) The sound vibrations vary the plate separation of a capacitance (called a capsule). The resulting change in capacity causes a flow and return of current when a d.c. potential is connected in series with the capacitance. Because the current variations are small, the first stage of amplification is built into the microphone housing, to allow for the losses in the lead to the main amplifier. The microphone gives high fidelity reproduction but its cost, including power pack, can be as high as £200 as compared to £1 for the crystal microphone used with many tape recorders.

Regenerating the Sound

Electrical impulses leaving the microphone are suitably amplified before being fed to a device

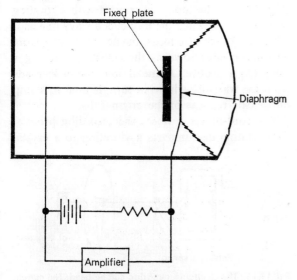

Fig. 19.7. The electrostatic microphone.

V. High quality.

for converting them back into sound vibrations. This is achieved by means of a speaker for powerful sound projection or an earphone for individual listening.

The moving-coil loudspeaker uses the principle of the moving-coil microphone in reverse. The alternating current is fed to a coil situated in the field of a magnet and attached to a diaphragm. (Fig. 19.8.) This produces a vibration in the cone-shaped diaphragm which, being large, can generate very intense sound waves.

The size of the diaphragm allows it to respond more easily to low frequency vibrations than to higher ones. To correct this, a smaller central

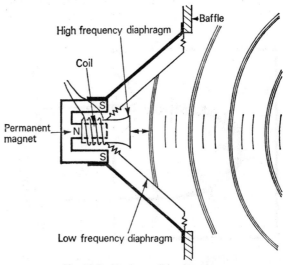

Fig. 19.8. Moving-coil loudspeaker.

cone is sometimes built into the larger one, as in Fig. 19.8, or a separate smaller speaker is used.

When a compression is generated at the point in front of the diaphragm, a rarefaction is generated behind it and so, to prevent the mutual cancellation of these two disturbances, the speaker is mounted in a baffle board, or in a box which keeps them separate. The tendency of the speaker to resonate at certain frequencies can be reduced by mounting it in a cabinet whose dimensions suppress these frequencies and promote others. (Fig. 19.9.)

The Telephone Earpiece

The incoming fluctuating current to the earphone passes through the windings of two electric magnets, causing their strength to vary. (Fig.

227

19.10.) A diaphragm made of a ferromagnetic metal (stalloy) vibrates in response to the varying fields and emits sound waves.

The permanent magnet at the base of the soft iron field pieces imposes on them a residual polarity, which can be increased or reduced by the current in the coils. If the polarity were allowed to reverse, the maximum attraction would occur at each peak of the current and the frequency would be doubled.

The diaphragm, being small and stiff, responds more readily to the higher frequencies. This makes it more effective for the reproduction of speech, because the clarity of speech increases when the frequencies below about 2000 Hz are absent. The diaphragm resonates at certain frequencies and

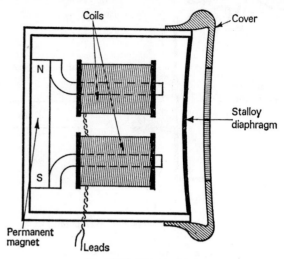

Fig. 19.10. The earphone.

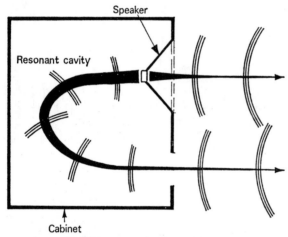

Fig. 19.9. The baffle or enclosure prevents the waves from the back of the cone cancelling those from the front.

does not reproduce accurately the wave form of the current input. However, its ability to convert very weak currents into audible sound makes it suitable for use in telephones and radio headphones.

Sound Recording

All methods of recording and reproducing sound rely on a sequence of reversible processes, with sound vibration at one end of the sequence and a lasting change produced in some other property at the other. The early systems had to be entirely mechanical and they are thus very restricted, but electrical methods of transmission and recording have revolutionized the process.

Our requirements of a recording medium are that it should accommodate a long period of recording time, and reproduce faithfully the original sound, though these requirements may be conflicting. At every stage in the process of recording, amplification and playback, care must be taken to minimize the loss of exact reproduction or fidelity.

Disc Recording

The gramophone disc is the most common means of sound recording for reproduction in our houses. At the recording studio, the output of a microphone, after being amplified, actuates an electromagnetic vibrator attached to a cutting tool. (Fig. 19.11.) The tool is in contact with a rotating wax disc, into which the tool cuts a wavy line as it vibrates. As the disc turns, the head traverses from its outside edge towards the centre, producing a long spiral groove. A metal impression is made from the wax disc which, in turn, is used to stamp out plastic replicas of the original disc.

A record-player reverses the recording process. The rotating disc imparts a vibration to a crystal

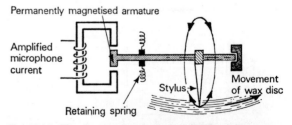

Fig. 19.11. The electromagnetic disc cutting head. The current gives a rotational vibration to a cutting stylus.

by way of a stylus held in the groove. The electrical output from the crystal pick-up is amplified and fed to a speaker. (Fig. 19.12.)

For good quality reproduction, the speed of rotation of the record must be sufficient for the stylus to follow the high frequency waves. The distance between the grooves must be sufficient to give the lower frequency waves the large amplitude they need to produce a loudness comparable with that of the higher frequencies. By using a diamond or a sapphire stylus, the point can be made sharper and more durable, which, in turn, allows us to use slower speeds and closer spaced grooves for the same quality of reproduction. High quality amplifiers allow separate controls of the bass notes

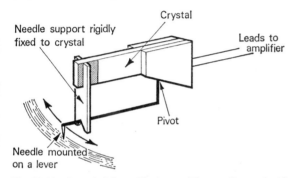

Fig. 19.12.   Crystal pick-up. The lever with a needle attached is a push-fit in the pivot and it can quickly be replaced.

to restore the intensity lost by the crowding together of the lines. The original records designed to play at 78 rev/min for only a few minutes, have been replaced by microgroove records rotating at speeds of 33⅓ and 45 rev/min. This gives high fidelity reproduction from discs which can store about twenty minutes listening time per side.

Tape Recording

Sound vibrations can be recorded as a pattern of varying degrees of magnetization on a plastic ribbon impregnated with a magnetic material. The tape moves at a constant speed across the poles of an electromagnet, which are less than 0·1 mm apart. The electrical output from a microphone is supplied to the electromagnet and controls the magnetic field between the poles. Thus, the section of tape bridging the poles at any instant is magnetized to a degree controlled by the sound vibration. (Fig. 19.13.)

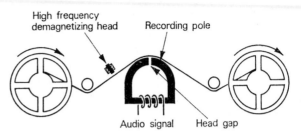

Fig. 19.13.   Tape recorder.

During playback, the magnetized tape recording is moved at the same speed past the poles of the magnet and induces a field in the magnet. This, in turn, induces a current in the windings, which can be amplified to reproduce the original sounds.

In practice, all these changes are superimposed on a very high frequency current of about 80 kHz, which acts as a carrier wave for the low frequency vibrations. Prior to each recording, the tape is wiped clean as it passes through a gradually diminishing field of a high frequency electromagnet.

The quality of reproduction from a tape is better at higher tape speeds and when the head gap is small. At the higher speed of 190 mm per second available on most instruments, its performance is equivalent to a good quality disc record. The advantages of the tape recorder are that it requires less skill in recording, no intermediate processing before playback, it is portable and inexpensive, and the tape can be used to record again and again. Specially wide tapes are being used increasingly for the recording of sound and vision for television. Perhaps in the future, we shall see them become as commonly used by the amateur as sound tape recorders are at present.

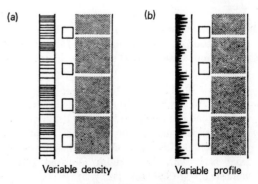

Fig. 19.14.   Film sound track.

Film Sound Track

In the case of sound cinematography, it is convenient to record the sound in the same way as the picture is recorded, that is, by the photographic process. The sound track of the film is a narrow strip down one side of the film, the opacity of which varies in accordance with the sound vibration.

One way of producing this track is to use the output from the microphone to vary the light emitted from a gas discharge tube, which is focused on the unexposed film. Development of the film produces a track of varying density. (Fig. 19.14a.) The output from the microphone can vary the sound track exposure in other ways; for example, it can vary the width of an aperture restricting the light source. Alternatively, the oscillating currents can be converted electromagnetically into the vibrations of a mirror, which directs a light beam to film the width of the track to varying degrees. (Fig. 19.14b.)

The method of regenerating the sound from this track is illustrated in Fig. 19.15. The density of the sound track at any point controls the amount of light shining on to a photocell. As the film moves, the current output from the photocell varies accordingly, and after amplification it is passed to the speaker.

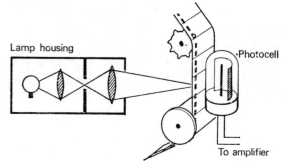

Fig. 19.15. Regenerating the sound from a sound track.

If several speakers are to be controlled separately, as in the case of stereophonic sound systems, several tracks are needed. This may restrict the space available for picture projection, and so magnetic sound tracks which can be fitted into about 1/5th of the space are fast replacing the optical ones.

Questions

1. Why is it that music needs a longer reverberation time than speech?
2. What are the properties required for a material to absorb sound well? And to reflect it?
3. Why is it more difficult to exclude low-frequency sound when soundproofing?
4. Why is it that ultrasonic vibrations can be used to abrade holes, etc., while sound waves cannot?
5. Early recordings were made by operating the cutting stylus mechanically from the vibrations which were to be preserved. What are the drawbacks of this system?
6. Why are loudspeaker diaphragms cone-shaped?
7. What qualities are required for a good pick-up and a good loudspeaker?
8. Why do you think disc recordings are more popular than tapes for music reproduction?
9. Why is it important that the motors used in record players and tape recorders should run at a very constant speed?
10. Is it possible to reproduce a piece of music exactly as performed? If not, why not?

Problems

1. A room, measuring $20 \text{ m} \times 10 \text{ m} \times 10 \text{ m}$ has a mean absorption coefficient of 0·15 and its reverberation time is 0·41 s. What is its Sabine absorption?
   Answer: 0·16 m ^{2}.
2. A room $10 \text{ m} \times 10 \text{ m} \times 10 \text{ m}$ has a carpeted floor and one end is a large window with heavy curtains. All the other surfaces are plastered. What is the reverberation time with the curtains drawn and what is it with the curtains removed and the window open? (See table 19.1.)
   Answer: 1·63, 1·08 s.
3. A sonar beam is radiated from a ship and an echo is received after 0·9 s. If the speed of sound in the water is 1400 m/s, how far away is the reflecting surface?
   Answer: $6·3 \times 10^2$ m.
4. An explosion on a water surface is heard twice by an observer some distance away. If the speed of sound in air is $3·4 \times 10^2$ m/s, and $1·4 \times 10^3$ m/s in water, and the interval between the arrival of the two sounds is 7·95 s, how far is the observer from the explosion?
   Answer: $3·57 \times 10^3$ m.

20 Gases and Vapours

Nearly all the matter in the universe is gaseous. The stars, which constitute most of this matter, are made of gas though in their interiors the density exceeds that of any solid we know on Earth. Across some areas of space stretch great clouds of gaseous matter, whose density is less than the most complete vacuum ever produced on Earth, and whose temperature is close to absolute zero.

Although the chemical properties of gases vary, their physical properties are very similar. They all spread themselves rapidly to every corner of a space into which they are introduced. They are all transparent and usually colourless. Although it sometimes happens that chemical reactions take place between them, usually they all mix quite easily together and, when mixed in this way, they exert pressures quite independently of each other.

A few simple laws, recalling the names of the scientists who formulated them, sum up the characteristic behaviour of gases.

Sometimes, two scientists, working independently in different countries, discovered the same law at about the same time. This has happened in all branches of science and you may, therefore, come across some of the laws given below, and others, under alternative names. It is natural for people to honour the scientists of their own country by associating with them the laws they helped to discover.

The Gas Laws

The gas laws express relations between the volume V, pressure p, and temperature T of a fixed mass of gas.

General Gas Law. The product of the pressure and volume of a fixed mass of gas is proportional to its absolute temperature, i.e.,

$$pV \propto T$$

The law is sometimes stated as three separate relations for a fixed mass of gas.

Boyle's Law

$$p \propto \frac{1}{V} \text{ at constant temperature}$$

for example, if the pressure on a gas is doubled its volume is halved. (Fig. 20.1.) At extremely low pressures all gases obey the law, but at higher pressures deviations may become significant. In

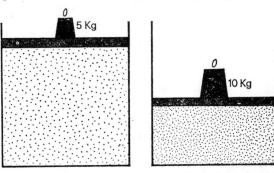

Fig. 20.1. A specific example illustrates the meaning of Boyle's Law.

one sense the law reflects the structure which all gases have in common. The concept of an *ideal gas* which obeys the law exactly is a useful one in thermodynamics. When we wish to emphasize that the behaviour of a gas does not accurately follow the law, we refer to it as a *real gas.*

Charles' Law

$$V \propto T \text{ at constant pressure}$$

Pressure Law

$$p \propto T \text{ at constant volume}$$

We should not be surprised to find that the pressure (or volume) of a gas is directly proportional to its absolute temperature, because temperature itself is defined in terms of the change in pressure of a gas. (chapter 2.) We may express the combined effect of the laws as an equation

$$pV = RT$$

where R, the constant of proportionality in this equation, is called the *gas constant* and applies to 1 g of a particular gas. The equation is not strictly accurate for gases at high densities and low temperatures but it is accurate enough for many purposes. For example, Boyles' law is accurate to 1 part in a thousand for such common gases as air, oxygen, nitrogen, hydrogen, at ordinary

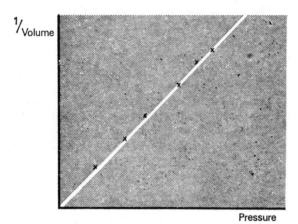

Fig. 20.2. Graph of 1/volume against the pressure of a fixed mass of a gas at constant temperature.

temperatures and pressures. The accuracy of the equation also depends on the way in which temperature is defined. Deviations from the laws are discussed later in more detail. For m kilogrammes of a gas the equation becomes

$$pV = mRT$$

A common use of the equation is to convert a measured volume of gas to the volume it would occupy under standard conditions of temperature and pressure (S.T.P.). *The standard conditions of temperature and pressure are 0°C and 760 mm of mercury pressure.* This pressure, exerted by a column of mercury 760 mm high, is referred to as one atmosphere.

1 atmosphere = $1 \cdot 013 \times 10^5$ N/m²

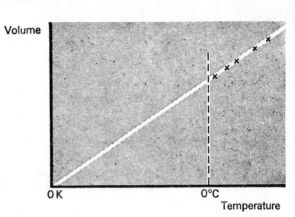

Fig. 20.3. Graph of volume against absolute temperature of a fixed mass of gas.

Problem: The density of oxygen at S.T.P. is $1 \cdot 43$ kg/m³ What mass is contained in a cylinder $1 \cdot 5$ m long and internal diameter $0 \cdot 3$ m if it exerts a pressure of 12 atmospheres at 15°C.

Solution: We change the volume to the equivalent volume at S.T.P. using $\dfrac{p_1 V_1}{T_1} = \dfrac{p_2 V_2}{T_2}$

$$\frac{12\left(\dfrac{\pi}{4} 0 \cdot 3^2 \times 1 \cdot 5\right)}{288} = \frac{1 \times V_2}{273}$$

$$V_2 = \frac{273}{288} \times \frac{12}{1} \times \frac{\pi 0 \cdot 3^2}{4} \times 1 \cdot 5 \text{ m}^3 \text{ at S.T.P.}$$

mass $= V_2 \times$ density at S.T.P.

$$= \frac{273}{288} \times \frac{12}{1} \times \frac{\pi 0 \cdot 3^2}{4} \times 1 \cdot 5 \times 1 \cdot 43 \text{ kg}$$

$$= 1 \cdot 73 \text{ kg}$$

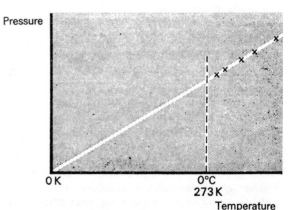

Fig. 20.4. Graph of the pressure against the absolute temperature of a fixed mass of gas.

We can also use the gas equation to determine the mass of a gas in a container by measuring the pressure, temperature, and volume of the gas. Although it is possible to measure the mass directly by weighing the container, first under vacuum and then filled with gas, this method is usually extremely inconvenient. An oxygen cylinder, for example, is a difficult object to weigh in this manner, whereas measuring the pressure and temperature of the gas inside it is easy.

Dalton's Law. In a mixture of gases, the total pressure is the sum of the pressures which each gas would exert if it alone occupied the total available volume.

$$p = p_1 + p_2 + p_3, \text{ etc.}$$

This statement may seem to be common sense, and you may think that making a scientific law out of it is making a fuss about nothing. It is important, however, when framing scientific laws to do so in such a way as to exclude all possible alternatives, and sometimes this inevitably means stating the obvious.

Atomic and Molecular Weights

The masses of atoms and molecules are not usually expressed in kilogrammes because they are such minute fractions. For example, the mass of an oxygen molecule is 53.5×10^{-27} kg. We prefer to express the masses of atoms and molecules in terms of a smaller unit. To make sure that the masses of atoms are expressed as a number greater than one, we make the smallest atom of all, the hydrogen atom, our unit of mass. The hydrogen atom thus has a mass of one *atomic mass unit* or 1 u. On this scale, then, the mass of an oxygen molecule is about 32 u, and the mass of a helium molecule is about 4 u.

Now 1 kg of hydrogen contains 6.02×10^{26} atoms. If we want to specify this same number of oxygen molecules we need 32 g of oxygen, while only 4 g of helium contain this number of molecules. In fact, the molecular weight in grammes (called a gramme molecule or mole for short) of any substance contains 6.02×10^{23} molecules. Knowing this number, called Avogadro's number N, we can calculate the mass of a substance which contains a given number of molecules.

If M is the molecular weight of the substance,

then M grammes contain N molecules. Suppose m grammes contain n molecules

then
$$\frac{M}{m} = \frac{N}{n}$$

and
$$n = m\frac{N}{M}$$

Problem: How many molecules are contained in 50 g of nitrogen (mol. wt. 28)?

Solution: $n = m\dfrac{N}{M}$

$$n = \frac{50 \times 6.02 \times 10^{23}}{28} = 10.7 \times 10^{23} \text{ mols.}$$

Avogadro's Law

The law states that *at a given temperature and volume, the pressure exerted by any gas depends only on the number of molecules present.* Neither the shape nor the size of the molecules of a gas influences the pressure they exert. Thus, the pressure exerted by a million molecules of hydrogen in a given container would be the same as that exerted by a million molecules of oxygen, or of chlorine, or of radon. Avogadro's law is sometimes stated as: 'Equal volumes of all gases under the same conditions of temperature and pressure contain the same number of molecules'. With a little thought you will see that the two statements of the law are equivalent. Again, the law is only exactly true at the lowest pressures. In calculations we often use the fact that a mole of any gas (6.02×10^{23} mols.) occupies 22.4 litres at S.T.P.

Problem: What volume would 20 g of helium occupy at S.T.P. (mol. wt. helium = 4)?

Solution: 4 g of helium occupy 22.4 litres.

∴ 20 g of helium occupy $\dfrac{20}{4} \times 22.4 = 112.0$ litres.

Universal Gas Constant

According to Avogadro's law, the pressure of a gas does not depend on the nature of the gas but only on the number of molecules for a given volume and temperature. If we could apply the ideal gas equation to a specific number of molecules, then the constant of proportionality between pV and T would be the same for all gases.

The number particularly convenient for specification is Avogadro's number, the number of molecules in a gramme molecule of any substance.

Thus, whatever the gas, 6.02×10^{23} molecules are described by the same equation.

$$pV = KT$$

This is an *equation of state*, the constant K being called the universal gas constant for one mole.

Vapours

In the minds of most people, the word 'vapour' conjures up an image far removed from the formal scientific meaning of the word. The mist that hangs over hollows in the early morning, for instance, is not a vapour, nor is the smoke that curls above volcanic craters, nor is the steam that rises from boiling liquids. These are in reality suspensions of liquid droplets.

Vapours are invisible, as gases are, and they resemble gases also in many other ways. Between the two states of matter, however, there are essential differences in behaviour which oblige us to recognize an essential difference in kind. For example, when a vapour is compressed, its pressure rises until it reaches a point at which the vapour condenses into a liquid. On the other hand, when a gas is compressed, it remains a gas, even when subject to very high pressures.

Because of the many similarities between their physical properties, the difference between gases and vapours can only be defined by a full description of their behaviour. In this chapter, we shall examine the process of evaporation in some detail, when the nature of matter in a vapour state will become clear. For the time being, we can define a vapour as matter in a gaseous state, existing at such a temperature that a sufficient increase in its pressure will result in condensing it into a liquid.

Evaporation

According to the kinetic theory of matter, the molecules within a liquid are continually on the move. Some molecules, which by chance collisions gain a velocity much higher than average, shoot off the surface of the liquid and escape to become vapour. The higher the temperature of the liquid, the greater the velocity of the molecules, and the greater the rate of evaporation.

If the space above the liquid is not bounded by a container, the molecules which escape keep right on going and diffuse away. Evaporation continues until all the liquid is gone. The process is accelerated if there is a movement of air above the liquid.

Exposed liquids are usually a few degrees below the temperature of their surroundings because of the extraction of latent heat of evaporation. After an initial drop in the temperature of the liquid, heat flows in from the environment at the same rate as it is lost by evaporation.

Saturated Vapour

If the space above a liquid is enclosed, then vapour molecules accumulate in the space. Occasionally, molecules from the vapour meet the liquid surface and return to the liquid. As the density of the vapour increases, a stage is reached when the number of molecules evaporating is equal to the number of molecules condensing in the same time. (Fig. 20.5.) Under these conditions, the space above the liquid is said to be saturated with the vapour from the liquid.

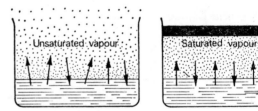

Fig. 20.5. In a saturated vapour, molecules leave and rejoin the liquid at the same rate.

The vapour molecules exert a pressure which increases as the density of the vapour increases. When the vapour is saturated, the pressure exerted reaches a steady value, called the saturated vapour pressure or S.V.P.

A vapour can exist when it is too cold for the liquid to exist, i.e., below the freezing point. In the polar regions of the Earth, the water vapour evaporates from snow and ice and falls again as snow. This immediate change from solid to vapour, which takes place without an intermediate liquid state is called sublimation.

Even solids, such as iron or copper, have vapour pressures, but at ordinary temperatures these are insignificant except in the context of ultra high vacuum.

Volume and Pressure Changes in Vapours

Consider what happens if the volume above the liquid is suddenly increased. The number of vapour molecules per unit volume decreases sharply, and the rate at which they return to the liquid also drops. The rate at which molecules leave the liquid continues as before, so that for a while a much larger number of molecules leave the liquid than return to it. This continues until the equilibrium density of the vapour is restored and the saturated vapour pressure is exerted once again. A reduction in the volume above a liquid produces condensation of the molecules from the vapour to the liquid and again the S.V.P. is restored.

The establishment of equilibrium between evaporation and condensation is a rapid process, and any confined volume at a uniform temperature

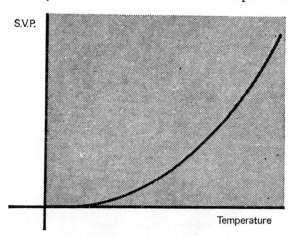

Fig. 20.6. Variation of S.V.P. with temperature.

in which there is an exposed liquid may be assumed to be saturated with the vapour from the liquid.

A rise in temperature causes a large increase in the rate at which molecules escape from the liquid. The increase in the rate at which molecules return to the liquid is not so marked and therefore at higher temperatures the vapour becomes much denser and exerts a higher pressure. The variation of S.V.P. with temperature for a typical vapour is shown in Fig. 20.6.

Relation between Pressure and Boiling Point

Imagine a bubble of vapour near the surface of a liquid. (Fig. 20.7.) The pressure tending to collapse the bubble is the same as that exerted

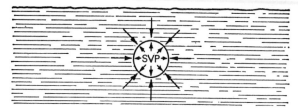

Fig. 20.7. The pressure of the saturated vapour in a bubble tends to expand it while the pressure of the liquid tends to contract it.

on the surface, i.e., atmospheric pressure. The pressure tending to expand the bubble is the S.V.P. of the liquid. The liquid begins to boil at the temperature at which the S.V.P. of the liquid equals atmospheric pressure. Thus, a liquid at a uniform temperature should boil first at the surface, where the pressure is least.

We have, in fact, neglected the surface tension of the liquid, which tends to collapse the bubbles. The contracting influence of the surface tension is greatest when the bubbles are small and has the effect of retarding the formation of the bubbles. Once formed, the bubbles grow very rapidly and may produce the 'bumping' associated with boiling liquid. In practice, irregularities in the vessel help bubbles to start forming below the surface.

When the source of heat is at the bottom of the vessel, the liquid at deeper levels will be above the temperature of the surface, because the increased pressure raises the boiling point. Water, as we know, boils at 100°C when atmospheric pressure is at the standard value of 760 mm of mercury. At

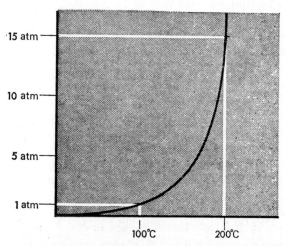

Fig. 20.8. Variation of the boiling point of water with pressure. (S.V.P.∼ temperature).

high altitudes, where the atmospheric pressure is below the standard value, the temperature at which the S.V.P. of water equals atmospheric pressure is less than 100°C. For example, at the top of Mount Everest, where atmospheric pressure is only 230 mm Hg, water boils at 70°C, so that, in addition to being unable to breathe enough air up there, you cannot make a decent cup of tea or coffee. For the same reason, a puncture in a spaceman's suit would be disastrous, because the pressure in space is almost zero and the temperature of his body is well above the boiling point of the body fluids. The S.V.P. of any substance at its boiling point is equal to atmospheric pressure. Thus, we can measure the variation of S.V.P. with temperature by determining the boiling point of a liquid for a series of pressures above and below atmospheric pressure. (Fig. 20.8.) The efficiency of steam engines and turbines improves as the temperature of the steam increases. Modern plants produce steam at pressures above 200 atmospheres and temperatures above 500°C.

Vapours and Gases

Are substances divided fundamentally into two groups, those which form vapours and those which form gases? This question is best answered by looking at the results of an experiment carried out by Andrews. He subjected carbon dioxide to a wide range of pressure, volume, and temperature changes and presented his results on a pressure–volume graph. (Fig. 20.9.)

Starting with the carbon dioxide at one of the temperatures on the right of Fig. 20.9, he reduced the volume and measured the resulting pressure while the temperature was kept constant. The lines are called isothermal curves.

Critical Temperature

One particular isothermal curve marks the difference between liquid and gas. This isothermal is the first one to have a horizontal section. The isothermal defines the critical temperature of the substance. *Above the critical temperature a gas cannot be liquified by pressure alone.* No increase in pressure will cause the gas to change into a liquid. It merely becomes a denser gas. Below the critical temperature a substance may exist as a solid, a liquid, or a vapour. The isothermals below

the critical temperature, at the bottom right of Fig. 20.9, represent the unsaturated vapour. No liquid is present at this stage and the isothermals are like those for the gas. An unsaturated vapour obeys the gas laws and is indistinguishable from a gas until it is subjected to high pressures, in which case the vapour condenses.

The isothermals for the saturated vapour are horizontal. During this stage, as the volume reduces, the pressure remains constant and the liquid condenses. When all the vapour has been condensed to liquid, the isothermals become nearly vertical; this indicates that the liquid state is almost incompressible. Any substance will behave like carbon dioxide as represented in Fig. 20.9, over an appropriate range of pressures and

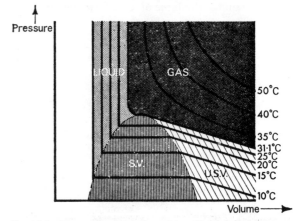

Fig. 20.9. The results of Andrews' experiments with carbon dioxide plotted on a p–V diagram.

temperatures, and provided, of course, the substance does not decompose. The critical temperatures of some substances are given in Table 20.1.

The critical temperature should not be confused with either the melting point or the boiling point, both of which can be influenced by the pressure or by impurity, whereas the critical temperature

Table 20.1. Critical temperatures

Element	K	°C
Hydrogen	33	−240
Oxygen	154	−119
Nitrogen	126	−147
Air	133	−140
Water	647	374
Aniline	699	426

does not depend on these factors. The only relation we can state is that neither melting point nor boiling point can be greater than the critical temperature.

The Kinetic Theory of Gases

Bernoulli, a Swiss scientist, first advanced the theory that gases were composed of particles in motion. This kinetic theory of the structure of gases is now accepted as fact, and it explains many of the properties of gases.

The continual bombardment of any surface by the gas causes a pressure to be exerted. The greater the density of a gas, the more frequent the bombardment and the greater the pressure exerted. Thus, the pressure increases either when more gas is pumped into a vessel, or when the volume of a certain mass of gas is reduced. When the temperature of a gas is raised, the speed of the molecules increases, causing an increase in both the number and the momentum imparted by each collision. This accounts for the increase in pressure of a gas with temperature. In 1860, Maxwell was able to explain some of the properties of a gas in more detail by making certain basic assumptions about its molecules.

1. The molecules of a gas make elastic collisions.
2. The molecules spend a negligible time actually in collision.
3. The attractive forces between molecules is negligible.
4. The molecules themselves occupy a negligible part of the volume of the gas.

Maxwell applied a rigorous mathematical treatment to these assumptions but we can achieve the same result by adopting a simpler approach.

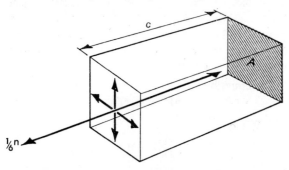

Fig. 20.10. In one second, one-sixth of all the molecules within a distance, c, of the surface strike the surface.

Consider a gas containing n molecules per unit volume each having a mass m. The molecules have a range of velocities and travel in random directions, but we will assume that they can travel in one of only six directions as shown in Fig. 20.10 and that they have a single velocity c which would produce the same pressure as the various velocities. On the average, $\frac{1}{6}n$ molecules per unit volume travel in any one direction. The molecules which collide with the surface of area A during one second are contained within a volume cA.

$$\text{number per second} = \frac{n}{6}cA$$

Each molecule bounces back from the surface exactly reversing its momentum from $+mc$ to $-mc$, thus involving a change of momentum of $2\,mc$ per collision.

Force on the surface

$$= \text{the rate of change of momentum}$$
$$= \text{No./s} \times \text{momentum change per molecule}$$
$$= \frac{ncA}{6} \times 2\,mc$$
$$= \frac{1}{3}nmc^2\,A$$

Pressure $= \text{force/area}$
$$= \frac{1}{3}nmc^2\,A/A$$
$$p = \frac{1}{3}nmc^2$$

Now $nm = \text{density } (\rho)$

Hence $p = \frac{1}{3}\rho c^2$

also since $\rho = \dfrac{\text{total mass}}{\text{volume}} = \dfrac{M}{V}$

$$p = \frac{1}{3}\frac{M}{V}c^2$$
$$pV = \frac{1}{3}Mc^2$$

If we write this as

$$pV = \frac{2}{3}\cdot\frac{1}{2}\,Mc^2$$
$$= \frac{2}{3}\ \text{kinetic energy of molecules,}$$

237

actual measurements show that

$$pV = MRT$$

Hence

$$\text{K.E.} \propto T$$

That is, the kinetic energy of the molecules of a gas is proportional to its absolute temperature.

The velocity c, which produces the same effect as the various velocities of the gas molecules, is not, as we might expect, the average velocity of the molecules. It is the velocity such that c^2 is equal to the average of the squares of the velocities of the molecules

$$c^2 = [u_1^2 + u_2^2 + u_3^2 + \ldots + u_n^2]/n$$

$$c = \sqrt{\frac{(u_1^2 + u_2^2 + u_3^2 + \ldots + u_n^2)}{n}}$$

c is the root of the mean of the squares of the velocities of the molecules called the *root mean square* or R.M.S. velocity.

Problem: Calculate the R.M.S. velocity of the molecules of hydrogen at 0°C. (Density of hydrogen at S.T.P. $= 9 \times 10^{-2} \, \text{kg/m}^3$; standard atmospheric pressure $= 1 \cdot 01 \times 10^5 \, \text{N/m}^2$.)

Solution: We use $p = \dfrac{1}{3} \rho c^2$

from which $c = \sqrt{\dfrac{3p}{\rho}} = \sqrt{\left(\dfrac{3 \times 1 \cdot 01 \times 10^5}{0 \cdot 09}\right)}$

$$c = 1 \cdot 8 \times 10^3 \, \text{m/s}$$

Graham's Law of Diffusion

The rate at which a gas diffuses through a restricted aperture or porous barrier is, as we might expect, proportional to the average velocity of the molecules.

mols. per second $\propto$ average velocity.

The average velocity is itself proportional to the R.M.S. velocity c.

Hence   molecules per second $\propto c$

but $p = \frac{1}{3}\rho c^2$ or $c = \sqrt{\dfrac{3p}{\rho}}$

$\therefore$ mols. per second $\propto \sqrt{\dfrac{1}{\text{density}}}$

This confirms Graham's law of diffusion, which he established experimentally; *the rates of diffusion of gases are inversely proportional to the square*

roots of their densities, measured under the same conditions.

Deviations from the Gas Laws

The experiments of Andrews show that, close to and below the critical temperature and density, substances do not obey the gas laws and, in particular, the equation $pV = MRT$. At higher densities, the gas molecules are sufficiently close together for the attraction between the molecules to reduce the pressure they exert, and for the volume of the molecules themselves to restrict the space in which they are free to move. Both these effects are illustrated in Fig. 20.11.

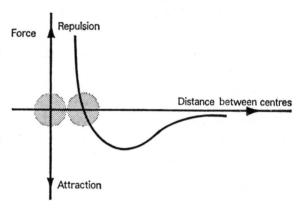

Fig. 20.11.   The attractive force between molecules and their volumes become significant at small separations.

Many scientists have attempted to find a single equation which will describe the behaviour of a substance in its gas, vapour, or liquid state. Of all the equations that have so far been proposed, Van der Waals' is the simplest and most accurate. The equation allows for the attraction between the molecules by adding a factor a/V^2 to the pressure, where V is the volume and a is a constant. The equation allows for the space taken up by the molecules by reducing the measured volume by a constant factor b.

The equation

$$pV = MRT$$

becomes

$$\left(p + \frac{a}{V^2}\right)(V - b) = MRT$$

To determine the constants a, b, and R for a gas, we measure the other quantities for three particular

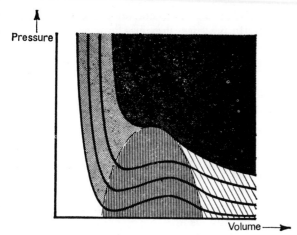

Fig. 20.12. The graphs of Van der Waal's equation shown here are similar to the isothermal of Fig. 20.9 determined by experiment.

sets of conditions, insert them in the equation and solve them simultaneously. We can then use the equation to predict the relation between p and V for a wide range of temperatures and pressures. When we plot a graph of the values of p and V, which satisfy the equation at several fixed value of T, we obtain the curves of Fig. 20.12. As you can see these curves approximate to the isothermals of Fig. 20.9 determined by experiment over the entire range.

Pumps

A pump is a mechanical device designed for transferring a fluid from one place to another by creating a difference in the pressures within that fluid. The most familiar type of pump to most of us is the kind used to inflate tyres. (Fig. 20.13.) This consists of a cylinder, inside which a plunger moves backwards and forwards, compressing air with each forward stroke, and forcing it into the tyre through a valve, which closes automatically with every return stroke of the plunger. When the pliable leather washer on the plunger is reversed, the pump can be used in conjunction with an appropriate valve to produce a vacuum.

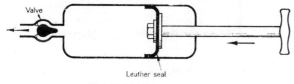

Fig. 20.13. Piston pump.

Rotary pumps are more efficient in producing lower pressures. (Fig. 20.14.) They work fast and last a long time, but, because they require very accurate machining, they are very expensive. Double vanes, fitting into slots in an eccentrically mounted rotor, press against the sides of a cylindrical barrel. As the rotor spins round, each vane in turn draws in a volume of the fluid on the intake side, seals it off, and then compresses it to a pressure at which it is expelled through a flap valve. The vapour from the special oil, which both lubricates and seals the pump, exerts a very low pressure. The pump produces pressures of about a millionth part of atmospheric pressure, i.e., about 10^{-3} mm Hg. (1mm Hg = 133·3 N/m²).

The *water filter pump* is a device for pumping a gas which uses something available in most places,

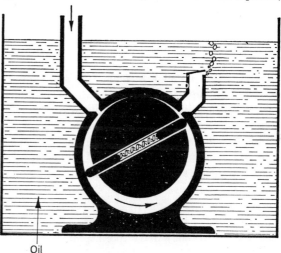

Fig. 20.14. Rotary pump.

a supply of water under pressure. Water passes rapidly across the end of a tube and knocks away any molecules of the gas which emerge. This continually extracts the gas molecules, even when the pressure of the gas inside the tube is a fraction of atmospheric pressure. (Fig. 20.15.) Since the pump relies on the diffusion of gas molecules, it is sometimes referred to as a water diffusion pump.

Figure 20.16 illustrates another form of diffusion pump which is used to evacuate vessels down to pressures as low as 10^{-5} mm Hg. It is used in series with a rotary pump to evacuate radio valves and cathode-ray tubes. The liquid, either

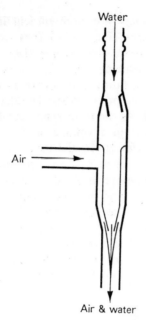

Fig. 20.15. Water diffusion pump.

mechanically and registers on a scale calibrated directly in pressure. Pressures in excess of atmospheric pressure—counting atmospheric as zero—are referred to as gauge pressures to distinguish them from absolute pressures.

$$\text{Absolute pressure} = \frac{\text{Gauge}}{\text{pressure}} + \frac{\text{atmospheric}}{\text{pressure}}$$

Moderate pressures comparable with atmospheric pressure can be measured by a U tube containing a liquid. (Fig. 20.18.) Low pressures cannot be measured by this liquid manometer, however, because the difference in liquid level is inconveniently small.

In the *McLeod gauge*, a gas of a very low pressure is compressed in a known volume ratio, to increase its pressure to a measurable level. (Fig. 20.19.) The reservoir is raised until the mercury fills the bulb of volume V, trapping the gas in the tube of

mercury or a special low vapour pressure oil, is heated and vaporized very rapidly. The molecules are deflected by the cowl and travel at very high speed away from the vessel being evacuated. Molecules of gas which diffuse from the vessel enter the vapour stream and get knocked downward towards the rotary pump inlet. The vapour molecules condense as they strike the water cooled surfaces, and return to the reservoir.

Valves and cathode-ray tubes are usually 'gettered' after they have been sealed. In this process, a reactive metal, such as barium, is evaporated inside the valve. The metal reacts with the residual gases and provides a final stage of evacuation. The lifetime and the efficiency of the filaments of valves and cathode-ray tubes are strongly dependent on the degree of evacuation which can be achieved and, indeed, the production of high vacua is a branch of engineering in its own right.

Pressure Measurement

Pressures up to several times greater than atmospheric pressure can be measured by the *Bourdon gauge*. Basically, the gauge is a curved bronze tube whose curvature varies with the pressure. (Fig. 20.17.) The movement is magnified

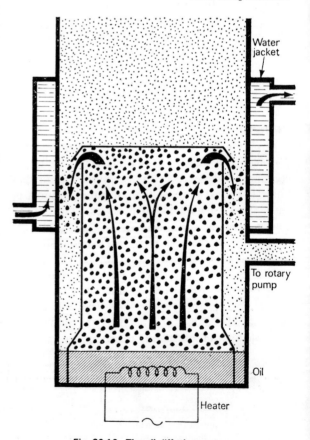

Fig. 20.16. The oil diffusion pump.

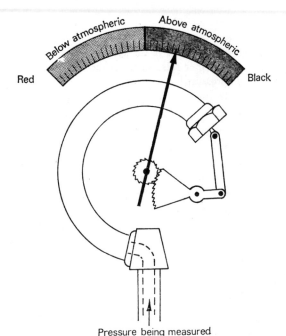

Fig. 20.17. The Bourdon gauge.

low pressures from 10^{-1} to 10^{-4} mm Hg is the *Pirani gauge*. It is based on the regular variations of the thermal conductivity of a gas with pressure. The conductivity of a gas affects the equilibrium temperature of a heated filament which, in turn, affects its electrical resistance. This is converted electrically to a deflection on a meter. (Fig. 20.20.)

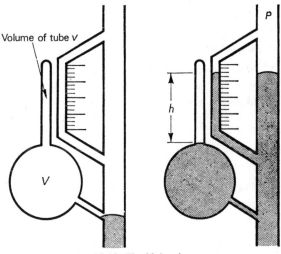

Fig. 20.19. The McLeod gauge.

volume v. Applying Boyles' law to the gas, which increases in pressure from p to $(p+h)$ (mm Hg),

$$p(v+V) = (p+h)v$$

$$\therefore \qquad p = \frac{v}{V}h$$

since v/V is constant $p \propto h$

The tube is calibrated directly in pressure.

The McLeod gauge does not give a continuous reading of pressure and is not suitable for registering rapid variations in pressure. A continuously reading gauge used extensively to measure very

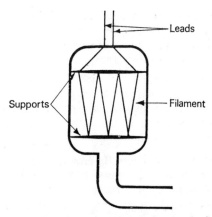

Leads

Supports

Filament

Fig. 20.20. The Pirani gauge measures pressure by its effect on thermal conductivity at low pressures.

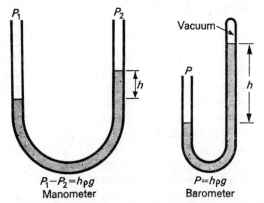

$$P_1 - P_2 = h\rho g$$
Manometer

$$P = h\rho g$$
Barometer

Fig. 20.18. The U tube manometer measures pressure differences; where one liquid column is bounded by a vacuum it measures absolute pressure.

Pressures as low as 10^{-13} mm Hg have been produced for the purpose of examining physically clean surfaces, i.e., surfaces completely free from absorbed substances. At the other extreme, pressures up to 400,000 atmospheres can be achieved. Astonishing effects occur at such high pressures, such as a 50 per cent reduction in a volume of water and an increase in the viscosity of machine oil to approach that of pitch.

Questions

1. Why do we measure atmospheric pressure as a depth of mercury?

2. Explain how the bombardment of the walls of a vessel by gas molecules causes a pressure.

3. Why does a gas diffuse through a porous material quicker than a liquid?

4. Explain how increasing pressure raises the boiling-point of a liquid.

5. What differences in properties would you expect between a substance in a solid state and the same substance above the critical temperature, compressed as a gas to the same density as the solid?

6. Why do high vacuum pumps present a lubrication problem?

7. What is the difference between boiling and evaporation?

8. Does water vapour in the space above the mercury in a barometer raise or lower the apparent atmospheric pressure?

9. What is the difference in behaviour between a saturated vapour and an unsaturated vapour?

10. Why do gases obey the gas laws better at low pressures?

11. What factors limit the degree of evacuation which can be reached by a pump?

12. Explain the difference between gauge pressure and absolute pressure.

13. A closed steel tank, filled with nitrogen, is heated. What happens to (a) the weight, (b) the density, (c) the volume, (d) the pressure of the gas?

14. A cylinder closed with a freely moving piston is heated. What happens to (a) the weight, (b) the density, (c) the volume, (d) the pressure of the gas? Suggest why liquids were at one time thought to be incompressible.

Problems

1. Express standard atmospheric pressure (760 mm Hg) in lbf/in^2, N/m^2, kgf/m^2.
   Answer 14·7 lbf/in^2, $1·013 \times 10^5$ N/m^2, $1·035 \times 10^4$ kgf/m^2.

2. An exhaust pump has a barrel with a volume of 10^{-4} m^3. If the pump is connected to a tank of $1·5 \times 10^{-3}$ m^3 volume at atmospheric pressure, what is the pressure in the tank after three strokes?
   Answer: 0·83 × atmospheric.

3. At 15°C and 750 mm Hg pressure, air weighs 1·26 g/litre. What is its density at 250 mm Hg pressure and −45°C?
   Answer: 0·53 g/litre.

4. An electric light bulb is filled with argon at 100 mm Hg pressure at 15°C. What is the gas pressure when the lamp is alight, at 400°C?
   Answer: 235 mm Hg.

5. A litre of hydrogen is collected under an inverted jar with the open end under water. The water inside the jar is 120 mm above the level outside and the atmospheric pressure in 750 mm Hg. What would the volume of hydrogen be, dry, at S.T.P.? (Saturated vapour pressure of water = 12·7 mm Hg, at the temperature of the gas.)
   Answer: $9·48 \times 10^{-4}$ m^3.

6. A litre of air saturated with water vapour at 100°C is cooled to 40°C. The pressure remains at 800 mm of mercury. What is the new volume of the air? (Saturated vapour pressure of water at 40°C =55·1 mm Hg. S.V.P. water at 100°C=760 mm Hg.)
   Answer: $4·51 \times 10^{-5}$ m^3.

7. If the outside temperature is 20°C at ground level and drops off 0·5°C for each 100 m rise, what height is the cloudbase when the dew-point of the air is 10°C?
   Answer: 2000 m.

8. What is the weight of 1 litre of air at 20°C and 755 mm Hg pressure, saturated with water vapour? (S.V.P. of water at 20°C=17·5 mm Hg. Density of air at S.T.P. = 1·293 g/l. Density of water vapour at S.T.P. = 0·8 g/l.)
   Answer: 1·186 g.

9. The following table refers to methane:

Temperature (°C)	−170	−165	−160
S.V.P. (mm Hg)	352	560	846
Temperature (°C)	−155	−150	
S.V.P. (mm Hg)	1230	1720	

What is the boiling point of methane at normal atmospheric pressure?
Answer: −161·5°C.

10. The length of an air column in a horizontal tube sealed in by water is 312 mm at 20°C and 514 mm at 70°C. Atmospheric pressure is 760 mm Hg throughout. What is the S.V.P. of water vapour at 70°C? (S.V.P. water at 20°C=17·5 mm Hg.)
Answer: 232 mm.

11. A hydrogen cylinder contains 1 m³ of gas at 120 atm pressure. If gas occupying 6 m³ at atmospheric pressure is released slowly, how much does the pressure in the cylinder fall?
Answer: 6 atm.

12. A car tyre is inflated to $28·5 \times 10^3$ N/m² at 12°C. Running on the tyre raises its temperature to 27°C. What is its pressure?
Answer: $3·0 \times 10^3$ N/m².

13. What volume per minute must be pumped if we want to pump 1 mole of nitrogen at 1 mm Hg pressure and 80°C?
Answer: 22,010 l/min.

14. A gramme of air at 0°C and 1 atm. pressure is heated to 100°C at constant pressure. What is the volume of the heated air and what pressure would be needed to bring the air back to its original volume if it remains at 100°C? (Volume of 1 g of air at 0°C and 1 atm pressure=$7·74 \times 10^{-4}$ m³.)
Answer: $1·06 \times 10^{-3}$ m³, 1·35 atm.

15. Six litres of air at 0°C and 1 atm pressure are heated at constant volume until the pressure becomes 5 atm. What is the temperature? This temperature is now kept constant and the pressure reduced back to 1 atm. What is the volume? If this pressure is maintained, at what temperature will the volume be 4 litres?
Answer: 1092°C, 30 litres, −91°C.

16. A non-leaking pump has a barrel whose effective volume is 1/10 of the space it is to evacuate. How many strokes of the pump are needed to reduce the pressure to 1/100 of its original value, at the same temperature?
Answer: 49.

17. A diving bell (an airtight tank with its bottom open, used for working on the sea bed) with a volume of 11·32 m³ is lowered into the sea on a day when the barometric pressure is 760 mm Hg, until the water level inside the bell is 12·2 m below the surface. How much water has entered the diving bell? (relative density of sea water= 1·03.)
Answer: 3·1 m³.

18. A vacuum pump has a barrel of 1000 mm cross-section and a stroke of 590 mm. It is used to evacuate a tank containing $2·36 \times 10^{-3}$ m³ of air at 760 mm Hg pressure. What is the pressure after the second stroke of the pump, and how much force is then needed to hold the piston still?
Answer: 486 mm Hg, 4 N.

19. 'Bottled gas' is stored in a steel cylinder at a gauge pressure of 125 lbf/in². When some gas has been used, the pressure falls to 40 lbf/in². What fraction of the original gas is still in the cylinder?
Answer: 11/28.

20. A diving bell of uniform cross-section and height 4 m is lowered into sea water until the open end is 20 m below the surface. If the bell was initially full of air at atmospheric pressure find the height to which the water rises in the bell. Show that the volume of air, measured at atmospheric pressure, which must be pumped into the bell in order that it may again be full of air, is approximately twice the volume of the bell. (relative density of sea water=1·02; of mercury=13·6; atmospheric pressure=760 mm Hg.)

(I.E.R.E.)

Answer: 1·5 m.

21 Heat Engines

Over a hundred years ago, Sadi Carnot, a young French engineer, approached the problem of steam engine design in a theoretical but simple way. While contemporary engineers were preoccupied with mechanical improvements, his theoretical deduction of the importance of inlet and exhaust temperature produced a leap forward in steam engine design and laid the foundations of the study of heat engines. Sometimes, the idealized approach, typified by weightless strings, frictionless pulleys, and infinitely slow movements, takes a situation so far from reality that any deductions made have no practical value. At other times, the simplifications clear the ground of worrying detail and allow us to see clearly the underlying realities. Before we describe the design and performance of particular engines, we will examine some basic principles of thermodynamics relevant to all engines.

First Law of Thermodynamics

The study of the relation of heat to other forms of energy is called *thermodynamics*. The sum total of the kinetic and potential energies of the molecules of a body is referred to as its *internal energy*. We cannot arrive at an absolute value for this internal energy but we can deal with differences in it. We can increase the internal energy of a body in several ways; for example, by adding heat or by compressing it. Commonly, an increase in internal energy shows itself as a rise in temperature but not always. It may show itself as a change of state as when ice turns to water.

When the principle of conservation of energy is stated with reference to heat and work, it is called the first law of thermodynamics. *The heat supplied to a system is equal to the rise in internal energy plus the work done by the system on its surroundings.*

$$\text{Heat supplied} = \begin{array}{c}\text{increase in}\\\text{internal energy}\end{array} + \text{work done.}$$

$$Q = U + W \qquad (1)$$

Commonly, the increase in internal energy U shows itself as a change in temperature. The work done W involves the movement of a force, for example, in thermal expansion which is resisted by atmospheric pressure. (Fig. 21.1.) Under these conditions, a gas expands about ten times as much as a liquid and thirty times as much as a solid of the same initial volume. For solids and liquids, the external work term W in equation 1 is usually negligible compared with the change in internal energy U. For gases, however, the work done in pushing back the surroundings becomes a significant factor in the energy equation.

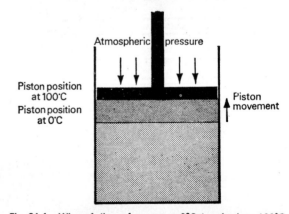

Fig. 21.1. When 1 litre of a gas at 0°C is raised to 100°C, the expansion against atmospheric pressure involves the performance of about 36 joules of work.

Thermal Expansion and Specific Heat

The specific heat of a substance is the heat required to raise the temperature of unit mass by one degree, i.e.,

$$\text{Specific heat} = \frac{\text{quantity of heat}}{\text{mass} \times \text{temperature rise}}$$

$$C = \frac{Q}{mt}$$

$$= \frac{U+W}{mt} \qquad (2)$$

Thus, the specific heat depends on W, the work done in expanding. Since the expansion is comparatively small for solids and liquids, their specific heats are only slightly affected by the work done. This is not so for gases, where the work done W is comparable with the change in internal energy U. Furthermore, the amount of expansion we allow a gas is a matter of choice and, by controlling the volume, we can vary the amount of work the gas does. Thus, the specific heat of a gas is not defined until we have specified the conditions of pressure or volume, which accompany the change in temperature.

Principal Specific Heats of a Gas

One way of avoiding the variability in specific heat is to keep the volume constant and thus allow the gas to do no work. An alternative is to allow the volume to change but in such a way that the pressure remains constant. We could define the conditions in other ways, but the specific heats in these two cases are of special interest, and are called the principal specific heats of a gas. The specific heat at constant volume is denoted by the symbol C_v and that at constant pressure by the symbol C_p. Since work is done under the conditions defining C_p, then $C_p > C_v$. The difference is equal to the work done in expanding unit mass of the gas at constant pressure.

$$C_p - C_v = \textit{work done}$$

$$C_p - C_v = W \qquad (3)$$

Reversible Change

We can deduce several important relations concerning energy changes if we consider a parti-cular kind of change. In this kind of change, movements occur so slowly that they involve negligible momentum and kinetic energy. At every stage of the change, the system is in equilibrium and it is possible to stop without overshooting. If the conditions are suddenly reversed, even by infinitesimal amount, the change will be reversed at the same instant and in every detail. This complete reversibility is not possible when friction is involved because it causes a loss of heat in both directions of change. Large temperature differences or pressure differences cannot be allowed in a reversible change because they are not in keeping with a state of equilibrium.

Needless to say, a perfectly reversible change is only a concept, and few real changes approach reversibility. The compressions and expansions in a sound wave are an example of a nearly reversible change.

Work done when a Gas Expands

First consider the simple case of a gas expanding reversibly at constant pressure in a cylinder from volume V_1 to V_2. (Fig. 21.2a.)

Force on piston = pressure × Area = pA.
W = work done = force × distance = $pA\,x$.
But Ax = change in volume = $(V_2 - V_1)$.
$W = p(V_2 - V_1)$.

This equation is equally true for solids, liquids, and gases, whether confined or not, which expand at constant pressure. (Fig. 21.2b.)

When the pressure and volume both vary, the total change may be considered to be made up of a number of small volume *changes* V', V'', V''', ... each occurring at constant pressures p', p'', p''', ...

$$W = \Sigma p'V + p''V'' + \ldots \text{ etc.,}$$

when the pressure can be expressed in terms of the volume, this becomes

$$W = \int_{V_1}^{V_2} p\,dV$$

Relation between C_p, C_v, and R

Consider unit mass of a gas under conditions p, V_1, T, which expands at constant pressure as its temperature is raised by 1K to conditions p, V_2, $(T+1)$

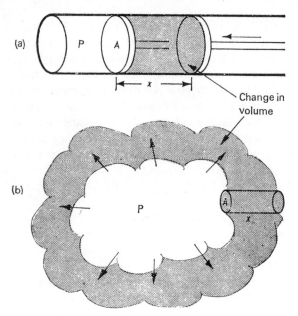

(a)

(b)

Fig. 21.2. Work done by expanding gas.

applying $pV = mRT$
to initial condition: $pV_1 = RT$
to final conditions: $pV_2 = R(T+1)$
subtracting, $pV_2 - pV_1 = R(T+1) - RT$
$p(V_2 - V_1) = R$

but $p(V_2 - V_1) = W$ the work done in expanding the gas

$\therefore \qquad W = R$

Hence from equation (3)

$$C_p - C_v = R$$

Adiabatic and Isothermal Changes

We have seen that when a gas expands it performs work. The work is done at the expense of the internal energy of the gas, which cools as a consequence. If no heat flows in or out of the gas during the expansion, the expansion is said to be adiabatic. An adiabatic compression adds to the internal energy of the gas and causes a rise in temperature.

The heat produced by repeated compressions may be felt in a bicycle pump barrel, while the cooling due to expansion is evident in the air escaping from an inflated tyre. An adiabatic

change could be produced if we had a perfectly insulated enclosure.

In practice, adiabatic conditions are realized where a change in volume occurs very quickly, allowing no time for heat to flow in or out. For example, along the path of a sound wave in a gas, adiabatic compressions and rarefactions follow rapidly one on the other and cause very small temperature changes. The changes in a sound wave are so very small that they also approach closely to being reversible changes. An adiabatic change does not obey Boyle's law but, if it is reversible, it follows the relation

$$pV^\gamma = \text{const.} \qquad (4)$$

where γ is a constant for a particular gas.

When the change in volume of a gas occurs very slowly, heat flows in or out before any appreciable temperature change can occur. This is an isothermal change, and it is described by Boyle's law

$$pV = \text{const.}$$

Both kinds of change are described by the ideal gas equation

$$pV = mRT$$

The value of the index γ in equation (4) is not a constant quantity for all gases but it is approximately constant for gases which have the same number of atoms in each molecule. It has values of about 1·6 for monatomic molecules, about 1·4 for diatomic gases, and about 1·3 for triatomic

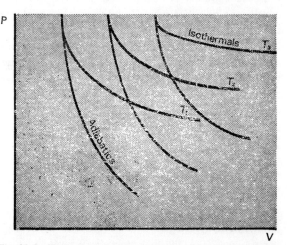

Fig. 21.3. The curves of adiabatic changes in a gas are steeper than those of isothermal changes.

gases. The constant, as might be expected, is related to the principal specific heats C_p and C_v:

$$\gamma = \frac{C_p}{C_v}$$

Because of the cooling which occurs, the pressure in an adiabatic expansion drops lower than it would in an equivalent isothermal change. The graphs of pressure against volume are steeper for adiabatic than for isothermal changes. (Fig. 21.3.)

Problem: Two cubic metres of gas at S.T.P. are compressed to 0·25 m³. Calculate the resulting pressure and temperature when the change is (a) isothermal, (b) adiabatic.

Solution:

(a) For isothermal change the temperature remains constant

$$pV = mRT$$

$$pV = \text{constant}$$

$$1 \times 2 = p \times 0.25$$

$$p = \frac{1 \times 2}{0.25}$$

$$p = 8 \text{ atmospheres}$$

(b) For adiabatic change

$$pV^\gamma = \text{constant}$$

$$1 \times 2^{1.4} = p\, 0.25^{1.4}$$

$$p = \left(\frac{2}{0.25}\right)^{1.4}$$

$$= 18.4 \text{ atmospheres.}$$

The final temperature may be obtained by applying the equation

$$\frac{pV}{T} = \text{constant}$$

which applies to both isothermal and adiabatic change

$$\frac{1 \times 2}{273} = \frac{18.4 \times 0.25}{T}$$

$$T = \frac{18.4 \times 0.25 \times 273}{2}$$

$$= 627\text{K or } 354°\text{C}$$

Heat Engines

A heat engine operates by changing heat energy into mechanical energy, and our three main requirements of a heat engine are:

(a) High efficiency.

(b) Large ratio of power to size.

(c) Operation on cheap fuel.

We will look at some common heat engines in the light of these requirements and ignore, for the moment, other important qualities, (such as long life, quietness in operation, low frictional losses, and ease of manufacture) which are common to all machines.

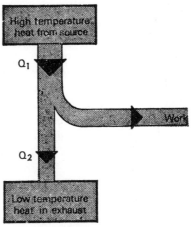

Fig. 21.4. Energy flow in a heat engine.

Efficiency of a Heat Engine

Of the heat supplied to a heat engine, only a fraction is converted into mechanical energy. The rest is finally rejected in the exhaust gases or conducted away to the surroundings. The principle of energy conservation still applies, and all the heat can be accounted for, but the efficiency of an engine is measured by the ratio of the useful work output to the total heat input.

$$\text{Efficiency } \eta = \frac{\text{work done}}{\text{heat supplied}} = \frac{W}{Q}$$

Now consider the idealized case where (a) the work is done very slowly so that no kinetic energy is involved, (b) heat flows in only from the source and out only in the exhaust and (c) there is no friction to convert work back into heat. If quantity of heat Q_1 flows in from the source, and quantity Q_2 flows out in the exhaust, then by the conservation principle

$$W = Q_1 - Q_2$$

and the efficiency generally becomes

$$\eta = \frac{Q_1 - Q_2}{Q_1}$$

We assume that the mass of the working substance remains constant, i.e., that the engine is not taking in more material than it is giving out. The quantities of heat flowing in and out are assumed to be proportional to the absolute temperatures of the source and the exhaust. ($Q \propto T$). The efficiency becomes

$$\eta = \frac{T_1 - T_2}{T_1}$$

Thus, we see how the efficiency of an ideal engine working reversibly depends on the temperatures of the source and of the exhaust. The efficiency is increased when the heat is supplied at a higher temperature and rejected at a lower temperature. In a real heat engine, the optimum efficiency is reduced because of frictional and conduction losses, but the theoretical efficiency is used as a reference figure against which real engines may be judged.

In fact, the efficiency of a heat engine is usually only about $\frac{3}{4}$ of the ideal or theoretical efficiency.

The equation for the efficiency is also important because it allows us to define a scale of temperature, the thermodynamic scale, which is independent of the variation of any particular physical property. If T_1 is defined by the icepoint, then T_2 is uniquely defined by the efficiency η of an idealized engine working between temperatures T_2 and T_1. It is not a scale which we can put to direct use but the idea is useful as you will see if you study thermodynamics at a more advanced level.

Problem: Compare the ideal maximum efficiencies of an engine when its intake and exhaust temperatures are respectively (a) 350°C and 100°C, (b) 300°C and 100°C.

Solution:

Efficiency $\eta = \dfrac{T_1 - T_2}{T_1}$

(a)
$$\eta = \frac{623 - 373}{623} = \frac{250}{623}$$
$$= 0.40 = 40 \text{ per cent}$$

(b)
$$\eta = \frac{573 - 373}{573} = \frac{200}{573}$$
$$\eta = 0.35 = 35 \text{ per cent}$$

The Second Law of Thermodynamics

Even under the ideal conditions specified above, the efficiency of a heat engine can never be equal to one. In other words *no engine can continually convert all the heat supplied to it into mechanical energy.* This is one way of stating the second law of thermodynamics. The validity of the law has been established by directly testing the predictions that can be made from it. The law predicts, for instance, that a machine cannot do useful work by extracting heat from the coldest part of its surroundings. It also predicts that heat cannot be made to flow from a cold to a hot body unless extra energy is supplied. It is a pity that these predictions turn out to be true. They mean that we must provide our engines with expensive high temperature heat, and that our refrigerators will never operate on the heat they extract from their interiors.

In short, the first law of thermodynamics states that energy cannot be created or destroyed, while the second law dictates the practical conditions under which energy can be changed from one form to another.

Steam Engines

Steam is an excellent working substance for a heat engine. Heat is supplied to a steam engine by introducing the steam into the cylinder. (Fig. 21.5.) The temperature of the heat source can be raised by producing the steam at higher pressures, e.g., 214°C and 20 atm pressure. The exhaust temperature is kept low by spraying the spent steam with water. (Fig. 21.6.) Although they can be used with the cheaper forms of fuel, such as coal, reciprocating steam engines are fast disappearing. Their theoretical efficiency is low, about 30 per cent, and they have a lower power-to-weight ratio than other engines. The frequent

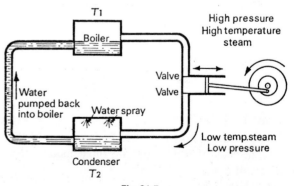

Fig. 21.5.

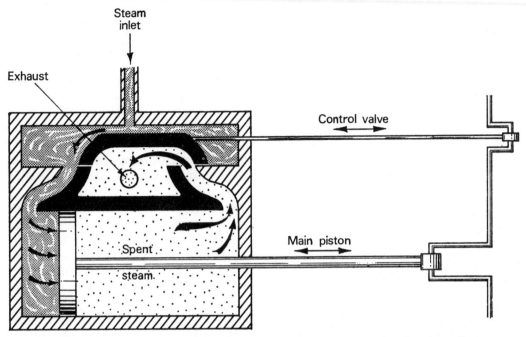

Fig. 21.6. Double acting steam engine. The valve is moved at the end of each stroke to direct the steam into the other half of the cylinder.

changes in the direction of a piston in a reciprocating engine causes both energy loss, due to friction, and vibration. These are reduced considerably in the steam turbine which can rotate at very high speeds.

Steam turbines operate at steam temperatures of 500°C and pressures of 200 atm and achieve actual thermal efficiencies of 35 per cent. (Fig. 21.7.) The thermal efficiency is the ratio of the heat input to the work output of the engine. (Table 21.1.)

Table 21.1. Typical thermal efficiencies

Engine	η Per cent
Turbojet aircraft engine	15
Petrol engine	15–20
Piston steam engine	12–27
Diesel engine	30–40
Steam turbine	30–50

The Internal Combustion Engine

Few events in history have changed man's life so much as the development of the motor car. The internal combustion piston engine has played an important part in this change. There were early types of steam motor cars which had quite amazing

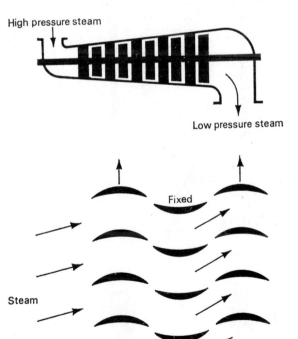

Fig. 21.7. Steam turbine showing the detail of the blades and the overall layout of a turbine.

performances, but the internal combustion engine has a higher power to weight ratio than the steam engine, which makes it more convenient for motor vehicles.

In the four-stroke petrol engine, an explosive mixture of air and petrol vapour is drawn into the cylinder through the inlet valve. (Fig. 21.8.) The valve closes and the mixture is compressed as the piston returns on its next stroke. As the piston reaches the top of its stroke, ignition is caused by an electric spark, and the mixture burns and expands rapidly, pushing back the piston. On the fourth stroke, the outlet valve opens and the burnt gas is pushed out by the piston through the exhaust pipe.

Notice that the thrust is only delivered on one stroke ($\frac{1}{2}$ revolution) while energy is absorbed on the other three strokes ($1\frac{1}{2}$ revolutions). This gives the crankshaft an irregular motion which can be reduced, to some extent, by a massive flywheel. A more even drive is obtained by using several pistons on the same crankshaft. Four cylinders provide a power stroke each half revolution. The power stroke itself, however, does not give an even thrust and power is only delivered during the first three-quarters of the stroke. To obtain continuous thrust from an engine, at least six cylinders are required.

Compression Ratio

Another important factor of the four-stroke engine is its compression ratio, that is, the ratio of the maximum and minimum volumes enclosed by the piston in its extreme positions. During the

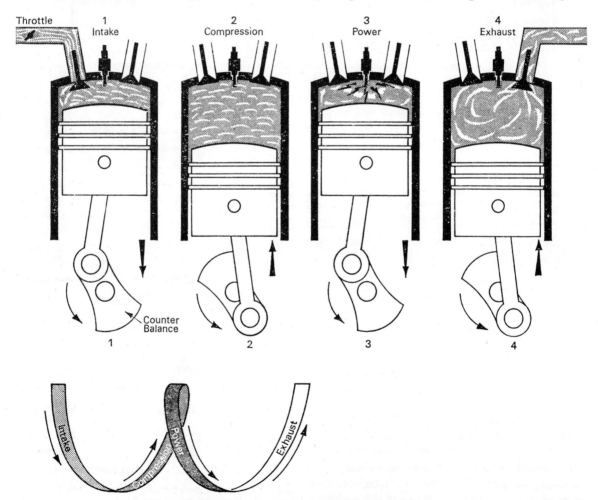

Fig. 21.8. The four-stroke internal combustion engine.

compression stroke, which is approximately adiabatic, the fuel and air mixture gets hot. The greater the compression ratio, the higher the source temperature becomes, and the greater the efficiency of the engine. A limit is reached when the temperature becomes high enough to ignite the mixture without the help of the spark. The pre-ignition of the charge may occur while the piston is still rising thus throwing great stress on the engine bearing and reducing the efficiency. A smooth thrust from the piston is obtained only when the gas burns gradually. In practice, the compression ratio must be well below the pre-ignition point because, when the gases are near the ignition temperature, the initial combustion may raise the temperature sufficiently to detonate the remaining gas. The condition can be recognized by the characteristic knock sometimes described as 'pinking'. The power to weight ratio of an engine is improved by raising its compression ratios, and fuels have been developed which resist pre-ignition up to high pressures. These fuels are classified according to 'octane ratios': A 90 octane fuel will serve an engine of compression ratio 7:1 without pre-ignition, and fuel of about 98 octane is needed for a sports car engine of, say, 10:1 compression ratio.

The octane ratio of a fuel is the percentage of iso-octane in a mixture of iso-octane and heptane which gives the same pre-ignition qualities. Fuels superior to pure iso-octane have been produced for special engines and these are given octane ratings above 100. Unfortunately, high octane fuels cost more, and the improved efficiency is offset by the increased cost. Certainly, there is nothing to be gained from the use of high octane fuels in low compression engines—a common habit among motorists.

The Diesel Engine

A variation of the internal combustion engine combines the efficiency of a high compression ratio with the economy of using low grade fuel. In the diesel engine, air alone is drawn into the cylinder on the first stroke and compressed on the second stroke. Because the compression ratio is of the order of 16:1, the air is raised to a high temperature. Instead of a spark triggering combustion, a measured quantity of fuel is injected under pressure into the cylinder at a controlled rate. This ignites rapidly to produce the power stroke.

The efficiency of the diesel engine is greater than that of the petrol engine and, since it operates on cheaper fuel, it is far more economical. The diesel engine must be designed to withstand the high pressures and is, therefore, heavier and more expensive than the petrol engine. The diesels are preferred for heavy motor vehicles where economy and long life are the more important qualities.

The Wankel Engine

Reciprocating engines have been highly developed and they have proved themselves to be excellent for many purposes, but they suffer from certain basic disadvantages. The pistons in a reciprocating engine may reach a speed of 150 km/h and reverse their direction up to 100 times per second. These rapid reversals produce friction and wear additional to those produced by the load. Many attempts have been made to produce a rotary gas engine but sealing problems have proved a great obstacle. Felix Wankel has invented a rotary engine in which effective sealing is possible and which is well on the way to being a commercial proposition.

In the NSU-Wankel engine a rotor, shaped like an equilateral triangle with curved sides, rotates eccentrically in a rigid casing. (Fig. 21.9.) The casing is shaped rather like a circle with a waist. More exactly the case shape is a double epitrochoid and the corners of the rotor touch the inside of it in any position. The sides of the rotor enclose three spaces, which vary in volume as it rotates. During a complete revolution, each space goes through the four processes of the piston engine. The two rotor positions in Fig. 21.9 indicate six different stages in the complete cycle. The engine fires three times per revolution, which in this respect is the same as a six cylinder piston engine. The centre of the rotor does not remain fixed, but moves in a circle round the drive shaft to which it is geared. The gear drives the shaft at three times the speed of the rotor.

The compression ratio of this rotary engine can be designed to operate on petrol or diesel fuel. Another advantage is that the engine has no valves or valve linkage. It will probably have a power to weight ratio double that of a piston engine. Several developments of the engine by individual manufacturers are in progress, but the details are not published. The piston internal combustion engine has been developed for three quarters of a century and the Wankel engine will not replace it overnight.

Aviation Engines

Two requirements of an aircraft engine are high power to weight ratio and a low air resistance. The petrol engine driving a propeller was at one stage used exclusively and it attained an output of 1·5 kW/kilogramme weight. Its frontal resistance is high, however, and it loses its efficiency at high altitudes.

The disturbance produced in the air by the engine and the propeller produces a drag on the plane which cancels out some of the power of the engine. At high altitudes, the engine loses efficiency as the pressure of the air needed for combustion reduces.

Jet Engines

The turbojet engine (Fig. 21.10) was developed to meet the need for a high speed high altitude engine. Air is drawn into the open front of the engine, compressed, mixed with fuel, and ignited in the combustion chambers. The high pressure exhaust from this chamber drives a gas turbine, which is coupled to the compressor by a central shaft, and then escapes at high speed at the rear of the engine. The turbine serves only to compress the incoming air while the propulsive force arises as a result of the reverse momentum of the exhaust material.

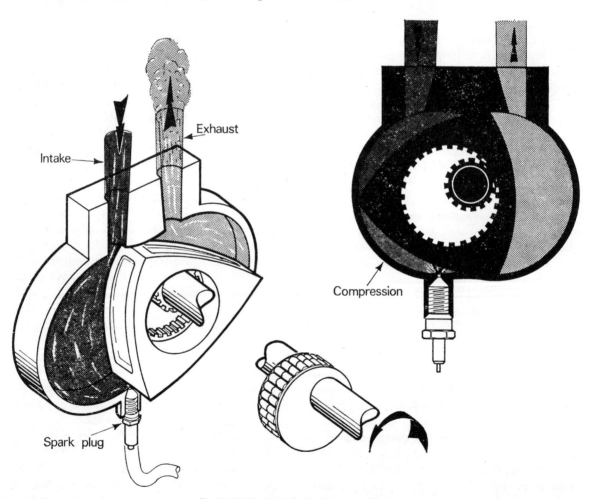

Fig. 21.9. The NSU-Wankel rotary engine.

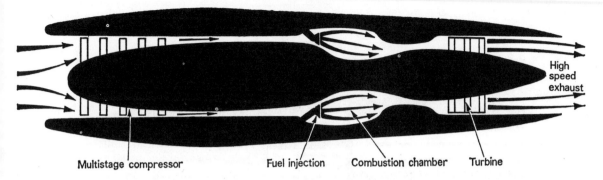

Fig. 21.10. Turbojet engine.

The advantage of the turbojet is its high power to weight ratio, which may be three times that of a petrol engine. The turbojet is most efficient between the speeds of 500 km/h and 1500 km/h, and it can operate at the reduced atmospheric pressure up to 20,000 m.

The turboprop engine is a modification of the turbojet in which a propeller geared to the turbine, provides the main propulsive force. (Fig. 21.11.) The result is an engine of reduced maximum speed and altitude, but of increased economy and range.

The ultimate simplification of the jet engine is the ramjet. (Fig. 21.12.) It is used to power unmanned missiles operating up to very high altitudes but still within the region of the Earth's atmosphere. The compressor propeller and turbine are all omitted to give an open ended duct. The forward motion of the engine at 500 km/h and above, compresses the air, the fuel is injected and the mixture burns as it passes through the combustion chamber. The exhaust matter streams from the nozzle-shaped rear of the duct and imparts a powerful forward reaction to the missile.

The Rocket Engine

A rocket engine is designed to operate in the absence of any atmosphere, and must carry both fuel and oxygen. (Fig. 21.13.) The oxygen and fuel, both in liquid form, are pumped into the combustion chamber where they combine to produce a high speed exhaust.

You may have noticed on films showing rocket launchings that the initial acceleration from the launching pad is small. This is due to the reduced efficiency of the jet engine at low speeds. As the rocket ascends, its acceleration increases, partly because the jet is more efficient at higher speeds,

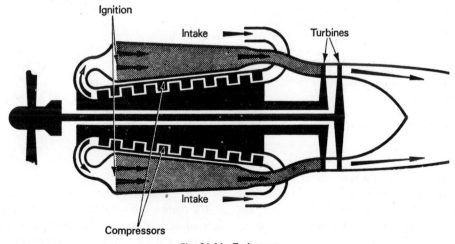

Fig. 21.11. Turboprop.

253

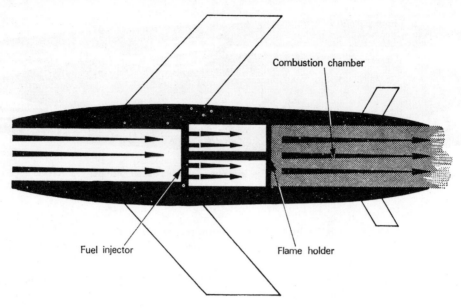

Fig. 21.12. Ramjet.

and partly because the rocket becomes light as it burns fuel.

When the fuel of a rocket has been used up, the fuel tanks become so much dead weight. Rockets are therefore built in several stages so that the empty tanks can be jettisoned as soon as they are empty. Each stage is designed to have the best

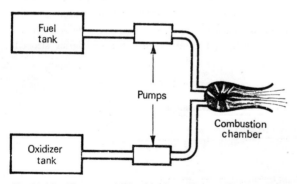

Fig. 21.13. The very high altitude rocket engine must be provided with both fuel and oxidizer.

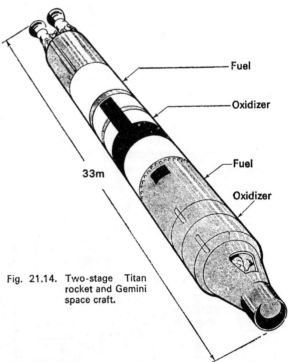

Fig. 21.14. Two-stage Titan rocket and Gemini space craft.

shape and propulsion system for its operational speed. For example the first stage must be streamlined to reduce atmospheric drag, while the final stage might be designed for controlled landing on the Moon or re-entry into the Earth's atmosphere. (Fig. 21.14.)

The Refrigerator

A refrigerator makes heat flow from a cold to a hot region contrary to its natural tendency. The second law of thermodynamics tells us that this cannot be done without the expenditure of work.

254

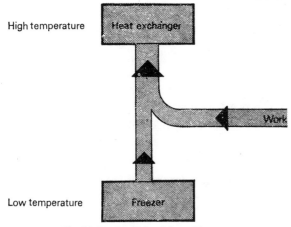

High temperature

Heat exchanger

Work

Low temperature

Freezer

Fig. 21.15. Principle of the refrigerator.

A refrigerator may therefore be considered to be a heat engine in reverse. (Fig. 21.15.)

All refrigerators have two stages of operation.

1. A spontaneously occurring change, which extracts heat from the interior of the refrigerator.
2. A reverse process, involving the expenditure of energy and the production of heat, which is dissipated outside the refrigerator.

In the most common form of refrigerator, a volatile liquid such as ammonia or sulphur dioxide is allowed to evaporate as it flows through pipes surrounding the freezing compartment. (Fig. 21.16.) This extracts the latent heat of vaporization from the liquid which cools to a low temperature and thereby cools the interior of the refrigerator. The vapour at low pressure is drawn into a pump, which compresses it. The work done by the pump in compressing the vapour is transferred to the vapour, which is raised to a temperature above that of the room. As this vapour slowly moves through the cooling pipes, it is cooled below its boiling point, and returns to the liquid state. The cooling is sometimes accelerated by an electrically driven fan blowing air over fins on the cooling pipe. A valve controls the flow of liquid to the low pressure section, where it evaporates, and the cycle is repeated.

The liquid must be below the critical temperature, or it will not liquefy, and it must be above the melting point, or it will solidify. Each liquid has a limited temperature range of operation. To obtain the lowest temperatures, a system using

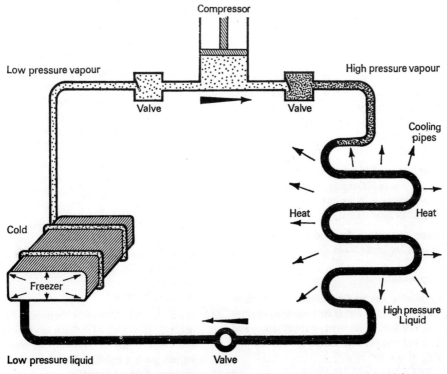

Compressor

Low pressure vapour

High pressure vapour

Valve

Valve

Cooling pipes

Heat

Heat

Cold

High pressure Liquid

Freezer

Low pressure liquid

Valve

Fig. 21.16. Refrigerator. Evaporation occurs as the working substance passes over the freezer.

one liquid is used to cool a second system below the critical temperature of its working substance. In the cascade process of liquefying air, several such stages are used.

The majority of refrigerators operate by the extraction of latent heat during evaporation. Other spontaneous processes which extract heat can be used. The expansion of a gas can produce a reduction in temperature because of the energy needed to force back the surroundings (external work) and to separate the gas molecules against the intermolecular attractions (internal work). Certain magnetic substances become heated when magnetized but cool on demagnetization. This is the process used to obtain temperatures near the absolute zero of temperature.

Questions

1. If you leave a refrigerator open, will the room be cooled or heated?

2. Why do we have to use the Sun's energy indirectly by burning coal, oil, etc., rather than directly?

3. What are the advantages and disadvantages of a turbine compared with a reciprocating engine?

4. Which is greater, the specific heat of a gas at constant volume or at constant pressure? Why?

5. The Royal Festival Hall is heated by removing heat from the water of the Thames. What is the main advantage of this system over conventional heating systems?

6. If raising the temperature of the power source of a heat engine increases the efficiency, what limits the increase of efficiency which could be produced?

7. How would you use the energy which is dissipated from the radiator and exhaust pipe of a car to increase efficiency? Why do you think car manufacturers do not do this?

8. Why is steam so useful as a working substance in heat engines?

9. How does a rocket provide a forward thrust in a vacuum?

Problems

1. When 1 g of gas is heated by 1°C at constant pressure, 0·42 joules of external work are done. What is its specific heat at constant pressure? Specific heat at constant volume $=840$ Jkg^{-1}°C^{-1}.)
   Answer: 1260 Jkg^{-1}°C^{-1}.

2. Twenty per cent of the energy available in the fuel is converted to useful work by a car engine. If the car does 6 km/litre, how much waste heat is produced each minute at 18 m/s? (1 litre of petrol produces $2·8 \times 10^7$ J.)
   Answer: $40·3 \times 10^5$ J.

3. Calculate the value of the gas constant per kilogramme for hydrogen. (Density of hydrogen under standard conditions $=0·09$ kg/m³.)
   Answer: $4·12 \times 10^3$ Jkg^{-1}°C^{-1}.

4. If the pressure of a gas is doubled by an adiabatic change, what is its percentage change in volume? ($\gamma = 1·4$.)
   Answer: 38 per cent.

5. If the volume of a gas under standard conditions is trebled isothermally, what is its new temperature and pressure? What is its new temperature and pressure if the change is adiabatic? ($\gamma = 1·4$.)
   Answer: 0°C, $3·38 \times 10^4$ N/m²,
   -97°C, $2·18 \times 10^4$ N/m².

6. If air at 30°C and 750 mm of mercury pressure is compressed adiabatically until its volume is halved, what is its new temperature and pressure? ($\gamma = 1·4$.)
   Answer: 127°C, 1980 mm Hg.

7. A steam engine takes in 10,000 J at a temperature of 490°C and gives out 8000 J at 290°C. What is the engine's efficiency and what would be the maximum theoretical efficiency of an engine working between these temperatures?
   Answer: 20 per cent, 26·2 per cent.

8. How much external work is done by a gas expanding isothermally from 1 litre to 2·5 litre against 2 atm. pressure?.(1 atm = 10^5 N/m².)
   Answer: 300 J.

9. An ideally efficient heat engine operates backwards as a refrigerator to take heat from a source at -3°C and deliver it to a room at 27°C. How much heat is taken from the source to supply 1000 J?
   Answer: 1111 J.

10. What is the difference between C_p and C_v for helium? (Density of helium under standard conditions = 0·18 kg/m³. Density of mercury = 13,600 kg/m³. $g=9·8$ m/s².)
    Answer: 2·06 kJ kg^{-1}°C^{-1}.

11. An atomic bomb is detonated and 100 ms later the fireball is 50 m across and has a temperature of 300,000 K. Estimate its radius when its temperature is 3000 K. ($\gamma=1\cdot4$.)

Answer: 1162 m.

12. Ten per cent of energy from the petrol is used in accelerating a car weighing 1000 kg. How much petrol is used in increasing the car's speed from 0 to 40 km/h? If the density of petrol is 0·75 kg/l and it costs 6p. per litre, how much does the acceleration cost? (Heat of combustion of petrol $4\cdot62\times10^6$ J/kg.)

Answer: 0·0133 kg, 0·106 p.

13. The heat of vaporization of water is 2268 kJ/kg. How much of this is retained as internal energy in water? (1 g of water vapour under standard conditions occupies $1\cdot672\times10^{-3}$ m³. Standard atmospheric pressure $=10\cdot1\times10^4$ N/m².)

Answer: 2100 kJ/kg.

14. If a gas at 760 mm Hg pressure is compressed isothermally to 10 per cent of its original volume and then expands adiabatically to its original volume, what pressure change at constant volume will restore the original conditions? ($\gamma=1\cdot4$.)

Answer: $6\cdot25\times10^4$ N/m².

15. A vertical tube closed at the bottom is fitted with a light piston which, situated below the top of the tube, encloses air at 1 atm pressure. The piston is pushed slowly down the tube by pouring mercury into the open end. If the temperature of the air stays constant, what is the length of the column of air when the mercury level reaches the top of the tube?

Answer: 760 mm.

16. Define the principal specific heats of a gas and describe briefly how one of them could be determined experimentally.

   Derive an expression for the difference between the principal specific heats of an ideal gas and calculate its value for hydrogen, given that the density of hydrogen at S.T.P. is 9×10^{-5} kg/l. (Density of mercury $=13\cdot6$ kg/l.)

Answer: 4·12 kJ kg⁻¹°C⁻¹. (I.E.R.E.)

22 The Earth and its Atmosphere

Up to now, man has been bound to the surface of the Earth, breathing its atmosphere, enjoying and suffering its weather. During his life on the Earth he has learned to understand and to master, to a very large extent, his environment, to live in the extremes of heat and cold, to travel with speed and safety on land, on sea, and in the air. But, living so close to the Earth, he has always been preoccupied with a close-up view of it. The sea, that shallow film of water covering three-quarters of the Earth's surface, he regards with caution and respect. Mountains, wrinkles of rock on the crust of the Earth, fill him with awe.

He is now entering a new phase, however, in which he will be capable of exerting an enormously greater influence on his environment than ever before. In the past he has learned, with ever-increasing success, to predict the weather, but one day nuclear power may enable him to influence it. He has continually improved his means of travelling from place to place on the Earth, but soon he will be able to travel away from the Earth completely.

The Earth's Interior

Our experience of the Earth is very much confined to its surface. On the scale of Fig. 22.1 the highest manned flight and the deepest borehole would be contained within the boundary line.

The temperature of the Earth is about 20°C at the surface and increases with depth by about 30°C/km. At a depth of 50 km, the Earth reaches a temperature of 1500°C, at which the rock would normally be molten. However, the pressure at this depth is very high, about 20,000 atm, and instead of becoming liquid, the rock remains solid.

In this state, which is similar to that of cold pitch, the rock transmits elastic vibrations like a solid but, under constant stress, it flows slowly like a viscous liquid.

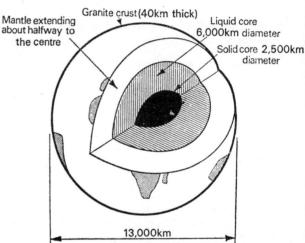

Fig. 22.1. The earth has a liquid core and probably a solid central kernel.

The vibrations produced by an earthquake or an explosion travel through the Earth and may be detected at many points of the surface. The highly sensitive instruments which record the Earth tremors are called seismographs. (Fig. 22.2.) One use of these instruments is to pinpoint nuclear explosions, a factor which will be important in the eventual control of nuclear weapons. Seismograph recordings of waves transmitted through the Earth also provide information about the structure of the Earth's interior. These recordings indicate a truly liquid core having about half the diameter of the Earth, surrounded by the solid mantle.

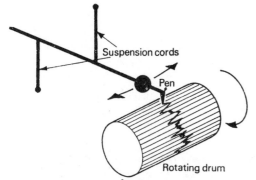

Fig. 22.2. The seismograph records Earth tremors. The pendulum supports vibrate with the Earth relative to the massive pendulum.

Table 22.1. Main constituents of the Earth's crust

Element	Per cent
Oxygen	47
Silicon	28
Aluminium	8·1
Iron	5·0
Calcium	3·6
Sodium	2·8
Potassium	2·5
Magnesium	2·0
Titanium	0·44
Hydrogen	0·14
Phosphorus	0·118
Manganese	0·1

There is a strong possibility that there exists a central kernel of solid matter at the centre of the liquid core. (Fig. 22.1.)

The Earth's Crust

The density of the Earth is greatest at the centre where there may be a greater abundance of nickel and iron. At the surface, there is a layer of lighter rock which is cooler, more rigid than the interior, and which forms a crust on the Earth's surface. The surface layer is mainly composed of granite resting on the denser basalt rock. (Table 22.1.) The solid crust varies in thickness from about 10 km under the seas to about 40 km under the mountains and may be considered to be floating on the semi-plastic mantle underneath. (Fig. 22.3.) Where the granite is thick, it floats high on the plastic rock underneath and gives the surface a higher elevation. The basalt, having a greater density than the granite, floats lower on the underlying rock and is to be found on the ocean beds. It is believed that the granite land masses, i.e., the

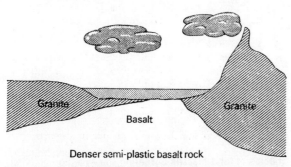

Fig. 22.3. Where the lighter granite is thick it floats high on the plastic material beneath.

continents, drift like rafts from one place to another on the Earth's surface. This theory is supported by the way in which the continental outlines can be fitted together, suggesting that, at one time, they were in contact. (Fig. 22.4.)

Source of the Earth's Interior Heat

The source of the Earth's interior heat is the radioactivity of substances in the interior. As each atom decays it produces heat and, because of the size of the Earth, the outer layers insulate the interior so that the centre of the Earth reaches a high temperature (4000°C).

One theory is that the Earth is getting hotter and, as a result, more of the mantle is melting into the liquid core. This produces a reduction in volume because the liquid is much denser than the solid. The semi-plastic mantle adjusts to this change smoothly but the more rigid crust cracks and crinkles to produce the geological features of the Earth's surface. Other, more recent, evidence suggests that the Earth is expanding. The whole question of whether the Earth is getting hotter or cooler, larger or smaller, is as yet not clearly established.

The Magnetic Field of the Earth

Convection currents, combined with the rotation of the Earth, produce a circulating electric current within the liquid core. The magnetic field of the Earth is the result. It does not produce a quite symmetrical pattern, partly because of the influence in some places of local magnetic rocks. The convection pattern moves slowly from East to West at the rate of 0·18° per year.

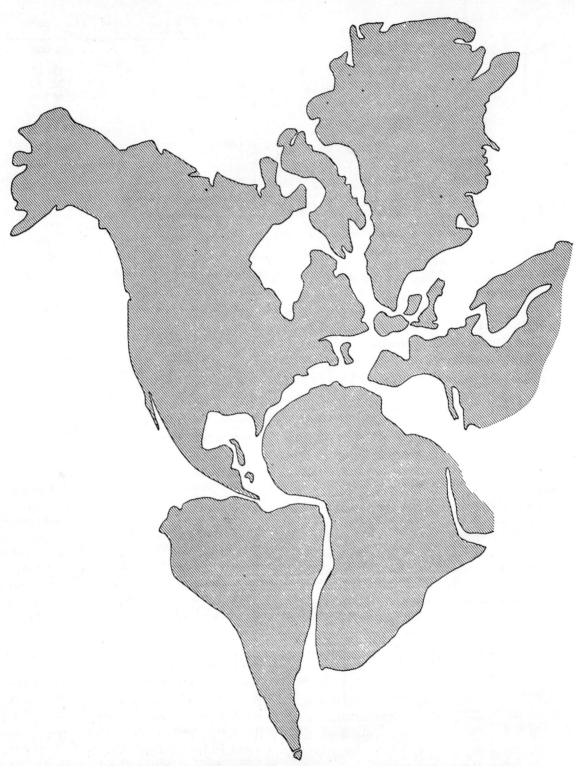

Fig. 22.4. The fit at the edge of the continental shelves of land masses bordering the Atlantic strongly suggests that they were once in contact. Convection currents in the more plastic regions of the mantle are thought to have carried them apart.

Electric currents in the Earth's atmosphere also produce a magnetic field at the Earth's surface. These atmospheric currents are affected by sunlight and they produce daily variations in the Earth's total magnetic field.

The Atmosphere

Only a minute fraction of the matter of the Earth exists in a gaseous state. Almost all the atmosphere exists below a height of 30 km and its relative size to the Earth might be compared to the fuzz on a peach. There is no real boundary to the atmosphere; it simply becomes less and less dense as the altitude increases. Eventually the density reaches the near perfect vacuum conditions of space where only a few molecules exist per cubic centimetre.

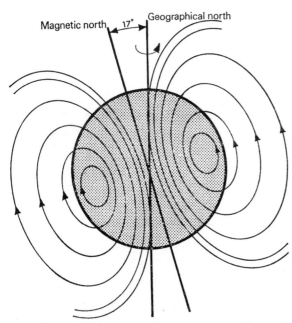

Fig. 22.5. The lines show the general direction of the Earth's magnetic field in the plane through the geographical and magnetic axes.

Composition of the Atmosphere

More than 99 per cent of the atmosphere is composed of two gases, nitrogen and oxygen, in the proportion of about 4:1. Traces of about a dozen other gases do exist, the most important one of which is carbon dioxide. (Table 22.2.)

We have excluded such variable components as water vapour, which may account for anything

up to 5 per cent of the atmosphere, and localized pollution. The pollution may occur naturally or be man-made, and includes poisonous sulphur compounds, radioactive substances, ozone, carbon monoxide, and even solids in suspension, such as soot. Some diseases flourish in polluted areas, and frequently control is delayed because there is a long lapse of time between exposure to the pollution and the acute stage of the disease, as is the case with cigarette smoking and lung-cancer, and also with radioactive exposure and anaemia. When cause and effect are separated by a long interval of time in this way, the scientist has a particular duty to perform in tracing, with meticulous thoroughness, the connections between them and then in persuading society to exercise the utmost caution.

The proportions of the most important atmospheric constituents—oxygen, nitrogen, and carbon dioxide—are maintained by cycles of interchange involving the Earth's surface and the life it supports. (Figs. 22.6 and 22.7.)

Table 22.2. Gases present in the atmosphere

Gas	Symbol	Per cent
Nitrogen	N_2	78
Oxygen	O_2	21
Argon	Ar	0·93
Carbon dioxide	CO_2	0·033
Neon	Ne	0·0018
Helium	He	0·00052
Methane	CH_4	0·0002
Krypton	Kr	0·0001
Hydrogen	H_2	0·00005
Nitrous oxide	N_2O	0·00005
Xenon	Xe	0·00001

Source of the Atmosphere

We can assume, since they are the commonest gases in the universe, that hydrogen and helium were the original gases surrounding the Earth. Being very light gases, however, they were lost into space in the early stages of the planet's life.

The present atmosphere has come from the Earth's interior. Intense volcanic activity first produced stable compounds, such as nitrogen, carbon dioxide, and water vapour. Later, as the planet cooled, the water vapour condensed and life developed. The oxygen in the atmosphere was originally produced, and is now maintained, by

261

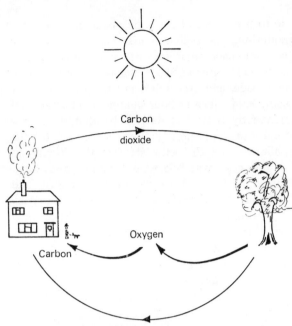

Fig. 22.6. The carbon cycle. Combustion, organic decay, and respiration produce carbon dioxide from oxygen and carbon and release energy. Plants use the Sun's energy to convert carbon dioxide into oxygen which is released, and carbon which provides material for growth.

the action of the plants which grow by absorbing carbon dioxide and releasing oxygen. The traces of the inert gases, argon, krypton, xenon, etc., in the atmosphere are a result of the radioactive decay or spontaneous fission of the elements present in the Earth.

The Troposphere

Air near the Earth is not heated directly by the Sun but by convection currents from the Earth. The temperature of the atmosphere decreases with altitude at the rate of 6°C/km down to −55°C. This drop in temperature is caused by the adiabatic expansion of the air as it moves into the lower pressure of high altitudes. Condensation and instability in these convection currents produce our clouds and, subsequently, our snow, hail, and rain. The region containing these weather phenomena is called the troposphere and it extends to a height of about 10 km (Fig. 22.8.)

The Stratosphere

Beyond the troposphere lies the stratosphere, a region where there is no water vapour. Aeroplanes

often fly on the fringe of the stratosphere to avoid the weather. To enable them to do this, their cabins must be pressurized, since atmospheric pressure decreases to one-half of its value with every 10 kilometres of altitude. The pressure of air in the stratosphere is too low for piston-engined planes, but jets are efficient there, and have reached altitudes of almost 40 km. Horizontal winds of high velocity blow in the stratosphere, and, when blowing in a favourable direction, can be used to advantage by the jet-pilot.

An important feature of the stratosphere is the *ozonosphere*, which is a layer in which the oxygen molecules contain three atoms (O_3) instead of the usual two (O_2). This form of the gas behaves differently from normal oxygen, and is given the name of ozone. Ozone has a characteristic smell, and is poisonous in high concentrations. It is produced in the stratosphere by the absorption of a component of the ultra-violet radiation from the Sun, and is to be found near some electrical equipment.

The Ionosphere

From 100 to 10,000 km above the Earth extends a very rarified but highly important region,

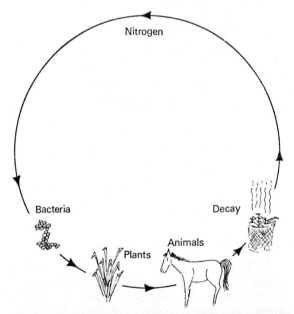

Fig. 22.7. The nitrogen cycle. *(a)* Bacteria extract free nitrogen. *(b)* Plants use this nitrogen from bacteria. *(c)* Animals eat the plants and gain size. *(d)* Dead plants and animals decay to release nitrogen.

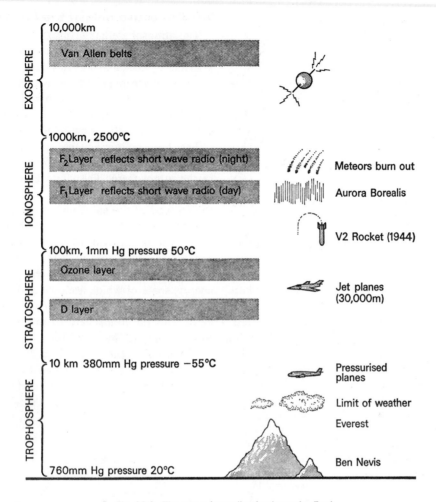

EXOSPHERE

10,000km

Van Allen belts

1000km, 2500°C

IONOSPHERE

F₂ Layer reflects short wave radio (night)

F₁ Layer reflects short wave radio (day)

100km, 1mm Hg pressure 50°C

STRATOSPHERE

Ozone layer

D layer

10 km 380mm Hg pressure −55°C

TROPHOSPHERE

760mm Hg pressure 20°C

Meteors burn out

Aurora Borealis

V2 Rocket (1944)

Jet planes (30,000m)

Pressurised planes

Limit of weather

Everest

Ben Nevis

Fig. 22.8. The space immediately above the Earth.

the ionosphere. The gas in this region is ionized by the absorption of the short wave-length ultra-violet radiation from the Sun. The energy from this radiation raises the temperature of the upper ionosphere to more than 2000°C. This represents no hazard to manned craft because the rate of heat transfer from the gas at this density is so very low.

The ionosphere is of great importance in radio communication because it acts as a reflector of radio waves. The waves, by repeated reflection between Earth and ionosphere, are propagated around the Earth's surface. (Fig. 22.9.) If it were not for the ionosphere, radio waves would only be detectable within 'seeing' distance of about 40 km like the shorter television waves which are not reflected by the ionosphere. Communication satellites, such as the ones poised above the Atlantic, are used to relay television waves across longer distances.

Variations in the layers of the ionosphere occur as it becomes shaded or exposed to the Sun's rays. This causes periodic variation in radio reception and in the electrical currents in the atmosphere which make a small contribution to the magnetic field at the Earth's surface.

The Exosphere

Between the ionosphere and true space is a region containing traces of hydrogen called the

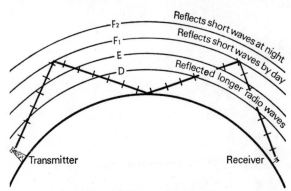

Fig. 22.9. Repeated reflections of radio waves by the ionosphere and the Earth's surface make possible long range reception. The **wave-lengths used for television are not reflected** by the ionosphere and long range reception is only made possible by artifical satellites, such as 'Early Bird'.

exosphere. The first satellites to enter the exosphere discovered two belts of electrons and protons (ionized hydrogen) called the Van Allen belts. (Fig. 22.10.) This ionized hydrogen will be harmful to interplanetary spacemen unless they are shielded from it. The investigation of the radio waves from outer space must be conducted through the windows framed by the Van Allen belts, because the ionization acts as a barrier to radiowaves.

The Protective Role of the Atmosphere

The atmosphere has several important functions in preserving the frail phenomenon of life. It provides oxygen, and acts as a barrier against harmful radiation from outside the planet. Almost all the uv light from the Sun is absorbed by the atmosphere. Even so, the fraction which gets through can afflict us with snow-blindness and sunburn.

The blue colour of the sky results from the scattering of the Sun's light by the gas molecules in the atmosphere. The white light from the Sun contains all the colours of the rainbow but only the red end of the spectrum of longer wave-length is transmitted directly. The shorter wave-length blue light is diffused to such an extent that it appears to come from all directions. (Fig. 22.11.)

The Sun also emits highly charged particles of energy, some of which are deflected by the Earth's magnetic field, towards the poles. These particles clash with the ionosphere to produce the Aurora Borealis or northern lights. Cosmic rays, those extremely high energy particles from outer space, are reduced by the atmosphere to tolerable levels of radiation at the Earth's surface. 'Shooting stars', or meteors, which are small particles of matter from the solar system, burn themselves out

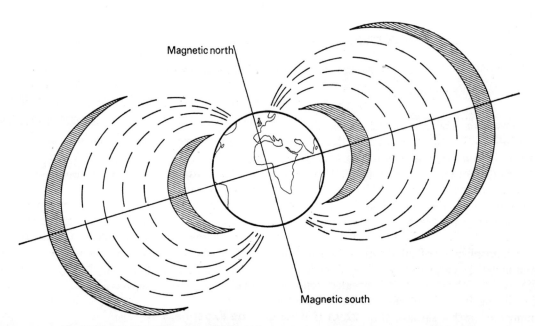

Fig. 22.10. The Van Allen Belts of ionized hydrogen occur at distances of about 3000 and 15,000 kilometres from the Earth's surface. They are produced by high energy particles which are deflected by the Earth's magnetic field.

by friction with the atmosphere. The atmosphere is not entirely a benevolent influence, however, as the storms and extremes of weather within the troposphere show, but life has evolved to survive in the conditions set by the Earth and its atmosphere. In the future, man's adaptation will proceed partly biologically and partly technologically.

Water in the Atmosphere

The water content of the atmosphere is small. In the hottest and wettest jungle air, the proportion of water vapour approaches a mere 5 per cent by weight. Elsewhere, the percentage of water in the atmosphere is less and in some regions is almost zero. If all the atmospheric moisture were to come

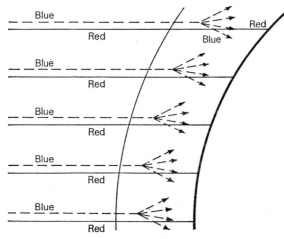

Fig. 22.11. The shorter wave-length blue light from the Sun is scattered in all directions, whereas the red component travels directly to the surface.

down in one torrential downpour, the surface of the Earth would be covered with a layer of water only one inch deep. This relatively small amount of water vapour, however, has far-reaching effects on life and conditions on the planet.

The amount of water vapour in the atmosphere is the result of the equilibrium between the processes of evaporation and rainfall. The rain falling on the land either re-evaporates from plains or lakes or returns to the sea by way of rivers. In its course to the sea, the water relentlessly erodes the land, and shapes the surface of the Earth. (Fig. 22.12.)

Clouds provide a barrier to incoming radiation from the Sun by day and to the Earth's radiation

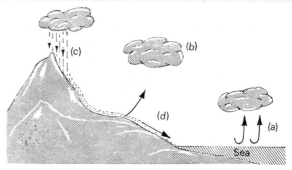

Fig. 22.12. The water cycle. (a) Evaporation from the sea and from plants later rises. (b) Clouds form and cool as they rise. (c) Supersaturated clouds precipitate rain. (d) Water returns to sea or re-evaporates.

into space by night. This reduces the difference between the daily extremes of temperature.

The major source of atmospheric moisture is evaporation from the sea, which covers more than two-thirds of the Earth's surface. The amount and the rate of evaporation increases rapidly with temperature, so that equatorial oceans provide the largest contribution of water vapour.

The warm air is cooled by expansion or carried by winds to colder regions, and the water vapour condenses into a suspension of droplets or ice particles. Light is strongly scattered by these droplets and a visible cloud is the result.

Weather Phenomena

Condensation does not occur immediately the air becomes saturated with water vapour. There is a tendency (which is greatest when the drops are smallest) for moisture to re-evaporate. Since large drops must start small, water persists in the gaseous form even when the air is super-saturated. The presence of microscopic particles in the air gives

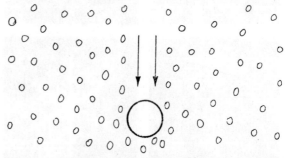

Fig. 22.13. A raindrop starts as an ice crystal which falls and grows by collisions with suspended droplets and eventually melts to fall as rain.

265

the drop a start and aids condensation. Near the Earth's surface, there are plenty of such particles but, at high altitudes, a considerable degree of super-saturation can occur. Once the droplets start to fall, they grow in size as they collide with other droplets on the way down. (Fig. 22.13.) It is thought that to provide some descending droplets the temperature of part of the cloud must cool down to below freezing.

A cloud which is formed near the ground, or which drifts into a hillside, is a mist. Air pollution provides an abundance of particles on which the moisture can condense. In industrial areas, the dirt renders the droplets more opaque and produces a fog called in extreme cases 'smog'. Because of air pollution, industrial populations tend to suffer from respiratory diseases and a period of freezing smog produces many deaths among the elderly.

When saturation occurs below the freezing point, the water vapour sublimes directly to the crystalline solid state and snow is formed. (Fig. 22.14.) When rain drops fall through a region below 0°C, they freeze and become hailstones.

The phenomenon of *freezing rain* is a great hazard to aircraft. Raindrops below their normal freezing point strike the aircraft and immediately freeze on to it, weighing it down, and jamming the control surfaces.

Fig. 22.14. Hexagonal crystal structure of snowflakes.

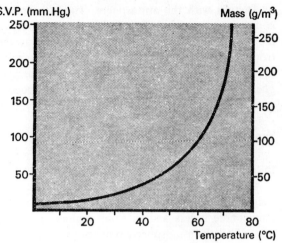

Fig. 22.15. The mass of water vapour required to saturate a cubic metre of air. The lower scale shows the pressure (S.V.P.) exerted by the vapour at these temperatures.

Humidity

Animals and plants depend on an interchange of moisture with the atmosphere. Sweating in mammals regulates body temperature. Transpiration in plants is a process whereby water is drawn in through the roots and evaporated at the leaves. Some industrial processes, such as cotton-spinning and paint-drying, are strongly affected by atmospheric moisture. The properties of certain organic materials, e.g., paper, vary with humidity so that control is necessary when testing or manipulating them.

The mass of water vapour contained per unit volume of air is the *absolute humidity*. Surprisingly, these processes are not influenced by the absolute humidity but by how close the air is to saturation. This is measured by the relative humidity, defined for a given volume, as follows:

$$R.H. = \frac{\text{mass of water vapour present}}{\text{mass required to saturate at same temp.}} \times 100$$

The relative humidity is usually referred to simply as 'humidity' and is expressed as a percentage. A 100 per cent humidity corresponds to saturation. The mass of water vapour required to saturate the air varies with temperature. (Table 22.3.) The pressure exerted by the water vapour at saturation is called the *saturated vapour pressure* (S.V.P.) and it has a variation with temperature similar to that of the mass required to saturate, (Fig. 22.15.)

266

Table 22.3. Mass of water vapour contained in one cubic metre of saturated air

Temperature (°C)	Water vapour content (g/m³)
0	4·84
5	6·76
10	9·33
15	12·71
20	17·12
25	22·84
30	30·04
35	39·18

The humidity can be increased either by the evaporation of more water or by a reduction in temperature. Thus, air approaches nearer to saturation as it cools. Eventually the air becomes completely saturated and water condenses into droplets which either remain suspended in the air or form on exposed surfaces as dew. This condensation begins at the *dewpoint, i.e., the temperature at which the water vapour present is just sufficient to saturate the air.* And cooling below the dewpoint produces further condensation.

Problem: If the humidity is 75 per cent at a temperature of 20°C, how much water will be condensed if the temperature drops to 5°C?

Solution: Referring to Table 22.3.

Water content at 20°C $= \dfrac{75}{100} \times 17 \cdot 1$ g/m³

Water content at 5°C $= 6 \cdot 8$ g/m³

Water condensed $= \dfrac{75}{100} \times 17 \cdot 1 - 6 \cdot 8 = 6 \cdot 0$ g/m³

Hygrometers

Hygrometers are instruments which measure humidity. We can measure the absolute humidity by passing a known volume of the air through tubes of material which absorb the moisture and can be accurately weighed. More often, however, we are interested in measuring the relative humidity. One accurate way of doing this depends on a determination of the dewpoint by cooling a surface until the water vapour condenses on to it. Dewpoint hygrometers vary in the detail of their design but all have the following features:

1. A polished metal surface which makes any condensation easily visible.

2. A means of gradually lowering the temperature of the surface.
3. A thermometer to measure the temperature of the surface at which water condenses.

In many designs of the instrument the evaporation of ether in a controlled stream of air bubbles cools the polished surface. (Fig. 22.16.)

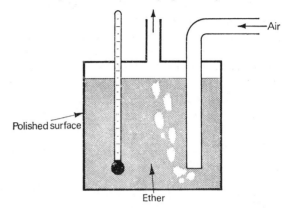

Fig. 22.16. The dew point is determined by cooling a polished surface to the temperature at which it mists over as the water vapour condenses.

Since the pressure exerted by the vapour is directly proportional to the mass per unit volume present, we can write

Humidity

$= \dfrac{\text{mass of water vapour present}}{\text{mass to saturate at room temp.}}$

$= \dfrac{\text{pressure exerted by vapour}}{\text{saturated vapour pressure at room temp.}}$

At the dew point, the actual vapour present saturates the air, i.e., it exerts a pressure equal to the S.V.P. at the dew point

$$\text{Humidity} = \dfrac{\text{S.V.P. at the dew point}}{\text{S.V.P. at room temp.}}$$

The S.V.P.s cannot be measured directly but they can be obtained from tables when the dew point and room temperature are known. (Table 22.4.)

Problem: Air at a temperature of 20°C has a dew point of 15°C. If the S.V.P. of water is 12·8 mm Hg at 15°C, and 17·5 mm Hg at 20°C, calculate the humidity.

Solution:
$\text{Humidity} = \dfrac{12 \cdot 8}{17 \cdot 5}$, i.e., 73 per cent

The Wet and Dry Bulb Hygrometer

The wet and dry bulb hygrometer is the most convenient instrument for measuring humidity. The method is an empirical one, that is, it depends on no exact theory. In the instrument, two identical mercury thermometers are mounted side by side. The bulb of one thermometer is enveloped by wetted fabric which has the same effect on the thermometer as wet clothing has on a person. It makes it cooler. The dryer the air, the more rapid the evaporation and the greater the depression of the wet thermometer reading below that of the dry thermometer. For a given dry bulb temperature, the difference in temperature of the two thermometers correlates with the humidity of the air. Sometimes, the thermometers are mounted in a sling which is rotated rather like a football rattle, before readings are made. (Fig. 22.17.)

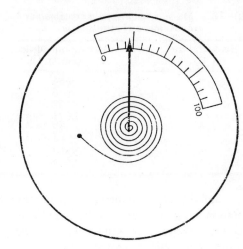

Fig. 22.18. The paper strip hygrometer uncurls when the humidity is high, giving a direct reading of humidity.

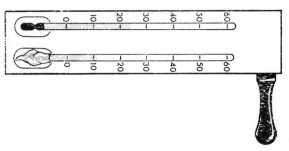

Fig. 22.17. The sling hygrometer (psychrometer) used to measure relative humidity ensures a rapid replacement of air near the thermometer bulbs.

Alternatively, they are mounted on a bracket and the water is drawn onto the wet bulb by capillary action from a container. Each particular wet and dry bulb hygrometer has its own empirical tables from which the actual humidity is obtained. (Table 22.5.)

For the recording and control of humidity in industry, hygrometers depending on the length of an animal hair or the amount of curl in a paper spiral are used. (Fig. 22.18.) They are convenient because they give a direct reading of humidity, but they need frequent recalibration.

Table 22.4. Variation of saturated vapour pressure of water with temperature

°C	S.V.P. (mm Hg)	°C	S.V.P. (mm Hg)
0	4·58	16	13·62
1	4·92	17	14·52
2	5·29	18	15·46
3	5·68	19	16·46
4	6·10	20	17·51
5	6·54	21	18·62
6	7·01	22	19·79
7	7·51	23	21·02
8	8·04	24	22·32
9	8·60	25	23·69
10	9·21	26	25·13
11	9·84	27	26·65
12	10·51	28	28·25
13	11·22	29	29·94
14	11·98	30	31·71
15	12·78	31	33·57

Table 22.5. Extract from wet and dry bulb humidity table

Dry bulb temp. (°C)	Depression of wet bulb									
	1°	2°	3°	4°	5°	6°	7°	8°	9°	10°
16	90	81	71	63	54	46	38	30	23	15
17	90	81	72	64	55	47	40	32	25	18
18	91	82	73	65	57	49	41	34	27	20
19	91	82	74	65	58	50	43	36	29	22
20	91	83	74	66	59	51	44	37	31	24

Humidity

The humidity of the air has an effect on how warm the air feels to the human body. Humid air always feels warmer than dry air of the same temperature. (Fig. 22.19.) Some respiratory conditions, such as bronchitis and hay fever, may be benefitted by high humidity. The central heating of our homes is rapidly replacing older and less effective methods of heating but the homes of the future will be air conditioned which, in addition to heating involves cooling, ventilating, and humidifying.

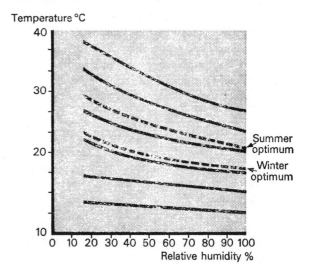

Fig. 22.19. The equal comfort curves show how the sensation of warmth varies with temperature and humidity.

Questions

1. Does the molten matter that erupts from volcanoes extend to the Earth's centre?

2. Why does it rain more on the windward side of mountain ranges than on the lee side?

3. Why does it feel colder when a wind is blowing than it does at the same temperature in still air?

4. What is the principle behind the 'seeding' of clouds to cause rain?

5. It has been suggested that flying saucers generate their lift by cutting the Earth's lines of magnetic force. Is this possible?

6. Under damp conditions, a clear cold night leads to the formation of mist. Explain this.

7. If the rate at which the air temperature falls with height is greater than that which would be caused by adiabatic expansion of the air, thunder clouds towering thousands of feet are caused. Why is this?

8. The fluffy white clouds which form on summer days (fair weather cumulus) have flat bases. Why?

9. Is our atmosphere leaking away into outer space?

10. The relative humidity is often maintained at a constant fixed level in an enclosure by circulating the air over a tray containing saturated solution of a salt. Different salts give different humidities—how does this work?

11. What is the relation between dew point and humidity?

12. Is the average temperature of the Earth increasing or decreasing?

13. Is the radius of the Earth increasing or decreasing?

14. If the temperature of the Earth's interior is several thousand degrees, why is it not gaseous?

15. Describe (a) the carbon cycle, (b) the nitrogen cycle.

16. What is the main advantage to a plane of flying in the stratosphere?

17. Why are certain wave-lengths of radio waves more effective than others for long range communication?

18. Why is more than one seismograph required to pinpoint an earthquake?

269

Problems

1. A humidifier raises the humidity of air from 30 per cent to 80 per cent at a constant temperature of 15°C. At what rate must water by supplied to the unit, if it passes 3 cubic metres of air per second? (see Table 22.3.)
Answer: 19 g/s.

2. The air conditioning of a house delivers air at 20°C and 70 per cent humidity when the outside temperature is 0°C. How much water is required per cubic metre of air if the air is initially saturated?
Answer: 7·14 g/m³.

3. A desert atmosphere contains 6 g/m³ of water. What range of humidity is produced when the temperature fluctuates between 10°C and 30°C?
Answer: 20–63 per cent.

4. At approximately what temperature would dew form in the situation described in Problem 3.
Answer: 3°C.

5. Estimate the force exerted by atmospheric pressure $(10 \times 10^4 \text{N/m}^2)$ on a television tube screen measuring 400 mm × 500 mm.
Answer: 2×10^4N.

6. Determine from Table 22.5 the humidity represented by a dry bulb temperature of 18°C when the wet bulb temperature is 14°C.
Answer: 65 per cent.

7. If the relative humidity in a closed room at 10°C is 50 per cent, what does it become when the temperature is raised to 15°C? (Saturated vapour pressure of water at 10°C = 9·2 mm Hg; Saturated vapour pressure of water at 15°C = 13 mm Hg.)
Answer: 35·4 per cent.

8. If the barometric pressure is 760 mm Hg, the air temperature is 20°C, and the relative. humidity is 65 per cent, what fraction of the barometric pressure is caused by the water? (S.V.P. of water at 20°C = 18 mm Hg.)
Answer: 1/65.

9. In a closed room, measuring 2 m × 3 m × 9 m, the relative humidity is 50 per cent at 13°C. How much water must be added to the air to maintain this relative humidity at 20°C? (S.V.P. of water at 13°C = 11·23 mm Hg; S.V.P. of water at 20°C = 17·51 mm Hg; Density of air at S.T.P. = 1·29 g/l; Relative density of water vapour with respect to air = 0·6.)
Answer: 0·154 l.

10. A volume of air at 20°C has a relative humidity of 60 per cent. What percentage of the water would condense if the temperature fell to 10°C? (S.V.P. of water at 20°C = 17·5 mm Hg; S.V.P. of water at 10°C = 9·21 mm Hg.)
Answer: 12·3 per cent.

23 Electrons in Action

Electrical engineering itself could be described as a study of the movement of electrons. A detailed examination of a basic process can give an insight into topics which may have previously been approached in quite a different way. In this chapter we will describe the conduction of electricity in solids and gases and some of the phenomena associated with it.

Conduction in Solids

In order that a current may flow in a medium, first of all charge carriers must be present, and, second, these charge carriers must be mobile. In its normal state, an atom is electrically neutral, the positively charged nucleus being surrounded by electrons which collectively carry an equal and opposite charge. Charge carriers are created, however, if electrons are detached from the atoms. To achieve this, work must be done to separate the electrons from the nuclei against the electrostatic attraction.

When an electron is separated from its atom, two kinds of charge carriers are created: the negatively charged electron and the positively charged ionized atom. Because of their size and mass, the ionized atoms are far less mobile than the electrons which, therefore, make the major contribution to conduction. The electrons nearer the nucleus are more tightly bound to the atom, than those in the more distant positions, and more energy is required to detach them. The situation can be represented graphically by Fig. 23.1 in which the nucleus is considered to be at the bottom of a potential energy well for electrons. The deeper an electron is in the well, the more energy is required to separate it from the atom. The motion of an electron about the nucleus prevents it from falling right down into the nucleus.

Band Theory

According to the quantum theory, an atom has well-defined energy levels (orbits) which the electrons can occupy, and they cannot possess

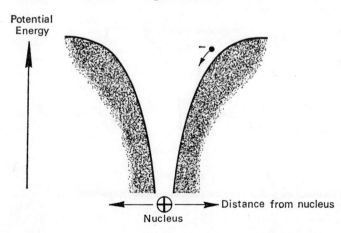

Fig. 23.1. The attraction of the nucleus acts as a potential well for electrons.

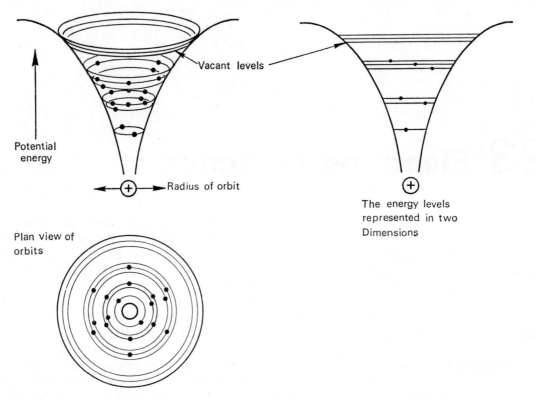

Vacant levels

Potential energy

Radius of orbit

The energy levels represented in two Dimensions

Plan view of orbits

Fig. 23.2. The permitted energy levels in an atom may be represented by circular orbits.

energies between these values. An atom has more energy levels than electrons to occupy them and the electrons tend to occupy the lower energy levels, leaving vacant the upper levels, which correspond to positions further from the nucleus. It will be of great help to our imagination if we represent the energy levels by circular orbits which the electrons can occupy (Fig. 23.2) (al-

though this picture of the energy levels would be inadequate if we wished to explain the situation in every detail).

The energy needed to ionize an atom is often expressed in terms of the potential in volts which would extract an electron, i.e., in electron volts.

$$1 \text{ electron volt} = 1 \cdot 6 \times 10^{-19} \text{ joules}$$

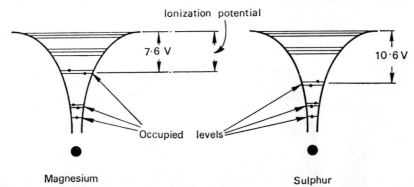

Ionization potential

7·6 V

10·6 V

Occupied levels

Magnesium

Sulphur

Fig. 23.3. The ionization potential of the metal magnesium and the insulator sulphur represented on a potential well diagram.

272

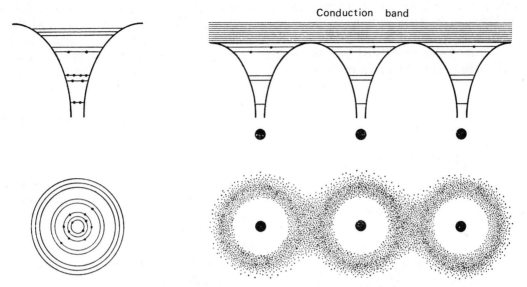

Fig. 23.4. Energy levels and potential barrier in a metal with occupied levels adjacent to the conduction band.

The ionization potential represented on the potential diagram is the distance from the outermost occupied orbit to the top of the potential well. (Fig. 23.3.)

When atoms assemble together in a solid, each single energy level of the isolated atoms is split into a range of levels, owing to the influence of the other atoms. (Fig. 23.4.) The potential barriers preventing electrons from passing from atom to atom in the solid are less than those preventing the escape of electrons from isolated atoms. The outer electron orbits overlap to such an extent in the solid that they may be considered to be common to all the atoms. Electrons which are excited into these orbits are not confined to a single atom but move randomly about the solid. These common levels are represented on the potential diagram by

a continuous band of energy levels called the *conduction band*. In metals, the occupied levels are continuous with the band of vacant levels and the potential barrier is zero. In insulators, the outer orbits are far from the occupied orbits and, on the potential diagram, this is represented by a large gap between the occupied levels and the conduction band. (Fig. 23.5.)

Variation of Resistance with Temperature

At very low temperatures, the electrons in a solid will tend to occupy the lower energy orbits which are confined to individual atoms and, therefore, few charge carriers will be available. At higher temperatures, the atoms vibrate more energetically and shake electrons into one of the bands of energy levels which continue through the material.

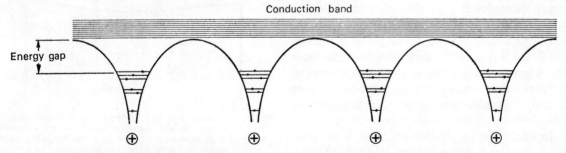

Fig. 23.5. Energy levels in an insulator with an energy gap which is greater than the energy of thermal vibration of the atoms.

Thus, the number of electrons free to carry charge through the solid increases with the temperature.

If an external potential is applied to a solid, electrons in the conduction band flow down the potential gradient. (Fig. 23.6.) From this diagram,

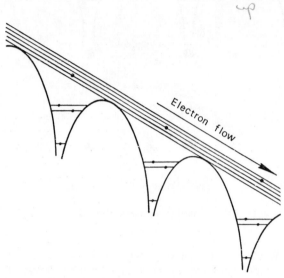

Fig. 23.6. Effect of an electric field on the energy levels in a solid.

it would seem that even the smallest field would cause a very large current to flow and that the electrons would continually accelerate without loss of energy. However, the potential diagram is imaginary and does not represent the atoms in three dimensions, and the electrons frequently collide with the atoms, converting their kinetic energy into heat energy. The frequency of these collisions increases with the thermal vibration of the atoms, i.e., with the temperature. Thus, an increase in the temperature of a solid reduces the mobility of the electrons.

In metals, the occupied levels are so near to the upper vacant levels that, at normal temperatures, a large proportion of the outer electrons are in the conduction band. The electrons move at random about the metal, as the molecules of a gas move in a container. Any increase in the temperature of a metal reduces the mobility proportionally more than it increases the number of conducting electrons and, therefore, there is a net increase in resistance.

In insulators, the conduction band is far from the energy level of the outermost occupied orbit. The energy of the thermal vibration of the atoms

is not sufficient to elevate more than a few of the electrons to the conduction band, and the resistance of the material is very large. Any increase in temperature increases the number of electrons free to move more than it reduces their mobility, so there is a net reduction in resistance. Insulators subject to high potentials sometimes break down at high temperatures and allow a substantial current to flow.

Superconductivity

At very low temperatures near absolute zero, certain metals and compounds completely lose their electrical resistance. The temperature at which this *superconductivity* occurs ranges from 0·3K for hafnium to 30K for niobium nitride. Currents set up in these materials will continue for years without attenuation. Another amazing property of materials in this superconductivity state is that magnetic fields cannot penetrate them (although a large enough magnetic field may destroy the super-conducting state). A spectacular demonstration of this is the suspension of a magnet above the surface of a superconductor. (Fig. 23.7.)

Superconductivity is thought to depend on a long range pairing up of electrons, which is associated with regular thermal waves in the

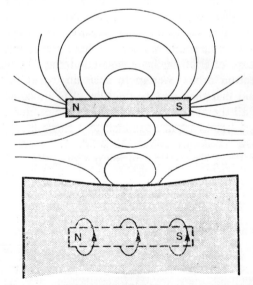

Fig. 23.7. The magnetic field inside a superconducting material is zero. As the magnet descends on to the surface, large induced currents exert a field externally which repels the magnet. This may be imagined as a reflection of the upper magnet in the surface of the superconductor.

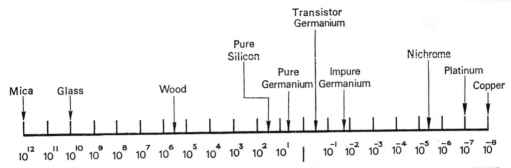

Fig. 23.8. Resistivities (ohm-metre) of conductors, semiconductors, and insulators at room temperature (300K).

material at low temperatures. At higher temperatures, thermal vibration breaks up the electron pairing and normal resistance is restored.

A similar effect to superconductivity is superfluidity, the state of zero viscosity, which liquid helium exhibits at low temperatures. Electrons in atoms and waves in space move without loss of energy, and there is evidence that matter has a wave nature which is exhibited in the atom and in the extraordinary behaviour of matter at low temperatures.

Semiconductors

Carbon, silicon, and germanium belong to a class of materials called semiconductors, which are intermediate in resistance between metals and insulators. (Fig. 23.8.) The atomic structures of these materials are similar to each other and, as one might expect, they are in the same group in the periodic table of the elements. (Fig. 8.9.) In a semiconductor, the energy difference between the upper occupied orbits and the conduction band is only about twenty times as much as the average energy of thermal vibration of the atoms. (Fig.

23.9.) Consequently, any increase in temperature produces a large increase in the number of electrons in the conduction band. The resistance of semiconductors drops rapidly as the temperature rises. Comparative figures are given in Table 23.1.

Table 23.1. Comparison of the resistances of metals, semiconductors and insulators, at different temperatures. (Figures are very approximate because they vary widely with the method of preparing the sample).

Material	Resistance in ohms between faces of a metre cube		
	0°C	500°C	1000°C
Copper	$1\cdot6\times10^{-8}$	5×10^{-8}	9×10^{-8}
Carbon	$3\cdot5\times10^{-5}$	$2\cdot7\times10^{-5}$	$2\cdot1\times10^{-5}$
Germanium	9×10^{-4}	—	—
Silicon	6×10^{-7}	—	—
Silica	10^{16}	10^{7}	10^{5}

Electrons and Holes

We will explain the behaviour of semiconductors, using as an example one of the most important

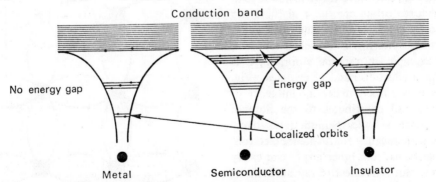

Fig. 23.9. The energy levels in a semiconductor, an insulator, and a metal compared schematically with the energy of thermal vibration of the atom.

275

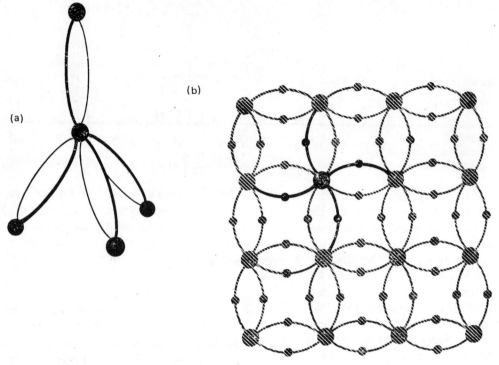

(a)

(b)

Fig. 23.10. *(a)* Germanium has a tetrahedral structure in three dimensions but *(b)* the fact that each atom shares one electron with each of its four neighbours can be represented in two dimensions.

semiconducting materials — germanium. The germanium crystal has a tetrahedral arrangement of atoms but we can represent this in two dimensions as a square lattice. (Fig. 23.10.) Each atom is bound into the lattice by the four electrons it shares with its neighbours. The rotating electrons exert a magnetic influence which couples them together in pairs. The electrons are called *valence* electrons and, although they are shared between neighbours, they do not move through the crystal because the valence orbits are full and there are no vacancies into which electrons could transfer.

When a valence electron is detached from an atom as, for example, by thermal vibration, it is elevated to the conduction band of energies. (Fig. 23.11.) It now moves freely under the influence of an electric field and contributes to the flow of current. The electron leaves behind a positively charged atom with vacancy for a valence electron, and valence electrons from other atoms can easily transfer into the gap. The effect of repeated movements of valence electrons in one direction is to move the positively charged vacancy in the opposite

direction. (Fig. 23.12.) Such a vacancy is called a positive hole and it behaves in some ways like a positively charged electron.

n-Type Semiconductors

If some atoms of the element arsenic, which has five valence electrons, are introduced into the

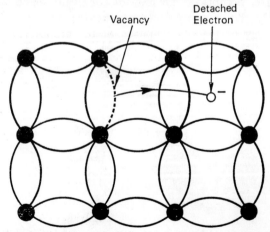

Vacancy   Detached
           Electron

Fig. 23.11. Some electrons may wander from their position linking two atoms.

276

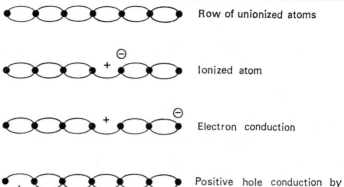

Row of unionized atoms

Ionized atom

Electron conduction

Fig. 23.12. Both electrons and holes can contribute to conduction.

Positive hole conduction by a shuffling along of electrons

germanium crystal, which has only four, every arsenic atom has one uncoupled electron. Because the electron is uncoupled, it is easy to detach from the atom by thermal vibration. On the energy diagram, this is equivalent to introducing an occupied level (donor level) just below the conduction band. (Fig. 23.13.) The charge carriers in this impure germanium are the negative electrons, as in a metal, and for this reason the material is called an *n-type* semiconductor. The conductivity of the material is still far from that of a metal, because the atoms of arsenic are relatively few and far between.

p-Type Semiconductors

When an impurity, such as boron, which has only three valence electrons, is introduced into germanium, it is unable to share an electron with all four of its germanium neighbours. It does not take much thermal vibration to shake an electron

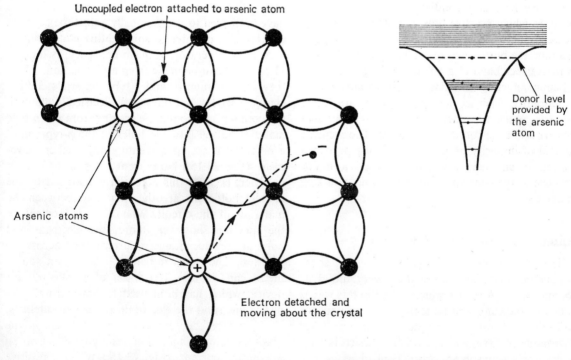

Uncoupled electron attached to arsenic atom

Arsenic atoms

Electron detached and moving about the crystal

Donor level provided by the arsenic atom

Fig. 23.13. The lattice and energy level diagram for *n*-type germanium with arsenic impurity.

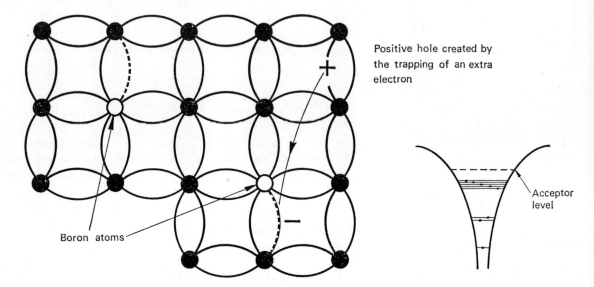

Positive hole created by the trapping of an extra electron

Acceptor level

Boron atoms

Fig. 23.14. The lattice and energy level diagram for *p*-type germanium with boron impurity.

coupling two germanium atoms into the orbit coupling the boron atom and an adjacent germanium atom. This creates a vacancy among the valency electrons of the germanium, which acts as a positive hole and conducts electricity. Germanium, in which positive hole conduction predominates, is referred to as *p-type* material. On the energy diagram, the boron has created receptor levels near to the valence band of germanium. (Fig. 23.14.)

Semiconducting materials which do not depend on impurity, such as pure germanium, are called *intrinsic* semiconductors. Impurity semiconductors are said to be *doped* with impurity. The accurate control of impurity of the order of one part in a million is no easy task and it posed a major obstacle to the wide application of semiconducting materials.

Applications of Semiconductors

The temperature sensitivity of some semiconducting materials makes them very useful as thermometers. A semiconductor used in this way is called a *thermistor* and its temperature response is calibrated against the reading of a conventional thermometer. Temperature sensitive resistors have many applications in automatic control systems.

The resistance of some semiconductors is reduced when they are irradiated with light, a phenomenon known as the 'inner photo effect'. By producing more free electrons or holes, the light provides more charged carriers in the material. Photoconductive devices made from semiconductors have been used to automatically adjust the contrast of television pictures to suit lighting conditions.

A solar generator, with an efficiency as high as 11 per cent can be made from a *pn* junction. When they are separate, *n*- and *p*-type materials contain charge carriers but they are electrically neutral. On coming into contact, electrons from the *n*-type material diffuse into the holes of the *p*-type, until a potential is set up preventing any further movement. (Fig. 23.15.) No current flows in the circuit, however, because this potential is matched by the contact potentials at other junctions between the materials of the circuit. When light is incident on the junction, however, more free electrons and holes are produced, and a current flows across the junction. The Sun's radiation falling on a square metre can provide 100 watts of power by this device, which has been used to power rural telephone lines and the electronic systems in satellites.

A junction between a *p*-type and an *n*-type semiconductor has a strong rectifying effect on an alternating current. (Fig. 23.16.) When a positive potential is applied to the *p*-type material, electrons

278

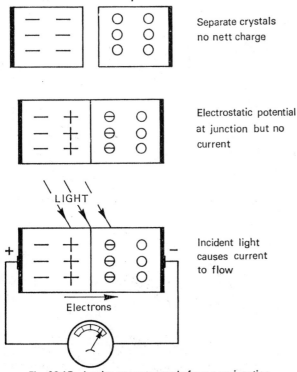

n   p

Separate crystals no nett charge

Electrostatic potential at junction but no current

LIGHT

+   Electrons   −

Incident light causes current to flow

Fig. 23.15. A solar generator made from a *pn* junction.

A transistor is a device for amplifying the power of an alternating electric current and it has revolutionized the electronics industry since its development in 1948. One form of the device is made up of a thin slice of *p*-type semiconductor between two pieces of *n*-type. (Fig. 23.17.) The incoming signal varies the negative potential of the emitter relative to the base and, thus, controls the number of electrons introduced into the *n*-type material by the emitter. Because it is thin, only a small fraction of these electrons are collected by the *p*-type base, the majority crossing the base and being attracted by the high positive potential on the collector. Thus, the current in the collector circuit is controlled by the current in the emitter circuit. Now, although the current in the output is only about 0·9 per cent of that in the input, the potential in the collector circuit is large so that the power (*IV*) is amplified. It is this transfer of current from the input to the output circuit which gives the device its name of transfer resistor or transistor. The same effect can be produced with a *p-n-p* junction. Semiconductor amplifiers, oscillators, and detectors consume far less power than the valve circuits which they have largely replaced.

Fluorescence and Phosphorescence

When certain materials are bombarded with fast-moving electrons, they emit electromagnetic radiation of a characteristic frequency. Glass, for example, emits green light. The bombardment first causes electrons to transfer to a higher energy

flow readily from the *n*-type, which contains many free electrons. On the other hand, when a negative potential is applied to the *p*-type material, the resistance is high, because there are few free electrons in the *p*-type to move across the boundary. Rectifiers are commonly made from a very thin layer (0·05 mm) of selenium sandwiched between two electrodes.

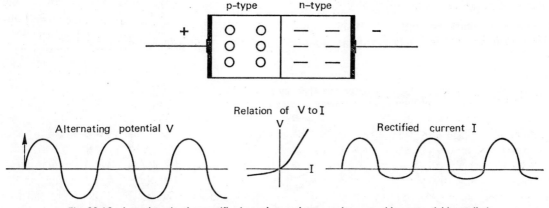

p-type   n–type

+   −

Relation of V to I

Alternating potential V

V

I

Rectified current I

Fig. 23.16. A semiconducting rectifier has a low resistance when a positive potential is applied to the *p*-type material.

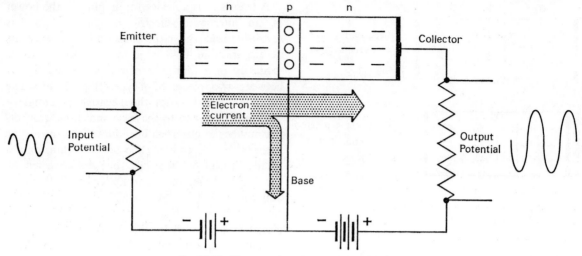

Fig. 23.17. The *n-p-n* junction transistor amplifier.

level in the atoms of the material, and then radiation is emitted as they return to their ground state.

This phenomenon of *fluorescence* may be caused by electron bombardment or else by e.m. radiation, in which case the emitted light is of longer wavelength than the radiation absorbed. (Fig. 23.18.) For example, ultra-violet radiation causes many substances to fluoresce and emit visible light.

In some materials, notably poor conductors, an ionized atom does not immediately recapture an electron and emit light. There is an interval between the absorption and emission of energy. This delay may cause a substance to be luminous for some time after its irradiation has ceased. This phenomenon is called *phosphorescence* and it may be considered as a special case of fluorescence.

Not all substances fluoresce, but those that do find a variety of uses. Fluorescent paint is used for roadway markers and advertising signs; fluorescent dyes and whitening agents are used in fabrics; and the front surface of the cathode-ray tubes used in television sets is coated with a fluorescent material to make the pattern of cathode rays visible.

The fluorescence of certain substances in ultra-violet light can be used as a means of quick identification of mineral ores and precious stones, such as diamond. A forged document may match the original in appearance, but under ultra-violet rays the differing fluorescence of the inks used will distinguish between them. A dentist may use ultra-violet rays to distinguish between a live tooth, which fluoresces and a dead one, which does not.

The most familiar application of fluorescent substances is in fluorescent lights, which are basically discharge tubes containing mercury vapour. As the vapour conducts the current it emits ultra-violet radiation which, of course, is invisible. The inside of the tube is coated with a

Fast electron or electromagnetic radiation

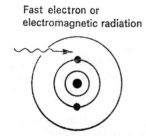

Electron in excited state and surplus energy absorbed by atom or carried away by electron

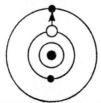

Radiation of longer wave length emitted

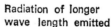
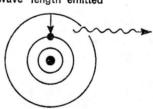

Fig. 23.18. Fluorescence

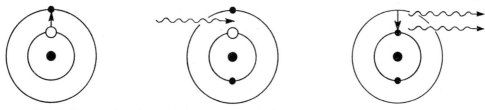

Fig. 23.19. Radiation of a certain frequency can stimulate the return of an electron to its ground state.

fluorescent powder, which converts the energy of the ultra-violet radiation into light. Fluorescent lamps operate at a much lower temperature than tungsten filament lamps, and they are about three times as efficient.

An electron excited into a higher energy level in the atom will eventually return to its ground state and emit a photon of e.m. radiation. In some cases this return of the electrons can be precipitated by irradiating the atoms with e.m. radiation of just the frequency which the transition would produce. (Fig. 23.19.) The atoms may be excited electrically and then triggered off by radiation which produces a cascade effect and is thereby amplified.

A device which amplifies radiation of microwave frequencies in this way is called a MASER (Microwave Amplification by Stimulated Electron Response). The equivalent device for amplifying visible frequencies is the LASER (Light Amplification by Stimulated Electron Response). Atoms of solids (e.g., ruby) and gases (e.g., neon) can be triggered in this way.

The radiation produced by these devices is coherent, i.e., of the same phase and frequency as the incident photon. The amplification can be greatly increased if the light is reflected back and forth in the material. For this reason lasers are bounded by parallel optical flats which are almost

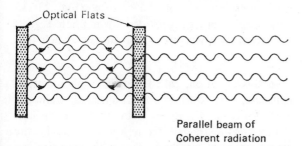

Fig. 23.20. In the laser a fraction of the light is reflected back to stimulate further emission.

perfect reflectors and reflect back a large fraction of the light. (Fig. 23.20.) These devices allow us to transmit powerful parallel beams of coherent radiation over long distances. The beams can be modulated and therefore made to carry signals in a similar way to radio waves.

Electron Emission

We have seen that all matter contains electrons which, in most cases, are bound to individual atoms and not free to move. In metals, however, a large number of electrons are not bound tightly to particular atoms and they move freely, rather like gas molecules, within the confines of the metal. The metal as a whole is electrically neutral but, as an electron moves away from the surface, it leaves behind an uncompensated positive charge. (Fig. 23.21a.) Work is needed to separate an electron from the surface against the attraction of this positive charge. We may consider there to be a surface barrier or retarding potential which deters electrons from leaving the surface. (Fig. 23.21b.) The minimum energy required to extract an electron is called the *work function* (W) of the surface.

At ordinary temperatures, very few electrons have the velocity necessary to carry them across the potential barrier but we can help electrons *to cross* the boundary in several ways:

(a) We can give more of the electrons the necessary escape velocity by increasing the temperature. (*Thermionic emission.*)

(b) We can apply a strong field which sucks out the electron from the surface. (*Field emission.*)

(c) We can knock electrons from the surface by bombarding it with other electrons. (*Secondary emission.*)

281

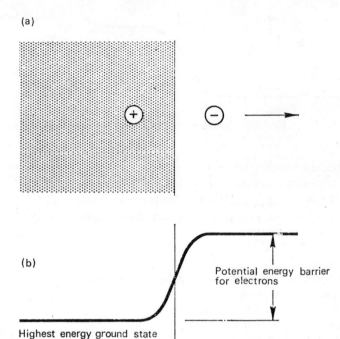

(a)

(b)

Fig. 23.21. Electron emission.

Potential energy barrier for electrons

Highest energy ground state of electrons in the metal (top of conduction band)

(*d*) We can give additional energy to the electrons by shining light on the surface. (*Photoelectric emission*.)

Photoelectric Effect

When light is absorbed by a surface, it causes the emission of electrons.

The emission can be explained in terms of the quantum theory of radiation. According to this theory, light is not a continuous train of waves,

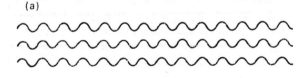

(a)

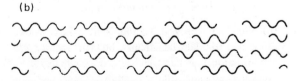

(b)

Fig. 23.22. According to the quantum theory, light does not consist of a continuous wave, as represented in *(a)*, but of a large number of discontinuous photons as in *(b)*.

as for example a liquid surface wave is, but consists of a large number of wavelets or photons. (Fig. 23.22.) The energy of a photon is proportional to its frequency, f

$$\text{energy} \propto f$$

or

$$\text{energy} = hf$$

where h is a constant (Planck's constant) for all electromagnetic radiation.

When a photon of sufficient energy is absorbed by an electron, it overcomes the surface forces and escapes from the metal. The electrons which are in the highest energy levels of the atoms, i.e., the conduction band, require the least energy to extract them from the surface. This energy is the work function, W, of the surface. (Fig. 23.23.) Any surplus energy provided by a photon gives the electrons a velocity, v, on emission such that

$$\tfrac{1}{2} mv^2 = hf - W$$

In this equation, called Einstein's photoelectric equation, h is constant for all surfaces, while the work function, W, varies from surface to surface.

Electrons extracted from lower levels in the atoms emerge from the surface with velocities less than v. The lowest frequency of radiation which

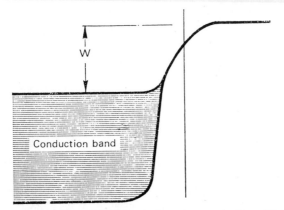

Fig. 23.23. The work function is the energy required to extract from the surface an electron at the top of the conduction band.

will extract electrons is called the threshold frequency, f_o, given by

$$hf_o = W.$$

In fact, at temperatures above absolute zero, some electrons emerge for lower frequencies because of their thermal energies. (Fig. 23.24.)

Problem: What is the minimum frequency of light which would produce photoelectric emission from a tungsten surface of work function 4·5 eV? Planck's constant $= 6·6 \times 10^{-34}$ Js; $e = 1·6 \times 10^{-19}$ C.

Solution: Work function $W = 4·5$ eV

$$= 4·5 \times 1·6 \times 10^{-19} \text{ J}$$

Electron energy $= hf - W$

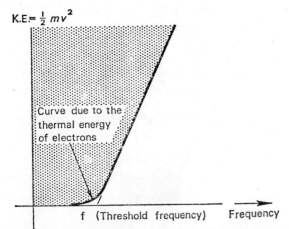

Fig. 23.24. The maximum energy of the electrons emitted from a surface when radiated with e.m. radiation of different frequencies.

When the electrons just emerge with zero velocity

$$hf = W$$

$$\text{and } f = W/h = \frac{4·5 \times 1·6 \times 10^{-19}}{6·6 \times 10^{-34}}$$

$$= 1·07 \times 10^{15} \text{ Hz}$$

The Thermionic Effect

When a metal is heated to about two thousand degrees, many of its electrons acquire energies which are greater than the surface potential barrier and they escape from the surface in large numbers. (Fig. 23.25.) The process may be compared with evaporation, where the faster molecules escape across the surface leaving it cooler. The latent heat extracted during evaporation is

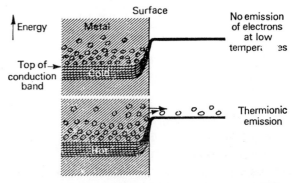

Fig. 23.25. The effect of increased temperature electron emission from a metal surface.

analogous to the work function in thermionic emission, and, in fact, an emitter is left cooler by the loss of its more energetic electrons.

Charge carriers are introduced into evacuated radio valves by thermionic emission of electrons from the cathode. For efficient emission, metal cathodes must operate at a high temperature, the limit being set by the melting point. Tungsten, with a melting point of 3400°C, is commonly used. However, by coating the metal with an oxide, such as barium oxide, the work function of a tungsten filament can be reduced from 4·5 V to 1·0 V, so that it gives the same emission at 1000°C as an uncoated tungsten surface at 2400°C.

Smaller valves use oxide coated nickel cathodes, because they are efficient emitters and withstand mechanical vibration. (Fig. 23.26.) Pure tungsten cathodes are less robust mechanically, but they are

283

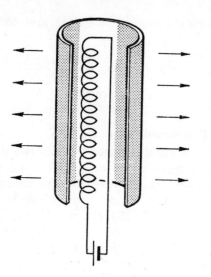

used in some larger valves, because they are not so easily damaged as the oxide coatings by operation at high voltages.

Secondary Emission

The energy required to overcome the potential barrier at a surface can be provided by the impact of basic particles, such as ionized atoms, or by electrons themselves. The energy of the incident particle may be sufficient to cause the emissions of several secondary electrons. The effect is used in the photomultiplier tube to amplify the electric current released by a minute flash of light up to a detectable size. (Fig. 23.27.)

In some cases, the incident particle may splash off atoms of the cathode itself. These atoms adhere to nearby surfaces, and often produce a silvering of the glass container. This process, called *sputtering*, is used to produce high quality mirrors.

Field Emission

If, instead of increasing the energy of the electrons in the metal, we lower the potential barrier at the surface, the same effect of increased emission will result. (Fig. 23.28.) This increase is called the *Schottky effect*. In the extreme case, where the field is sufficient to extract electrons at normal temperatures, it is called cold cathode emission. This takes place in a discharge tube,

where several thousand volts, applied between electrodes in a vacuum, cause a current of electrons to flow.

Conduction in Gases

Gases are usually excellent insulators but, under certain circumstances, they do conduct electricity. A lightning flash is the most spectacular evidence of this conduction but to produce it requires a potential difference of some 100 million volts. Over a shorter distance, a spark can be produced between two flat surfaces in air at atmospheric pressure by applying a potential of about 3,000,000 volts per m. If the gas is reduced in pressure, its conductivity increases and an electrical discharge occurs at a much lower potential gradient.

For electricity to flow in any substance there must be some free charges available. In a gas, these free charges are produced by the ionization of the gas atoms. The detailed observation of the conduction of electricity through a gas under reduced pressure is historically important because it led to the discovery of electrons and X-rays, and to the development of the cathode-ray tube.

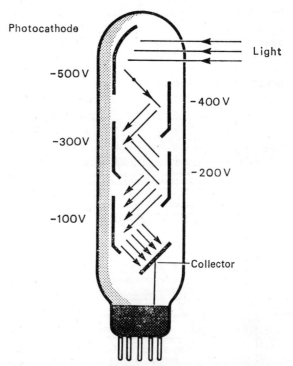

Fig. 23.27. Each electron released by the light at the photo-cathode produces a cascade of secondary electrons.

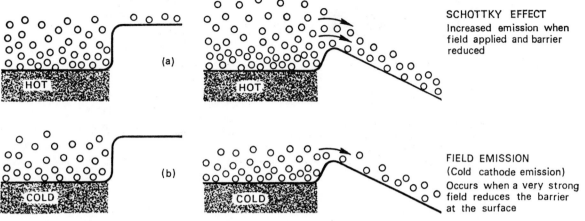

SCHOTTKY EFFECT
Increased emission when field applied and barrier reduced

FIELD EMISSION
(Cold cathode emission)
Occurs when a very strong field reduces the barrier at the surface

Fig. 23.28. The effect of an electric field on electron emission. *(a)* Schottky effect increases emission when field applied and barrier reduced. *(b)* Field emission (cold cathode emission) occurs when a very strong field reduces the barrier at the surface.

The Discharge Tube

If a potential of about 10,000 volts is applied between electrodes situated about 150 mm apart in a glass tube, and the pressure is slowly reduced by a vacuum pump, a discharge of electricity takes place. (Fig. 23.29.) The appearance of the tube follows a well defined sequence of visible patterns as the pressure drops. At a pressure of a few mm Hg, the current takes irregular paths through the gas and these show up as continuous streamers. The conductivity increases as the pressure reduces and the streamers widen, become more stable, and break up into a pattern of light and shade. The colour of the light emitted is characteristic of the gas or vapour in the tube; for example, sodium lamps are yellow and neon lights are red. Further reduction in pressure reduces the conductivity of the gas and the pattern moves towards the anode until the Crookes dark space fills the tube. At this stage, the end of the glass tube opposite to the cathode glows with a greenish colour.

Cathode Rays

The greenish glow of the glass was originally attributed to 'rays' which were radiated from the cathode. A series of experiments carried out on the rays showed them to have momentum, to carry negative charge, and to be deflected by electric and magnetic fields. (Fig. 23.30.) These properties were compatible with the rays being a stream of fast moving electrons, and quantitative measurements confirmed that this was the case.

When cathode rays strike a solid, such as the glass tube or the anode, most of their energy is converted into heat. Some materials fluoresce when cathode rays are directed at them, that is, they emit light of a characteristic colour. The green light from the glass discharge tube is an example of this fluorescence.

In addition to the visible radiation, the glass tube and anode of the discharge tube emit radiation of a much shorter wave-length of about 10^{-10} metres. (Fig. 23.31.) These X-rays are produced whenever cathode rays are absorbed by matter, but denser materials, such as metals, are more effective X-ray producing targets.

X-rays are very penetrating, and, since they can cause damage to animal tissue, care should be taken when experimenting with cathode rays. The X-ray sources used in medicine and crystallography are cathode-ray tubes designed to control the wave-length and intensity of the X-rays.

The Discharge Tube Pattern

The pattern of light seen in the tube at higher pressures is caused by electrons colliding with the atoms of the gas at high speed. An electron may strike a gas atom with such energy that it knocks an electron out of the atom. There are then three charged particles which can contribute to the current; the original electron, the electron ejected from the atom, and the ionized atom, which has a net positive charge, because of the electron it

285

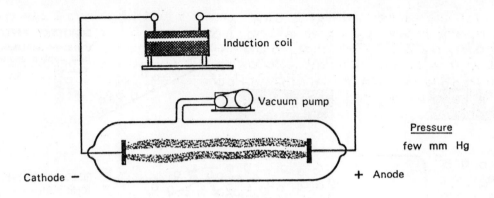

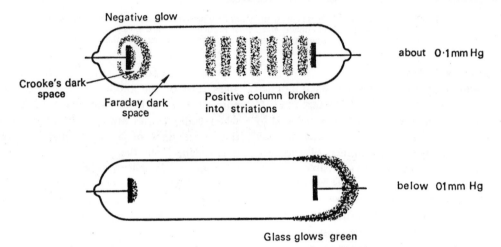

Fig. 23.29. Discharge tube patterns at different gas pressures.

has lost. The relative difference in mass gives the electrons a greater mobility than the ions, and conduction in gases is mainly due to the electrons.

The original electron must be sufficiently accelerated by the electric field to acquire the speed to ionize the gas atoms. Thus, electrons starting near the cathode drift some distance down the tube before causing ionization. At this stage, they have imparted their energy to the gas atom and they must be accelerated again by the field before they can provide further ionization. The regions of strong ionization emit light which is characteristic of the gas and which is caused by the recombination of ionized atoms and electrons. This stop-start motion of the electron accounts for the striations along the tube. The electric field is not uniform along the length of the tube, which explains why the pattern is not uniform.

The tube blacks out at low pressures because there are so few gas atoms that electrons travel the whole length of the tube without making a collision. These electrons (cathode rays) are emitted by the cathode itself as a result of positive ion bombardment, and their energy is dependent on the potential applied across the tube.

The Cathode-Ray Tube

In the cathode-ray tube, electrons are emitted by a heated cathode and pass through a hole in the grid. (Fig. 23.32.) A pair of anodes at successively higher potentials accelerate and focus the electrons on to the screen, which has a fluorescent coating. The direction of this fine pencil of cathode rays is controlled either by two pairs of electrostatic deflector plates or two pairs of magnetizing

286

coils. Alternating potentials, applied to these deflectors, swing the pencil up and down and from side to side and, thus, when their frequencies are related, they trace a pattern on the screen. In the cathode-ray tube, we deduce the nature of the potential applied to one set of plates from the pattern it produces, when a known alternating potential is applied to the other plate. In the television tube, the deflection is controlled by a magnetic field provided by two pairs of external coils. The luminous spot traverses the screen horizontally 625 times (or 405 times), as it moves

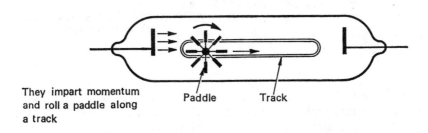

They impart momentum and roll a paddle along a track

Paddle   Track

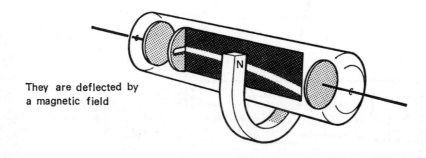

They are deflected by a magnetic field

They travel in straight lines as shown by the sharp shadow cast by an obstacle

Fig. 23.30. Properties of cathode rays.

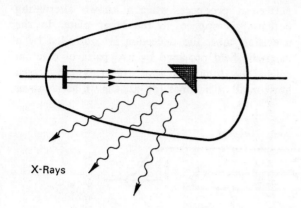

X-Rays

Fig. 23.31. X-rays are produced when cathode rays are absorbed by matter.

once from top to bottom. At the same time, the intensity of the cathode rays varies according to the potential applied to the grid and, thus, they can be made to build up a picture on the screen. The vertical movement repeats at a frequency which gives about 25 pictures per second.

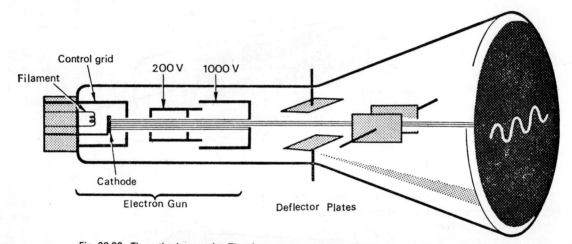

Fig. 23.32. The cathode-ray tube. The electron gun produces a fine beam of cathode rays which are deflected horizontally and vertically to produce a trace on the fluorescent screen.

Questions

1. What are the advantages and disadvantages of transistors compared with thermionic valves?

2. Explain why a plastic rod attracts pieces of paper after being rubbed on a sleeve, while a metal rod does not.

3. Explain how a 'hole' can transfer charge in a semi-conductor.

4. Why are small quantities of radioactive materials included in luminous paints?

5. What characteristics are needed for a television tube coating?

6. How does the beam from a laser differ from the beam from a searchlight?

7. Would it be possible to remove all the conduction-electrons from a piece of metal so that it became an insulator?

8. Explain the terms *fluorescence* and *phosphorescence* and account for the occurrence of these phenomena.

   Discuss the functions of, and the factors affecting the choice of material for: (i) the coating inside a 'fluorescent lamp'; and (ii) the coating inside a cathode-ray tube screen.

(I.E.R.E.)

Problems

1. What is the energy of ultra-violet light of wave-length 5×10^{-7} m?
   Answer: $3 \cdot 97 \times 10^{-19}$ J.

2. What is the velocity of photoelectrons emitted by sodium under the effect of incident ultra-violet light of wave-length 3×10^{-8} m? (Assume the work-function is negligible.)
   Answer: $3 \cdot 81 \times 10^{6}$ m/s.

3. If a photon has a wave-length of $7 \cdot 5 \times 10^{-7}$ m, what is its energy?
   Answer: $2 \cdot 65 \times 10^{-19}$ J.

4. If light of wave-length 6×10^{-7} m causes a metal surface to emit photoelectrons at $2 \cdot 5 \times 10^{5}$ m/s, what is the longest wave-length which causes photoelectric emission?
   Answer: $6 \cdot 55 \times 10^{-7}$ m.

5. Describe briefly one application of photo-electric emission. Define work function and state Einstein's photo-electric equation. Draw a graph showing how the energy of photo-electrons varies with the frequency of the incident light.

   Calculate the minimum value of the frequency of light which would cause emission from a surface, if light of wave-length 3×10^{-2} m causes photo-electrons to be emitted with a maximum velocity of 2×10^{5} m/s. (Velocity of light $= 3 \times 10^{8}$ m/s, electron mass $= 9 \cdot 1 \times 10^{-31}$ kg, Planck constant $= 6 \cdot 6 \times 10^{-34}$ Js.)
   Answer: $7 \cdot 2 \times 10^{13}$ Hz.

6. Give an account of the production of cathode rays and describe experiments which demonstrate their properties.

   A potential of 1000 V is applied to a cathode ray tube. What is the greatest velocity that an electron could acquire in the tube, and what would be the shortest wave-length of the X-rays that could be produced? (Planck constant $= 6 \cdot 6 \times 10^{-34}$ Js, electronic charge $= 1 \cdot 6 \times 10^{-19}$ C, electronic mass $= 9 \cdot 1 \times 10^{-31}$ kg.)
   Answer: $\lambda = 12 \times 10^{-10}$ m.

Appendix

Physical Constants

Acceleration due to gravity	$9 \cdot 80665$ m/s
Avogadro's number	$6 \cdot 02 \times 10^{23}$ molecules/gramme molecule
Electron charge	$1 \cdot 602 \times 10^{-19}$ C
Electron mass	$9 \cdot 109 \times 10^{-31}$ kg $= 0 \cdot 000548$u
Electron volt	$1 \cdot 6 \times 10^{-19}$ J
Planck constant	$6 \cdot 625 \times 10^{-34}$ Js
Proton mass	$1 \cdot 6725 \times 10^{-27}$ kg
Mass of hydrogenatom	$1 \cdot 6734 \times 10^{-27}$ kg
Speed of light (in free space)	$2 \cdot 998 \times 10^{8}$ m/s
Speed of sound (dry air at 20°C)	344 m/s (1240 km/h)

The Elements

List of the elements showing atomic weights, melting and boiling points. (Values of m.p. and b.p. are given to the nearest degree at 1 atm. Above 1500°C, they are not known accurately.)

At. No.	Element	Sym.	At. Wt.	m.p. (°C)	b.p. (°C)
1	Hydrogen	H	$1 \cdot 0078$	-259	-253
2	Helium	He	$4 \cdot 002$	-270	-269
3	Lithium	Li	$6 \cdot 940$	180	1330
4	Beryllium	Be	$9 \cdot 02$	1280	2450
5	Boron	B	$10 \cdot 82$	2300	2550
6	Carbon (graphite)	C	$12 \cdot 01$	3500	3900
7	Nitrogen	N	$14 \cdot 008$	-210	-196
8	Oxygen	O	$16 \cdot 000$	-219	-183
9	Fluorine	F	$19 \cdot 000$	-220	-188
10	Neon	Ne	$20 \cdot 183$	-249	-246
11	Sodium	Na	$22 \cdot 997$	98	883
12	Magnesium	Mg	$24 \cdot 32$	650	1100
13	Aluminium	Al	$26 \cdot 97$	660	2400
14	Silicon	Si	$28 \cdot 06$	1410	2480
15	Phosphorus	P	$31 \cdot 02$	44	280
16	Sulphur	S	$32 \cdot 06$	119	445
17	Chlorine	Cl	$35 \cdot 457$	-101	-34
18	Argon	A	$39 \cdot 944$	-189	-186
19	Potassium	K	$39 \cdot 096$	63	760
20	Calcium	Ca	$40 \cdot 08$	850	1440
21	Scandium	Sc	$45 \cdot 10$	1400	2500

At. No.	Element	Sym.	At. Wt.	m.p. (°C)	b.p. (°C)
22	Titanium	Ti	47·90	1680	3300
23	Vanadium	V	50·95	1920	3400
24	Chromium	Cr	52·01	1900	2600
25	Manganese	Mn	54·93	1250	2100
26	Iron	Fe	55·84	1539	2900
27	Cobalt	Co	58·94	1492	2900
28	Nickel	Ni	58·69	1453	2820
29	Copper	Cu	63·57	1083	2550
30	Zinc	Zn	65·38	419	907
31	Gallium	Ga	69·72	30	2250
32	Germanium	Ge	72·60	958	2880
33	Arsenic	As	74·91	Sublimes at 610°C at 1 atm	
34	Selenium	Se	78·96	217	685
35	Bromine	Br	79·916	−7	58
36	Krypton	Kr	83·7	−157	−153
37	Rubidium	Rb	85·48	39	710
38	Strontium	Sr	87·63	770	1460
39	Yttrium	Yt	88·92	1500	3000
40	Zirconium	Zr	91·22	1850	4400
41	Columbium (niobium)	Cb	92·91	2420	5100
42	Molybdenum	Mo	96·0	2620	4600
43	Technetium	Tc	97·8*	2700	—
44	Ruthenium	Ru	101·7	2400	3900
45	Rhodium	Rh	102·91	1960	3900
46	Palladium	Pd	106·7	1552	3200
47	Silver	Ag	107·88	961	2180
48	Cadmium	Cd	112·41	321	767
49	Indium	In	114·76	156	2000
50	Tin	Sn	118·70	232	2606
51	Antimony	Sb	121·76	630	1440
52	Tellurium	Te	127·61	450	997
53	Iodine	I	126·92	114	183
54	Xenon	Xe	131·3	−112	−108
55	Caesium	Cs	132·91	29	713
56	Barium	Ba	137·36	850	1140
57	Lanthanum	La	138·92	920	4200
58	Cerium	Ce	140·13	804	2900
59	Praseodymium	Pr	140·92	935	3000
60	Neodymium	Nd	144·27	1024	3170
61	Promethium	Pm	146·0*	—	—
62	Samarium	Sa	150·43	1052	1600
63	Europium	Eu	152·0	900	1400
64	Gadolinium	Gd	156·9	1320	2700
65	Terbium	Tn	159·2	1450	2500
66	Dysprosium	Dy	162·46	1500	2600
67	Holmium	Ho	163·5	1500	2700
68	Erbium	Er	167·64	1525	2600
69	Thulium	Tm	169·4	1600	2100
70	Ytterbium	Yb	173·04	824	1500
71	Lutecium	Lu	175·0	1700	1900
72	Hafnium	Hf	178·6	2000	5100
73	Tantalum	Ta	180·88	3000	6000
74	Tungsten	W	184·0	3380	5700
75	Rhenium	Re	186·31	3170	5900
76	Osmium	Os	191·5	2700	4600
77	Iridium	Ir	193·1	2443	5300
78	Platinum	Pt	195·23	1769	3800
79	Gold	Au	197·2	1063	2660
80	Mercury	Hg	200·61	−39	357
81	Thallium	Tl	205·0	304	1460
82	Lead	Pb	208·0	327	1750
83	Bismuth	Bi	209·0	271	1530

At. No.	Element	Sym.	At. Wt.	m.p. (°C)	b.p. (°C)
84	Polonium	Po	210·0	254	960
85	Astatine	At	210·0*	—	—
86	Radon	Rn	222·0	−71	−62
87	Francium	Fr	223·0*	—	—
88	Radium	Ra	226·0	700	1140
89	Actinum	Ac	227·0	1050	—
90	Thorium	Th	232·0	1700	4200
91	Protactinium	Pa	231·0	3000	—
92	Uranium	U	238·0	1133	3800
93	Neptunium	Np	237·0*	640	—
94	Plutonium	Pu	242·0*	—	—
95	Americium	Am	243·0*	850	—
96	Curium	Cm	248·0*	—	—
97	Berkelium	Bk	247·0*	—	—
98	Californium	Cf	249·0*	—	—
99	Einsteinium	Es	254·0*	—	—
100	Fermium	Fm	253·0*	—	—
101	Mendelevium	Md	256·0*	—	—
102	Nobelium	No	253·0*	—	—
103	Lawrencium	Lw	257·0*	—	—

* Isotope of longest known half-life

Conversion Factors

Length:

1 inch $=0·0254$ m
1 foot $=0·3048$ m
1 yard $=0·9144$ m
1 mile $=1·6093$ m
1 Angstrom unit $=10^{-10}$ m

Mass:

1 pound $=0·45359$ kg
1 ton $=1016·05$ kg
1 metric ton $=1000$ kg
1 unified atomic mass unit $=1·66 \times 10^{-27}$ kg

Force:

1 kilogramme force $=9·807$ N
1 pound force $=4·448$ N

Energy:

1 calorie $=4·1868$ J
1 British thermal unit $=1055·06$ J
1 kilowatt-hour $=3600$ J

Power:

1 horsepower $=745·7$ W

Pressure:

1 torr $=133·322$ N/m²
1 mm Hg $=133·322$ N/m²
1 bar $=10^5$ N/m²
1 atmosphere $=101325$ N/m²
1 pound per square inch $=689·5$ N/m²

Fuel consumption:

1 mile/gallon $=0·354$ km/litre

Capacity:

1 litre $=10^{-3}$ cubic metres
1 gallon $=4·54596$ litres
1 pint $=0·568245$ litres

Multiples & Fractions

Multiple	Prefix	Symbol
10^{12}	tera	T
10^9	giga	G
10^6	mega	M
10^3	kilo	k
10^2	hecto	h
10	deka	da
10^{-1}	deci	d
10^{-2}	centi	c
10^{-3}	milli	m
10^{-6}	micro	μ
10^{-9}	nano	n
10^{-12}	pico	p
10^{-15}	femto	f
10^{-18}	atto	a

Index

REPRODUCED PHOTOLITHO IN GREAT BRITAIN BY
J. W. ARROWSMITH LTD., BRISTOL